SHARK

THE SHADOW BELOW

D1559539

SHARK

THE SHADOW BELOW

Hugh Edwards

HarperCollins*Publishers*

HarperCollins*Publishers*

First published in Australia in 1997
by HarperCollinsPublishers Pty Limited
ACN 009 913 517
http://www.harpercollins.com.au

A member of HarperCollins*Publishers* (Australia) Pty Limited Group
Copyright © Hugh Edwards 1997

HarperCollins*Publishers*
25 Ryde Road, Pymble, Sydney, NSW 2073, Australia
31 View Road, Glenfield, Auckland 10, New Zealand
77–85 Fulham Palace Road, London W6 8JB, United Kingdom
Hazelton Lanes, 55 Avenue Road, Suite 2900, Toronto, Ontario M5R 3L2
and 1995 Markham Road, Scarborough, Ontario M1B 5M8, Canada
10 East 53rd Street, New York NY 10032, USA

National Library Cataloguing-in-Publication data:

Edwards, Hugh, 1933–.
    Shark: the shadow below.
    ISBN 0 7322 5790 5
    1. Sharks – Australia. I. title.

597.30994

Cover photography by Hugh Edwards
All photographs reproduced in this book were taken by Hugh Edwards, unless credited otherwise.
Every effort has been made to contact copyright holders of material quoted in this book. Any
inquiries should be addressed to the publisher.
Material from Peter Benchley's book *Jaws* is reprinted by permission of International Creative
Management, Inc. Copyright © 1997 Peter Benchley

Printed in Australia by McPherson's Printing Group on 79 gsm Bulky Paperback and 115 gsm Matt Art
5 4 3 2 1
01 00 99 98 97

CONTENTS

About the author		vi
Preface: The Shadow		vii
1	Honeymoon Island	1
2	'The Ravin'd Salt Sea Shark'	16
3	The Great Shark of Jurien Bay	35
4	In the Shark Cage	43
5	The Blood-stained Sea	56
6	A Different View of Sharks	82
7	Patterns of Attack: The Serial Killers	99
8	The Real Risk of Shark Attack	127
9	Great Whales, Giant Squid	160
10	The Shark That Attacked a Submarine	183
11	Adventures on the Shark Circuit	205
12	The Gentle Giants of Ningaloo	237
13	How Sharks Compare with Other Dangerous Creatures	262
14	The Global Scene: Shark Attacks Around the World	302
15	The Search for a Shark Repellent	322
16	Sharing the Planet	344
References		354
Index		356

About the Author

Hugh Edwards is a Western Australian author of 23 books, many of them with maritime themes. Nine of his books have been published overseas, with editions in the United States, Canada, Britain, France and the Netherlands and translations in Russian and Japanese.

Sharks swim through the pages of some of them, though he initially was best known as a wreck explorer. In the 1960s he led a number of diving expeditions in search of sunken 17th-century Dutch treasure ships off the coast of Western Australia. His book, *Islands of Angry Ghosts*, about the 1629 Batavia wreck off the Abrolhos Islands and the expedition that raised cannon and coins and found the skeletons of the mutineers' victims, won the Sir Thomas White Memorial Prize for 1967. A classic of its kind, it has been continually in print for the past 30 years.

Hugh Edwards's first view of sharks was as a seven year old, and from an unusual angle — held upside down by the heels over the side of a steamer above a pack of feeding whaler sharks. It is not a position he recommends. But the experience did not give him an aversion to sharks; rather the reverse. As a diver he has had a lifelong interest in sharks, dolphins, whales and other denizens of the oceans. Early chapters of *Shark: The Shadow Below* deal with a diving expedition to the Albany Whaling Station in 1976 to film *Carcharodon carcharias*, the Great White shark, from underwater cages. 'It was the first time I ever heard my own heart beating,' he recalls. 'It sounded like a diesel motor!'

This book also covers other 'man-eating' sharks — tigers and whalers — as well as the majestic whale shark, the largest fish in the sea which eats only plankton. It also looks at other species harmless to humans, which far outnumber the dangerous sharks.

Many of the photographs in this book were taken by Hugh Edwards over years of diving since the 1950s. Combined with Edwards's thrilling and evocative text, they give a unique personal insight into one of the world's most misunderstood creatures: the shark.

PREFACE: THE SHADOW

THE PREDATOR

Tiger! Tiger! burning bright
In the forests of the night,
What immortal hand or eye
Could frame thy fearful symmetry?

…

When the stars threw down their spears,
And water'd heaven with their tears,
Did he smile his work to see?
Did he who made the Lamb make thee?

From 'The Tiger'
William Blake, 1757–1827

THERE IS A SHADOW AT THE BACK OF THE HUMAN MIND. THE FEAR OF A PREDATOR, unseen, beyond the boundaries of our senses.

Dormant in daylight, this irrational apprehension may visit us in darkness or come to dog us in our dreams. It rises ghost-like from the misty pool of ancestral memories. Unwelcome relic of a time when there were dangers real enough beyond the flickering circle of our forebears' firelight.

In our artificial modern world, where steel and plastic and touch-button technology have replaced the leaves of the forest, such primal fears should logically be out of context. After all, road deaths occur so regularly that unless there is some freakish aspect they do not make the news. Though children of the future may have their nightmares of squealing tyres and shattering impacts, they are not a part of today's bad dreams. But mention the word *shark* and it can cause a quickening of the pulse even in people who don't go near the water.

We are very aware of sharks. A shark-caused fatality is guaranteed television news time and column space in most newspapers. Repeats of the *Jaws* films show knifing dorsal fins and gnashing triangular teeth endlessly on late night television.

For the individual there may be solace in statistics. These indicate that the possibility of suffering a fatal shark attack is comfortably remote. But that is because the statisticians include everyone in their figures, even non-swimmers and people who never go near the water. Once you become a surfer or a diver and enter the ocean the odds begin to shorten.

And if a shark should appear, the ultimate predator gliding smoothly on outstretched pectoral fins, long tail moving with broad sweeps, nostrils dilating, dark eye calculating...then 10 000 years of civilisation are swept away in an instant. The hair freezes on the scalp, the heart thuds. The ancestor instincts return with a sudden rush of adrenalin. We are face to face, one to one, with a primitive creature who may want to eat us.

HONEYMOON ISLAND
chapter one

HONEYMOON ISLAND, A WAVE-WASHED GRANITE OUTCROP IN THE SOUTHERN Ocean, has a pleasant and romantic-sounding name. But the events of 11 September 1995 had more of a nightmare quality.

The island lies a kilometre offshore and 40 kilometres east of the fishing hamlet of Hopetoun. It can be found as a speck on the Admiralty charts, past Starvation Bay on the southern coast of Western Australia. A lonely and isolated rock, with white sand beaches and the ammoniac smell of resident gulls, fur seals and sea lions. Below the tidemark the kelp weed surges restlessly to and fro in the swells from the Southern Ocean.

Among the roots of the kelp, down in the dark fissures of the rock and under ledges, large southern abalone cling limpet-like to the rough-textured granite, their shells like oval shields. It was the larger green-lip abalone, the kind most prized by Asian markets, which brought abalone diver David Weir and his deckhand David Lashman to Honeymoon Island on that fatal Monday.

Shucked abalone in 1995 were fetching a price of $80 a kilogram to the fisherman. A good diver on a good day could gather enough green-lips to make up a handsome catch. Worth as much money, perhaps, as an average wage-worker might take home in a month. A balance against the frustration of bad weather spells when the Southern Ocean is a foam-streaked wilderness and diving is impossible. On the South Coast, good days in winter are the exception rather than the rule.

Good divers like David Weir, 29 years old, with ten seasons under his belt, could make $150 000 a year. That was a figure which put them among the State's top income earners. The State Premier, in 1995, had a salary of $170 000. It was good money provided the diver was prepared to work hard and put up with cold and discomfort. Provided he also accepted certain risks, because there were occupational hazards that went with the job.

Abalone was overexploited in the early days of the diving industry. By 1995 the Western Australian Fisheries Department had limited the number of professional divers and placed conditions on their operation. Only 26 divers were licensed to fish abalone in Western Australia, in a season which extended from May to November. Only eight divers held licences for Zone 2. This was the area from Busselton on the west coast to Shoal Cape near Esperance on the south coast. The demand for licences naturally greatly exceeded their availability and they seldom changed hands. A Zone 2 licence sold in 1993 for $2.45 million.

David Weir lived at Margaret River with his wife Caroline and two young daughters, Julie aged three and Melanie, 13. He leased a Zone 2 licence and considered himself fortunate to have the opportunity of earning a good living diving in the ocean, which he loved. He had been a fisherman since leaving school, following in the footsteps of his father, Ted.

The green-lip abalone *Haliotis laevigata* that he sought are found in colonies over a wide range of coastline. The scientific name of the genus, *Haliotis*, means 'sea ear' — from the inside shape of the shell. Abalone are found worldwide in various sizes from tiny thumbnail-sized shells to barnacled specimens as big as soup plates. Technically speaking they are a gastropod, which means 'stomach foot', and they have a body and means of locomotion somewhat like that of the garden snail. The green-lip abalone is one of the world's bigger varieties, growing to 23 centimetres (9 inches) across the shell.

As a marine snail, abalone forage at night, crawling on their 'feet', eyes out on long stalks, browsing on seaweed while their natural enemies the blue groper and the stingrays sleep. Sometimes they simply stay put, lifting their shells to trap strands of seaweed drifting past. By day they clamp tightly to the rock, preferring granite shelves and ledges. Underwater, with their shells pulled down around them, they look like a series of limpet mines on the hull of a ship. The outside of their shells is rough and usually grown over with weed or barnacles. But the inside is brilliant mother-of-pearl, second only in beauty to *Pinctada maxima*, the famous Western Australian pearl shell of tropical waters.

Abalone meat is greatly prized in Asian markets. Apart from a delicate taste it is supposed to have aphrodisiac qualities.

Divers use a metal lever to prise the green-lips off the granite. For the inexperienced it takes force and effort to dislodge a determined abalone. But a proficient diver like Dave Weir could flick them off with ease — there was a knack. The divers were allowed an annual quota of 2.5 tonnes of abalone meat per season, the biggest and best Grade 1 abalone running at about two to a kilogram. But sometimes even bigger ones were found on virgin ground.

The limiting factor, apart from the quota restrictions, was that which affects all fishermen. The weather.

Weather on the south coast in the winter months can be vile. The area of the two Capes at Australia's southwest corner, Cape Naturaliste and Cape Leeuwin where the Indian Ocean meets the Southern Ocean, is notorious among sailors as one of the roughest tracts of water in the world. Giant swells shouldering up from the Antarctic and the Roaring Forties crash in bursts of violent spray along the length of the south coast when the winter cold fronts move through. One gale after another — with the spray blowing off the tops of the waves, and the giant albatrosses and petrels riding the wind like Valkyries or storm spirits.

The south coast is sometimes called the 'Rainbow Coast' because of the number of rainy days. But visitors to the region are compensated by its natural beauty and its rich sea life. Sperm whales, humpbacks and right whales pass by in season, together with pods of their predator — orca, the killer whale. There are schools of dolphins and pilot whales, massed formations of tuna and salmon and sometimes vast shoals of herring and squid so thick that they look like banks of seaweed in the water.

The sharks follow them all, preying on the sick, the weak or the unlucky. For that is their ordained role in the cycle of life in the sea.

Abalone divers customarily work the rough water along granite outcrops because the abalone themselves prefer the most turbulent conditions. Most divers use trailer boats from 6 to 8 metres in length for mobility and for ease of launching off isolated beaches.

In winter there are many days when the boats cannot go out at all. Sometimes the divers are forced to work less productive ground in shallow sheltered water because they are unable to anchor in the heavy swells and breaking seas at their preferred diving spots.

The late winter of 1995 saw a series of exceptionally savage storms and strong depressions lash the south coast. The swell stayed high week after week, making it difficult to launch the trailer boats through the prevailing surf. Heavy seas closed out areas which ordinarily gave the highest yields.

The swell was still up on the weekend of 9–10 September 1995. On the Monday, Dave Weir and another abalone diver, Darren Adams, decided that they would 'give Honeymoon a go'. The water was shallow and the abalone

3

were generally well scattered. But Weir had once found a patch where, he estimated, there were 120 kilograms of abalone. He hoped he could locate it again. The island provided shelter from the swell and there was reasonable anchoring ground inside the island. At least a diver could get into the water and work, even though the visibility would probably be poor.

The early part of Monday was uneventful, much like many other days in the accustomed grind of abalone diving along the south coast.

By the middle of the day Darren Adams, who had been having sinus problems, decided he had had enough. Dave Weir was pleased with his morning and figured on having one more dive. He had done well in the circumstances, gathering a reasonable haul of abalone in water discoloured by the recent storms.

Like all the abalone divers, he worked with a 'hookah', an air compressor powered by a petrol motor in the boat, pumping air down a nylon hose to the diver. It was his umbilical cord. At the end of the hose he breathed on the same mouthpiece 'demand' valve used by SCUBA divers. A thick-skinned neoprene wetsuit protected him against the worst of the cold.

He also carried a small 'pony bottle' of compressed air for emergencies as an alternative air supply in case the hookah motor should fail. The rig was similar to those used by pearl divers in the tropics and by other working divers. In Weir's case the emergency bottle was basically for deep water and was hardly necessary in the shallows inside Honeymoon Island. But his harness was set up to accommodate it, and he decided to leave the rig as it was.

At 3 p.m. Weir prepared to make his last dive for the day. By the time he had gathered another bag of green-lips they would have to be on their way. Otherwise, by the time they reached Hopetoun, the light would be gone and they would get back to town in the dark.

A diver would be chilled at the end of successive dives, despite the heavy wetsuit. The scalding hot shower at the end of the day, a hearty hot meal, a couple of cold beers and a warm bed were the only luxuries in a hard life. After a day in the ocean, weary abalone divers fell into instant sleep. Dave Weir was looking forward to the end of the day as he prepared for the dive.

'Righto!'

He made the signal to David Lashman, his 21-year-old tender and deckhand. The hookah motor started, Weir clasped his abalone iron and net bag and splashed over the side of his aluminium runabout with its black Mercury outboard motor. He entered the water as he had hundreds, perhaps thousands, of times before. An enveloping cloud of his own entry bubbles surrounded him as he broke the surface.

4

Some people might have had concerns diving at Honeymoon Island. There were seals on the rocks. Sea lions snorted through their whiskers and gave gruff, dog-like barks. No great distance away, right whales had been calving, the water around them slicked by the blood and mucus of afterbirth. Any of these natural events could have attracted the interest of sharks and perhaps made a casual diver think twice about a swim.

But Dave Weir was a professional. He had been diving since his teenage years, and sharks were a part of the ocean. If you wanted to dive, he would have told you, especially if you wished to have the benefits of being a professional diver, you shared the ocean with the sharks and whatever else might be around. They had a right to be there too.

In any case the chances of a serious attack were statistically low. The last fatality south of the tropics had been back in 1967. Twenty-eight years was a long time ago; Dave had been one year old at the time. Too young to know of the horror of that year's death.

Three weeks before 11 September, in the Hopetoun area, another abalone diver had been frightened out of the water by a huge shark. It was a number of days before he was able to dive again. The other abalone divers laughed and made sympathetic jokes. A shark scare was something which happened to all abalone divers sooner or later. They made light of it because to dwell too much on the possibility of becoming a shark fatality would make their work impossible. They preferred to put a brave face on it instead.

'Breaks the monotony,' they said with a grin, raising their beers in the pubs. 'Here's to Whitey!'

The toast to 'Whitey', the Great White shark, sometimes known as the White Pointer or 'White Death', was spitting in the eye of the Devil.

Carcharodon carcharias, the Great White shark, *was* the Devil in the minds of many Australian divers. The species had a dark record in eastern Australian waters.

But so far as the abalone divers were concerned there was a lot of salt water between attacks. Spearfishing had been a common factor in most of them, and that didn't apply where abalone were concerned. And it didn't do to linger on morbid recollections of events which had happened somewhere else, some other time. They had a job to do, and needed to get on with it.

Nevertheless, each man carried something of a shark shadow at the back of his mind. They would not have been human otherwise.

After a fatal attack in South Australia, years previously, Port Lincoln divers had invented mobile cages, powered by propellers driven by compressed air, as a protection against sharks. Dave Weir had operated with

5

a cage for a time. But when he switched to a smaller boat he had found it too cumbersome, and asked himself whether it was really worth the hassle.

On that Monday, 11 September, they followed a practised routine. Lashman had steered the boat close to the reef and the turbulent white water preferred by abalone. After going over the side, Weir spent 10 to 20 seconds on the surface, as he usually did. Then he dived and was lost to sight, in water about 8 metres deep.

Lashman moved the boat to a safer spot, already thinking about what needed to be done at the end of an operational day. Soon they would be coiling air hoses, sorting the catch, and…

'Oh my God!'

There was an enormous swirl where Weir had dived and a violent thrashing. Lashman saw a tail nearly 2 metres across break the surface. A huge fin knifed the water, and a cloud of blood burst from below.

'Dave!'

Lashman gunned the boat back to the spreading bloodstain in the foam and leaped to grab the air hose, to draw the diver in. But the line came in slack, with the harness still attached but shredded. The emergency bottle showed gouges and teeth marks. Then the diver's body came to the surface, without a head, shoulder and arm. A corpse in crimson water, shockingly mauled.

'Oh God!'

Lashman gagged in horror. He reached for the body spouting blood from the dreadful wounds. But he was unable to drag it into the boat. It was too heavy for him. David Weir had been over 1.8 metres tall, a muscular man, and he was wearing a 13.5 kilogram lead belt and heavy fins. Lashman tried to lift him first by the weight belt, then by the legs, but he slipped and lost his grip. The body sank and it would have been foolhardy beyond belief to dive into the water to try to recover it. David Weir was obviously beyond all help.

'Oh God!' Where was the shark? Would it attack the boat? What should he do?

David Lashman was only 21 years old, and he had been a deckhand less than a year. But he took the only course possible in the nightmare situation. He gunned the motor and, with the Mercury outboard screaming at full throttle, ran from Honeymoon Island to nearby Starvation Bay in less than eight minutes. There he ran the boat through the shallows and up on to the beach. He jumped ashore and stumbled into the camp of some startled amateur fishermen.

The fishermen did not need to question him to ascertain the truth of the story. It was written on his face. They drove him at once to Hopetoun to report the tragedy. All the way along the bumpy dirt road, that ghastly scene in the water — the blood, the mutilated body — would not leave his mind.

Weir must have entered the water almost on top of the shark, with no visibility and no chance of avoiding it in the dirty water. The attack was so sudden, so unexpected that Lashman had trouble grasping the grim reality of it.

'He was distraught and going into shock when he arrived,' said Roger Veen, owner of the Hopetoun general store. Lashman at that time still could not give a coherent account of what had happened. Except that Dave Weir was dead and a shark had killed him. Veen sensibly did not press him and drove him a further 50 kilometres to Ravensthorpe Hospital. There the young deckhand was placed under heavy sedation. On the following day he was still too distressed to give a report to police. Roger Veen and many others in Hopetoun, a town of 300 people where David Weir was well known, were also distressed.

'David was a very genuine fellow,' Veen told reporter Susan Brockman of the *West Australian* newspaper. 'I've dealt with him in business and as a friend and he was always a marvellous chap. The town is in shock after the attack. It cleared the bar at the hotel. A lot of people there heard the news, put down their drinks and headed for home.'

Police divers and four abalone boats went to Honeymoon Island the next day to search for Weir's remains. But the water was too dirty to allow a proper search. A mobile cage was brought from Esperance and police divers prepared for a lesson in its use so that they could search the Honeymoon Island seabed. But there was no need. A beach patrol, mounted on four-wheel motorcycles, by friends of David Weir found his body at Munglinup Beach early on the morning of Wednesday 13 September. An unlucky day indeed.

The body had washed ashore about 15 kilometres from the scene of the attack. Rob McWilliams was first on the scene and, though he had not expected to view a pleasant sight, he found the shark-mauled remains extremely distressing. Though they knew that what they found must be David Weir it was not possible to make a positive identification. The remains were taken to Ravensthorpe hospital where David Lashman was still undergoing treatment for shock.

'We believe this is the body of David Weir,' Sergeant Phil Clews of Ravensthorpe police told Torrance Mendez of the *West Australian*. 'The weight belt is missing and we will have to conduct further inquiries.' The body was taken to Perth, the State capital, for autopsy.

There was a bizarre postscript months later when a human arm and portions of a wetsuit were found washed ashore at Munglinup Beach in late December, a few days before Christmas 1995.

Other abalone divers in Hopetoun, who had known David Weir well, believed that the shark may have mistaken him for a seal or sea lion in the dirty water that September day.

'It could have happened to any of us,' said Darren Adams, who had been diving near Weir. 'Sharks are something we have to live with and this was just a case of the worst kind of bad luck.'

In previous years, following a shark attack, there had usually been a hunt for the killer. Professional fishermen put out baited lines, boats patrolled with harpoons and guns. But 1995 was a different year. There was to be no revenge. Darren Adams shook his head when asked by newspaper and television reporters whether a reward would be offered.

'There's no bounty on the shark's head,' he said. 'They live in the ocean and we work in it.'

When I first heard the news of the tragedy on the radio I was working on my dive-boat, preparing for a sortie to photograph right whales in Southern Ocean waters. Naturally the news caused some deep thought. I knew at once which species of shark would be involved. *Carcharodon carcharias*, the Great White shark, needed no introduction to divers.

There was one chilling aspect to a *Carcharodon* attack. Few of the victims ever saw the shark coming. The initial impact was usually devastating and overwhelming and in most cases it came completely without warning. As it had with David Weir.

There are, of course, exceptions to every rule.

Damon Edmunds, a 25-year-old abalone diver working off South Australia's Purdie Islands, some hundreds of kilometres east of David Weir's last dive, was one of the lucky ones. He saw his shark in time, its attention diverted by his air line.

Edmunds was diving on 'hookah' apparatus in 17 metres of water early in May 1996. It was seven months after Weir's tragic death. Looking up to the surface he was horrified to see a 5 metre Great White circling above him. It was nosing at his air hose, his vital link to the boat.

Edmonds knew that Great Whites often attacked sea lions from below. Instead of swimming up towards the boat he braced himself in a rocky crevice in the bottom, hoping that the shark would go away.

'But it just kept circling. Every time I moved or made an attempt to make ground towards the boat, the shark was back again with its big black eye.

'I could tell that it was in a serious attacking mood because when I sent the abalone bag up to the surface it attacked the bag.

'My brother Dion was on the boat. I sent the bag up by air-filled parachute and he sent me down another one, in the usual way. I kept sending the empty bag back until he realised I had a problem and guessed what it was.

'Meantime the shark bit through the bag rope. Lucky it wasn't the air line!'

Damon Edmunds was trapped by the shark for three hours and was suffering cold and hypothermia when his brother managed to attract the attention of another abalone boat. A diver with a self-propelled shark cage went down to rescue him, arriving like the cavalry at the point at which Edmunds felt he could not hold out any longer.

'Boy, was I glad to see that cage!' Edmunds had a very fortunate escape. A reprieve he will remember all his life.

But for Pat Bowring, 45 years old, who went to dive on the wreck of the paddle steamer *Koputai*, 6 kilometres off Sydney's Bondi Beach, on 24 May 1996, there could be no happy ending.

Bowring, a well-known Sydney journalist and the husband of Nene King, editorial director of the *Australian Women's Weekly*, was an experienced diver. He was one of an elite group of less than 20 divers in Australia who made deepwater dives breathing mixed gases in order to avoid decompression sickness, or the 'bends'. They were known as 'technical divers,' because any dive over the normal safe SCUBA limit of 50 metres is called a 'technical' dive.

Bowring had made similar dives off Florida and Mexico.

The old paddlewheeler, sunk in the 1920s, lay in her sea grave at 79 metres — more than 250 feet — a depth regarded as well beyond ordinary safe limits. But Bowring and his friends had made similar dives before. Yet it was a grim fact that in the previous year the wreck had claimed the lives of two other divers.

In March 1994 Bowring's close friend Paul Cavanagh, manager of television's Channel Seven, had drowned while diving with Bowring off Sydney's Long Reef. Bowring had taught Cavanagh to dive and was greatly affected at witnessing his companion's death. But he refused to give up diving, saying that every diver had to live with some degree of risk.

Because of the depth and the *Koputai's* fine state of preservation, Sydney divers regard the wreck as 'the Everest of dives'.

'Only a handful of divers have ever managed to actually reach the wreck,' explained Manly Dive Centre manager Joe Ellams to a *Daily Telegraph* reporter. 'It's the pinnacle of wreck diving. To see the *Koputai* sitting out on the sand, untouched and untampered with, is one of the great diving experiences.'

On the *Koputai* dive, on 26 May, Bowring and two other divers descended down a 'mermaid' line linking their vessel to the wreck. At the 20 metre mark Bowring signalled that he was having some difficulty and would return to the surface. The others acknowledged with the diver's 'OK' signal — the finger and thumb in a circle. They continued on their descent to the wreck.

Bowring regained the surface and signalled to the people on board the boat that he was all right. 'I'm OK!' However, he then seemed to be having difficulty with his mask. Heavy swells washed over him and he appeared to have trouble reaching the safety line astern.

Two of the people on board the boat dived into the water to assist him. But by the time they reached the spot, only 15 metres astern, Bowring had vanished down into the depths.

When he failed to resurface and his two companions had returned from the wreck because of his non-appearance, the alarm was raised. A major search was undertaken. By 4 p.m., after a full day's searching which included police launches and helicopters circling the area, it was officially reported that Pat Bowring was missing. He was believed drowned or possibly the victim of a heart attack.

But 48 hours later, on Sunday 26 May, a dramatic discovery was made.

Bowring's deepwater drysuit, ripped from neck to stomach, with the zip still done up was recovered near the wreck in 80 metres of water by a group of divers including Joe Ellam. The suit was black, with light blue arms and shoulders. The centre section had been torn out, leaving ragged edges.

There was no sign of Bowring's breathing apparatus, with its four gas tanks, or of his buoyancy compensator vest, weight belt, mask and fins. Or of his body.

'It was quite bizarre,' one of the police officers said. 'There is no way he could have got out of the suit himself without taking off his equipment and undoing the zip.'

The torn condition of the suit pointed to another possibility. By Monday police agreed that a shark was probably responsible. But they said that Bowring could possibly have died beforehand. The following day a Sydney pathologist confirmed that Bowring's suit had indeed been ripped by a shark.

The search continued for his equipment. It was hoped that this might give clues from teeth marks on fabric or rubber, or gouges in his tanks, which would identify the species of shark involved.

But some divers already had their own opinions.

There was one species of shark which had the brute strength, the wickedly sharp teeth and the lethal capacity. It was a shark which could cut through a nylon weight belt and equipment harness straps with ease. A shark which was big enough to shake a diver out of his suit like a dog skinning a rabbit.

Carcharodon carcharias had previously figured in attacks on SCUBA divers in South Australia, Tasmania and New South Wales. In some of these incidents no body was ever found. Only severed weight belts and torn and scattered pieces of equipment were recovered. Evidence of a devastating attack, and a sad ending for a lost diver.

Tiger sharks, common off Sydney Heads, are also large predators. But unlike Great Whites, *Galeocerdo cuvieri* had not previously figured in attacks on SCUBA divers, live or dead. At least not on the record.

The key question in the *Koputai* case was whether Pat Bowring was alive when his suit and body were savaged by the shark.

In most instances of past diving accidents, or drownings, bodies recovered by the Water Police had usually been unmolested by sharks. But there were some exceptions, including Sydney's notorious Shark Arm Murder case.

Prior to Pat Bowring's fatal dive, Great Whites had been involved in the 1990s in savage attacks on SCUBA divers in Australian waters. Two such tragic deaths occurred within days of each other in 1993.

Therese Cartwright, a 35-year-old mother of quadruplets and one other baby, was attacked near a seal colony off Tenth Island on the northern Tasmanian coast on 5 June 1993. As she dived with SCUBA equipment, following two other companions down, a Great White struck her in midwater, shearing her leg from her body and making off with her remains.

On 9 June a honeymoon couple, John and Deborah Ford, were decompressing below a boat after a SCUBA dive at Julian Rocks, near Byron Bay, New South Wales, when John Ford saw a huge Great White, mouth open, charging towards his new bride. In a heroic gesture Ford pushed his wife aside and took the charge himself. He was killed and eaten by the shark.

Scientific research at the Farralon Islands, rocky peaks in United States waters about 42 kilometres west of San Francisco's Golden Gate, where Great Whites congregate each year to prey on young elephant seals, has identified a particular pattern of *Carcharodon* attack.

The seals and sea lions are apparently too agile for the sharks *below* the surface. But the animals are vulnerable for a few seconds when they go to the surface to breath. The Great Whites' *modus operandi* is apparently to wait in ambush on the bottom and then drive up at a 45 degree angle, at great speed, when they see an elephant seal or sea lion taking a breath. If successful they strike the prey with such force that it is immobilised by the impact. Then they return to finish off the helpless and wounded animal.

In experiments at the Farralons, Great Whites vigorously attacked surfboards, with built-in video cameras, which were towed behind boats. This indicated that they may be attracted by any movement at or near the surface, even if it does not bear a close resemblance to a sea elephant.

Human divers — whose fins may make them look like seals or sea lions — are most at risk near the surface, whether descending or ascending. This is the danger zone where the majority of recorded Great White attacks have occurred.

When Pat Bowring had problems with his equipment, or his health, he was in a vulnerable situation. A lone diver separated from his companions, sending out vibratory signals of distress or anxiety in midwater and silhouetted against the surface, could perhaps be a prime target for a prowling Great White.

It could have happened so swiftly and unexpectedly — hallmarks of a *Carcharodon* ambush — that no one else would have been aware of it. He would have been desperately unlucky, of course, to have a Great White in the vicinity, just when he was experiencing his problems.

But Great White sharks are not uncommon in the deep water off Sydney, and perhaps 'the worst kind of bad luck', as fellow abalone diver Darren Adams said of David Weir's death, is a fair description of the circumstances in any shark fatality. A diver unlucky enough to be in the wrong place at just the wrong moment.

The ragged-edged section torn from Pat Bowring's drysuit (heavier than an ordinary wetsuit) took in a region from the chest below the neck to the hip. A typical Great White strike. Yet, as we've noted, Bowing may have died from a heart attack. And a further possibility is that Bowring, who had a theoretical four hours' breathing time below the surface with his tanks, died from a problem with his equipment. An overdose of oxygen might have caused convulsions, unconsciousness and drowning.

Either way, some time in the next 48 hours — most likely on the Friday night because sharks have a preference for fresh prey — a shark may have scented the body from a distance and ripped the dead diver out of his suit. In

12

this event it might have been thought that some of his heavy equipment, particularly his gas tanks and weight belt, would have been found not far from the suit. His buoyancy compensator vest, which normally covered the torn area of the suit, would also carry indications of what might have occurred.

The search for Bowring's equipment, and for clues to the cause of his accident, continued in the days following the discovery of the suit by deep divers of the Manly technical diving group.

The 79 metre depth was a major problem because police and navy divers were not permitted to go beyond 50 metres for reasons of insurance and service regulations. Aside from the extreme depth, the currents and poor visibility made the *Koputai* wreck a deadly hazardous dive. Police diver Sergeant John Marshall, who knew Bowring and described him as a physically fit man and a diver with seven years experience, told the *Sun Herald:* 'The water down there is very dark. There's very low visibility. I wouldn't do that dive. It's too deep.'

The prospect of further efforts by technical divers raised a valid question about the wisdom of risking further lives for one already lost.

A commercial ROV (remote-operated vehicle), a robot machine with a video camera linked to the surface, owned by Dusty Miller's Western Australian commercial diving firm Contract Diving Services, was sent down to scan the seabed. But the results were negative.

'This is the most baffling case I have ever worked on,' a frustrated Sergeant Terry Ervin of the Sydney Water Police told Nigel Vincent of the *Daily Telegraph.* 'We have a suit, but no body.'

The Bowring case was unusual but it was not unique. The police in Miami, Florida had an identical case on record. The shark attack on William Covert, a 25-year-old unemployed marine biologist and recent graduate of Michigan State University occurred on 13 September 1995. Covert disappeared while diving for tropical fish off the Florida Keys. He had been in Florida for a month working to earn money for a return to college to further his studies.

No body was found. All searchers found was his weight belt, still buckled but bitten through, fragments of a T-shirt, sweat pants with the front chewed away and his teeth-marked SCUBA gear. 'We think he was attacked and eaten by a 10 or 12 foot [3 or 3.7 metre] bull shark, based on [the opinions of] two experts who examined the clothing,' the Miami Sheriff's Office told Reuters News Service.

As in the Pat Bowring case, the police had torn clothing and a well-founded suspicion, but no body.

Western Australian police have the case of the missing windsurfer, listed as a fatality without a body.

In January 1997 a group of German windsurfers joined other international sailboarders at the port of Geraldton in Western Australia. All were eagerly looking forward to tackling Geraldton's famous surf break at Lighthouse Reef, 2 kilometres off Point Moore. One of the group, Werner Schonhofer, was a 41-year-old dental technician who had been windsurfing for more than 20 years. He had ridden some of the world's hottest sailboarding spots, including the breaks at Hawaii's famous 'pipeline'.

On Monday, 20 January 1997, the conditions on the west coast were severe. The meteorology bureau put out a strong wind warning indicating they expected southerly winds exceeding 30 knots with a 3 metre swell. These conditions would keep most sailors inside the harbour, but to the windsurfers they presented an exciting challenge. Werner Schonhofer was among the windsurfers who launched their sailboards from the beach, near the lighthouse, and skimmed out to where the wind-whipped surf was roaring across the outer reef. The rainbow-coloured sails made a pretty picture as they danced across the foaming crests. Some of the riders made spectacular leaps and somersaults using the dark faces of the breakers as launching pads.

Late in the afternoon, around 6 p.m., Schonhofer's friends saw him experience a severe 'wipe-out' on a huge wave. This was not an uncommon event in such severe conditions. Usually the windsurfer recovered his gear, water-started the board again and was back in the thick of things within a few minutes. If any of the gear was damaged — a mast or boom broken or a sail ripped — the rider swam the board and rig back to the beach to ruefully examine the wreckage. In Schonhofer's case he appeared to be washed into the channel between the reef and the shore. No one saw him after that.

When Schonhofer failed to return to the beach his friends became concerned. Darkness fell and there was still no sign of the missing boardrider. His travelling companions, including Klaus Maier and Leonhart Kohwagner, contacted the police who began a search. They were hampered by the strong winds and darkness, but at first light the skipper of a crayfishing boat reported by radio a sighting of a wetsuit and sailboard harness floating 2 kilometres offshore from Coronation Beach, north of Geraldton. Schonhofer's drifting sailboard was sighted by a helicopter and recovered.

The zip fasteners of the blue and yellow short-legged wetsuit were still fastened, but the suit was shredded by shark bites. The harness also bore the marks of shark teeth. The sailboard was undamaged, but a dent in the mast

14

may have been caused by Schonhofer striking his head during the wipe-out. 'He was probably unconscious, incapacitated or drowned before the sharks got to him,' said veteran local windsurfer Rik Engstrom. 'I'd say that was exactly how it did happen. Let's hope so.'

Experienced windsurfers said that their boards moved too fast for a shark to catch them in ordinary circumstances, but a rider could be vulnerable in the water, particularly if he were injured. Local fishermen said that the teeth marks were most likely to be those of tiger sharks, which were common in the area. Rik Engstrom said he believed that the largest bite indicated a shark of about 4.5 metres in length.

The Geraldton police, like their counterparts in Manly, New South Wales and Miami, Florida, had shark-torn clothing as evidence and a basis for theory, but they had no body to finalise the case. Werner Schonhofer's fate, like that of Pat Bowring, will continue to be a matter for surmise.

Were tiger sharks, the striped predator species *Galeocerdo cuvieri*, the likely villains in the Schonhofer mystery? If the windsurfer had been knocked unconscious and drowned, tiger sharks would quite likely have been attracted to his body since they play a major role as ocean scavengers. But if he were attacked near the surface — and the same applied with William Covert — then the more likely aggressor would be *Carcharodon carcharias*, which has the darker record for attacks on living humans, especially divers.

Carcharodon carcharias has been around for some 60 million years. The species is the apex predator in the shark world. Humans entering the shark's domain become just another marine mammal and so share the risks of the sea, including the possible unwelcome attentions of the Great White.

'THE RAVIN'D SALT-SEA SHARK'

chapter two

I HEARD THE FIRST REPORTS OF DAVID WEIR'S DEATH OVER THE RADIO WITH A certain sense of *déjà vu*. There was a tragic familiarity about what had occurred. The circumstances surrounding the attack were similar to others in the past. The unexpectedness, the shock, the fearful physical damage — all pointed to a particular species of predator. *Carcharodon carcharias* — 'Old Ragged Teeth' — was back in the news, and when that occurs it is almost always bad news for a diver. Somewhere.

I had had my own acquaintance with the Great White shark, spanning 40 years, and David Weir's sad demise awakened old memories. Turning the radio off I walked slowly down to the jungle end of my garden in Swanbourne, a sleepy beachside suburb of Perth, in Western Australia.

Neighbours used to joke that a lost tribe of pygmies lived at the overgrown back of the garden and that there were monkeys swinging in the palms. There was certainly a nautical graveyard, with bent whaling harpoons grown over with grass. Brass portholes and ballast bricks from ancient shipwrecks lay about, together with bits of boats and sailboards. They were relics of past expeditions and forays to distant shores, kept out of a certain nostalgia. Perhaps they would be recycled again one day. More likely they would continue to recline in honoured retirement. But each object had its own story and was regarded with affection on that account.

On David Weir's day I had one particular piece from the past in mind. Leaning against the back fence were some oblong aluminium panels. Their functional outline was softened by a covering of wide green leaves. Nasturtium creepers with their pretty red flowers twined their way through the mesh. Only a handful of divers would have recognised the panels in that dismembered and apparently derelict state. But scrubbed with a wire brush and bolted together they would take on the familiar shape of a shark cage, complete with camera gaps and quick-release bottom panel. With a bit of elbow grease, I told myself, it could be as good as new.

The cage had been waiting through the winter rains and summer suns of the years for some future unspecified adventure. I ran a finger over the gouges in the 45 centimetre (18 inch) camera gap and wondered whether indeed there would be another day in its working life.

The scrapes and notches in the soft metal had been made in a manner which could hardly be forgotten: scored by the serrated teeth of *Carcharodon carcharias* in the blood-murked water off the Albany whaling station.

Great Whites had been framed in those camera gaps. Sometimes they had shoved their noses, uninvited, inside the cage, raking the bars with their teeth while our hearts beat like drums. The cage had enabled us to observe at first hand the behaviour of a species of shark that had long fascinated me. So much of a spurious nature had been written about Great Whites; so little was positively known about them. The cage offered an opportunity to distinguish between some of the myths and the realities.

Great Whites have a dark reputation as the ultimate predator, magnificent yet sinister beasts. But because they are denizens of the deep seas practical observation of them has been extremely limited. Most actual experience with humans has been through tragedies on the horrific side. As with David Weir.

However, there was one location that provided a dramatically different perspective to the general rule.

Albany, a town on King George's Sound on the south coast, where the Cheynes Beach Whaling Co. had established operations, was a rare exception to the shark's preference for deep water. When the whalechasers towed dead sperm whales into the Sound they left a broad bloodslick behind them and the sharks followed in the wake. There in sheltered waters they finned around the carcasses, occasionally tearing out great gobbets of whale flesh and blubber in massive bites.

Set beside the dead Albany whales, the cage had provided a window by which to look in on the life of the greatest shark in the ocean. The bites on the bars were the price of curiosity.

'Is it a shark cage or a diver's cage?' the welder had asked me with a grin when I first took the plans to him. 'I mean, you're on the inside looking out...' He stubbed a gloved finger on the drawing. 'And how are you going to stop them getting at you through this bloody great hole here?'

The hole he referred to was the 45 centimetre camera gap.

'They're too big to get through,' I replied.

17

He looked at me thoughtfully and didn't ask any more questions.

While the welder adjusted his handpiece and the cage took shape in arcs of flying sparks, his goggles reminded me of my own first dive.

In 1946 I was 12 years old and the dive was in humble circumstances. The ex-Army gas mask I tried out at Rottnest Island, illegally combined with my mother's laundry hose, smelled of rank raw rubber. It was hardly the use for which it had been designed and the misted eyepieces sometimes popped disconcertingly out of focus. Often I had to shut one eye to see. When the mask flooded I choked on salt water.

But it opened for me a world of mystery and magic. Half a century on, I have seen many changes in the world. Seen many miracles of technology become commonplace. Now when the beat of a helicopter approaches and passes overhead we don't even bother to look up. But in the realm below the surface, beneath the silver skin, the wonder is still there.

In 1946 computers, television, transistors, microwave ovens, video cameras and mobile telephones were generations away from general use. Some of Britain's senior scientists declared as late as 1949 that the notion of putting a man on the moon was 'the purest folly'. People travelling overseas mostly went by steamship because intercontinental air travel could only be afforded by the wealthy and was something of an endurance test in any case. It took the better part of a week from Australia to London, with overnight stops along the way. In unpressurised propeller-driven aircraft airsick bags were in frequent use. The ears rang from engine noise for days after.

In 1946 radios had valves, we had to wind our watches every day and took them off before swimming. Our first 'fins' were bits of plywood nailed to sandshoes. But the primitive means were incidental. The magic was there to see. If I were asked which of all the wonderful postwar inventions have made the most significant difference in my life, my answer would come without a moment's hesitation. Self-Contained Underwater Breathing Apparatus has enabled us to swim with the fish and become a part of the ocean.

Sharks, of course, had a bad name in those early days. The reason for the negative attitude was ignorance. People saw only the surface of the sea and knew little or nothing about what went on below the waves.

SCUBA became freely available after the Second World War, allowing ordinary people the experience of discovering a new world below the waves. The period of less than 50 years since then has seen a turnabout in our attitudes to animals. The unexpected beauty and the wonderful diversity of underwater life have led to a better understanding of the creatures that live in the sea, together with an enhanced appreciation of our own role on the planet.

The Second World War was a time of great human ugliness. When it was over, people wanted to put the death camps, the burnt and bombed-out cities, the millions of dead in unmarked graves behind them. For the moment it hurt too much to look back. Humanity looked to the future hoping to rediscover some beauty in life, and the natural world provided some of the answers. Especially the underwater experience. Sharing the coral reef scene of corals and fish and sharks and sea creatures of so many differing colours and shapes and sizes was like travelling to another planet.

Nonetheless it was impossible to escape the influence of the war entirely. There were always reminders, sometimes in unexpected places. The 'tank' of my first SCUBA unit, for example, five years after Victory in the Pacific Day, was an ex-USAAF Liberator bomber oxygen bottle, bound with copper wire. I sometimes wondered whether it had made sorties over enemy territory. As children we had spent Saturday afternoons at the cinema with a regular diet of war movies, perched on the edge of our seats, breathlessly watching films like *Coming in on a Wing and a Prayer*. Consequently I had no difficulty imagining the flak bursts, dark bruises against the clouds. The gunners in their harness in plastic bubbles swinging twin 50 calibre machine guns in slow arcs. The nervous sweat beading their foreheads as they searched a hostile sky for the swastika insignia on enemy fighter aircraft . . .

The surviving bombers were scrapped at war's end. I saw fields filled with them out of Melbourne. Wings, tailfins, broken bodies of once sleek ships that had been the pride of their squadrons, now pushed carelessly into piles by bulldozers — their aluminium skins going to fill a duller peacetime role as domestic pots and pans. The steel oxygen cylinders necessary for high altitude flying went to salvage yards and some were recycled to the new world of SCUBA.

My B 29 bottle would have been instantly condemned by any responsible air-filling station today. But it did its job for me. At night as a teenager I dreamt of adventures to come in a sea which at the time was perceived to be a place of lurking dangers. Responsible people warned us of the horrors we could expect to meet below.

In the long ago 1950s manta rays were 'Devil Fish'; barracuda were considered voracious killers; moray eels sought human flesh and were poisonous to boot; and giant cod were supposedly more feared by pearl divers than sharks were. In the Errol Flynn movie *Reap the Wild Wind* a giant octopus reached out with 10 metre tentacles to thrill moviegoers. It was

19

generally believed that a diver might expect to run into a similar monster in the wild. As for sharks, they were evil, sharp-toothed vermin of the seas.

The only good shark was a dead one.

Game fishermen and others who caught and killed sharks were heroes. Personalities such as Sydney radio's Bob Dyer and his wife Dolly of 'Pick A Box' fame, Alf Dean of South Australia, and the celebrated American westerns writer Zane Grey were applauded by the press and the public every time they landed a 'man-eater'. The headlines usually described them as 'Ridding the Seas of a Menace!'

Even where events were accurately described, there was a different perception about sharks, as typified in the book *Shark: The Killer of the Deep: Zane Grey*, featuring the fishing exploits of Zane Grey.

In 1937 Grey hooked a large tiger shark outside Sydney Heads. The shark was finally gaffed and secured by the tail alongside the boat. Grey wrote:

The huge tiger rolled over, white underneath, and he opened a mouth that would have taken a barrel. I saw the rows of white fangs and heard such a snap of jaws as had never before struck my ears. I shuddered at their significance. No wonder we shot and harpooned such vicious brutes!

The shark was towed ashore to Watsons Bay, there to be hauled up by the tail — still alive — on a tripod to be weighed. It tipped the scales at 1036 pounds — 470 kilograms. Grey wrote triumphantly of his dying captive:

I had one good long look at this tiger shark while the men were erecting a tripod and I accorded him more appalling beauty and horrible significance than all the great fish I had ever caught.

'Well, Mr Man-eater, you will never kill any boy or girl!' I flung at him. That was the deep and powerful emotion I felt — the justification of my act — the worthiness of it and the pride in what it took.

Ironically, a shark caused Grey's own death in October 1938. After battling unsuccessfully in Australian waters with a Great White estimated to be over 800 pounds (362 kilograms) in weight, Grey suffered a stroke and died a few months later, leaving behind him the legacy of his prolific writing both on game fishing and the American West.

In Australia in the 1930s the acknowledged shark expert was Gilbert Perry Whitely, ichthyologist at the Australian Museum in Sydney. He wrote a book on sharks and rays, published in 1940 with the title *The Sharks, Rays, Devil-Fish, and other Primitive Fishes of Australia & New Zealand*.

He wrote of the Great White:

The White Shark or White Pointer is the maneater par excellence and is credited with being the most ferocious monster of the seas. Museums all over the world proudly portray specimens with gaping jaws and upstanding triangular teeth. One can picture this monster (if one had not been fortunate enough to see it in life) following a ship in the hope that someone would jump overboard and provide it with lunch. This shark is said to grow to a length of 40 feet [12 metres] and has been known to devour man. But it lives in the open oceans and I have no record of it ever having been responsible for a tragedy on our Australian beaches… It is a very voracious species.

Whitely suggested that the Great White Shark 'might, in fact, be the origin of the legend of Jonah and the Whale… The White Shark could easily swallow a man whole, in the unlikely event of it wanting to do so'.

Gilbert Whitely, in his era, was deferred to on all shark matters. But his views on sharks nonetheless illustrated something of the general lack of knowledge during that time. The word 'Devil-Fish' in the title of his book is indicative. Today we call the beautiful and harmless plankton-eating rays of tropic seas 'mantas'. Their scientific name is *Manta birostris* and comes from the name Spanish-American fishermen gave the giant rays. 'Manta' means 'blanket' in Spanish. Sharks are no longer considered 'Primitive Fishes' but rather as splendidly evolved creatures superbly adapted to their marine environment.

Whitely mistakenly condemned the grey nurse shark. 'Its swift and savage attack is justly feared by bathers,' he wrote. 'At the time of annual salmon runs surf-bathing is certainly attended with risk, as the majority of attacks on human beings take place at such times.'

By sharks, yes. But the culprits were Great Whites, whaler sharks and sometimes tigers. The grey nurse, *Eugomphodus taurus*, was an innocent bystander, known today to be harmless to humans.

The brief passage quoted above on the Great White shark also contains some errors. There are no specimens 40 feet (12 metres) long — and a good thing too. By 1940 there had already been more than 200 shark attacks in Australian waters, and despite Whitely's disclaimer ('no record of it ever having been responsible for a tragedy'), a significant number of the fatalities — we recognise now — bore the hallmarks of *Carcharodon carcharias*.

The death of a Melbourne youth, Norman Clarke, on 15 February 1930, which Whitely listed in his book, was a classic *Carcharodon* attack. It was the first recorded shark incident in Victorian waters in 50 years. Interstate dinghy

21

races were being held on Port Phillip Bay that weekend, and a crowd had gathered at the deepwater end of Middle Brighton pier, about 400 metres from shore. About 4.30 p.m. Clarke, aged 19 years, dived from the pier, as boys will. Surfacing, and no doubt feeling pleased with himself, he swam back towards it. Three metres from the pier his expression changed. He suddenly raised his arms high as though reaching out to those on the pier. He called for help, but was plucked below the surface in an ominous swirl of water.

Moments later he reappeared with a giant shark gripping him by the leg. He was sitting across the shark's snout beating at it with his fists. The shark went down again to the cries of the onlookers, and poor Clarke was never seen again.

The tragedy was witnessed by a large crowd of horrified people. They said that the shark was at least 16 feet (nearly 5 metres) in length. At the time one of the 'experts' asserted that it was a grey nurse. But there can be no question that it was a Great White.

This is not intended to disparage Gilbert Whitely. Wisdom is easy in hindsight. Today we have the advantage of a greatly expanded base of knowledge and research. Whitely's own research into sharks and fishes in an early period was most valuable, and his findings were accurate where he had full opportunity for study. But the larger sharks lived in the mysterious world of deeper water and a good deal of what was written about them in earlier days was necessarily surmise. Today SCUBA allows scientists the advantage of being able to study sharks in their own environment.

However, in times when the experts were in error, it can be understood that there were many popular misconceptions. The Great White in particular, with its huge size and spectacular armoury of triangular teeth, looks a nasty brute when hauled ashore as a corpse. It has not had many friends through the centuries.

In his *History of the Fishes of the British Isles*, Jonathan Couch wrote in 1867:

> *The White Shark is to sailors the most formidable of all the inhabitants of the ocean... For in none besides are the powers of inflicting injury so equally combined with the eagerness to accomplish it. The White Shark is 'the dread of sailors who are in constant fear of becoming its prey when they bathe or fall into the sea'.*

The British zoologist, Pennant, wrote in a similar vein about *Carcharodon* in 1776:

> *This fish grows to a very great bulk, Gillius says to the weight of four thousand pounds [over 1800 kilograms]; and that in the belly of one was found*

22

an entire human corpse, which is far from incredible considering their vast greediness after human flesh.

They are the dread of the sailors in all hot climates, where they constantly attend the ships in expectation of what may drop overboard; a man that has that misfortune perishes without redemption; they have been seen to dart at him like gudgeons to a worm.

A master of a Guinea [West African] ship informed me that a rage of suicides prevailed among his new-bought slaves from the notion the unhappy creatures had that after death they should be restored again to their families, friends and country.

To convince them that at least they should not reanimate their bodies he ordered one of their corpses to be tied by the heels to a rope and lowered into the sea. Though it was drawn up again as fast as the united force of the crew could exert, yet in that short space of time the sharks had devoured every part but the feet, which were secured at the end of the cord.

Swimmers often perish by them; sometimes they lose an arm or a leg and sometimes are bit quite asunder, serving but two morsels for this ravenous animal.

Sailing ships moved at a slow pace, particularly the square-riggers of the 16th and 17th centuries, and in equatorial regions they often *crawled* along in the light tropic breezes. This meant that sharks of several 'man-eater' species could follow sailing ships long distances. The Australian shark researcher Victor Coppleson recorded that the crew of the 870 ton (884 tonne) *Rose of Sharon* hooked a 16 foot (4.8 metre) shark, almost certainly a tiger given the locality, while anchored in the Torres Strait on a voyage from Sydney to Calcutta in the 1880s.

The head and entrails were thrown overboard and the shark was eaten. They sailed 80 nautical miles (148 kilometres) the next day before anchoring once more for the night, a sensible precaution in the treacherous coral-studded water. They fished again and caught another tiger shark which, when its stomach was opened, was found to contain the head and viscera of the one caught the previous night. It had also swallowed tins, chicken carcasses and other rubbish thrown over during the day's voyaging, showing that it had been shadowing the ship.

Modern raft expeditions like the Kon Tiki moving slowly across oceans have often reported attendant schools of sharks swimming with them, and among their regular ship-followers were blue sharks, oceanic whitetips and other members of the *Carcharhinus* family.

23

Thor Heyerdahl, leader of the Kon Tiki expedition, had ample opportunity to study sharks as his raft moved at its snail's pace across the wide Pacific:

We have sat with our legs in the water to test them, and they have swum towards us until they were only two or three feet [90 cm–1 metre] away, only to turn their tails to us again. But if the water was in the least blood-stained as it was when we had been cleaning fish the sharks' fins came to life, and they would collect like bluebottle flies from a long way off. If we flung out sharks' guts they simply went mad and dashed about in a blind fury. They savagely devoured the liver of their own kind and then, if we put a foot in the sea, they came for it like rockets and even dug their teeth into the logs where the foot had been.

To sailors the names were unimportant. They were all sharks. 'Murderous devils' — whatever their shape or size or their unpronounceable scientific names. In fact, humans of any occupation have never much cared for sharks. William Shakespeare, in *Macbeth*, expressed the general view when he referred to their kind as 'the ravin'd salt-sea shark'.

The masters of slave-ships recorded in their journals that sharks regularly followed their vessels, waiting for a death, and considered them creatures of ill-repute. The slavers, hardly salubrious gentlemen themselves, wrote that the ship-following shark was a 'monster' which gorged on human flesh. Whether the victim was alive or dead, they said, scarcely seemed to matter. The first recorded attack victim was a sailor from a Portuguese vessel sailing to India in 1580. The man fell overboard but managed to grasp a rope thrown to him. As his shipmates hauled him in, 'there appeared from below the surface of the sea a large monster called Tiburon. It rushed at the man and tore him into pieces before our very eyes. That was a very grievous death'.

Sailors' dislike of sharks stemmed from the natural fear of falling overboard. During calms or when anchored in tropical harbours they would set to shark fishing for sport. In a spirit of revenge they hauled hooked sharks on deck with block and tackle, there to beat them with cutlasses and iron bars as 'punishment' for being what they were. Sometimes they blinded or disembowelled sharks and threw them back as a 'warning' to others of their kind. Unreasoning cruelty in return for cruelty perceived.

Sharks were a particular pest to old-time whalers, who hunted Leviathan under sail. The sharks gathered in shoals as the whales were dismembered at sea alongside the mother ships. Sometimes the exasperated crew slashed at them or speared them with whale-killing lances.

24

In his epic novel of the legendary white whale, *Moby Dick*, Herman Melville wrote of sharks wounded by whalers' flensing knives while feeding on whales at the vessel's side:

They viciously snapped not only at each other's disembowelments but also at their own. Like flexible bows they bent round, and bit their own; till those entrails seemed swallowed over and over by the same mouth, to be oppositely voided by the same wound… It was unsafe to meddle with the corpses and ghosts of these creatures. A sort of generic or Pantheistic vitality seemed to lurk in their very points and bones, after what might be called their individual vitality had departed.

Melville, drawing on his own whaling experiences, was perhaps the first popular writer to describe the Great White shark at a time when few people knew such a creature existed. Moby Dick is, of course, the monster sperm whale whose malignant spirit surges with its milk-white hump throughout the novel's pages. At one point in the novel, Melville dwells on the significance of the colour white, musing on the accepted contrasts of colour relating to good and evil, or rather about our human perceptions of those colours — white for purity and good; black for evil. White bulls, white horses and white elephants were sacred in ancient times. White was the colour of the Pope's cassock, of the robes of priests and nuns. White maintained the faith; it was the colour of honesty and truth.

But what if those perceptions were reversed? Because we accept so readily that white is the colour of good, when it becomes the colour of terror we are thrown all the more off-balance. When Santa Claus fires the gun or the murderers come dressed as policemen, the resulting fear is actually more devastating. In such circumstances, Melville writes, the colour white:

strikes more of a panic to the soul than that redness which affrights in blood…
Coupled with any object terrible in itself, whiteness heightens that terror to the furthest bounds.
Witness the white bear of the poles and the white shark of the tropics. What but their smooth, flaky whiteness makes them the transcendent horrors that they are?

It was the contrast, Melville said, the shock that the colour of innocence and love could be worn by such deadly creatures. He had a special word about the White shark, based on his time aboard the Yankee whaler *Acushnet* in the 1840s:

25

As for the white shark, the white gliding ghostliness of repose in that creature when beheld in his ordinary moods, strangely tallies with the same quality in the Polar quadruped. This peculiarity is most vividly hit by the French in the name they bestow upon that fish. The Romish Mass for the dead begins with 'Requiem eternam' (eternal rest)... Now in allusion to the white stillness of death in this shark and the deadliness of its habits the French call him 'Requin'.

In the 1950s I spent some time on the tilting decks of Ted 'Sharkey' Nelson's commercial shark-fishing boat *Shaleen*. There I saw numbers of sharks and heard Sharkey's accounts of some of the great fish he had caught himself. To Sharkey and the other professional fishermen a shark was always referred to as a 'fish'.

Shaleen was a clipper-bowed 30 footer (9 metre vessel) with a wooden carvel-planked hull — ridiculously small by the standards of today's aluminium and fibreglass fishing boats. Western Australian professional fishing craft in the 1990s are twice her length, run at three times her speed and locate their grounds by GPS, radar, echo-sounders and other electronic marvels. By today's standards *Shaleen* would be considered quite unsafe, and would not be allowed to put to sea.

But Sharkey, singlehanded, took her 50 kilometres out to sea, into the wild wastes of the Indian Ocean. He would go out in rough westerly weather, and well out of sight of land on days when others stayed home in harbour. He scorned such 'newfangled nonsense' as ship-to-shore radio, and pulled his long miles of shark lines on his own, with no crew to help him.

Long-line shark fishing, especially singlehanded, is among the more dangerous fishing operations because of the possibility of being accidentally hooked and dragged overboard by the line. But Sharkey was a marvel of dexterity, baiting his lines with quick, sure hand movements, and seeing the shiny-tipped hooks flick overboard, one after the other. Few could match his own skills and he was impatient with lesser mortals on his quarterdeck. Though he employed deckhands from time to time they seldom stayed long. 'They just get underfoot,' he grumbled. 'A man's better off without 'em.'

I have my own memories of the hundreds of hooks and wire traces coming in over the gunwale when the line was pulled. The winch groaning, and glittering droplets of water flying off the bar-tight sisal rope. Rows of floats, piled high in the stern, miles of shiny coils of green line, and the spiked fins of the catch lying belly-up on the deck, coal-scuttle mouths part open. Sharkey presiding over all like the Devil amongst the sinners in an old-fashioned Hell.

He caught hundreds of sharks of many species. Whalers, grey nurse, makoes and carpet sharks. There were blues, too, and occasionally threshers, which came up on the line. Most were dead, caught during the night. But the tiger sharks, worthless commercially because of their rank ammoniac flesh, were always alive. Hate glowed red in their dark eyes.

'Too mean to die,' Sharkey would say. But he unhooked them and let them go, unless they were line-robbers. Stingrays too. There was a soft side to him which he kept well hidden.

It was what he called the 'Big Fish' that provided the highlights for him in his routine of battling big waves and long shark lines. Because his hooks were small and his gear light, in order to catch the small sharks required by the market, it was not often that he caught a Great White. They broke the light tackle with contemptuous ease. When he did succeed it was usually because the huge shark had swallowed a hooked 7 or 8 foot (2 or 2.4 metre) grey nurse or whaler whole and choked on its meal. Sometimes he only caught one of the big sharks every couple of years. But when he did it was an event.

In the 1950s I saw my first Great White shark hanging up on a block and tackle under the Fremantle railway bridge, and I still have a picture with Sharkey standing proudly beside it. He had caught much bigger ones, he told me at the time. But to me it seemed huge, bigger than anything I could have imagined. Even in death the power of the muscular body was evident. As a spearfisherman, it sent a shiver down my spine.

'Different from other sharks?' I suggested.

'Different?' Sharkey said, pausing knife in hand. 'Now there's a bloody understatement, Hughie! There's no other shark in the sea can compare with these buggers!' He shifted his cigarette from one side of his mouth to the other with shark-slimed fingers, surveying his 'fish'.

'See that big dark eye there? When you bring 'em up on the line they watch you every second, waiting for you to make a mistake. Sets the hairs up on the back of your neck, it does, when you're out fishing on y'r own!'

If Sharkey had disappeared, swallowed up by the sea one day with *Shaleen* no one would have been very surprised. But the ocean was his friend and, though a Viking funeral might have been more appropriate, he died ashore in his own bed. It was Cancer, the crab, which killed him.

Another person I met who had first-hand knowledge of Great Whites was Peter Goadby, a famous gamefisherman with Australian and international experience in marlin and shark fishing. He had hooked several record-breaking Great Whites and made a personal study of them. He was also

27

author of *Sharks: Attacks, Habits, Species* — the most practical and sensible book on sharks I had seen to that time. He wrote:

> *The feature most noticed and remarked on by those who have seen big White sharks in action is the great dark eye which forces itself into the human mind by its apparent intelligence, ferocity, and a constant watchfulness.*
>
> *If one were superstitious it would be easy to believe that the White Death is guided by evil supernatural spirits as fables sometimes say. When attacking it resembles a silent giant bomber with its graceful pectoral fins and effortless, lithe manoeuvring.*
>
> *The silence ends when it attacks the baits hanging over the side of the boat. Then, if its head is out of the water, the growls and ripping sounds are never forgotten. These sharks are inquisitive and at times fearless in their attacks on boats...*

So is *Carcharodon carcharias* the supershark? The prince of the *Selachimorpha*, that cartilaginous family of the sharks and rays and sawfishes?

Physical statistics alone would suggest that this is so. The Great White is a creature dominant among other sharks in the same way that the terrestrial Bengal tiger is 'Lord of the Jungle' in Asia or the African lion is 'King of the Beasts' on the plains of Africa.

Like the sperm whale, and the orca, the Great White shark is the apex predator of its food chain.

In terms of sheer dimensions the Great White stands out among other shark species. It is by far the largest and the heaviest of the predatory sharks, and significantly bigger and bulkier than either of the other two major man-eater species — the tiger, *Galeocerdo cuvieri*, and members of the whaler family, the *Carcharhinidae*. Great Whites may grow to more than 6 metres (20 feet) in length. At that size they can weigh as much as 3200 kilograms (7000 pounds).

The largest Great White I have seen myself was one which we caught at Albany in 1977. A huge female, she was 5.6 metres in length — 18 feet 4½ inches to be precise — and weighed more than 1800 kilograms. She was almost 3.6 metres in girth. More significant was the distance from the tip of one pectoral fin to the other. If she had approached you head-on in the water her width, or 'wingspan', would have been over 3 metres. An interesting sight for a diver to see. Her teeth measured 65 centimetres and her jaws today are in the Western Australian Museum. A big shark, but by no means the biggest of her species caught at Albany.

28

In the 1950s Clem Hill, a fisherman friend of mine, shot a Great White at the Babbage Island Whaling Station at Caernarvon in Western Australia. The shark measured 19 feet 6 inches. 'There were other sharks in the same school which were bigger,' he recalls.

The largest Great White caught at the Cheynes Beach Whaling Co. Station, in a location where big sharks regularly gathered, was measured at just under 6 metres (actually 19 feet 6 inches). It was claimed that much larger specimens had been seen, by whaling men at sea, feeding on the bodies of harpooned whales. I have no doubt that this is a correct statement. The gunners on the whale-chasing ships were expert at gauging the length of whales by eye. Both they and the company faced heavy penalties for taking undersized whales and with long practice they could correctly assess the size of marginal whales to within a few inches. These were whales of around 10 metres in length.

Their estimate of shark sizes would be not far off the mark, and the gunners spoke of Great Whites in the 6 to 9 metre range. However, sighting is one thing, actual physical measurement another. Without a scientifically accurate measure — hardly possible at sea — the claim remains unproven. Since whaling has finished forever, it must be set down as a legend rather than a proven fact.

But Master Gunner Ches Stubbs recalled one Great White so big that it was actually harpooned with a shot from the whalechaser *Cheynes II*. The harpoon itself was a massive steel projectile, almost 2 metres long and 100 kilograms in weight, and the gunner's aim was true. Unfortunately the shark slipped off the harpoon as it was winched alongside. It may have been the largest Great White ever taken in Australia — though Ches, who liked to have the last word, said he had seen even bigger ones than that.

By comparison, tiger sharks are generally in the 4 metre range, with some growing to 5 metres. There have been one or two claims of exceptional individuals up to 6 metres.

The Great Whites at the Albany whaling station regularly reached 15 to 16 feet (to use fishermen's measurements), or more than 5 metres, with bigger specimens at 6 metres and perhaps even exceeding 7 metres at sea.

But remember that weight and length do not necessarily increase in graduated proportion. A 4.8 metre Great White for instance, enormously more bulky, may be twice the weight of a 4.2 metre member of the same species.

Great Whites of the same body length as tiger sharks tend to weigh much more. The White has an exceptionally powerful tail with exaggerated keels of muscle, the caudal ridges, running the length of the body. A section

29

immediately ahead of the caudal fin (tail) will still be as thick as a man's body. By comparison, a comparatively large tiger shark's tail junction can often be circled with both hands.

The largest tiger shark on record was caught off Newcastle in 1954 in a beach shark net. It weighed 1527 kilograms (3360 pounds) and was 5.4 metres (18 feet) in length. This was obviously a beast of considerable size, and not one you would wish to share a swimming pool with. But it was still less than half the weight of the largest specimens of *Carcharodon carcharias*.

Young tigers, with their pronounced stripes, are pretty fish. But big tigers, especially those from areas of dirty water, lose their stripes and become dark on the back. They are often potbellied and skinny-tailed ugly brutes, whereas Whites retain a grace and majesty even when they grow to great size.

The Great White is streamlined with a cone-shaped nose, the bottom rows of teeth are always visible, and it appears to fly through the water on outstretched pectoral fins. Like an aircraft in a heavier element. The classic shark.

The other members of the man-eater club are the numerous subspecies of the whaler family, the *Carcharhinidae*. These include *Carcharhinus leucas*, common in Australian estuarine and inshore waters, and known in North America as the bull shark. It is a worldwide species, as can be seen from its many local names — Zambezi shark in South Africa, Ganges shark in India, Nicaraguan shark and Amazon shark in South America.

The whalers are medium-sized sharks growing to a maximum of about 3.6 metres and 450 kilograms, but are more commonly seen at around 2.4 metres. Despite their lesser size they are still extremely dangerous and they may have killed more human beings worldwide than either Great Whites or tigers.

In Australia whalers have been responsible for most of the attacks in Sydney harbour. In Western Australia there have been more shark attacks in the Swan River, on which the capital of Perth is situated, than in any other single location in the State. The culprits have undoubtedly been whalers and the list includes at least one fatality. A 13-year-old Scotch College schoolboy, Charles Robinson, was mauled off the school rowing shed in Freshwater Bay in 1923 and died from shocking leg injuries.

Whalers, or Zambezi sharks, have probably also been responsible for many of the attacks off the Natal beaches of South Africa, a region which earned the grim title 'shark attack capital of the world' in the 1950s.

The greatest human toll of all may have been on the coasts of India. In estuary river mouths like the Ganges whaler sharks became accustomed to feeding on human flesh, gorging on part-burned bodies washed downstream from the funeral ghats. Pilgrims bathing in the river as a religious exercise also fell prey to the sharks. Attacks through the years have been very numerous, though no accurate record of such incidents has ever been kept, perhaps because they have occurred so frequently that they were not considered anything out of the ordinary.

There was an additional bizarre touch to the relationships of sharks and humans in the Ganges. Besides the bodies from the ghats and unlucky pilgrims making their devotions in the river, some cases were people who offered themselves as sacrificial suicides.

The European traveller Samuel Purchas wrote in 1617 of the Ganges delta: 'There are many fishes here called Sea Dogs [sharks]. They who are weary of this world and desire to have a quick passage to Paradise cast in themselves here to be devoured of these fishes.'

This practice was confirmed 20 years later by another traveller, Sebastian Manrique. He observed Hindu pilgrims at the mouth of the Hooghly River make a vow to priests and then 'enter the sea up to their breasts and [be] very soon seized and devoured by certain ferocious . . . sea monsters which we call sharks'.

Carcharhinus leucas often frequents shallow water, an environment where there is the greatest chance of coming across humans — bathers or net fishermen. This is the reason for the extensive tally of attacks. Other members of the *Carcharhinidae* — closely related — such as the grey reef shark, *Carcharhinus amblyrhynchoides*, and the lemon shark, *Negaprion brevirostris* are also dangerous shallow water sharks of the Pacific and the Caribbean.

Deepwater *Carcharhinus* species of the Atlantic, Pacific and Indian Oceans include the blue shark, *Prionace glauca*, the oceanic whitetip, *Carcharhinus longimanus*, and the silvertip, *Carcharhinus falciformis*. These all grow to be good-sized sharks of 3 to 4 metres and may have been responsible for mid-ocean attacks on humans in shipwreck or aircraft-crash situations.

Scientists surmise that many of the river and estuarine attacks on humans by whaler sharks are a form of territorial aggression — like a dog biting a postman — rather than an attempt to eat the victim. Unfortunately, when a whaler shark bites, its teeth are so sharp that even quite a small specimen can do fearful damage slicing through human flesh. Most bites are in the thigh or lower leg. If an artery is severed a fatality may result.

Darren Good, a Sydney 24-year-old, who dived naked from Parramatta's Charles Street wharf for a bet on the night of 26 February, 1996, won more than the money. He was bitten on the left leg and right testicle by a whaler

31

shark. The wounds required 50 stitches and some recovery days in Westmead Hospital. There he probably had time to reflect that things could have been a good deal worse.

The mako shark, *Isurus oxyrinchus*, looks very similar to the Great White on the surface in both shape and colouration and the two are often confused by fishermen. The mako also has the same distinctive mackerel tail as *Carcharodon*. However the essential difference is the teeth which indicate a different diet. The White has serrated triangular teeth for rending the flesh of large prey, a mako's teeth are hooked and sharply pointed for catching and holding medium-sized, fast-swimming school fish such as tuna, bonito and large trevally. Curiously, although makos grow to considerable size and are certainly well enough equipped to be a danger, there is no record of a human fatality caused by a member of this species.

Makos are famous for their high leaps when hooked or gamefishing tackled. The name comes from the Maoris of New Zealand, who greatly admire the shark for its courage. Maori chiefs often wore necklaces of mako teeth.

Another admirer of makos was the famous writer and fisherman Ernest Hemingway. His book, *The Old Man and the Sea*, won the Nobel Prize for literature in 1954. It contains a description of one of the most beautiful of sharks:

> He was a very big Mako shark built to swim as fast as the fastest fish in the sea and everything about him was beautiful except his jaws. His back was as blue as a swordfish's and his belly was silver and his hide was smooth and handsome.
>
> He was built as a swordfish except for his huge jaws which were tight shut now as he swam fast, just under the surface with his high dorsal fin knifing through the water without wavering. Inside the closed double lip of his jaws all of his eight rows of teeth were slanted inwards.
>
> They were not the ordinary pyramid-shaped teeth of most sharks. They were shaped like a man's fingers when they are crisped like claws. They were nearly as long as the fingers of the old man and they had razor-sharp cutting edges on both sides.
>
> This was a fish built to feed on all the fishes in the sea, that were so fast and strong and well-armed that they had no other enemy. Now he speeded up as he smelled the fresher scent and his blue dorsal fin cut the water.

Regardless, none of the other species can compare with the Great White in size or strength. The proportion of human fatalities in Great White attacks is understandably higher than in other cases. It is clearly the most dangerous shark in the oceans of the world and also the most widely travelled shark, being found in a great diversity of environments.

Despite its wide distribution not a great deal was generally known about Great White sharks prior to the 1970s. The first underwater film of White sharks was taken by Australian cameraman Ron Taylor at Dangerous Reef in South Australia in 1964. In 1969, Taylor did most of the underwater filming for Peter Gimbel's outstanding documentary production, *Blue Water, White Death*. The film received accolades from the critics, but is today best remembered as being the scene-setter for *Jaws*.

Peter Benchley's novel *Jaws*, published in 1974, was the most successful fiction work of the decade. It sold hundreds and thousands of copies and received enormous publicity. Benchley wrote in a tight, succinct style and his descriptions of a Great White attack were well researched and graphically described:

The fish was about forty feet away from the woman, off to the side, when it turned suddenly to the left, dropped entirely below the surface and with two quick thrusts of its tail was upon her.

At first the woman thought she had snagged her leg on a rock or a piece of floating wood. There was no initial pain, only one violent tug on her right leg. She reached down to touch her foot, treading water with her left foot, feeling in the blackness with her left hand. She could not find her foot. She reached higher on her leg and then she was overcome by a rush of nausea and dizziness. Her groping fingers had found a nub of bone and tattered flesh. She knew that the warm pulsing flow over her fingers in the chill water was her own blood.

Pain and panic struck together. The woman threw her head back and screamed a guttural cry of terror.

At that point the reader might also scream a cry of terror; indeed terror was the major theme of *Jaws*.

The book and film introduced *Carcharodon carcharias*, the Great White shark, to the world. If you were to suggest that in 1970 one per cent of educated people would have heard of the Great White shark — as distinct from other shark species — it would probably have been an over-generous estimate. Ten years later, everyone who could read or owned a television set knew something about *Carcharodon* — even if their perceptions were larger and angrier than the real-life creature.

Jaws, the first film increased the size of the novel's shark by 30 per cent. *Jaws II*, *Jaws III* and the final effort in 1987, *Jaws IV — the Revenge*, further expanded its bulk and nastiness. Finally the subject could swim no further, and the *Jaws* fictional freak mercifully died of sheer exhaustion. But it has had its effect. Swimming pool sales boomed as never before; skinny-dipping in the ocean was out for a decade. For at least one generation, millions of people around the world who had previously swum in the ocean without a care now found that salt-water swimming was not quite the same. *Jaws* had brought the shadow too close for comfort.

In the real world *Carcharodon* cruised on, unaware of the fuss, maintaining its forage and attack patterns of millions of years, including in its hunter's diet the occasional human victims over a world-wide range.

Carcharodon-caused fatalities have been listed in both warm and cold waters. Fatalities are on record from the coasts of Newfoundland and North America to Turkey and Italy in the Mediterranean. (One of the sad stories from the Mediterranean was that of Maurizzio Sarra, a distinguished writer and photographer and a pioneer of Italian SCUBA diving. Author of *My Friend the Shark*, Sarra was fatally mauled by a Great White in the Tyrrenian Sea off Monte Circeo on 2 September 1962.) Great Whites have taken other human victims in the Adriatic Sea and in the Bosporus. They have killed humans in Korean waters and in the Sea of Japan. *Carcharodon* may have been responsible for a dramatic series of attacks in Hong Kong in the 1990s. There have been similar Great White deaths of swimmers and divers off the Californian coast, off Mexico and Chile and off Hawaiian, New Zealand, Australian and South African shores. Other listed fatalities have occurred as far south as Tasmania and the South Island of New Zealand.

Despite its vast range the Great White does not come into contact with humans as often as we might expect. It seems to generally prefer to swim a deepwater path of its own choosing. This is fortunate when we consider its formidable capacity as a predator.

But when it does enter regions frequented by humans, the meeting may have an ending that sends shivers up the spine of every swimmer and diver. In the 1960s there was a series of chilling attacks on divers in southeastern Australia. I met the survivors, Brian Rodger, Rodney Fox and Henri Bource (who lost a leg), and heard their stories, their first-hand accounts of the ferocity of *Carcharodon carcharias*.

And, as a diver myself, I wondered who would be next .

THE GREAT SHARK
OF JURIEN BAY
chapter three

O N 19 AUGUST 1967 TWO SPEARFISHERMEN SWAM SEAWARDS FROM THE
limestone bluff of North Head at Jurien Bay, a remote spot on the coast
of Western Australia.

Their names were Robert Bartle and Lee Warner. Both men were clad in
the black neoprene rubber suits with hoods that were standard among divers
at the time. Their full face masks glinted in the pale August sun. Bartle had on
a short suit, cut off at the knees, a factor which may have had some later
significance (see p. 328). Warner wore a full suit, for the water still had a
winter chill about it, together with the green-yellow tinge and poor visibility
that went with the time of year. Clear blue water and the warmth of the
Leeuwin Current would come with early summer. But that was still two
months away.

The divers were heading towards some reefs marked by the white spray
of breakers more than a kilometre offshore. They swam with their powerful
single-rubber spearguns held out in front of them and with the steady,
economical fin strokes that eat up distance. Glancing back from time to time
to check their distance from the shore, they could see the vehicles parked at
random angles on the scrub-covered heights above the grey headland.
Bartle's Volkswagen, with its familiar beetle shape, was among them.

The two swimmers were contrasts in physique and personality. Bob Bartle
was a pleasant-faced fellow, 24 years old, short but strongly built. He worked
hard in his family's hardware business but in his spare time he lived, breathed
and dreamed diving. A natural organiser, he was secretary of the Western
Australian Council of Underwater Activities.

Lee Warner was 26, a former school teacher who had taken time off from
the classroom to pursue his passion for underwater sport. Warner had an

impressive natural physique, piercing blue eyes and a black bushy beard. He had a devil-may-care attitude to life, casual and carefree. But he was very serious about his diving. He could free-dive on a breath to 30 metres (100 feet).

Each man towed a float with a blue and white diver's flag at the end of a long cord. The floats were dual-purpose. The flag warned boats of the diver's position, and wire toggles hung from the float to hold the fish he had speared. To left and right of Warner and Bartle other flags moved out to sea. They were towed by divers from the other vehicles on the headland. They would be their opposition in the spearfishing competition to be held on the following day, Sunday 20 August.

This day, the Saturday, was scheduled as a practice day. Divers entered in the competition had come 240 kilometres north from Perth for the event. Now they had the opportunity to swim over the ground, to note the underwater terrain, and hope that the fish they saw would still be there on the morrow when points would be scored for their catch. Not all the divers took the practice swim seriously. But Warner and Bartle had a strong sense of purpose. They were working to a long-term plan which included contesting the State Pairs Championships later in the year and the Australian Championships early in the new year of 1968.

The regular competitions held throughout the year were not especially important in the overall scheme of things. But, as every athlete knows, there is no practice like an actual contest. Warner and Bartle were hardening their bodies and sharpening their skills for the more important events ahead.

Warner was the more brilliant diver of the two. But Bartle had endurance and determination. Together they made an excellent combination as a pairs team. By August 1967 they had made hundreds of dives together and were among the top echelon of Australian spearfishermen.

None of the divers swimming at Jurien Bay used SCUBA because it was outside the rules. In competition, spearfishermen had to dive holding their breath. Some of the top Australian divers could take fish at 25 to 30 metres below the surface. But it took long practice, skill and a certain courage to reach those depths. The water at Jurien Bay, inside the reef, would be comparatively shallow. But breath-holding 'blackout', a sometimes fatal affliction among competition divers, could occur in shallow water as well as in the deeps.

In the distance the smooth winter swell broke with a sullen booming sound. There were distant feathers of spray on the outside reefs, the mist of the breakers hanging on the air. It was a light hazy day with a promise of spring about it. But down below the silver surface the surges restlessly sweeping the kelpweed showed that winter still held a grip.

The ground was barren some distance from shore. But the divers noted the positions of smaller fish such as red morwong, scaly-fin, silver drummer and zebra fish. Nothing much to cause excitement there.

What every spearfisherman hoped to see that day was jewfish. The Western Australian jewfish is a silver-scaled sea perch. Occasional specimens grow to 30 kilograms but they are more commonly seen at from 5 to 20 kilos. They are the State's premium table fish and a prestigious catch. Jewfish are most often found in caves and reef gullies with sandy bottoms. Underwater they have a characteristic black vee stripe across their heads which fades when the fish is taken from the water.

Warner and Bartle were seeking jewfish ground, and their thoughts were on finding broken country in the limestone reef bottom with holes and caves. Neither they nor any of the other divers had been concerned about sharks when they entered the water and the thought did not trouble them as they swam.

Both had had shark experiences. As a youth Warner had shot grey nurse sharks and some whalers and sold them to fish and chip shops for pocket money. The fish shops presented the fillets fried in batter as 'snapper' or 'kingfish'. Shark actually tasted fine but the customers (who mostly knew what they were getting) preferred it under another name. With shark, you never knew what it had eaten!

Bartle had had to fight off an aggressive bronze whaler shark at Dunsborough earlier in the year, jabbing it away with his speargun as it charged him repeatedly.

'If anyone asks me if I'm scared of sharks I wouldn't shrug my shoulders after Dunsborough,' was his comment afterwards.

But the expert opinion at the time was that the danger of sharks was high only in summer. Statistics seemed to show that it was warm water and high temperatures which triggered attacks. Jurien Bay, in Western Australia's temperate zone, was cold in August. No question about that. 'Cold enough to freeze the balls off a brass monkey,' the first divers on the day reported, making wry faces as they walked into the water. Rough diving talk was a part of the camaraderie of competition.

In nearly 20 years of diving there had never been a fatal shark attack on a spearfisherman in Western Australia. It was not something that was regarded as a matter for concern. In eastern Australia, where there was a different record, boats patrolled vigilantly while spearfishing competitions were being held. But at Jurien Bay there were no boats because there seemed to be no need.

About 700 metres from the shore Bob Bartle gestured ahead with his speargun and Lee Warner, swimming beside him, saw a hint of white sand in the distance. As they came closer they saw a depression in the seabed. It was a sunken sandy saucer, a hollow some 12 metres across, in about 8 metres of water with overhanging ledges.

Jewfish are nocturnal and often hole up under ledges during the day. The spot seemed barren of other fish species. But it was the kind of place where a jewfish might be hovering on silvery fins in the darkness under the overhangs.

'Better have a look,' said Bob.

'Right oh.'

There was a routine procedure. Bartle glided down in a shallow dive to peer under the ledges, dropping the lead anchor weight of his float as he did so, for greater freedom of movement.

Warner watched from above. Sometimes jewfish which had hidden came out from curiosity to look at the silver flash of the anchor weight, or followed a spearfisherman up after a dive. On a lucky day there might be two or more in a cave to share. But the second diver had to be quick because companion fish tended to 'spook' after the first shot. Warner watched closely.

Bob examined the caves, disappearing at times under the ledges, but making a final 'negative' sideways sign with his hand as he began to ascend. No jewfish. Well, that was not totally unexpected. They would have to look at the reefs further out as they had intended. Warner turned to swim on while Bartle dived again to retrieve his float weight.

Suddenly, and without warning, a huge dark shape hurtled under Warner's fins. It was so big, and moving so fast, that he cried out involuntarily: 'What the bloody hell…!'

Without slackening speed, the creature — Warner had not yet identified it as a shark — struck Bartle with tremendous force. The impact was so severe that his mask was dislodged. Then Bartle was seized between the hip and shoulder and shaken violently, like a dog shaking a rabbit.

Watching from above, Warner was frozen with horror. The attack was so sudden, so totally unexpected, that for a moment he could not grasp the reality of it. At that point, his eyes wide in shock, everything appeared to him to be happening in slow motion. The period of frozen immobility, of indecision, probably lasted only a few moments. To Lee Warner it seemed an eternity. But the discipline of years of diving rapidly returned and Warner saw what he had to do.

38

With his speargun held in front of him, he filled his lungs with a deep breath and began his dive towards the struggling forms, that nightmare scene, below him.

He had killed sharks before and knew the vital spot behind the eyes. A spear piercing the brain there could kill any ordinary shark. He had never seen — or even imagined — a beast of this size before. But there was still a chance he might kill or immobilise it. Or at the very least distract it from its deadly purpose. In any case there was no option — apart from fleeing and leaving Bob Bartle to his fate, and that was unthinkable.

Bartle was still gripped in the jaws, dwarfed by the huge bulk of the creature which continued shaking him mercilessly from side to side. Warner closed to firing range and took aim. Then he squeezed the trigger. The gun bucked in his hand and the stainless steel spear thudded home.

'I fired the spear into the top of the shark's head, where I figured the brain should be. It hit with a solid clunk, but it didn't seem to affect the shark. Except that it attracted its attention to me. It sort of shook its head and then rose up towards me.'

As the monster angled up towards the surface it bit Bartle completely in half.

Warner gagged in horror as a cloud of blood welled upwards. Then the shark came up through the blood straight towards him.

In its mouth it still gripped the lower part of Bob Bartle, his fins protruding.

'Christ!' Warner screamed, eyes bulging behind his mask. 'Jesus Christ Almighty!'

As the shark closed he pushed it away desperately with his unloaded speargun. Jabbing at the great black eye.

A detached part of his mind noted that the eye rolled white. 'I didn't think sharks could do that,' he would say later. Then he was back to stark reality. The water was murked with blood. Shapes were distorted, grotesque in the darkened twilight sea. The huge shadow of the shark moved through it all.

'Never in my life have I seen anything so chilling as watching that shark circling around me with the body of Bob still in its jaws. From less than a metre away I could see the terrible wounds which had been inflicted. I felt helpless. I could see Bob was dead. That was only too obvious. I thought I was soon to follow. I simply cannot describe the terror which flowed through me.'

The shark continued to swim around him.

'It kept circling about 3 metres from me. Its body looked about 5 feet [1.5 metres] thick from top to bottom. I didn't really get a good idea of its

39

length — I couldn't see its extremities and I don't remember seeing the tail. All I could see was the eye and what it had in its mouth.'

Then his gaze was attracted to something else. 'Out of the corner of my eye I saw Bob's gun which was still loaded and floating just below the surface. I grabbed it thinking, here was another chance! Swinging it around I tried to belt the spear into the shark's eye.

'But the eye was set close to the top of its head and somehow the spear just whistled over it and missed everything. It was the worst shot of my life. I don't know how I could have missed a target of that size and I've cursed myself for it a thousand times since.

'It was my last real chance to get back at the shark.'

Now the shark was tangling the float and spear lines and there was a new danger.

'It kept circling round and round. It was tied to my gun from the first spear and the gun picked up the float lines and the line from Bob's gun. It all was just one big tangled mess.

'I was afraid of getting caught up in the lines myself.

'The shark was black on top, white on its guts, a sort of mottled pattern. It looked weird in the bad winter light and the blood-reddened water. The jaw looked wider than the body. It seemed at least a metre across. Maybe more.

'I knew Bob was dead, and then there was the thought of other sharks. A little bronze whaler came and began darting around in the blood. I wondered whether there were any more big ones…'

Warner had no gun now, and no defences of any kind. He began to swim backwards, breaking away from the shark.

'I felt pretty bloody helpless, I can tell you. I swam backwards at first, FAST. Looking back I could see the shark still swimming around tangled in the lines and floats at the same spot. Once I lost sight of it I began freestyling for shore. Now and again I looked back to convince myself that the shark wasn't following. I was still frightened.

'It wasn't too far to shore, but it seemed miles. I swam away from a friend and diving companion of seven years. Now that's something I'll never forget. Not as long as I live.'

He ran stumbling from the water and looking back saw the flags of other divers out in the water, the swimmers still unaware of what had happened. He knew that he had to get help, and fast. Had to find someone with a boat to get the other divers out of the water.

It all seemed unreal — in fact the sense of nightmarish unreality never left him. It was such a short time since he and Bob had walked down to the water's edge with their fins and guns and gear. Laughing and joking, kidding each other about the cold swim.

Now that time seemed a whole world away.

Up on the bluff of North Head, his breath coming in gasps, Lee Warner searched frantically for the keys to Bob Bartle's Volkswagen. And could not find them. But he did find a key to one of the other cars. It started at the first turn of the key. 'Thank God for that!' Then he drove skidding around corners on the gravel road, at breakneck speed, and kicking up fishtails of dirt on the turns. Heading towards the little fishing settlement at Sandy Cape, 10 kilometres away.

The fishing season was over but there were still a few boats in the anchorage. Some of the fishermen were relaxing, having a Saturday afternoon beer and listening to the football on the radio. Their peace was shattered at the sound of an approaching vehicle driven by an apparently crazy man. 'Who the hell...?'

Warner skidded to a halt and gasped out his story.

'Got to get them out of the water.' His face showed the urgency. 'Those other blokes. They don't know what's out there!'

The fishermen understood at once. They put their beers down. 'What about your boat, Harry?'

'Let's get going, then!' said Harry Holmes. He was skipper of the 13.5 metre steel rock lobster boat *Gay Jan*, the most suitable boat in the bay. They all ran to his dinghy on the beach and in a short time the *Gay Jan* was off on her way to North Head at full throttle, exhausts blowing black diesel smoke. Soon she was rolling in the swell and picking up divers off the headland.

'Get out of the water, quick! There's been a shark attack!'

'Shark? Where...? Who...?'

Some of the divers were incredulous, finding it hard to believe. Until they saw Lee Warner's eyes.

A little later they saw something else.

The floats were still there, still attached by the tangled lines, the dark shape of the giant shark swimming beneath them.

There was also another object floating. When they brought the *Gay Jan* alongside the floating torso of Robert Bartle, some of the divers choked with nausea and could not look. The body was cut clean through the breastbone by one tremendous bite. Strangely enough the expression on Bob's face was peaceful, as though he had simply drifted off to sleep. His lungs were still filled with air, which showed he had not even cried out.

Death must have been very quick. It is possible that he was never aware of what had happened to him. His friends always hoped so in the aftermath.

Those aboard the *Gay Jan* caught hold of the lines and floats and tried to draw the shark in. But it was incredibly strong. As it began to swim away the lines snapped one by one, the metal fittings on the spears straightened and broke. Then it was gone. The shadow disappeared.

The divers held a wake that night at the Jurien Bay Hotel, drowning their sorrow in the traditional way. Some of them wept. Next day they held their spearfishing competition as scheduled. Their thoughts as they entered the water may be imagined. But they explained the reason: 'Bob would have wanted it that way.'

On that Sunday, 20 August 1967, the news was on the radio, Statewide. Like every other diver who had been in the Indian Ocean that weekend I asked myself the same question: 'What if it had been me?' I had known Bob Bartle well. Lee Warner too.

There were other questions to be answered. I knew I would be going north to Jurien Bay on the following day.

It was a road that would take me to other places as well. A long and winding trail following *Carcharodon carcharias*, the Great White shark.

Malevolent man-eater, or simply misunderstood? That was something I hoped one day to find out.

IN THE SHARK CAGE
chapter four

I THOUGHT OF ROBERT BARTLE AGAIN NINE YEARS LATER ON A BRIGHT MORNING ON King Georges Sound in the far south of Western Australia. A day in July 1976. The sun glinted on the wet granite slopes of the headland sheltering the Sound. The air was clean and fresh off the Southern Ocean, and the mist was still rising from the tea-tree gullies on the shore.

It was an altogether idyllic scene. Even the steam clouds drifting above the Cheynes Beach Whaling Station had little rainbows which were pretty too. So long as you didn't look too closely.

It was one of those blue-sky golden days that sometimes come on the south coast in midwinter. Days with the light mellow colour of chardonnay wine which make you feel that it is good to be alive. A stimulant to the senses in any ordinary circumstances.

But my own mood did not match the magic of the morning and the reasons were close to hand. I was standing in full wetsuit and diving gear on the duckboard of my boat *Beachcomber II*. Dabbing at a floating shark cage with my finned foot and asking myself the rhetorical question: 'Why am I doing this?'

My reflective gaze rested on some dead sperm whales which were floating nearby, their rippled stomachs distended. The white splotches on their flanks were a series of shark bites. It was these scalloped indentations with their ragged edges which had caught my eye. Some of the bites had taken out a scoop of blue skin, white blubber and red whale meat probably half the body weight of a human being. They indicated Great White sharks of somewhere in the 5 to 6 metre range.

Sharks as big as that would be the equivalent in weight of a medium-sized delivery van. Being hit by one in full charge, I thought to myself, would be like stepping out in front of the van on a freeway.

An image of the picture I had seen of Bob Bartle's body, bitten in half at the breastbone, returned and flashed unwelcome through my mind.

Was the monster shark that had inflicted those bites on the sperm whales still out at sea on the whaling grounds? Or was it, even at that moment, finning under our boat? An immense shadow invisible to us in the dark water below? It was a question of more than passing interest for anyone about to go below. To me, at that moment, the trapdoor entry in the top of the cage looked about as inviting as a gallows drop.

The cage had been lightly built with the comforting and entirely theoretical thought that if something went wrong below it could be winched back on board complete with its human cargo. Plucked out of the deeps to safety. It was comforting to think that we could, literally, be snatched from the jaws of death. But now there were problems.

Because of time pressures in preparing the boat and equipment, and getting the gear and people to the Southern Ocean port of Albany, the first dry test of the cage had not been made until a couple of days previously.

It was a less than auspicious occasion. While lifting the cage, with the boat on its trailer, the davit had bent under the weight — the steel tube taking the shape (and the apparent strength) of a ripe banana. The test showed that we required a bigger davit and winch. To accommodate them we would need a bigger boat, and that was quite impossible for reasons of time and money. We would just have to make do with what we had.

That was a hard truth. It meant that if things got bad in the cage we would have to bale out into open water and get back to the boat past whatever was causing the crisis. The problem would have sharp teeth and a large dorsal fin.

I looked at the bites on the whales again. But there could be no turning back at that point. Weeks of preparation had brought us to this moment and pride would permit no flinching from the purpose.

'OK?' I asked my co-diver Peter Newstead, whose expression was as bleak as my own.

He gave me a thumbs-up signal. 'After you,' he said with a half smile.

Fair enough. It had been my idea after all. I stepped off the duckboard and sank at once into the dark and evil-looking water. Down into another realm bounded by the steel mesh walls of the shark cage and the purple, blood-murked water beyond. A twilight world where every shadow seemed sinister in the first nervous moments.

It was always interesting going down in the cage.

The bubbles of entry — like soda fizz — obscured your vision until they cleared and the inability to see anything hardly helped your nerves. There was the shock of icy winter water flooding your wetsuit before it warmed next to the skin. The darkness and the restricted vision beyond the cage bars made a dramatic contrast with the world of light and air above. In that other world, where the sun shone, you could see for miles instead of only a few metres. That other upper world, you were always reminded, was where you really belonged.

And what was it like, that world above?

The boat, the faithful *Beachcomber II* — built for just this purpose by Laurie Chivers who made the strongest boats in Western Australia — was moored alongside a bunch of dead sperm whales. Her 23 foot (7 metre) length, which seemed such a bulk on the trailer, was dwarfed by their size. The ivory-toothed jaws of the whales lolled unnaturally loose. But their white rippled bellies were drum-tight from the compressed air which had been pumped into them to keep them afloat. On the light swell they jostled the boat and each other in a weird, posthumous dance of death.

Each whale was tethered by an individual wire strop around its tail, hooked over a bollard on a pontoon anchored a short distance off the Cheynes Beach Whaling Station. From time to time a little green tugboat puffing black diesel smoke would head out towards us. A crewhand would lean out with a gaff, dexterously hook a wire strop over the tow bollard, and another whale would be towed away to shore to be hauled up on to the blood-slippery flensing deck at the station.

There a team of men in spiked boots would climb over the carcass like mountaineers, gripping flensing knives shaped like ice-hockey sticks with razor edges. They would swing their sticks and make chopping cuts at selected points. Then a groaning winch with a hook on a wire peeled the blubber 'blanket' back to reveal the raw and naked flesh.

In surprisingly short time a 50 tonne whale would be chopped, sawn and dismembered, hacked apart to disappear down various holes in the upper deck. The blubber was fed into vats to be rendered down into fine oil for automatic transmissions, watches, soaps, perfumes and lipsticks. The rest was roasted in ovens and ground down to become fertiliser and chicken feed. Soon the living whale was only a memory, vanished like the misted spray from its final spout.

While the rest of King George's Sound was a picture to inspire poets on that sunny winter's day, the whaling station itself was less than postcard-pretty in appearance.

Unless, of course, you were a vampire.

A red river of blood ran down the flensing deck, staining the sea crimson for hundreds of metres around. It was a gigantic open-air slaughterhouse, no better or worse than any other abattoir. Just bigger in scale. The blood reflected pink on the silver oil storage tanks, and little blood-red rainbows danced in the steam rising from the winches and from the mechanical head saw which decapitated the dead leviathans.

The pontoon was far enough offshore to avoid the worst of the blood contamination. But blood still leaked in clots and strings from the gaping harpoon wounds in the dead whales around the boat. Gobbets of blubber floated about, coagulating on the cage and everything below water. Including our wet suits and diving gear.

'Shark fin soup,' someone in the surface crew said with a guffaw, and they all broke up in laughter at the wisecrack.

Peter and I did not join in the general merriment. Smelling like a dead whale is not every diver's fancy when *Carcharodon* is about.

We had had our warnings. Whaling skippers had spoken of Great Whites so huge that they had mistaken them for whales. What if one of *those* monsters decided to turn up at our cage?

Sinking until I felt the mesh of the cage floor beneath my feet on that first day I took stock of my situation. Once the bubbles of the descent had cleared, I found the water surrounding the cage disconcertingly darker than I had expected. The sun was still too low for the shafts of sunlight to penetrate below. We also had the shadowy shapes of the boat and dead whales above our heads, further robbing us of light.

Light and visibility — the distance you can see under water before objects become shadows or disappear entirely — are naturally of prime importance in underwater filming and photography. In the clear blue water of tropical atolls in the Pacific and Indian Oceans and the Caribbean — those places nearest to paradise for divers — visibility may exceed 70 metres (225 feet). In the tannin-stained depths of some inland freshwater lakes among the sunken logs and snagging tree branches you are lucky to be able to see your hand in front of your face. Far less enchanting.

On that morning under the dead whales at Albany the visibility was about what I had expected. Some 5 or 6 metres. This was marginal for filming. The cage and its immediate environs could be seen clearly enough, but the water was thick with particles of whale. Though the depth under the pontoon was only about 12 metres we could see no sign of the bottom below. It was lost in the subsurface fog.

The sharks would have to come very close for good photography. A distance of an arm's length would be about right. But for a shark to come as close as that meant that he would have only one thing on his mind.

Better not to think about it. Instead I let technical matters occupy my thoughts. The cage reflected silver, much brighter than I had expected, contrasting with the dark background. This was a nuisance because it upset the balance of cameras on automatic aperture settings. While I pondered all this, and wondered whether a black or blue cage would have been better, there was a bang on the cage top and a flash of red. The 400 foot (122 metre) load motion picture camera in its underwater housing was being passed down to me. Then there was another *woosh!* of bubbles and Peter settled in the cage beside me.

He gave the traditional divers' finger-and-thumb signal: 'Are you OK?'

I returned it: 'I am OK.'

The sound of our underwater breathing was harsh below, and I noticed that we were both breathing faster than normal.

We busied ourselves with checking the cameras, reading the brightness — or lack of it — with the light meters, and adjusting the pull-pins on the bangsticks — those underwater explosive-headed defences we hoped we would never have to use. Always we had half an eye on the camera gap.

Suddenly I sensed rather than saw Peter stiffen and there it was. A shark, framed in the camera gap, seemingly grinning at us with his bottom teeth. He was poised on his pectoral fins and regarding us intently with a black glistening eye. *Carcharodon carcharias*, the Great White shark, in person. The creature I had been waiting to see alive and below the surface all these years!

The shark was a young male, medium-sized. He was no monster, at least not compared to whatever had made the bites on the whales. Nonetheless, at 4.2 metres, deep-chested and thick through the body, he was still larger than any shark I had seen swimming before.

We regarded each other from a distance of 2 or 3 metres. The shark's mouth was half open, showing us the bottom rows of triangular teeth like a pitful of ivory daggers. His body was muscular and powerful. Grey-green on top and creamy white on the underparts, where trailing twin 'claspers', the bottle-shaped sex organs, showed his masculinity.

The shark stayed for what seemed minutes but could only have been a few seconds. Then he worked his jaws slightly and rolled away to one side of the cage with an easy motion of powerful fins. For a moment he glided toward the edge of visibility, then a quick movement of the tail sent him skimming away out of sight.

In all our lives there are milestones, important moments we remember long after. This was one of them.

I drank in every detail of the shark. His eyes were black as night. His body, torpedo-shaped, magnificent, the dark-tipped pectoral fins jutting out like the wings of an aircraft. But above all there was an impression of poise and confidence. The shark was good, and he knew it.

In fact he appeared quite different from the other sharks I had seen throughout 25 years of diving. Tiger sharks, whalers, hammerheads, rare makoes, snaggle-toothed grey nurse. They had all seemed instinctive animals. I had the impression that this one was different. A creature of vitality and intelligence.

I had seen dead Great White sharks before, of course, on a number of occasions — like that first one of Sharkey Nelson's, hanging head down from the Fremantle bridge. I'd taken the opportunity to study the teeth structure, fin and body shapes and physiology of the dead specimens so far as was possible. They had always been out of their true element and no dead shark, flaccid on the back of a truck, blood oozing in patches through its skin, mouth chocked open with a slimy piece of wood to show the teeth, can give any idea of the majesty of the living creature. Any more than a human corpse on a slab can be beautiful.

When we had been building the cages, making our plans, I had had a secret fear of anticlimax. A concern that I might have built up in my mind the myth of a supershark that was larger than the reality. What if *Carcharodon* turned out to be simply a bigger and bulkier shark? Fat but stupid? Unremarkable for anything except its size?

Now, in the moment of truth, there was no disappointment. For the time being all fear and apprehension had vanished. I became anxious now for the shark to return, straining my eyes into the purple gloom searching for shadows which might swing our way. Transforming into the real thing. The genuine one-and-only Great White shark.

Peter Newstead was also peering out through his face mask into the murky distance. Catching my eye he looked at me inquiringly and pointed to the camera. An unspoken question. Had I got the shot? I shook my head and tapped the light meter, indicating the needle on the low end of the scale. There was still not enough diffused sunlight in the water to allow shooting.

But even if the light had been right, I doubt that I would have shot a single frame. At that first encounter I had been too fascinated, mesmerised in fact, by that face at the window. My first live sighting of *Carcharodon carcharias*. While we waited for the shark to reappear, or another to turn up, the cage was lifting and jerking with a motion that was to become familiar but never comfortable, and the mind raced.

There was euphoria that the system was working. The transition from armchair theory to field operation is not always smooth. So many things could have gone wrong. But now the needle on the light meter was slowly climbing. Soon it would reach F4, an acceptable level for shooting. The sharks were there and we had seen that they would come close enough for filming after all.

I could sense the sweet smell of success — at least so far as the cage operation was concerned — and I gave a mental three cheers.

With the excitement of the first encounter there was also a feeling of relief. Sharks were the most difficult creatures to film in their own environment. The Great White was the hardest of them all. If we succeeded it would be a considerable achievement.

It was curious, too, that once the shark appeared there had been no immediate sense of danger.

I knew that this was deceptive. It would be too easy to become lulled into a sense of false security. The Great White deserved our respect and was subject to moods and the necessity to eat like any other creature. A shark could be placid enough to pat on one occasion. The next time you tried it he'd snap your arm off. Or he might just yawn and go on his way. That was the danger. The complete unpredictability.

The Whaling Station was a controversial location. Some said it was far too dangerous. We had chosen it because we knew the sharks were there. But there were other factors to consider. Would the sharks be gorged on the whales, uninterested in all other potential prey? Or would they be hyperactive, excited by the blood into a feeding frenzy and likely to bite or snap at anything live that moved?

That had also been put forward as a possibility.

'You'll need to watch it there, you boys,' one old whaler had said with a serious expression, puffing on his pipe in the pub. 'You don't know what you're taking on with those mean devils. I seen 'em strip a humpback whale to the backbone in 20 minutes at Point Cloates. Give 'em half a chance, they'll snap you up too!' He made a snapping motion with his forefinger and thumb, and then jabbed his pipe stem in our direction for emphasis. 'They'll have you too, boy, so quick you won't even know what happened!'

His opinion had to be respected.

But the fact was that until we went down in the cage by the whales no one really knew what would happen, because no one had tried it there before. For reasons which hardly require explanation.

What had brought us to test our luck in these questionable circumstances?

One answer was that we were to make a film. Vic Martin, a Brisbane producer of documentary films for television, had been commissioned to make a one hour program for the Nine Network. We had worked together

49

before, at the Abrolhos Islands on a documentary film on the wreck of the 1629 Dutch East India Company treasure ship *Batavia*. I had played a part in the wreck's discovery and had written a book on the experience titled *Islands of Angry Ghosts*. As a follow-up, a shark film seemed a good idea, and the timing was right, with the mega-film *Jaws* due for release soon.

When Vic rang me to ascertain my interest, I had already been considering an expedition to Albany to dive with the Great Whites. Brian Greenhalgh, a diving friend in Albany, had been urging me to come down for some time. From that aspect Vic Martin's telephone call seemed fortuitous. The underwater photography would be a challenge. It was agreed that I would provide the boat, the cage and all the underwater gear including cameras. And man the cage. Vic would be producer and director and raise the capital.

There was one problem, I warned Vic. Success could not be guaranteed. Sharks were notoriously hard to film. Unlike sedentary fish such as giant cod, which stayed inside a territory, sharks were free-ranging creatures. They were shy of contact with strange air-breathing individuals almost their own size. In the past, sharks I had tried to film had shown a natural tendency to be wary of divers as something outside their ordinary experience. The human eagerness to get close for a camera shot was taken as a threatening gesture and they were usually off with a flick of their tail, presenting an unflattering posterior profile to the lens. Unsatisfactory, because it was the sharp end of the shark, and particularly the teeth, which moviegoers wanted to see.

Few people had filmed sharks successfully. To get the kind of pictures which 'filled the frame', in the moviemaker's phrase, the photographer had to take pictures no more than 1 to 3 metres away from the subject. This was inside the personal space of most sharks.

A land photographer had all the advantages. He could stand off with a tripod and telephoto lens to take shots of something like a lion, with teeth and whiskers sharp and full-frame, from 100 metres distance.

But it was impossible to use a telephoto lens in a similar way under water. There were visibility restrictions for a start. (Or stop.) A telephoto picked up all the plankton and tiny objects floating in the water. When the film was screened it looked like a snowstorm of celluloid dandruff. The only option for the photographer was to be eyeball to eyeball with his subject, in a real sense. That was not easy with flighty subjects like sharks. With Great Whites there were other reasons why close proximity could be a problem.

Photographers do not give up easily and a good deal of ingenuity had been exercised in efforts to overcome the difficulties. One system, used in a number of Hollywood productions, was to catch sharks on a line, drug them by injection and render them 'safe'. Some sharks were filmed in tanks at various 'Sea Worlds' and 'Marine Worlds' in the United States and elsewhere. Filming was even tried through tank viewing ports so that the photographer did not have to get wet at all.

But the drugged sharks, wobbling pathetically by on unsteady fins, never looked the part. Tank shots were also unconvincing, in the same way that shots of lions in a zoo have never had the same impact on the screen as lions in the wild.

So how can you film wild sharks convincingly?

Since no human can swim fast enough to catch up with a shark, the necessity is to bring the shark to the camera.

Most of the well-known undersea photographers, like Ron Taylor, who had a deserved reputation as the world's best camera operator with sharks, have used 'berley' or baiting with fish chum to bring sharks to them. Sometimes animal blood and carcass remnants from slaughterworks were employed. If sharks can be attracted from down-current by blood and entrails they may abandon their natural caution, forget about the photographer and come close enough to be photographed. The situation suits both parties.

On the down side, the blood and body bits can trigger what is called a 'feeding frenzy'. Getting sharks overexcited in this way carries its own risks, and some people, including Ron's wife Valerie Taylor, have been bitten and seriously injured. But there have been few other effective and realistic means to catch sharks on film.

At Albany there was no need for any of that. The dead whales were already the greatest shark attraction that could be devised. They provided a unique situation with *Carcharodon carcharias*, ordinarily the most difficult shark of all to locate and film.

'Of course you'll have a problem yourselves,' Vic Martin pointed out when I spoke of the difficulties of shark filming.

'How's that?'

He laughed: 'You might get eaten!'

I tried to think of a funny answer in reply and failed. It was not, actually, a funny subject where we divers were concerned.

'You realise,' Vic continued, 'I'm talking seriously now. If there's any blood, if anyone gets bitten, we have to film it. The crew will have instructions to keep the cameras rolling no matter what happens.'

'Sure. We're there to make a film,' I replied.

'No, I mean it. No matter what sort of trouble anyone gets into, the cameraman and sound recordist have to stay at their posts and keep working.'

51

The thought occurred to me, as it had already undoubtedly occurred to Vic, that it would be a very much more saleable film if someone *did* get eaten and the horror was recorded live (and dead?) on camera.

I tried to put that from my mind. If staying alive involved a conflict of interests it was better not to think about it until the time came.

Down in the shark cage we rocked and rolled with the swell, in rhythm with the boat above, and peered through our camera gaps. Waiting for 'Whitey' and trying to think positive thoughts. Above, the surface crew watched the cage and our vague and distorted shapes in its depths. Watched too for other vague and distorted shapes. Longer ones, outside the cage.

The camera gap was one of our concerns. The 400 foot load movie camera was 80 centimetres (more than 30 inches) high in its bright red aluminium case. The red colour was designed to attract sharks towards it. The gap was necessary so that the camera could pan freely without the lens being obscured by bars and mesh. That meant a correspondingly large undefended space in our protective structure.

'Can't sharks get their noses in?' people would ask.

We would nod our heads. 'Sure they can.' We knew they could. Vic Martin was more forthcoming to the enquirers. 'Makes great footage,' he would say, with rather too much of a grin. 'Be sure you keep the cameras rolling, boys!'

'Yes, Vic.'

The sharks often caught us unawares. Though we strained our eyes in the underwater twilight, watching for long-finned shadows, they frequently surprised us by appearing suddenly beside the cage.

One moment there was nothing there. The next an involuntary physical start, a muffled exclamation, 'God Almighty!' through a mouthpiece, and a Great White would be grinning in the camera gap. They seemed almost to be able to materialise without warning.

On the second morning conditions were better for photography. The light meter needle quickly reached the magic figure of F4 and, as it did so, a shark appeared obligingly as though on cue. It was a male with the familiar trailing claspers. I wondered whether he was the same shark we had seen previously.

I pressed the trigger and heard the reassuring whirr of the Beaulieu R16 camera running, the shark bright and clear in the viewfinder. Then I cursed as a curtain of blood drifted through from the whales above.

The blood created strange effects. The shark came through it like the Devil from behind a crimson curtain. It made me think of the people who had been attacked and who must have had the same vision of *Carcharodon* through their own blood. A thought I tried to put aside.

The new shark surveyed us, his black eye wicked and bright, the glint of white spear points in his lower jaw. The mouth was partly open as before, and he had neat black tips to the white undersides of his pectoral fins. Another young male. He was a pretty-boy, a snappily dressed young fellow. But, despite his style and elan, when I looked into his eyes and he looked into mine there was that age-old relationship between predator and prey. No pity there. No mistaking the reason for his interest.

There followed a strange sound like a distant diesel motor and for a moment I looked for the dark underwater silhouette of the tugboat, propeller spinning in an arc of bubbles as it came to fetch another whale.

Thud! Thud! Thud!

There was no tugboat and I realised suddenly and with a shock that the thudding beat was the sound of my own heart. But when I tried to mentally control it my heart simply beat faster. 'Shh! He'll hear you!' I spoke sternly to myself, trying to slow it, to will it to beat more softly. To no avail. In contrary fashion it actually speeded up.

The shark heard it too and cocked his grim head inquiringly. *Carcharodon carcharias* feeds on seals, dolphins and marine mammals, as well as fish. To him the heartbeat meant that whatever the strange thing was in the cage it was edible. The nostrils in his pointed nose contracted and expanded delicately, inhaling our scent and trying to separate it from the all-pervading odour of whale.

In the shark's world there are two important kinds of creatures to consider. There are those which might eat him — a short list where the Great White is concerned. And those he can eat himself. An infinitely longer list for *Carcharodon*.

Our shark didn't appear in much doubt about our category. But we were unusual and the cages were something he had not encountered before. So he swam backwards and forwards, coming a little closer each time, figuring us out, graceful and quite unhurried.

It made good film, and the camera whirred away. He was so lithe and beautifully balanced. When I took my eye away from the camera viewfinder for a better look, his fluid grace took the breath away.

As he worked closer, making up his mind about us, we were able to make closer inspection of the wicked armoury of teeth designed for the particular function of tearing large prey to pieces. Pretty or not, he was designed by Nature as a predator, a killer, and all the while he watched us with that palm-sized intelligent black eye.

I looked at the film counter and saw with satisfaction that I had shot 350 feet (107 metres). Good stuff too, most of it. As I glanced up there was a sharp crack from our shark's tail and he torpedoed off and out of our vision — his haste a contrast with his previously leisurely movement.

That provoked some thought. What could have frightened him? A shark so big, so well equipped? The answer came from behind the cage. *Bang!* The bump took us completely by surprise, throwing us off balance so that in turn we bumped each other, SCUBA tanks clanging. All the while we tried to look over our shoulders to see what was happening.

'What the blazes was *that*?'

At first the solidness of the bump seemed to indicate some connection, a collision perhaps with the boat above. But when we regained balance and reorientated ourselves, the sight that met our eyes resulted in an instant contraction of the abdominal muscles.

'Jesus!'

A great dark head was there. A female shark. Huge! Seemingly as wide as the cage. She had ragged fins and scars on her gills and upper body, and floppy pectorals. But it was the enormous bulk of her that made our eyes pop wide open behind our masks.

There was a clear signal of danger in her expression and she was as ugly as our previous shark had been beautiful.

Bang!

She gave the cage another rap with her conical snout so that it spun a half-turn, regarding us always with that large dark eye.

'God damn!'

This was a much larger, a much more dangerous shark than any we had seen before. She swam past us heavy, almost lumbering, and then performed a figure of eight with surprising agility, fins streaming, and came straight back at the cage in a direct charge.

'Christ!' There was an explosion of bubbles from my mouthpiece. She was coming straight for the camera gap!

Scrunch!

There was a crash so violent that the cage and our teeth rattled together in time to the sandpapery noise of the collision. Then the cone of her nose was through the gap, inside the cage.

Peter and I fell backwards in unison.

'The hell with this!' I thought, keeping the camera between myself and the shark. 'You'll have to eat aluminium, lady, if you want to get to me!' I had a sinking feeling that she might just do that.

Teeth tinkled against cage aluminium. I kept my finger on the button, the camera still whirring. At least if someone found the camera afterwards they might know what had happened! If they salvaged the film maybe all the effort wouldn't have been wasted...

A strange thought under attack.

Why should it matter posthumously?

The cage bucked and rocked and then all was quiet again. Shakily we got back to our feet as a vast tail like the rudder of a ship disappeared on the edge of visibility.

'There she goes/On her toes/Where and why nobody knows...'

The nonsense rhyme ran through my head as I checked the footage counter on the camera. I found that I still had 30 feet (9 metres) of film to shoot. About a minute's worth. Enough for a good squirt if...

BANG!

I saw Peter's eyes widen again. No need to ask this time. The shark was back and once again she had caught us unawares, thumping the cage with her tail in passing.

'Bugger this!'

It was becoming too hard on the nerves. She did her figure of eight turn again and was back this time chewing on the red fibreglass cage floats, as though they were a cherry on a cocktail stick. Pushing the cage backwards.

Off balance in the canting cage, I fell sideways into the camera gap. The top of my SCUBA tank hooked into the mesh of the cage wall and locked solid. My head, shoulder, arm and the camera were all outside the cage protruding through the cage gap. I was unable to move.

'Peter!'

I was held fast in a half-Nelson by the harness of my tank. There was an involuntary explosion of bubbles from my mouthpiece. This was serious. Perhaps a quarter of my body — a very important quarter — was sticking out of the cage for any interested shark to chew on.

While clear speech is impossible through the standard SCUBA mouthpiece, you can make certain sounds if the need is great. The need was great.

'Peter, for Christ's sake!'

Peter heard the sound. But he was understandably concerned at that moment with the shark, which was trying to get in through his side of the cage. He thought that he must have been obscuring my camera shot and so obligingly ducked his head.

The shark grinned horribly at him and me, showing all her teeth and the furry burr-like parasites sticking to the roof of her mouth.

Then she began to move round to my side of the cage.

THE BLOOD-STAINED SEA
chapter five

WHY TAKE THE RISK? WHY TAKE ANY RISK?
As the huge female shark began to circle the cage towards me there was no time for reflection.

'Peter!'

I had perhaps a couple of seconds to make up my mind. Of course I could jettison the camera, which would free my right hand and enable me to reach the release buckles on the SCUBA harness. Or I could hang on and hope that the shark wasn't hungry.

Letting go of the red case, containing the Beaulieu R16 movie camera which had cost every spare dollar I had, and having the painful experience of seeing it disappear into oblivion, could mean the end of filming. Without it we would probably have to abort the exercise and go home with our tails between our legs. Failure was not a pleasing prospect, particularly if there were to be a suggestion of cowardice attached.

On the other hand, if I continued to cling to the camera and the shark came around the cage and bit my arm off we would still be losers. The red case would go to the bottom anyway and it would be the end of my personal trip on this planet.

Did having your arm ripped off hurt much?

'P-E-T-E-R! For Christ's sake!'

Another burst of bubbles and desperate underwater noise.

The shark was now turning the corner of the cage and as Peter turned with it he looked up as though seeing me for the first time. Realising my predicament at once, he came across and slowly and carefully unhooked my tank top from the wire mesh. Cool under pressure as always.

Released, the warm flush of relief was almost euphoric. I had a glimpse of the shark disappearing into the distance with a capricious flick of its tail. Why she had abandoned her circumnavigation of the cage I could never tell. But I was certainly glad to see the back of her at that moment.

Closer to hand, Peter was giving me the diver's finger-and-thumb sign: 'Are you OK?'

I responded, 'I am OK'.

Yeah, just fine…

But my heartbeat was at a machine-gun rate. My hand shook as I readjusted the camera aperture. A lesson had been learnt, and fortunately not the hard way. From that time on we would secure our tanks on the mesh barrier of the cage with octopus straps, and be free to move about without tank or harness. We had to double the length of our regulator hoses, but the move prevented the possibility of getting hooked up again.

We also stopped using fins, since these also were too cumbersome in the cage. Instead we put mini-weightbelts around our ankles, 3 kilograms on each. Together with our standard 8 kilo waist-weightbelts the foot-weights made for better balance. This ingenuity, the ability to improve our situation, was one of the differences between ourselves and the sharks we had come to study.

Sharks are born perfectly evolved to fill their place in the ocean. They come into the world equipped with all the instinctive knowledge they will ever need to live out their predatory lives. They are the product of 60 million years of evolution.

In contrast, we *Homo sapiens* are physically insignificant creatures. But this weakness has turned out to be a long-term strength. To survive, our ancestors had to use their hands and brains. They learned to improvise, to utilise artificial means to make them strong. Now, facing the Great Whites, we epitomised the rise of *Homo sapiens*. We had a boat to carry us; SCUBA to breathe underwater; wetsuits to keep us warm; cameras to capture the images of the sharks on film; the television systems that would send the same sharks swimming through to thousands of homes in different parts of the world… These were all part of the miraculous technical advances of modern life.

So much, in fact, has happened in our own lifetime. Television, computers, space travel, the invention of SCUBA equipment that allows us to breathe underwater and study the sharks so closely — all of these were unknown when I was born.

But our bodies inside the wetsuits, hearts beating hard at the sight of the predator, were essentially similar to those of the animals around us. The sharks, the whales, the dolphins in the Sound. The albatrosses and black petrels and skua gulls which clamoured around the dead whales… Each species had evolved in its own unique way to fill niches in the environment of land, sea or air. Naked, we were just another creature on the earth. Prey or predator.

Why take the risk?

Why take ourselves back a few thousand years to the daily situation of ancestors who regularly faced being eaten by stronger predators? Who could not even dream of the safety and security we enjoyed as their more technically literate descendants? It was a question we asked ourselves at times of stress. 'What the bloody hell am I doing here?' — as a shark struck the cage and sent it spinning and we fell in a sorry heap on the mesh floor.

It was a rhetorical question and, once the stress situation was resolved and we had ceased being animals trying to survive a predator attack, we were again the technically superior species able to rationalise our behaviour. A rationale which would have seemed incomprehensible to a shark, and indeed to a large percentage of our own human species.

The great British mountaineer Leigh Mallory, who attempted to climb Mt Everest on nine occasions, was asked why he did it. Why he continued to risk his life on what was essentially just a bigger and more lethal snowbound rock.

'Because it's there,' he said.

Humans do things far outside the scope of ordinary species' behaviour. For other animals life is basically a matter of finding food and shelter, breeding, and surviving. That is the difference between *Homo sapiens* and the other animals. We do all kinds of crazy and sometimes unnecessarily life-threatening things beyond the primary requirement. Like mountaineering, and getting too close to sharks. The need to do these things is mental rather than physical. The mind drives the body.

Curiosity, the desire for knowledge and experience out of the ordinary, is one of humankind's characteristic traits. Curiosity, basically, was what had got us into the shark cage. The challenge was what kept us there, and the possibility of some future financial return hardly came into consideration.

'Curiosity,' I also reminded myself from time to time 'killed the cat'. I was never sure where the old saying came from — along with the 'tradition' that a cat has nine lives. We were reminded often enough in the shark cage that we humans had only one life to trifle with. High on Mt Everest, on 8 June 1924, closer to the peak than anyone had ever climbed before, Leigh Mallory finally lost his life. His body was never found.

'What are you trying to prove?' That was another question he may have been able to answer on that sun-sparkling day in the snow with the summit in sight. His companions later speculated that he may have made it to the top, only to fall victim to the mountain on the euphoric descent. What an irony if it were true!

But if someone *needed* to ask that question of why he was there, then there was no answer that would satisfy them. In our case, to paraphrase Leigh Mallory, the sharks were there. But the questioner would still not understand.

It was not about proving we were braver or better than anyone else. Courage is often a matter of circumstance. I get nervous climbing the 150 foot (46 metre) mast of the sail training ship *Leeuwin*. Or sitting in a motor car driven by someone else at 150 kilometres per hour. A bucking horse is not really my idea of fun and just watching bungy-jumping on television makes my toes curl. The sea, on the other hand, is a familiar environment for me and has been so since childhood. But with familiarity comes the knowledge that the sea has many moods and strengths that must be respected. Where the ocean is concerned there is a limited future for risk-takers. I always remember the lore of fisherfolk:

Those who be not afraid of the sea will soon be drowned. For they will put to sea on a day that they should have stayed ashore.
But those of us who be afraid of the sea be only drowned now and again.

or the helmet divers' traditional caution:

There are old divers and bold divers
But no old bold divers.

We took pains to eliminate as many of the risks as possible in filming the sharks. The operation could never be 100 per cent safe because of the unforeseen. There was also no opportunity for preliminary testing to find the weaknesses. You can't have a practice run with Great White sharks. It is the real thing or nothing.

If there were any possibility of complacency creeping into our daily stints in the shark cage, we needed only to recollect what had happened to others in less favourable circumstances.

It was true that the sharks sometimes looked so beautiful, so majestic, cruising past the cage with golden dapples of sunlight on their backs that the sense of danger receded. There was an occasional irrational urge to swim out through the camera gap and dance with them.

But when our sharks came so close that we could touch them, when we saw the rows of ivory daggers in their mouths, and looked deep into their eyes, then we read something there that made us shiver inside our wetsuits.

59

It was a sense of implacable and merciless purpose. To those watching from the boat above the sharks looked so graceful that their smooth beauty of movement was sometimes confused with benign motivation.

'Aren't they gentle?' someone suggested.

Again, it was a case of the eye deceiving the head. Polar bears look cuddly, too. But they are efficient terrestrial carnivores, eating seals and people too, if they can catch them. The blood and entrails, crimson on the snow, belie the beauty of the beast. In the cage we were closer than those above the silver surface, and we looked directly into the dark eye of *Carcharodon carcharias*. What we read there was far from gentle.

It was also suggested by a visitor that since the sharks appeared so 'safe' we should abandon the safety of the cage and swim freely with them.

Why not?

'It's up to you guys,' said Vic Martin, the surface cameraman, hopefully. 'But it would be a World First. Great film!'

We thought about it. Worked out how it could be done. And what could go wrong. Having something go wrong, of course, would make the 'best' film of all. A guaranteed sale in every country that sported a television network. Terrific, from a production point of view, we agreed. Just so long as it was someone else who got chopped up in those particularly efficient predatorial jaws.

A Great White shark attack is not a pretty sight. There is so much blood in the human body.

During the preceding decade there had been a series of horrific attacks on Australia's southeastern coast, and as divers we probably related more closely to them than those who stayed dry on the deck of the boat above. We were also that critical distance closer to *Carcharodon* in the physical sense.

The first of the attacks, which shocked all Australian divers, was at Aldinga Beach in South Australia. With its fringing reef, Aldinga lies in St Vincent's Gulf, about 88 kilometres south of Adelaide. It is one of a series of southern curving beaches with high red bluffs on the peninsula that ends with Cape Jervis; Kangaroo Island standing high across the water.

Aldinga is a pleasant beach, a favourite with families and, up to the 1960s, regarded as entirely safe from sharks. The offshore reefs provide good ground for fishing and it used to be a popular choice for spearfishing competitions because it pleased both the reef-swimming divers and their friends and families who spent the day on the beach.

The area's notoriety began on Sunday 12 March 1961, when the Cuda Spearfishing Club and the Underwater Sporting and Photographic Association were holding their annual spearfishing competition.

The president of the Association, a South Australian State champion and one of Australia's top competitive divers, was Brian Rodger. At 21 years of age, 2.3 metres in height with a huge frame and impressive physique, he was at a physical peak after a summer-long diet and exercise program.

South Australia's last shark attack had been in 1946, and only three other attacks had been recorded since 1836. It was thought that divers were immune to shark attack — though there had been occasional incidents when whaler sharks stole speared fish from the floats that divers trailed behind them. But they were regarded as being more of a nuisance than a danger.

Only the week before at Aldinga, Brian Rodger had a 2.7 metre whaler — the biggest shark he had seen up to that time — make a pass at his fish as he was threading one on to his float. And another shark of unknown size had gobbled 23 kilos of fish, plus a pair of plastic shoes, off another diver's float.

Rodger remembered being annoyed about that incident because the shoes had belonged to him. But at the time, the size of a shark which could bolt down all that fish (and the shoes) in one mouthful carried no significance for him.

On the Sunday, the competition was drawing to a close. By lunchtime, after four and a half hours in the water, Rodger already had a good bag of fish. About 2.30 p.m. he was making his way back towards the shore a kilometre distant. Suddenly he was surprised to see two large mulloway kingfish, 25 to 30 kilos in weight, flash beneath him.

'Now there's an unusual thing,' he thought. In his years of diving in South Australian waters he had not seen these kingfish in open water before. They passed too quickly for a shot. But there was always the chance they would come back, since kingfish are inquisitive creatures. He prepared to dive after them, relaxing to take a good deep breath, when suddenly he screamed through his snorkel. Something sharp and ragged and terribly heavy had struck him with tremendous force, throwing his whole body into a fearful spasm of pain.

He felt the pressure of a tremendous weight and was aware that something huge had seized his leg and hip. It was shaking him violently from side to side.

As the teeth tore through flesh and sinew he twisted round to find himself looking into the black eye of a Great White shark, which had the lower part of his body gripped in its jaws.

61

'I read once about jabbing a thumb into a shark's eye to make him let go, and tried to reach around with my left arm. Instead of getting his eye I jammed it down his throat, and slashed the arm to the bone on his upper teeth…

'"You'll have to be good to get out of this one!" I thought.

'Surprisingly the shark did let go, and then came back in a fast, tight circle for another bite. That was really terrifying because now I could see the whole shark and the size and enormous power of him.

'But at least I had my gun and now I had room to use it. As he came around I slammed a spear into the top of his head, about 7 centimetres behind the eye…

'It hit him hard, stopping his charge while he threw his head from side to side to shake out the 1.5 metre stainless steel spear. He managed this soon enough. But it was strange how even though I knew I was badly hurt myself I got a thrill from planting the spear into something so large and powerful.

'It was quite irrational, but for a moment that was all that mattered and I felt pleased and excited.

'Then his tail flicked away into the murk, and left on my own I realised just how serious my position was. Looking down at my leg laid open to the bone — in enormous rents from which the blood clouded — and at my shredded and lacerated arm, I knew that unless I could stop the bleeding I wouldn't make the distant shore. The actual wounds wouldn't kill me. But the loss of blood would.

'For a moment or two I wasn't sure what to do. But I found, astonishingly enough, that I could still move my leg, and I figured that if I could swim maybe I still had a chance of making shore.

'I'd done a first aid program as a part of the State's Underwater Emergency Rescue Squad course, and the knowledge I'd picked up there was pretty useful.

'About halfway back to the beach I realised that I was weakening from loss of blood. It occurred to me that the rubber from my speargun made a natural tourniquet, and I twisted it tight over my upper thigh with my knife, jamming the handle under the bottom of my wetsuit jacket. That stopped the blood flow a bit, and I began the longest swim of my life.

'It seemed to take forever. I kept watching the beach, and it didn't seem to be coming any closer. Gradually I was getting weaker and weaker.

'I'd ditched my gun and lead-belt and the float with all my fish. I hated doing it. Silly how a few points for a competition and a few dollars' worth of gear still seemed so important when my own life was at stake. The fish float was borrowed and I had to really force myself to abandon that.

62

'So I plodded along, weaker and weaker, keeping going until it became difficult to breathe even through a snorkel. I rolled on my back and kicked along that way for a while.

'As the land came closer it looked beautiful. I waved and yelled, "SHARK!"

'But it seemed to have no effect on the people on the beach. I was about at the end of my strength and was just despairing at the waste of vital energy when a rowboat appeared with two young spearfishermen rowing for all they were worth.

'"Hang on! We'll be right with you!"

'It was only a 7 foot [2.1 metre] boat. I'm pretty big and heavy and it was obvious we couldn't all fit in. Without hesitation one of them jumped out into the bloodied water — where the shark might have still been lurking for all he knew — and helped heave me in. He swam behind pushing to help the boat along. Pretty brave stuff, I thought.

'From then on everything was OK. A whole lot of divers ran across the reef and picked the boat up bodily to carry it to shore. There was a St John's Ambulance man there. They rigged an old door as a stretcher and hauled me up the cliff — white and blue around the face by this time from loss of blood — and the police organised an ambulance dash to Royal Adelaide Hospital.'

Rodger had lost 4 litres of blood. Only his strength and fitness saw him through. He had more than 200 stitches in a three hour operation.

The effectiveness of the repair work done by Dr Matuzek and Dr Hyde was shown when, after 16 days in hospital and two months recuperating at home, Rodger was back diving again. Later in 1961, he set a new Australian free-diving record by swimming down 45.4 metres (149 feet) in a Mt Gambier lake, on a single breath. A year later he ran a close second to Ron Taylor, later world champion, in the Australian Spearfishing Championships in Western Australia, and won the championship aggregate.

Rodger's attack, not surprisingly, shook the confidence of South Australian divers. But as months passed the memory faded and it began to be treated as a freak occurrence, unlikely to be repeated.

A perception which was to change dramatically in the following year.

On Sunday 10 December 1962, 16-year-old Jeff Corner and a friend, Allen Phillips, were taking part in a spearfishing competition at Caracalinga Head, 22 kilometres south of Aldinga where Brian Rodger had been attacked in the previous year. Jeff Corner, the South Australian junior champion, and Phillips were swimming about 182 metres offshore with a surf ski, in water about 8 metres deep and with fair visibility, about 1 p.m.

Phillips had just dived not far from Corner, looking for crayfish, when he saw a disturbance in the water near his friend. At first he was pleased, thinking Corner had speared a large fish — then he saw the tail of a big shark break water.

'Probably pinching fish off the float,' he thought, but as he swam across and ran into a welling cloud of blood he realised with dread certainty what had happened.

He turned and swam for their surf ski nearby, then desperately paddled to Corner who was surrounded by a pool of his own blood, with the shark gripping his leg.

'I grabbed Jeff and tried to pull him onto the ski. But the shark, which I recognised at once as a White Pointer from its pointed snout and black eye, tugged him down and out of my grasp, under the ski.

'Jeff came up again on the other side of the ski, and I caught him by the shoulders. The shark still refused to let go, and I banged it with the paddles. Hard.

'Then for no especial reason it released its grip and just lay on the surface watching us. I tried to pull Jeff onto the ski. He just looked at me, unable to speak, and his eyes rolled back. I think he was dead then. His leg was terribly mutilated, stripped of flesh from the hip to the knee.

'The White Pointer just lay there and watched, cold and calculating. I cut the fish off the float and threw them over to distract him, but he took no notice of them, just kept watching us. Then I found Jeff's handspear was stuck in his good leg, and jerked it free and prodded at the shark with it. But he didn't even seem to feel it.

'I couldn't get Jeff right onto the ski, and so I paddled for all I was worth with one leg hooked round his body. The shark followed. At any moment it could have made a rush and tipped us over, or dragged us off the ski.

'Then another spearfisherman, Murray Brampton, came paddling across on a ski.

'"Keep going!" he shouted, and I saw him lift his paddle and bang it down on the shark. That gave us the break we needed.

'Soon after, I reached the beach, and they said Jeff was dead.'

Corner's parents and Phillips's own wife and child were on the beach.

A year later, on another Sunday morning, 8 December 1963, the third attack in the series took place.

This time the scene was Aldinga again, close to the spot where Brian Rodger was attacked in 1961, and the occasion was the 1963 South Australian State Spearfishing Championships. The victim was

Rodney Fox, the 1962 South Australian champion, strongly favoured to retain his title in 1963.

It may be that he had unwittingly saved Rodger's life in 1961. Fox was swimming near him when Brian was attacked and though he was unaware of Rodger's desperate situation he himself was circled by a large and aggressive Great White which came so close at times that he could have touched it with his gun. He kept diving to the bottom, edging shorewards, and the shark stayed with him ten minutes or more.

Fox thought later that it was probably the shark that had attacked Rodger, following the now-diffused blood trail. The distraction offered unintentionally by Rodney Fox may have allowed Rodger to escape.

In 1963 at Aldinga, Fox was about a kilometre from shore, on the edge of a deepwater drop-off from 7 to 18 metres, with less than an hour of the competition left to go. As his finger tensed on the trigger he sensed, rather than felt, everything go still in the water around him.

'It was a silence. A perceptible hush. . . Then something huge hit me on the left side with enormous force and surged me through the water. I knew at once from the previous incidents what had happened — and was dazed with horror.

'I felt sick, nauseous. My mask was knocked off, and everything was blurred, and there was a queer sensation as though all my insides were squeezed over to one side. I reached out behind and groped for the shark's eyes. At that point it let go of me, and I pushed my arm down its throat by accident.

'With the release of the pressure uncontrollable agony swept over me in waves. But at least I was free. As I kicked for the surface and air I felt the shark under my flippers all the way. As I gulped air I felt the scrape of his hide and wrapped myself around him so he couldn't bite again.

'The shark took me back to the bottom. We rolled around scraping rocks and weed and I let go, desperate again for air.

'On the surface there was red everywhere. My own blood. And through it the head of the shark appeared, conical snout, great rolling body like a rust-coloured tree trunk.

'Indescribable terror flowed through my body, but just before it reached me, it veered away and I felt the tug of the fish float on my belt. The shark had grabbed my fish float and suddenly I was jerked below again, and towed 10 or 12 metres or more on my own line. It seemed ridiculous to die of drowning after all I'd been through. But my fumbling fingers couldn't undo the belt to which the line was attached.

65

'Then the line parted — perhaps on the shark's teeth — and I floated up to the surface…'

At Aldinga that year, 1963, because of the previous attacks the organisers of the competition had boats picking up competitors' catches in order to avoid attracting sharks.

A boat was close to Fox, whose total of fish already made him a likely winner, when they heard the scream, 'Shark! . . . Shark!' and saw him threshing in blood-stained water.

They dragged Fox into the boat and the men there, friends of his, were almost sick when they saw the extent of his injuries. His rib cage, lungs and upper stomach were exposed, with great flaps of skin and sinew flayed back. His arm was ripped to the bone. His lungs were punctured, the ribs crushed from the enormous bite of the shark.

His friend Bruce Farley kept him bending forwards, huddled in the bow of the boat to keep the wounds closed.

'We knew he was bad. But we didn't open up his wetsuit to find out the full extent. We made that mistake with Brian Rodger in 1961 and his leg fell apart.' Keeping the suit on was to be a vital factor.

Farley organised the beach rescue, finding a policeman almost as soon as he jumped ashore. 'He knew all the right numbers to ring.' They got Fox into a private car and began driving him towards Adelaide while an ambulance dashed south to meet them. He was in hospital, 55 kilometres away, less than an hour after being picked up by the boat. He was lucky enough to find a surgeon on duty who had returned that day from doing a specialised course on chest operations in England.

Rasping and choking in his own blood, Fox was so close to death that he heard someone at the hospital suggesting they should call a priest.

'But I'm a Protestant,' he choked indignantly, before the significance of the suggestion sank in.

Fox's toughness and physical fitness carried him through. But there is no doubt that if it had not been for the speed with which he and Brian Rodger were got to the operating theatre they would have shared Jeff Corner's fate. Both were on their last reserves of strength with such severe loss of blood that another hour without expert aid and transfusion would surely have been too much even for their exceptional constitutions.

It was significant that neither of them went into shock — a factor which kills many shark victims. Apart from their superb physical fitness this may have been because, as divers, they were familiar with sharks and had, without realising it, psychologically prepared themselves for surviving an attack.

In 1964 the South Australians won the Australian Spearfishing Championship teams event. In the South Australian team were Brian Rodger, Bruce Farley and Rodney Fox.

With Fox's experience the series of Great White shark attacks in St Vincent's Gulf ended. It may have been partly because the third attack was the last straw for many South Australian divers, who turned to safer sports. Spearfishing competitors dwindled in numbers to a few diehards. Or it may simply have been part of the unpredictable pattern of attacks experienced in other parts of the world. No one really knows why they start, or why they stop. Except the sharks.

Shark attacks, like those in South Australia, attract all kinds of theories. The common factors at Aldinga and Caracalinga were spearfishing competitions. Ironically, all the victims were champions, seized, possibly, because they were swimming furthest out.

It seemed likely on analysis of the attacks that the sharks had been attracted by the blood and vibrations from the struggling fish. This was a comforting thought for divers using SCUBA and who were more interested in photographing fish than killing them.

'No blood, no sharks.' That was the general opinion.

But with sharks, and especially the Great White, it seemed that as soon as people believed they knew their behaviour patterns then sharks did something different.

Henri Bource, a Melbourne musician aged 25 in 1964, was a keen underwater photographer. For Henri, 26 November 1964 began as a pleasant sort of day, the kind he most looked forward to. With 40 other divers and friends from several clubs, including his own Victorian Aqualung Club, he was one of a party aboard the fishing boat *Raemur-K*.

They were heading out from Port Fairy bound for Lady Julia Percy Island and the deck was crowded with divers and their gear. It was a scene typical of many weekend dives as they approached the island. People struggling into wetsuits, adjusting harnesses, fiddling with gauges and loading cameras. All the last minute things.

Henri, who was meticulous, had his gear ready early. In fact, most of it had been ready long before the trip. In the wheelhouse of the fishing boat he listened to the skipper Walter Kelly talking about the island with its colony of seals. The conversation inevitably turned to sharks. 'I've seen some big ones out here from this boat,' said Kelly, telling them about some of his experiences. 'There's one in particular called Big Ben. He's been hanging around here for years.'

Henri Bource had never seen a shark previously, and had no reason to be afraid of them. He was fascinated by the fisherman's account and one of his ambitions was to get a really good shark sequence on film with his camera.

They reached the island, about 8 kilometres offshore and 22 kilometres from Port Fairy, an hour and a half after leaving the wharf. Kelly dropped anchor in the bay in the lee of Lady Julia Percy. The island was rocky with spectacular cliffs, and there were at least a thousand seals on the lower slopes. The acrid smell of ammoniac seal droppings drifted offshore on the light breeze.

The fur seals set up a tremendous din, barking, squealing and baying, as the boat approached. When Kelly anchored about 180 metres offshore, scores of them splashed into the sea and came out to meet them. 'It was everything an underwater photographer could wish for,' Henri recalled, 'and I could hardly wait to get into the water.'

The first divers were soon sporting with the seals.

Henri's time of entry was listed as 12.45 p.m. by his girlfriend Jill Ratcliffe, who was safety officer for the day. The club's safety regulations required him to swim with a partner if he wanted to use breathing apparatus. Since he was keen to get a camera record of the seals, and preferred to go on his own, he went free-diving with a snorkel.

But the visibility was disappointing so he decided to change his technique, instead silhouetting the seals against the surface to get a better result.

'The visibility was even worse than I had thought. But the seals were helpful. I kept diving to a small ledge just below the rock and there I was able to film a number of seal cows, as they darted and spiralled through the long strands of kelp.

'All too soon I was out of film, so I swam back to the boat.'

He had hoped Jill would be able to have a dive. But at 1.30 p.m. she was still logging other divers and he decided to do some more free-diving with the seals, joining two other snorkel divers, Fred Arndt and Dietmar Kruppa. Together they found a large bull seal floating on the surface, lying on his back with a hind flipper sticking out of the water, and soaking in the sun. A seal at peace with the world.

'When we turned up he rolled a wary eye at the three of us but seemed too lazy to move. Fred was the first to actually touch him. After a cautious ten minutes he accepted Dietmar and myself as well. It was one of those rare moments of communication with wild creatures. We thought it was pretty wonderful. Something to tell the others about when we got back.'

They began diving with him, and scratching him under the flippers. Suddenly without warning the bull and all the nearby seals disappeared.

68

'The water was quite empty. There was a split second of eerie silence, and our instinct as divers warned us that something was wrong.'

They dived down about 10 metres again, hugging the bottom and looking around them. But they could not relocate the seals.

'The premonition of imminent trouble was still very strong and as I came to the surface I lifted my head out of the water, looking around to locate Fred and Dietmar. I was going to suggest that we'd better get back to the safety of the boat.

'Without any warning something hit me with tremendous force. I threw my arm up in the diver's signal for "Help!" and screamed "Shark… Shark!"

'I was torn through the water with enormous power and dragged below. The force of the attack ripped off my mask and snorkel. I could only make out a blurred shape, a huge shadow, as the shark took me down to the bottom, gripping me by the leg.

'As it dived deep, the shark shook me the way a dog would shake an old slipper. The pain was unbearable. I found myself reaching for the shark's eyes in a desperate attempt to escape. But I could barely reach my arm around his gigantic snout, and I just scrabbled helplessly across the monster's muzzle.

'There was another sensation in which the pain and fear were almost forgotten. I was drowning. I needed air — suffocating as I was tugged and rolled from side to side.

'Then suddenly it all stopped. The shaking and the turmoil ceased.

'There was a moment almost of peace. Then I realised, as I groped for the surface, that I had just had my leg bitten off.

'The air was wonderful as I gasped on the surface. Then I felt down to the remains of my left leg. I was quite calm. Shock, perhaps. But I found it hard to focus clearly. There was a curious division in which my body tended towards natural animal panic. But my mind remained quite detached.'

Dietmar Kruppa was the first to Henri's side. The injured diver clutched at his shoulder, trying to catch his breath. He tried to speak but no words came. The blood tasted sweet in his mouth as it clouded the water. Then he realised the shark would attack again and, afraid they would not be able to see it coming in the blood, he tried to push himself away from Dietmar so that he would not be hit too.

The shark came back at least five times. But Fred Arndt and Dietmar Kruppa showed tremendous courage, fighting the monster off with their light metal handspears. They were spears meant for little fish, not sharks a tonne in weight. The spears were bent and twisted out of shape afterwards. But despite their repeated jabs the shark did not attack either Arndt or Kruppa.

Now the *Raemur-K* was bearing down on them.

69

As soon as the cry 'Shark!' was heard and the welling cloud of blood was seen from the boat, Walter Kelly had hit the starter button of the motor and surged the boat towards them without even waiting to pick up the anchor. He dragged it with the boat's power. As they drew close, Jill Ratcliffe grabbed the safety line and without hesitation jumped in and swam towards the struggling group in the blood-stained water. Others jumped in alongside her with no thought of their own safety.

At the side of the boat, Jill called for a rope. Quickly, two of the divers entered the water and fastened the line around Henri. But they couldn't lift his weight out of the water. 'In a last desperate attempt,' Henri recalled, 'I slid my arm up the rope, and I felt a hard grip on my wrist. Colin Watson, a policeman, grabbed my arm and jerked me on board, spraying blood across the deck.'

The sight was almost too much for some of the others on board, who had been unaware that Henri Bource had lost his leg. It was hardly pleasant for those in the water. Apart from what must have been a ghastly sight, they realised that they were left in the water in a pool of blood with the shark still around.

Colin Watson and others carried Henri to the middle of the deck and immediately began to apply a tourniquet and first aid.

'I remember only the dark shapes of wetsuits and the occasional face above me, registering horror. Not until the moment I'd been taken on board did anyone realise the terrible extent of my injury. The shark had severed my leg at the knee.

'My most vivid recollections now are of the faces; they all looked at me with disbelief. Their shocked expressions seemed to say: "This couldn't be happening. This is the sort of thing you only read about!"'

Despite the horror of the situation the helpers' first aid was coolly and efficiently applied, and the swift placing of the tourniquet was to prove vital in the drama that followed. There was an agony of indecision while they decided whether to pick up people who were still on the island. They decided to head for port and explain later. Then, on the way back to Port Fairy, Walter Kelly dodged through reefs and lines of craypots on the shortest possible route home. As it turned out, every minute counted in what was literally a race for Henri Bource's life. After the cruel ill-chance of the encounter with the shark he did have some lucky breaks.

By the time they got under way the initial shock had diminished and Henri could distinguish voices. Somebody was at the radio, calling for an ambulance and a doctor to be standing by at the Port Fairy landing. He heard them tell the shore-based operator that his blood group was unknown.

Lifting his head a little, he managed to whisper the blood group to somebody above him and a moment later heard it radioed ashore. This was one of the things which made the hairline of difference between life and death.

Strangely his mind was still clear, and he was aware of the people around him. But his vision was fading, and as his strength ebbed from shock and loss of blood, he knew he was approaching closer to death.

An ambulance met the *Raemur-K* at the wharf. Henri's next sensation was of the rubber suit being cut away from his arm, then a needle being inserted to allow him to receive a life-sustaining transfusion.

Henri did not know at this stage that he had lost 3.5 litres of blood. Taken from the normal 4.5 litres held in the human system, it didn't leave much to go on with. Doctors said later that if the journey had taken a little longer, or if he had lost a fraction more blood, he would have passed the point of no return.

The ambulance rushed him to the new Warrnambool Hospital.

From there on Henri's recollections were hazy. A hospital corridor. The faces of nurses looking down at him. The rubber suit being cut away. 'That hurt a bit because it had cost hard earned savings.'

When he awoke from the anaesthetic of the operating theatre, it was still only 19 hours since the shark had gripped his leg.

As consciousness returned he became aware of a cage holding the bedclothes high at one end of the bed. It covered an empty space, the place where only the day before Henri Bource's left leg had been.

'My leg had gone and there wasn't a damned thing I could do about it.'

There were a number of common factors in these attacks on divers in southeastern Australia.

All of them were in cold water locations. They were contrary to accepted wisdom which believed that shark attacks were triggered by warm water and rising temperatures. No one knew at the time that some sharks, including the Great White, are warmblooded.

None of the victims saw the shark before they were hit. *Carcharodon* apparently had the ability to charge from outside the divers' vision and to catch them unawares. All who survived remarked on the severity and disorienting effect of the impact.

'You don't see the shark that gets you!' became a grim divers' maxim in southern Australian waters.

Another interesting statistic was that all the survivors — who might have been expected to quit the ocean and go no deeper than a bathtub for the rest of their lives — actually went diving again.

71

Brian Rodger and Rodney Fox became spearfishing champions on the national scene. Bruce Farley, who helped save Fox's life, became one of the most successful pearl divers in Broome in Western Australia. Henri Bource overcame the loss of his left leg to become an underwater welding specialist on oil rigs in Bass Strait. Lee Warner, who had witnessed Bob Bartle's horrific death, became an abalone diver in the Great Australian Bight — that cold, kelp-grown coast, where Great White sharks are most frequently found.

None of them would ever forget the incidents with which they were involved. The shadow was always there, even years later.

But it says a great deal for the courage and determination of the particular divers that they lived with the image that haunted them. And managed to exorcise it through the ocean.

Down in the shark cage dipping in the swells in the dim-lit world below the dead whales at Albany we sometimes thought of these other incidents too. Wondered how it had been for those divers at other times. Thoughts flickering at random while we waited for *Carcharodon* to put his face into our camera gap with that deadly bottom-toothed grin. To catch us unaware again and make our stomach muscles contract like elastic bands going *snap*!

And of course, having the time, and the particular situation, we pondered the relationship of human and shark. And considered the reports we had studied of White Shark attacks — the epithets applied to the sharks in newspaper and television reports were thought-provoking.

'Bloodthirsty killers,' for example, was a description that could be applied to some of the many many humans who have committed unspeakable and 'inhuman' deeds in crime or war. But in terms of the shark's role in the ocean, which we were beginning to understand, the labels seemed inappropriate.

There was an opposite view as well.

Those people who had seen from the safety of the surface the lithe beauty of the sharks, their smooth passage through the ocean, and their unhurried grace, deduced from this that they must be serene and 'gentle' creatures. But they had also wandered from the path of reality into the world of fairy tales. To the realm of *Bambi* and *The Lion King*, those delightful but utterly unrealistic Walt Disney fantasies, in which animals think and talk like humans.

From our vantage point in the shark cage we could see that none of these human perspectives about sharks, ascribing 'good' or 'evil' qualities to them, were valid.

Top and bottom: *Carcharodon carcharias, compact and confident: the ultimate shark.*

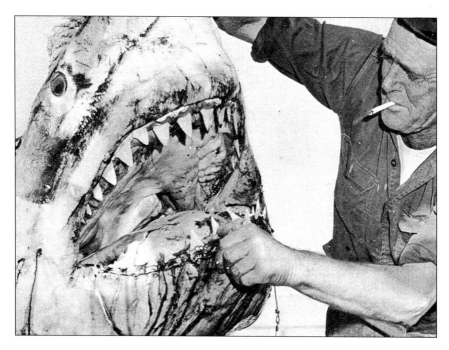

Opposite: *Werner Schonhofer vanished on Monday 20 January 1997 at Lighthouse Reef, Geraldton, Western Australia. His death officially remains a mystery since all that was found of him was the shredded remains of his wetsuit. (Photograph: Ron D'Raine. Courtesy the West Australian.)*

Above: *Sharkey Nelson and catch. Ted 'Sharkey' Nelson was a shark fisherman who worked out of Fremantle and off the shores of Rottnest Island, Western Australia. He provided me with the sight of my first Great White shark, in the 1950s.*

Above: *Clem Hill and an almost 6 metre long Great White in the 1950s at Carnarvon Whaling Station, Western Australia. 'It wasn't the biggest shark in the school,' said Clem.*

Top: *Beachcomber II anchored at Cheynes Beach Whaling Station, Albany, Western Australia. We set up next to the corpse of a dead whale in the hope that it would attract sharks to the cage where Peter Newstead and myself were waiting to film them. The cages (and divers) were perpetually coated in a film of blubber grease and blood from the dead whales. Breathed in with air through the SCUBA mouthpiece it tasted terrible.*
Bottom: *White gouges on these dead whales are shark bites scooped from the outer blubber. Some indicate Great Whites in the 5–6 metre size range.*

Top: *Testing the fibreglass floats around the top of the submerged cage, this Great White gives us, in the cage below, a fine view of its snow-white underbelly. (Photograph: Marilyn Edwards)*
Bottom: *The cage was an eerie perch in the gloomy light below the surface, beside the dead sperm whales. Shoals of herring and mackerel swam through the bars. When they vanished with an instant, collective swish of tails, our stomachs tightened. We knew what was coming next. (Photograph: Vic Martin)*

Top: *The black eye of Carcharodon carcharias is a dominant feature of the species. 'Like a black hole in a shroud' was how Peter Matthiessen described it in his book, Blue Meridian: The Search for the Great White Shark. (Photograph: Peter Newstead)*
Bottom: *A Great White comes in for a closer look. Without the intervening cage bars such proximity would be fatal. Down there, face to face with these sharks, we had occasional doubts about the bars' strength. (Photograph: Peter Newstead)*

Top: *The sharks seemed intrigued by the propellers and often nudged and 'tasted' the stern-drive and Mercury outboard motor. Later we learned that the interaction of the zinc anodes with other metals — a battery effect — sent an electronic signal to their sensory organs.*
Bottom: *A Great White female inspects the cage lines. Minutes later she tried to chew through the nylon rope. Who said sharks don't think? (Photograph: Marilyn Edwards)*

They were simply sharks and, like most other creatures in the sea, survival was the name of their game. Eat or be eaten. That was the truth of the matter.

The sharks showed us a side of Nature not many people have had the privilege of observing at close quarters. The Great Whites were elite beasts on the highest scale of predators. There was no question what they thought about us.

We were prey. It was as simple as that. And we were about to learn more on that aspect of life below the waves.

A DIFFERENT VIEW OF SHARKS
chapter six

IN MY OWN FIRST EXPERIENCE OF SHARKS I WAS IN A POSITION I WOULD NOT recommend to anyone: hanging upside down by the heels with the sharks snapping immediately below.

I was a small boy aboard the Blue Funnel Line vessel SS *Themistocles*, bound from Cape Town to Australia via Durban on the east coast of South Africa. The year was 1941, during the darkest days of the Second World War. At that time a Nazi victory over Britain seemed a dread probability. German surface raiders and U-boats were harrying Allied shipping in the Indian Ocean. Sinking hapless merchantmen by torpedo and gunfire.

Themistocles had a naval auxiliary gun mounted on her stern. It made for a brave showing, but the gunners cheerfully remarked that if we did encounter the enemy the piece would be 'about as much use as a ruddy popgun!'.

As a small boy I had a right of entry to the gun platform denied to adults. The excitement for a seven-year-old can be imagined. This was a *real* gun! With shining eyes I helped grease the mechanisms and imagined U-Boats in my sights.

Themistocles made her run up the South African coast by night, with all lights extinguished, in radio silence and an atmosphere of nervous tension, and on the way we passed the sea grave of the 1852 troopship *Birkenhead*.

For those who knew the story it was a grim reminder of what could happen if we were torpedoed. The *Birkenhead* had gone down soon after striking an uncharted rock. There was only enough room in the lifeboats for women and children and the troops were formed up on deck as though on parade. They stood rigidly to attention as the ship went down.

No man broke ranks until the waves lapped the decks. An example of bravery in the best British tradition. As the poet Rudyard Kipling wrote:

To stand and be still
To the Birkenhead drill
Is a mighty tough bullet to chew!

But it was in the water that the real ordeal began. Those struggling in the sea were attacked by hundreds of sharks. Of 680 soldiers, women and children, and crew, 455 people died. The majority of those who did not find a seat in the lifeboats perished.

The proportion of people who drowned to those who became victims of sharks has never been established. But the few who did reach the beach a mile (1.6 kilometres) away, through heavy surf, told horrific tales of companions torn to pieces beside them. They described a sea that was red with blood, shark fins darting between the swimmers.

Lieutenant Frank Giradot, a fortunate survivor, wrote to his father later: 'Nearly all those that took to the water without their clothes on were taken by sharks. Hundreds of them were around us and I saw men taken quite close to me. But as I was dressed, they preferred the others.'

Some South Africans still call Great Whites 'Tommy Sharks', in recollection. 'Tommy Atkins', of course, being the nickname of the British infantry soldier, like 'G. I. Joe' for American 'foot sloggers'. However, it is likely that several species of sharks were involved in the Birkenhead tragedy, with whalers probably the most numerous.

The *Birkenhead* passed into nautical legend and the disaster was still well remembered in South Africa 90 years later. But it was to be eclipsed by an even worse shark tragedy when the British vessel *Nova Scotia*, carrying 750 Italian prisoners of war, was torpedoed off the South African coast on 28 November 1942. Ironically, the Germans aboard the U-boat that sank her were the Italians' wartime allies.

There were 900 people aboard the *Nova Scotia*. The survivors in lifejackets, clinging to rafts and floating debris, were attacked by sharks in similar fashion to the *Birkenhead* nightmare, in a feeding frenzy which continued for nearly three days. When a neutral Portuguese sloop finally and fortuitously came by, only 192 men were still alive. More than 500 had perished from exposure or from the sharks. As the Portuguese rescuers dragged men from the water they had to fend off giant sharks with boat hooks and oars.

The Natal coast, up which we steamed in the *Themistocles*, would become known as the 'shark attack capital of the world' by reason of the number of attacks on surfers and swimmers.

I was too young at the time to know about the saga of the *Birkenhead* — my father had firm views about *that* kind of bedtime story. Nor was I aware of the notoriety of Natal beaches. The *Nova Scotia* was yet to make her fatal rendez-vous with her U-boat.

But I did know one thing about sharks. I had been told that they had to turn on their backs to eat. This seemed to me to be a very unusual thing, and it became fixed in my juvenile mind, joining a portfolio of animal curiosities which I carried in my head. Camels, for instance, had humps and could go without water for weeks. Giraffes had such long necks that I hoped none of them would ever have a sore throat. Elephants had long trunks and used them to pop sticky buns in their mouths. *'Beware the smile of the crocodile...He doesn't want to greet you. He only wants to eat you.'* Sharks ate belly up. And so on.

At Durban there were lots of sharks. Packs of them in fact.

We anchored outside the harbour and the *Themistocles'* cooks emptied the galley slop bins over the side from a door in the ship's side down close to the waterline. The sharks came swimming from ship to ship in the anchorage, feeding on the floating offal and scraps. Passengers on our ship, in the vessel's waist, were lining the bulwarks and craning their necks to see the spectacle.

'Sharks!'

At the cry I rushed on deck. But I found that I was too small to peer over the chest-high bulwarks. I bobbed about between the grownups' legs in increasing desperation until I plucked up courage to ask someone to lift me up.

'You want to see the sharks?' cried a jovial male passenger. 'I'll show you the sharks!'

With that he picked me up by the legs and dangled me over the side. Then he laughingly pretended to slip and lose his grip. This alarmed me so much that I screamed and kicked out, and he very nearly *did* drop me on to the sharks below.

My mother, who had just arrived on deck, came rushing forwards in alarm and yelled even more loudly than I did. I had a confused topsy-turvy image of wide, wet backs, jostling each other in the water by the side of the ship, heads making unmistakable snapping and gobbling motions.

Rescued and turned right side up, and after the hearty passenger had been roundly admonished by others for his foolish prank, I had a more orthodox view of the sharks. As I suspected, from that first inverted view, something was wrong. I was fascinated but there was still a sense of disappointment.

There were somewhere between a dozen and 20 sharks feeding on the rubbish below. They had light brown backs, rounded snouts, long fins.

Members of the *Carcharhinus* or whaler family, as I found out many years later when I became interested enough in sharks to identify species.

At Durban the sharks were bunting and butting at the floating food debris, occasionally gulping down pieces. I watched them with an increasing frown before turning to my mother.

'Sharks eat on their backs, don't they?' My voice had the querulous note of a small boy when some long-cherished belief is under threat.

'*Don't* they?'

'Yes, dear.'

'Well, these sharks don't seem to be doing that? Why aren't they?'

'You'll have to ask the sharks, dear.'

In later years I found out that it was the Greek philosopher Aristotle who may have been responsible for the story that sharks eat belly up. He put forward the notion in his epic *Historia Animalium*, a history of the animal world, in 330 BC. 'The mouths of sharks are placed not at the front,' he wrote, 'but at the underside of the head... So that these fishes turn on their back in order to take their food.'

The Roman, Pliny the Elder, in his own *Natural History* 400 years later, came to a similar conclusion. He made the interesting statement: 'Divers have fierce fights with dog-fish [sharks]; these attack their loins and heels and all the white parts of the body. The one safety lies in going for them and frightening them by taking the offensive; for a dog-fish is as much afraid of a man as a man is of it.'

Pliny's divers, of course, were the pearl divers of the Persian Gulf and Red Sea, where sharks were prevalent and confrontations not uncommon. The Romans were excessively fond of pearls. The divers were darkskinned, except for the palms of their hands and the soles of their feet — those 'white parts' which flashed in the water and attracted sharks.

Curiously, this suggestion that a show of aggression was the best means of defence against sharks was similar to the opinion of the modern Austrian diver Hans Hass. 'Shout at the sharks underwater,' claimed Hass in his 1950s books *Men and Sharks* and *Under the Red Sea*, 'and they will go away. Leaving you with a great story to tell your friends!'

Later Hass tried the theory on the denizens of the Great Barrier Reef and was disappointed to find that Australian sharks did not respond at all in the approved fashion. Some actually forced him to do his shouting out of the water.

'Australian sharks are somewhat different,' he concluded.

Perhaps, as my mother might have remarked, the sharks had not read the right books.

85

As a child in the golden pre-television days I was a voracious reader, as interested in factual accounts as I was in fiction. At Geelong Grammar School, where I was incarcerated as a boarder, I found a treasure trove in the school library. The Durban shark incident had made a profound impression on me, and I read avidly any book which had to do with the sea, and especially if it included sharks. There was always one question at the back of my mind, which remained unanswered, and while it was far from being an obsession it nagged unsatisfactorily at me. Did sharks ever eat on their backs? Or didn't they?

Nothing in the school library seemed to hold an answer. During my Ancient History studies I was taught to respect Aristotle. He was the first of the rational scientists, and much of what he had written about sharks and other creatures was accurate. In fact his studies were more useful than anything else that was done for the next 1600 years. He lived in Macedonia by the sea and was able to make practical observations. A good deal of additional information must also have come to him from sailors and fishermen who had seen with their own eyes what they reported to him.

Aristotle gave sharks and rays the name *Selache*, which is perpetuated in the modern term *Selachimorpha* and which differentiates them from the fishes with bones and scales. But where the upside-down eating was concerned, feeding was such a basic requirement for sharks, such a primary behavioural act . . . How could he be wrong?

Strangely, when I asked people who knew a good deal about sharks, including 'Sharkey' Nelson, none of them could give me a straight answer either. They agreed that sharks ate on their backs. Everyone knew that. But, come to think of it, none of them could recall actually seeing it happen.

In time I saw a lot of sharks myself, and caught quite a few in particular circumstances. The only time any of mine turned on their backs was when they were dead.

It was in the shark cage that I was at last able to settle the question and see feeding sharks turn belly up, and partially prove Aristotle's point.

In the cage we were always looking for different patterns of shark behaviour. Seeking camera shots which would illustrate the way the great sharks lived. The way they responded to the various situations in their lives.

Vic Martin had made a number of successful nature documentaries for television. He had his own standard list of types of behaviour which he believed made a well-rounded natural history film. 'Look for feeding,' he said, 'nest-building, locomotion, courtship, mating, birth, care of the young, prey and predators, displays of fear and aggression. Get all those and you've got it!'

In theory, after you'd ticked off each item on the list all you had to do was to add commentary of a not too inane nature, some music, and presto! — you had a nature movie. It was a useful practical guide.

One of Vic's more recent films had been on raptors — eagles and hawks — and he was inclined to quote this when listing his requirements for the sharks.

It made me instantly uneasy.

Birds, like most other live subjects, required skilled camerawork, no question about that. But there was one aspect which almost guaranteed success. Birds had nests.

Once a cameraman set up a 'hide' or a 'blind' so that he could film unobserved the result was reasonably assured. The birds would return to the nest on a regular basis and interact with each other. The young would go from the egg stage to hatchlings, to sibling competition, to learning to fly. The adults would bring food, indicating feeding habits and prey. Their comings and goings gave good opportunities for shots of flight.

And moving from one part of Australia and one species of bird to another, showed stunning tracts of the great Australian landscape.

As easy as falling off a log? By no means. Apart from camera skills a lot of ingenuity was required in constructing hides, and background knowledge of the birds was a necessity. For instance, when the photographer took up position he sometimes needed others to assist. Eagles would be nervous if they knew a human was in their proximity. But they could be fooled. 'Eagles can't count,' Vic said. 'If a couple of other people go into the hide with me and then leave, Mother Eagle is satisfied that all the pesky humans have gone and she starts to do her natural thing. I film it. Simple.'

Vic's general formula could be applied to filming all kinds of land creatures from kangaroos and koalas to crocodiles — whatever took your fancy in the natural world.

But not sharks.

I tried to explain the difficulties to him. No one had ever recorded shark courtship in the wild, let alone mating. Where and how would you expect to film births? Shark babies hurried off on their own to do battle with the world as soon as they were born. So there was no opportunity to study maternal behaviour as there was with dolphins, dugongs, whales and other mammals which shepherded their young and nursed them at the breast.

It would be difficult if not impossible to record sharks hunting natural prey because of the distracting factor of the camera and the human operator. The alien intrusion, impossible to conceal.

The list of negatives could have been continued, but I felt that it was long enough. If we were going to make a film we should rather be looking for positives.

Vic was understandably frustrated.

'For Christ's sake!' he said. 'You could at least get some goddamn feeding shots! They're biting at the bloody whales all the time!'

Sure they were. The bites were there for all to see. But that was another problem. *Carcharodon carcharias*, we learnt to our surprise, are somewhat nervous eaters. In their eagerness to get a mouthful of whale the sharks would sometimes slide up and expose themselves, half out of the water on the whales' backs.

But they were always looking around. If another fin appeared, if there was another swirl in the water, they would break off and hurriedly retreat. We surmised that this was because they felt exposed and vulnerable in the unnatural situation.

Sharks eat sharks, after all, and they appeared to be defensively aware of what was going on around them. Always deferring to a bigger shark.

Out at sea, where the buoyed whales floated on the swells, the sharks were sometimes on their flanks like a row of cattle at a trough. But in the more confined spaces off the Whaling Station their watchword was caution. When the cage was stationed alongside a whale they infuriatingly moved to the other end to eat. Move the cage and they responded by going to the opposite side of the whale to work their jaws in decent privacy. We were able to watch them feeding only at a distance. But film shot over any space was disappointing. The gore and debris in the water blotted out the scene as great clouds of crimson blood were pumped out of the feeding shark's gills.

It was awesome to watch.

The Great Whites struck with their bottom teeth. They then protruded the top jaw with its triangular, slashing blades, and sank those upper fangs deep into the whale's flesh. Then, using their tail as a lever, they spun in a corkscrew action, tearing out a great gobbet of blubber and flesh. As they turned over, their white bellies flashed in the sun so brightly they almost hurt the eyes.

It answered the question.

In certain circumstances, with very large prey, sharks do bite and twist and roll. Giving rise not only to the legend that they feed on their backs, but also to the reason for the name 'White Shark' as applied to *Carcharodon* — something which we had also wondered about. For Great Whites may be gold, grey, charcoal or even indigo blue on their upper parts, and white only on the belly.

The name almost certainly came from the 19th century whalers. They had the same opportunity of watching *Carcharodon* in action on dead whales alongside their ships as we did at the Albany Whaling Station.

We were also able to see the reason for the particular shape of Great Whites' teeth. The top teeth, as is well known, are the classic triangular shark teeth — each side serrated like a steak knife and for the same reason of slicing readily through flesh. Except that our steak knives are a recent innovation, and the sharks have had theirs for 60 million years.

What is less well known is that the teeth in the bottom jaw of a Great White are different from those of the top jaw. They are thicker through and rounder at the base, rising to spikes and needle tips. They still have serrations on their edges, but their purpose is to drive deep into the flesh of the prey and hold the shark there while the top teeth do the cutting. The top teeth are kept folded back except when needed.

If the prey is a fish, a seal or a human it is shaken like a rabbit in a dog's mouth and dismembered by the action. The roll, exposing the belly, is usually employed only with very big prey, like a whale. A situation in which the shark wants to tear a chunk out of something immovable.

The difference between the top and lower teeth is not generally understood, though it is logical once the purpose becomes evident. While all the rows of fearful spikes of the lower jaw are used in an attack, only the front row of the upper teeth are unfolded and used for the slashing cut.

Where a human only gets to have 52 teeth — including baby teeth — a shark continually replaces its teeth and may use 24 000 in a lifetime. A very useful capacity for a predator whose teeth are at constant risk of damage.

Aristotle's information from his observation of the shark's head shape may have been supplemented by sailors or fishermen telling him of the behaviour of sharks around a dead whale. What he couldn't have deduced from looking at dead sharks is that live sharks can dramatically project their whole jaw forwards, so that their bite is full-on frontal and not from underneath. But he is not the only one to have erred in his interpretation.

One of the problems with the *Jaws* film series, for people who know sharks, was that the teeth of the plastic monsters were all wrong. Similar-sized triangles were used for upper and lower jaws, and the fibreglass models always 'swam' with their mouths open and all the teeth, including those in the top jaw, protruded and projected forwards at an unnatural angle. A real Great White shows its top teeth only in the actual motion of biting. Not in the approach.

A minor point, perhaps, but something of a shame when the studio spent so many millions of dollars to produce a 'real' effect in other respects.

But it is a fact that humans are ignorant about many aspects of sharks. They continue to confuse us, and the myths continue to dominate over reality. As we found in the cage at Albany.

For instance, do sharks have feelings? That was a question I sometimes asked myself while watching the huge spectral shapes of Great Whites drift past the cage. We wondered about the lives they led in the mysterious depths of the ocean.

'Feelings? What an absurd suggestion!' the reader might respond with a laugh of scorn. 'Surely sharks just live to eat and eat to live?' That is certainly the theory of the Dark Ages — man, in his or her eternal conceit, believing that *Homo sapiens* alone has the superior being's capacity for love or friendship. But watching the sharks and seeing one preconceived notion after the other being demolished before our eyes, I wondered whether the possibility of shark friendships was as outlandish as it seemed.

Usually the big sharks came singly, but sometimes they were in pairs, often of the same sex. Our worst time in the cage was when two huge females (Grandma and Dangerous Mabel we christened them) ganged up on us for a concerted and methodical attack. Did that pair of old *Selachian* harridans swim the ocean in permanent company? Buddies, in the human sense?

Friendships occur among many animals, sometimes with oddly assorted couples. Any farmer will tell you that horses, sheep and cattle often have associates within the herd with whom they prefer to graze. I have known a horse and a goat that were inseparable and have heard of other similar 'friendships', even one between a cockatoo and a cat. My own Dalmatian dog, Roger, declared war on all cats except for one — Bluey, a semi-wild part Burmese who would lie belly-up between Roger's paws while the dog washed him and fussed over him in the most unlikely fashion.

It is an undisputed fact that sharks, too, have their own travelling companions. Tiger sharks in particular often swim with an assortment of fish followers. These include pilot fish, cleaner fish, remoras and cobia. The motley school swims along with the tiger shark, like a retinue out for a stroll with the prince. Such associations — aside from the obvious role of the cleaner fish — are not always clear. Pilot fish, striped distinctively like a footballer's jersey, got their name because sailors long ago believed they guided the shark to its prey. In fact, it is probably the other way around. The shark, far from being half-blind and stupid as was previously thought, actually has superior senses of smell and detection than most fish. Today's marine biologists speculate that the distinctive stripes of the pilot fish may actually be to prevent the shark from confusing it with other species and gobbling it up — a sort of reverse camouflage. So the pilot fish benefits from the shark's protection, but what it does to earn its keep is still unknown.

Remoras, or sucker fish, with their black and white longitudinal stripes are the other famous shark companions. The remora's dorsal fin has been modified to form a suction pad — surely one of evolution's more extraordinary adaptations — so the fish can suck onto the shark's back or underbelly and get a free ride. There are eight species of remora or 'shark-suckers'. Some have specialised into 'whale-suckers' and attach themselves instead to the baleen whale. Others swim with manta rays and other large denizens of the deep. The shark's usual companion is *Remora remora*, but a larger species, *Echenis naucrates* — the white-striped shark-sucker — is also quite a common rider on the shark bandwagon. The tiny white remora, *Remora albescens*, has a short body and fins and spends a good deal of tie actually inside the gills of sharks and rays. When danger threatens it rushes inside the shark's mouth to hide. A reverse of the usual scenario.

Why don't sharks eat members of their band of faithful followers? Presumably there are benefits for both parties. The remoras eat parasites which attach to the shark's skin. Those that swim inside the mouth and gills, pecking off pests, perform what must be a very welcome task. The others may act as extra eyes and ears for the shark, warning of danger. In return they receive protection and scraps from the master's meal. A good deal all round.

Remoras do venture off on their own in brief independent bursts and it is a little unnerving for a diver to find one accompanying him. It usually means there is a shark around somewhere, short of a follower — for the moment. Since the biggest remoras — 60 centimetres or more in length — seem to tag along with the biggest sharks, a large remora is scarcely a welcome sight for a diver.

There is a story told about Pacific Islanders catching turtles by tying a cord to a remora's tail, throwing it in the water and waiting for it to attach to the turtle's shell. It's a tale I personally view with suspicion. The suckerfish would have difficulty swimming with a cord around its tail, and even if it did attach to the turtle, the pull would be so great that, unless the fish was smart enough to let go, it would be torn in half. But it makes a good story.

The cobia kingfish, *Rechycentron canadum*, is another example of Nature's ingenuity. Young cobia, with their black and white stripes and flattened head look very similar to the remora; they even have a rounded tail to complete the resemblance. Only the sucker pad is absent. The disguise presents the juvenile cobia to the shark as a remora. Using this fake identity the cobia lives under the shark's protection and, as the shark grows accustomed to it, becomes one of the family.

91

The adult cobia loses its stripes, and its tail changes to the V-shape of most ocean speedsters. Eventually it will become a large and powerful creature, nearly 2 metres long and weighing as much as 55 kilos (120 pounds). A recognised gamefish and a great fighter on rod and reel. But the cobia puts in its kindergarten years with sharks and often remains in company with a particular shark well into its adult life.

The question remains as to whether the shark's followers are merely useful companions? Or does the shark become fond of the various individuals in its little family? After all, dogs were hunting companions to humans before the domestic bond of devotion was established. 'Dogs, yes; sharks, no!' Before the reader utters this cry of derision, let me tell a story from the Dampier Archipelago off the Western Australian coast.

In the 1960s, before we ourselves began to see sharks in a different light, my friend Maurie Glazier and I hooked a 13 foot (4 metre) female tiger shark and towed it into the beach at Thevenard Island. The shark's retinue of pilot fish and remoras followed, showing increasing agitation. They were pitifully aware that some disaster had struck their host and were probably, and rightfully, concerned for their own future.

As the water became shallower, the followers turned away one by one to swim back into the depths. At last, with the tiger shark hauled out into the sunlight, its stripes gradually fading in death, there remained only one faithful friend. It was a cobia, a handsome fish, well grown into the adult phase and more than a metre in length. This fish showed evidence of distress, sometimes almost grounding itself in its endeavour to reach the dead shark.

'Shoot it,' someone suggested. 'With a speargun. Cobia steaks go well on the barbecue.'

Maurie and I, who had caught the shark and held the cobia's fate in our hands, shook our heads. The fish was like a dog whose master has been cruelly struck down. It appeared to courageously disregard its own danger in the shallow water, ignoring the threat from the strange two-legged predators from the world of air, who had already killed the tiger shark. Why it wanted to reach the shark we could not understand, but its grief was obvious.

'I never thought that a fish could care so much,' Maurie said with regret.

'I didn't know they cared at all,' I replied, feeling more like a murderer every minute.

For more than an hour the cobia swam up and down erratically, a few metres from the beach. At length, it slowly swam away as though uncertain which direction to take. We did not see it again.

The one shark I have never seen with an accompanying remora, pilot fish or cobia is the Great White. Symbiosis, a beneficial association with other creatures, was underlined on our shot wish list at the Albany Whaling Station. But it never occurred in our view, despite the fact that our sharks did have furry parasites in their mouths and *coepeds* hanging from their fins and may have welcomed a good clean-up. I have never seen a suckerfish or pilot fish in company with Great White sharks in other films or photographs either. It may be that the Great White truly does swim alone.

Since that day at Thevenard Island I have often wondered whether the tiger shark would have been as distressed if the cobia had been hooked and caught. In short, do sharks have 'pets' of a different species? Do they feel affection in their company; *Selachian* sorrow at their loss?

We have so many preconceptions about sharks, yet our actual knowledge is so limited. We are told, for example, that sharks have no fun (except, presumably, taking off the legs of bathers). They don't sport like dolphins or sea lions, play like puppy dogs or fool around like human beings. Or do they? Perhaps the accepted wisdom that sees the shark only as a merciless killing machine is just another erroneous perception on our part.

The passage of the Great Whites by our cage was mostly smooth and graceful. Peter Newstead and I seldom saw them move quickly. But on the few occasions when they did, the contrast was dramatic. There would be a sharp, audible 'crack!' of the tail which produced instant acceleration. The shark would become a sleek-finned torpedo hurtling away out of our circle of vision in a white rush of bubbles. This could occur when a smaller shark sighted a larger one coming too close for comfort or when the tug boat came alongside the pontoon and took in tow two of the floating whales tethered there.

The wire strops holding the whales' tails were hooked with a gaff and dropped over the towing bollard of the tug. This was invisible to us below. But we could tell when the transfer was completed because the propeller on the tug would spin faster, becoming a silvery whirr leaving a spiral track of bubbles. And because the sharks surrounding the whales would instantly stop whatever they were doing and dash off after the tug boat. We watched them go, their tails beating furiously, often 'porpoising' in the boat's wake, their dorsal fins cutting the water. They swerved and zigzagged, forming their own torpedo-wake trails of white bubbles.

'Like dogs chasing a motor car,' Peter remarked once after observing the phenomenon. 'You almost expect to hear them bark.'

It was a fair comparison. There was no real reason for the sharks to chase the tug boat — the pickings were easier from the stationary whale carcasses tethered to the pontoon, and the sharks returned to the pontoon as soon as the tug had delivered its carcasses to the slip. Chasing it was simply a diversion. Was it evidence that sharks really do have a lighter side?

At Albany we had an animal behavioural problem with our filming because of our compulsion to impose human plans on wild, free-ranging creatures with no interest in our schedules. As the Scots poet Robbie Burns wrote: *The best laid schemes o' mice an' men / Gang aft a-gley.*

As a producer and director, Vic had worked out a program and a shooting schedule in the best traditions of the motion picture industry. We would dive at various locations, including Moreton Bay near Brisbane, for film of the grey nurse shark so popular in aquariums like Sea World at Surfers Paradise. The Great Barrier Reef, it was hoped, would provide tiger, whaler shark and wobbegong action. On the reef we would work with Ron Isbel and his charter boat, *Sea Hunt*.

Ron had a big reputation for turning on spectacular shark shows. Several international film crews, Italian, American and Japanese, had already used his services with success.

The film would open, Vic said, with the lesser sharks — though he hoped for something spectacular on tigers on the Barrier Reef — and conclude with dramatic scenes with the Great Whites. He had clearly in mind what he wanted.

At Albany the problem was that, as the days ticked away, the Great White sharks were not co-operating in providing the requirements he had listed. We were getting a good deal of the same kinds of shots of bland scenes of Whites swimming past the cage. There was some good footage of sharks with their noses in the cage, rolling evil eyes at us. But not enough of that. Anyone who has made nature films will appreciate the dilemma.

We needed more confrontation and we needed variety.

'Action!' said Vic, pounding a fist into his palm. 'Drama! That's what television is all about! We've got to give it to them!'

I bit my tongue to avoid saying, 'Tell the sharks!'

I did point out, though, that we could only film what we were seeing. If the sharks were ignoring the script requirement for *Selachian* villainy and behaving themselves like ladies and gentlemen, it was regrettable. But what was the alternative?

'Suggest something,' I said to Vic. He shook his head. I was glad he did not say, 'Swim out of the cage'. He was fair about that.

'We'll just have to all work harder at it,' he said. 'Let's go one hundred per cent for a good feeding shot.'

'Dinner in the diner,' I replied, trying to lighten things up and quoting that old favourite song *Chattanooga Choo Choo*, 'Nothing could be finer.'

When the opportunity did come, we fumbled it.

We were something of a circus. The rule was that we had no more than six people on the daily shoot. Even with this limited number, by the time the camera and sound gear and spare tanks were on board, the 23 foot (7 metre) *Chivers Safari* was seriously overcrowded.

Vic was director and cameraman. John McCabe was the sound recordist. We liked to have two deckhands to work the cage outriggers and ropes and the boat moorings — though a good deal of the time Peter Grace did it on his own. Peter was an ocean-racing yachtsman and good at making sense of an odd assortment of lines and avoiding tangles. Maurie Glazier was a fisherman friend of long standing, very experienced with sharks. Since we never knew when we might have to evacuate the cage in an emergency, it was important to have someone who knew the right rope to pull in a hurry.

Peter Newstead and I manned the cage. I operated the movie camera and we shared a couple of Nikonos still cameras. Peter's job was back-up. When all else failed he would operate the powerhead, the explosive-headed spear that was our only defence. We prayed we would never need it.

Qualifications?

Vic had been a television news cameraman with a Brisbane channel before branching out on his own. His pretty wife Annette was the weather girl on Brisbane Channel Nine. John was from Gladstone in Queensland and one of the original 'Greens'. Vic had met him when John was organising a protest to save a mountain cave threatened by a mining company. The cave sheltered a unique species of bat. Vic was short of a sound recordist, and John — attracted by the idea of touring Australia making nature films — took on the job. He had a cheerful personality and the knack of finding the right humour to suit the moment.

Peter Newstead used to joke that his qualification was as my next door neighbour and being out of work at the time. Originally Brian Greenhalgh, who had got me interested in the Albany sharks in the first place, was to have shared the cage. But unfortunately he couldn't take full time off from his job, so we had him only at weekends and on odd days.

Peter turned out to be an excellent cage buddy. He was short and stocky with black curly hair and glasses. He was actually a trained geologist with a university degree. When the mining slump in Western Australia came after the nickel boom of the late 1970s his company dispensed 'for the time being' with field geologists.

'Come to Albany,' I said. 'It will be fun.'

'Can you guarantee I won't get bitten?'

'No guarantees.'

'Then I'll come. When do we go?'

I knew already that Peter was a good SCUBA diver. The other quality essential in the cage was coolness under pressure. Something that comes naturally or not at all. Peter was never flustered, even later when we were to have some bad moments.

Along with Peter came his delightful wife Susan. She would be company for my wife Marilyn, a journalist with the *Sunday Times*, and our year-old daughter Petrana. And of course our Dalmatian dog Cinders, sometimes known as 'the spotted rat' for her charming but devious habits, could not be left behind. We rented two houses at Middleton Beach in Albany. As there were always visitors from Perth coming and going, it was a busy time.

'Does it take 15 people to put one man in the water to photograph a shark?' Vic groaned in mock dismay one busy mealtime. A chaos of abalone stew and bottles of red wine cluttered the table. We counted heads. Yes, it did. Not including Cinders the spotted dog.

The perfect feeding shot came on a perfect day when the sun was shining, and the sharks were there. Everything we could have asked for. For once Vic had allowed visitors aboard, and there were people climbing all over the boat, tripping over gear and photographic equipment. They included Marilyn's great friend Catherina Ingleman-Sundeberg. A Swedish marine archaeologist working on shipwrecks with the Fremantle Maritime Museum, she had come to Albany for a brief visit.

Catherina had brought her diving gear. 'I'm going to dive,' she said brightly. 'To see these sharks you talk so much of.'

We looked at Vic. The rule was that only working parties went into the cages. Other requests had been refused. It was a professional operation, not a fun show, and every day cost money.

'OK,' said Vic to our surprise. 'But just a quick look. You come out as soon as we say so. Right?'

'Of course.'

'I'm going too,' said Marilyn, who had been dying to have a turn in the cage but had needed moral support. 'Wait till I get my suit on!'

We had just had a session in the cage and shot a 400 foot (122 metre) roll of film. Peter and I welcomed the chance for a break in the sunshine. The camera had been passed up for loading. The girls settled themselves into the cage after a hesitant start, equipped with our foot weights and weight belts.

Peter and I were blinking in the sunshine, feeling the warmth permeating into our bodies.

'Good God! look at *that*.' Peter was suddenly pointing.

A Great White, about 4.5 metres long, had charged the whale right next to the cage and had begun feeding. Just as we had always prayed one would.

Bubbles burst to the surface from the girls in the cage.

'Quick, the camera!' I shouted. 'Where's the goddamn camera?'

It was another strict rule that the underwater camera was instantly reloaded ready for any similar circumstance as soon as it came aboard. Loading was a tricky job because the camera was a hybrid 16 mm. The magazine was a 400 foot load German Bolex operating on 12 volts. The camera and lenses were French Beaulieu R16, running on 7.5 volts. Astonishingly, they worked perfectly in tandem. But feeding the film up through the gooseneck to the magazine had to be done with dry fingers and took several minutes. Only Vic or John could do it.

'The camera!' I cried again.

'It's not loaded!' Vic grabbed his own 16 mm Eclair surface camera and dashed to the stern of the boat.

'It's not *what*?'

'Sorry. It's just not loaded!' He put the Eclair to his eye and began shooting. '*Jeez!*'

Well, at least we would get surface film.

The shark was fantastic. It bit and rolled, and spouted blood through its gills. It put its head out of the water, shaking and tearing at the whale. At one stage it had its tail in the cage as it lay belly-up. We could only watch from the boat.

It made tremendous surface footage. It would have been fantastic underwater too. A lesson learnt.

We banged on the cage, of course, to get the girls to come out. No chance. All promises were forgotten. They weren't going to come out when something as exciting as that was going on. No way!

They finally emerged, shaking and breathless. 'Did you see *that*?' — eyes shining with excitement.

Yes, we had seen it.

'The shark had her tail in my cage!' exulted Marilyn. Suddenly it was her cage. 'I had to push it away.'

'Did you bite it?' I asked dryly.

'Did I what?' She looked puzzled.

'You're a journalist. You know the definition of news given to every new cadet who joins a paper.'

'Yes. Dog bites man, no news. Man bites dog, that *is* news. What's that got to do with it?'

'Well, you just passed up the chance of a lifetime. If you'd grabbed that tail and bitten it instead of pushing it away, you could have gone into the Guiness Book of Records. The first person in the world to bite a Great White shark underwater and live!'

'Win some, lose some,' said Vic, shaking his head over the empty magazine on the underwater camera. 'It just got overlooked. We got the top stuff. Them's the breaks!'

'Spend 100 hours in a cage' — Peter had his back turned, staring fixedly out to sea — 'waiting for a bloody shot. And what happens...?'

I was equally disappointed, mentally chiding myself. We had realised early in the filming that we could not expect the sharks to run to our schedule. If something extraordinary occurred, the only way to be sure of getting it on film was to be always prepared for immediate action.

The extraordinary *had* occurred, and right under our noses. And we had missed it.

We would never have as good a chance again. But the girls did add variety to the film, with their excitement bubbling over in their interview. A fantastic experience for them, and the different angle added an extra dimension to the film.

When the shark had bitten and rolled for the last time and finned on its way replete, I thought I heard something inside my head. Something like a peal of ghostly laughter.

Aristotle, perhaps?

PATTERNS OF ATTACK: THE SERIAL KILLERS
chapter seven

EACH OF THE MAN-EATER SPECIES HAS ITS OWN USUALLY DISTINCTIVE PATTERN OF attack. A trademark approach to its victim.

There are only three species regularly implicated in fatal attacks on humans. On this basis it might be considered that identification of the perpetrator in the various attacks is a relatively simple matter.

On the contrary. There are few areas where reports have been as muddled and contradictory as the accounts of shark attacks through the years. The reason for this is the 'human' factor. Shark attacks are customarily sudden, and unexpected. They involve so much horror and emotion in observers and survivors that it is understandable that there can be confusion in the aftermath.

Take for example Lee Warner. In 1967, though only 24 years of age, he was a very experienced diver. In his world of elite spearfishing competition each species of fish counted for differing degrees of points. He had developed a practised eye for underwater detail. But after seeing his diving companion Robert Bartle bitten in half and devoured on Sunday 19 August 1967, he was quite unable to give a full description of the monster responsible.

Since the shark had circled him for several minutes, with Bartle's legs and fins protruding from its mouth, it might have been thought that Warner could recollect such aspects important to identification as the shape of the tail, the head, the teeth.

Some 'experts' were insistent after the attack that the creature responsible must have been a tiger shark, a very different-looking animal from the Great White. *Galeocerdo cuvieri* has a blunt square head as opposed to the cone-shaped nose of *Carcharias*. The tiger's distinctive stripes may fade with age. But it has a tail with the upper lobe angled and much larger than the lower lobe. The Great White in contrast has the powerful mackerel vee-shaped tail of the *Lamniformes*. A tiger's teeth are scimitar-shaped, while the White's are perfect triangles.

What did Warner see?

'Never in my life have I seen anything so chilling as watching that shark circling around me with the body of Bob still in its jaws. From less than a metre away I could see the terrible wounds which had been inflicted. I felt helpless. I could see Bob was dead. That was only too obvious. I thought I was soon to follow. I simply cannot describe the terror which flowed through me.'

Horror and terror, then, were the most vivid recollections. What about the shark itself?

'It kept circling about 3 metres from me. Its body looked about 5 feet [1.5 metres] thick from top to bottom. I didn't really get a good idea of its length — I couldn't see its extremities and I don't remember seeing the tail. All I could see was the eye and what it had in its mouth.'

Warner had a reputation among spearfishermen of being courageous to the point of recklessness. But what he had seen left him so shaken that he could only shrug helplessly when shown pictures which might have helped identify the species of the shark.

The mode of attack, in a direct charge with no preliminary circling, was classic *Carcharodon carcharias*. Judging from the straight line across Bartle's sternum — no angle to the bite — where the shark severed his thorax from the remainder of his body it must have been an immense creature, probably in excess of 6 metres (20 feet) in length.

As a professional abalone diver, Lee Warner has seen other Great Whites since that black day at Jurien Bay. He now recognises the species responsible. His last sighting was his last day as an abalone diver.

Sydney Harbour, home to another shark species, had an evil reputation in earlier years, though many people ignored the risk and swam in its waters.

Theo Brown, whom I knew in the 1950s as a rescue and recovery diver with the Western Australian Police Force, grew up as a boy in Sydney's East Lindfield, and swam every summer afternoon upstream from the Roseville bridge.

After 11 years away, including a spell with the Northern Territory Police, he returned to Sydney. In January 1960 he took two young boys, Ken Murray aged 13, and Gary Hopkins, 16, to Middle Harbour (an offshoot of Sydney Harbour) to practise snorkelling and duck-diving. On the following day he hoped to introduce them to SCUBA diving at Manly.

They went by rowboat to a small inlet opposite Middle Harbour's Killarney picnic reserve. It had a yellow sand beach where bush came right down to the water.

Theo Brown recalled later: 'The boys entered the water . . . I followed and was disappointed to find it warm and turbid. Even with my face mask I could see no more than a foot [30 centimetres] or so underwater.'

The boys played in the shallows for a while. Then Brown and Ken Murray swam deeper and practised some snorkel dives. 'Peering through the surrounding gloom we saw the bottom of fine grey sand dotted with an occasional shell. We could see nothing more, the water was too dirty.'

Brown went ashore. 'As I turned back to Ken I was in time to see him surface with his face mask hanging near his chin. I think I laughed as I called out to him, "What's the matter, Ken?"'

'He didn't answer but just looked at me and gave a soft groan. Again I called out, "What's the matter?" Again he didn't answer and just kept treading water and looking at me as he gave another soft gasp.

'I could see something red in the water. His bathers, I thought, they're red. But then I saw the red starting to spread through the water under him and suddenly I knew it was blood! I shall never forget the horror of that moment!'

Yelling to the other boy that there had been a shark attack, Brown plunged in and dragged the boy from the water. He found that Ken's right leg had been bitten off above the knee. 'The shattered bone was protruding through the remaining flesh... The water was red with blood. Blood was streaming through the wet sand, and it seemed to be everywhere.'

Brown's police training was an advantage. He managed to wrap a towel around the wound and stem the bleeding. Another boat came to help, and someone got to the boatshed to ring for an ambulance.

Brown recalled: 'While the other man rowed I held the towel tightly over Ken's wound and managed to control the bleeding. I fought to control myself and kept telling Ken that he would be OK. "Does it hurt very much, Ken?" I asked. He replied that it did and closed his eyes. I couldn't stop the tears. I tried to hide my face because I didn't want to upset Ken; but each time I turned he was quietly looking into my eyes, never complaining.

'I have never felt so helpless. So filled with despair...'

Ken Murray died, after lingering on for a week in hospital, from complications arising from his severe injury.

Brown recalled: 'There followed weeks of unimaginable despair, flooded with periods of such utter loneliness that my very existence seemed threatened. I couldn't forgive myself for what had happened. Why hadn't I thought of sharks? Why Ken and not me? Always the plaguing doubts and questions...'

Theo Brown's trauma was typical of many survivors of a shark attack in which someone else died. It was similar to Lee Warner's reaction in the case of Robert Bartle.

The incident changed Brown's life, as he recalled in 1973 in his book *Sharks — the Search for a Repellent*. Ken Murray's sad death lead to Theo Brown's subsequent obsession with finding an answer to shark attack. It was a search which took him to Rangiora Atoll in the Pacific to set up a research station to test his theories on the responses of sharks to sonic signals. Theo Brown died in the 1980s without achieving his objective, driven always by the recollection of that dreadful day in January 1960.

Three years after Ken Murray's tragedy a pretty Sydney actress Marcia Hathaway, her fiance Frederick Knight and four friends went by boat to Sugarloaf Bay, a little north of Balmoral Beach in Middle Harbour, for a picnic.

It was the Australia Day holiday, 28 January 1963. A hot humid day on which the *Sydney Morning Herald* had run the headline 'AUSTRALIA DAY SURFERS WARNED OF SHARKS'. Two of the Hathaway party went off to the rocks to pick oysters. Others lay on the beach. Marcia and Frederick Knight went swimming in water so shallow — about 75 centimetres, not more than knee deep — that they assumed it must be safe.

Suddenly the peace of the afternoon was shattered by Marcia's screams. 'I've been bitten by an octopus!' she cried.

Knight was close by her when the shark — not an octopus — bit the actress first below the calf on her right leg, then inflicted a second larger bite on her thigh. Others from the picnic party rushed to help as Knight tried desperately to drag Marcia from the shark's grasp, but already the water was stained red with the actress's arterial blood.

There was no road to Sugarloaf Bay so Marcia, losing more blood with every minute that passed, was taken by cruiser to the nearest boatshed. Frederick Knight, ignoring the risk that the shark might also attack him, dived into the water and swam to the nearest house to telephone for help. Aid came quickly — an ambulance was waiting at the jetty when Marcia's boat drew up.

But luck deserted her there. The first ambulance burnt out a clutch climbing the slippery hill, while volunteers exhausted themselves trying to push it over the rise. A second ambulance was called. But by the time it arrived it was too late. Though help came less than half an hour after the attack, Marcia Hathaway had died from shock and massive blood loss by the time she reached the hospital.

It was the second bite which caused the damage, severing the femoral artery and almost tearing the 32-year-old actress's leg off.

Hers was the fifth fatal shark attack in Sydney Harbour and its offshoots in the 21 years since 1942, and there had been 19 non-fatal attacks in the inland waters around Sydney. Eleven of these attacks were in Sydney Harbour and Parramatta River, five in Georges River, two in Botany Bay and one at Port Mackay.

Twenty years after Marcia Hathaway's death, and a long way from Sydney's harbour and surf beaches, a prawn trawler was in trouble in Great Barrier Reef waters north of Townsville.

The 14 metre *New Venture* capsized and sank near Lodestone Reef. The accident happened so quickly that the *New Venture* took her dinghy and all her safety gear to the bottom with her. The crew — skipper Ray Boundy, deckhand Dennis Murphy, aged 24, and the 21-year-old cook Linda Norton — were thrown into the water. But they managed to salvage a surfboard, a lifebuoy and some pieces of foam from the wreckage.

At about 1 p.m. on Monday 25 July 1983 they began to swim with the help of this flotation gear towards Lodestone Reef, where there were some sand cays and where they were confident that they would be found.

Darkness fell. Fortunately the tropical water was warm and they were encouraged by the progress they were making. Suddenly Boundy called out, 'There's a shark!'

The fin of the shark and the phosphorescence of its passage through the water showed all too clearly. At first it was tentative, surfacing from time to time and bunting alternatively at the foam pieces, the lifebuoy and the surfboard. By now they were only 8 kilometres from the reef and kept on swimming, ignoring the shark in the hope that it would 'just go away'.

Suddenly the shark broke off from one of its regular passes and seized Ray Boundy's leg. 'I gave him an almighty kick,' Boundy recalled. 'He got such a fright we thought we'd got rid of him altogether.'

No such luck.

Soon after, the shark returned more determined than before. It seized Dennis Murphy's leg and dragged him struggling down into the depths. Murphy surfaced gasping, 'He's got my leg!'

He told Boundy and Lindy Norton that his leg was off and he had no hope. 'Go on without me!' he called. 'Save yourselves!'

'We hated to leave him,' Ray Boundy said. 'We paddled off, like he said, and heard a lot of screaming and kicking and punching. 'Then we saw the shark take his body right out of the water upside down and eat it!'

103

Later in the night, closer to the reef, they were dismayed to see the fin of the shark again. Linda Norton, terrified, was sitting in the ring of the lifebuoy with her feet on a piece of foam. The shark, bolder now, grabbed Linda across the chest, shook her from the lifebuoy, and dived below the surface. Boundy never saw her again.

Ray Boundy, alone now, swam on desperately for the reef, sighting it soon after daylight. He also saw the unwelcome sight of the shark's fin behind him, zigzagging in his wake. The last few strokes were desperate indeed. But at last he reached the sawtooth coral edge of the outer reef and dragged himself over its rough surface to safety. Later that morning he was rescued by a searching helicopter. A man with a terrible tale to tell.

The separate instances — the attack on Robert Bartle at Jurien Bay in Western Australia; the Middle Harbour attacks in Sydney on Ken Murray and Marcia Hathaway; the stalking of the defenceless trawler crew near the Great Barrier Reef — were each characteristic of situations involving a particular member of the man-eater species.

Each shark has its own method of approaching prey or protecting territory. As police detectives say, when investigating a murder, they look for the MO of the perpetrator. The *modus operandi*, the method of operation which may carry the signature of a known prior killer.

Carcharodon carcharias, the Great White shark; *Galeocerdo cuvieri*, the tiger shark; *Carcharhinus leucas*, the bull shark. All are proven killers.

The tragedies quoted are typical of the three species.

Robert Bartle was killed by a Great White which hurtled from beyond visibility at express speed. It hit the diver so hard that his face mask was dislodged. Then it shook him like a dog with a rat, and bit him in half.

It was an attack exactly similar to others by Great Whites: on Shirley Durdin near Port Lincoln, in 1983; on Therese Cartwright in Bass Strait, in 1993; and on John Ford at Byron Bay, also in 1993.

All were divers. All were wearing fins which may have made them look rather similar to sea-lions or other seals. The sound of their breathing and heartbeat may also have been indicative of mammals. Mammals, of course, are the preferred prey of large Great Whites.

Divers seldom see the Great White before it strikes them. 'It came out of the blue like a thunderbolt...' is the common recollection of those who survived. The Great White does not circle and show itself before attacking, as other shark species do. There is good reason. The prospective prey comes in the shape of seals which are swifter and more agile than the shark. And *Pinnipeds* can scamper up the rocks and find sanctuary ashore. If the shark showed itself to seals before attacking they would simply laugh at him. His one chance is surprise, an ambush.

A seal has to go to the surface to breath and at that moment is at its most vulnerable. The White shark makes its charge from below and beyond the circle of vision, always hoping to catch its intended victim unawares, and to cripple it with a massive first strike.

Many human victims of Great Whites are taken on the surface or while ascending in this way.

Now let's turn to the tiger shark.

The tiger is a very different creature from the Great White. But while it is generally less physically impressive, a tiger can grow to 5 metres and can be very dangerous in circumstances that favour it.

On the Great Barrier Reef, in 1994, filming tiger sharks with Australian filmmaker Ben Cropp, I had some excellent opportunities to study the attack patterns of *Galeocerdo cuvieri*. Unlike the *Carcharhinidae*, the whaler sharks, which dash in when a fish is speared, a tiger comes to a food source slowly and cautiously.

But once it has made up its mind to press an attack it is pugnacious and determined and very difficult to deter. My longtime diving friend, fisherman Maurice Glazier, has observed tiger sharks feeding off dead humpback whales in the Abrolhos Islands. Once he stabbed a huge tiger through the brain with a shearblade knife lashed to the end of a pole.

'It made no difference,' he said. 'That shark kept tearing away, chomping at the whale until it rolled over dead. It still had a mouth full of whale meat when it went belly up. Nothing would stop the other tigers or turn them away from the whale. As long as they were alive they'd keep on at that humpback. If you killed one the others alongside took no notice either. They kept on feeding. But once they'd finished with the whale they'd go for the livers of the dead sharks.'

As in the case of Ray Boundy and his unfortunate crew, tigers will circle for a long time prior to making an attack. Tigers very often approach a bait in company, with two, three, even half a dozen sharks of their own species circling at different levels. It is my own belief that there was more than one shark involved in the *New Venture* incident. One shark would not need to feed again after consuming a human being. But if several sharks were involved in Dennis Murphy's unfortunate death then the pack would follow on. Or others would come on the scent to join them. The wretched swimmers would not be able to see the other sharks in the darkness and would assume that the fin and the bulk of the animal making a particular pass were always the same shark. In fact, the aggressive moves may have come from several individuals.

The favourite food of tiger sharks is turtle. In northwestern Australia and the Great Barrier Reef, green turtle abound. Turtles are swift swimmers when alarmed. But they spend a good deal of time sleeping on the bottom. In mating season they are so distracted by lovemaking that divers can swim right up to courting couples and slap them on the shell. Females regaining the water after egg-laying, if caught by the sun, are sometimes weak and exhausted. Easy prey, it would seem.

I have often wondered why turtles, with those kinds of vulnerabilities, have not been exterminated by their arch enemy, the tiger shark. Yet the healthy do survive. It seems that it is the young, the old, the sick, the weak that fall victim to *Galeocerdo's* scythe teeth. Even if a healthy animal is exposed to risk it seems to be ignored. But if it should sustain any form of injury then woe betide it.

I once read a true story of an attendant at a private zoo in California. He had a particularly good relationship with the lions, and used to handle and fondle them like pet dogs. They were his friends, rubbing against him and showing all the signs of lion affection, and he was able to take all kinds of liberties with them. One day he had a motorcycle accident and when he limped into the pen the lions attacked him at once, mauling him so severely that he was fortunate to escape with his life. Even when he was fully recovered the lions would growl and roar and throw themselves against the wire if they saw him. He could no longer even approach the pen.

He lost his job — but he lived on. In the *natural world*, a limp, or its equivalent, can be a death sentence. Nature, it seems, provides for the culling of the unfit, the incapacitated, the aged or the unlucky.

There are a lot of tiger shark victims, of course, besides turtles. The tiger's turtlefest appears to take place during the summer breeding and hatching season. At other times tigers eat fish, stingrays, seabirds, even conch shells and crabs, and certainly anything dead or floating. Shark fishing in northwestern Australia, we often found the unexpected in the stomachs of captured tigers.

There were often dolphin remains. There were also sea snakes and several varieties of seabirds. From time to time we found cormorants and quite often shearwaters, or muttonbirds. Whether the sharks had intercepted these while the birds were diving or had snatched victims from among the rafts of birds resting on the sea is open to question. And tigers seasonally eat baby frigatebirds and gannets which fail on their first flights.

Tigers are the garbage gobblers of the sea and often have old bones, lobster bait baskets, aluminium cans and other assorted rubbish rattling around inside them. My shark-fishing friend Ted 'Sharkey' Nelson once found a woman's handbag in a tiger shark's stomach. The bag had evidently fallen from a passing ship. It contained a passport and valuables. He posted it to the address shown and a long time later received a letter of thanks.

Though tigers seem slow and cautious in their initial approach to prey, they can move fast at times. In the lagoon at Thevenard Island I once saw a disturbance from the beach that was as disturbing as it was unexpected.

A turtle came rushing into the lagoon in desperate flight from the open sea as though the Devil were after it. The sea boiled behind the fleeing reptile and I saw the fin and tail of a large tiger shark moving at express speed in pursuit. Entering the reef opening the turtle swerved at right angles and dived under the shelving reef to escape. The thwarted tiger lashed the water to foam with its tail for some minutes, its body coming half out of the water and stirring sand and coral. It was evidently trying to drag the turtle out from its place of refuge.

I never established the actual outcome of the chase. The tiger, about 3.6 metres in length, muddied the water so much that it was impossible to see from the beach, and the only way to satisfy my curiosity would have been to swim out and find out first hand. Common sense suggested it would be wiser to keep my feet on the shore. The tiger might have been a sore loser.

But what concerned me most at the time was the fact that, only a short time before, I had been hunting lobster on the reef where the turtle dived for cover.

Whaler sharks are a different kettle of fish from either Great Whites or tigers. They are smaller, and more explosive and erratic in their movements. Though some specimens can exceed 4 metres and 300 kilograms, most whalers you meet underwater are in the 2 metre range.

A shark expert would say: 'Which whaler are we talking about?'

There are so many species of *Carcharhinidae*, the far-flung whaler family, that they could almost fill a book on their own. Each of the species, from the oceanic blue to the grey reef shark or the bull shark of beaches and estuaries, has its own habitat and characteristics.

The dangerous whalers are *leucas*, the bull shark; *longimanus*, the oceanic whitetip; *albimarginatus*, the silvertip; and *amblyrhynchos*, the grey reef shark. The lemon, dusky and silky can cause problems too.

While many whalers do not grow beyond 2 metres, all *Carcharhinidae* family members have sharp teeth capable of causing serious injury. Even a mere metre-long *Carcharhinus* shark can bite a human arm or leg to the bone. It may well be that, though the bull shark (*leucas*) lacks the size and bulk of Great Whites and tigers, it is the world's most dangerous shark. We have already noted its depradations in the Ganges, India's holy river, and in other Indian estuaries.

Whalers are the most numerous sharks, often found in shallow waters, bays, estuaries and far up rivers. They frequent the kind of places where they are likely to encounter humans.

Bull sharks make some extraordinary journeys including the 3700 kilometres (2300 miles) from the sea to the upper Amazon, and the thousands of kilometres from the Atlantic to fresh water in Lake Nicaragua, where numbers of fatal attacks on humans have occurred.

It was originally thought that the Lake Nicaragua shark was a separate species which had adapted to fresh water. But the tagging of bull sharks in the Atlantic provided the answer. It was proved that *leucas* ascended shallows and rapids to reach the lake and also made the return journey back to the sea.

The deaths of Ken Murray and Marcia Hathaway in Sydney's Middle Harbour were almost certainly caused by bull sharks. In Western Australia there have been more attacks in the confines of the Swan River than in the open ocean. The wounds, characteristically, have been similar calf and thigh injuries. *Carcharhinus leucas* again. One victim who survived had 400 stitches in a thigh wound. A 13-year-old boy died.

The curious thing is that, while the Great White and the tiger shark attack their victims with the apparent intention of eating them, this does not seem to be necessarily the case with *Carcharhinus leucas*.

Why would a shark attack unless it were hungry?

Why indeed. But it is a fact that the people struck by sharks in rivers, estuaries, and confined waters such as Sydney Harbour are usually bitten and let go free. There does not seem to have been an attempt by such sharks to feed, though one poor woman, Zita Steadman, may have been an exception. The tragedy is that the whalers have such a powerful and effective bite and that humans are so vulnerable in the thigh region that the femoral artery is often severed. The victim bleeds to death.

Scientists have surmised that the attacks may be territorial gestures. Whalers will ascend to almost fresh water, out of range of other sharks, to have their young. An attack may be a matter of maternal protection, the shark seeing human swimmers as a potential threat and treating them accordingly.

Or it may be purely territorial: 'This is my space!'

It is interesting that pregnant sharks have a hormonal influence that removes the urge to feed. Nature's way of protecting the newborn young from parental cannibalism. This may be the reason why some victims are not eaten and why attempts to catch sharks involved in river and harbour attacks with baited lines are so often unsuccessful.

Grey reef whaler sharks in Pacific atolls and on the Great Barrier Reef are very territorial and often act aggressively towards divers. In certain circumstances they will readily attack. But they do telegraph a warning beforehand, humping their backs and dropping their pectoral fins and swimming erratically. If you see that kind of pattern, with a shark of any kind, move elsewhere. Fast.

Whether *leucas* gives a similar warning is a matter for speculation. Estuarine and inshore waters are usually so muddy or turbid that there is no visibility, as recalled by Theo Brown. Most whaler victims never see the shark at all.

None of this should be taken as suggesting that whaler sharks do not eat human flesh. Like all sharks they are opportunistic feeders. In open sea disasters like those of the 1852 *Birkenhead* and 1945 *Indianapolis*, whalers were undoubtedly eager participants in the feast.

There is also the error factor to consider. In shallow dirty water the splashing of humans at play, the white flesh of calves and the soles of feet may look like fish. Limbs may be bitten through mistaken identification.

But we need to know more about the shallow water attacks involving *leucas* before we come to hard and fast conclusions. Are there overlapping areas between the territories of the various sharks?

Certainly. Great Whites, tigers and whalers have all been involved in attacks at surf beaches. Sometimes it is hard to decide which shark may have been responsible. Where Great Whites are involved, their typical charge and great weight often lift the victim clear out of the water. The attacker is frequently seen from the beach or by other swimmers nearby. Injuries are typically to the upper leg, waist and chest. The fatality rate is high.

Whalers may not be seen at all. The victim screams or shouts and is found to have calf or thigh injuries when dragged from the water. Shock and loss of blood are the most frequent causes of death. The survival ratio is higher than with Great Whites.

Tiger attacks are rarer in southern Australian waters, though there may be many more in the tropics than are recorded. While tiger sharks are slow to attack, when they do make up their minds they are very determined and persistent. As with Simeon Ettelson at Cottesloe, in Western Australia, in 1925.

Though they are the common large shark of the tropics, seemingly more at home in warm water, it is not unusual to find tigers in the temperate zones of New South Wales and southern Western Australia.

Sharkey Nelson sometimes had his own private war with big tigers. 'Line robbers,' he called them, 'thieving striped bastards!' And other unprintable names. A large tiger would live off his long lines set near Rottnest Island, for days, biting smaller sharks off at the gills and mutilating other 'fish' it did not eat. The only solution was to catch the culprit with special baits and larger hooks. The big striped body would be discarded to be eaten in its own turn because the flesh was too rank and ammoniac for human consumption. Whereas other sharks usually drowned on the line, the tigers were alive and came up fighting, hate in their black eyes.

There were often tiger teeth embedded in the wooden hull of Sharkey's boat, *Shaleen*.

Whalers have been the sharks most frequently encountered by spearfishermen, especially in the 1950s and 1960s, when hunting was the major reason for diving and when there were far more sharks about than there are today. Most spearfishermen of that era have their own shark stories. These range from fending off sharks with spearguns to being physically bumped by aggressive whalers. I have been bumped hard on at least three occasions by whalers.

Physical contact with a large shark usually means a serious situation. But such confrontations used to be so common among spearfishermen that they usually laughed them off. In later years we went actively hunting whalers with 'smokies', explosive-headed spears.

Nonetheless, an encounter with a mean whaler without that kind of weapon can be unnerving. I remember a typical encounter from 1963 — a year that stuck in my mind for other reasons. It was the year we found the wreck of the 1629 Dutch East India Company treasure ship *Batavia* in the Abrolhos Islands, off the Western Australian coast.

We saw no sharks at the wrecksite — there was too much diver activity there in raising bronze cannon, silver coin and other relics. But there were plenty of sharks in the other deeps and shallows of the Abrolhos. I wrote about one incident in my 1966 book on the wreck, *Islands of Angry Ghosts*.

Max Cramer and I had gone to our jewfish hole at the end of Seals Island with spearguns to catch our dinner. There the water sloped away over an underwater cliff from green shallows to a 70 foot [21 metre] ledge and away from that again into who-knows-what depth of murky black water.

110

It was close to sunset. I made a dive to 60 feet [18 metres] and, peering about in disturbingly dark water, saw no tell-tale silvery jewfish tails waving in the current. Max gave up and swam back to the boat. 'Better pack it in,' he said. 'Too late in the day to be diving in this kind of water.' I dived again, poised over a volcano-like knell at the edge of the 70 foot [21 metre] ledge — dark, evil water misty below me — when the shark appeared on the edge of my vision, coming up out of the deep and moving fast.

I swung to meet him, following the routine which had proved itself dozens of times before. Stick your speargun out in front; make yourself look as big as possible; growl to convince yourself, if you like; then swim right at your shark as though you mean to eat him!

He will depart, convinced you are a crazy or dangerous animal. This shark was one of the exceptions.

He stood my bluff with yellow, watchful eyes, and as I closed simply turned his head up towards me in a horrible inquiring manner. He was about 8 or 9 feet [2.4 or 2.7 metres] long, thick as a barrel with long gill slits. A whaler shark, genus Carcharhinus, with the words 'Dangerous to Man' written against his name in the text books. He was about to prove it.

Out of breath, I rose to the surface, still watching him closely. Suddenly, without warning or any of the usual preliminary circling, he attacked.

A tremendous lunge of his squat body had him inside my guard and smashing up under my fins from behind before I could bring my speargun around to fire. I heaved and squirmed trying to find room for my 5 foot [1.5 metre] spear between me and him. Kicked my fins in desperation to prevent him getting to my thigh and taking that fatal artery-slashing bite into the hamstring muscles at the back of the leg.

Somehow I got the gun around and sent the spear thudding into his side through his left pectoral fin and out again. There was no chance to reload.

He swirled me aside in an explosion of muscled power and I tensed for a continuation of the attack. Instead he sounded down into the deep water, shaking his head like a groggy boxer and trailing blood. I had hurt him more than I thought. I retrieved my badly bent spear and retreated to the boat.

'Cheeky bastard!' I said, sitting on the gunwale. But my hands were shaking when I took my mask and fins off.

I often wondered in later years how I would have fared if I had had no speargun.

The *Batavia* survivors, in 1629, reached the safety of the island only to suffer mutiny and massacre. We found the skeletons of some of the victims with sword-chopped skulls, buried in shallow graves. Most of the others had had their throats cut and were thrown in the sea. Some swam off, risking drowning and the threat of shark attack in their desperation to escape the murderers.

What triggers a shark attack? Scientists can only shrug their shoulders. They may speculate, but there are no definite answers.

Helicopter patrols sometimes see large sharks swimming past surf beaches, showing their interest in the swimmers. The bathers themselves continue to splash around, blissfully unaware of the shark's proximity.

The tiger shark is one species definitely known to kill and eat humans on occasion. But there are some amazing stories of humans swimming in complete harmony with tiger sharks in the wild.

Valerie Taylor has always had an unusual rapport with sea creatures of all species and particularly with sharks.

While Ron Taylor was filming at Marion Reef, off North Queensland in the Coral Sea, for one of the Taylors' television specials on sharks, a female tiger joined the usual school of whaler sharks.

'She seemed interested in us without being threatening,' Valerie recalls. 'So I tried handfeeding her with pieces of fish. She accepted the fish from my hand and, for the rest of the time we were there, came so close that on occasions she actually bumped me. It was pure magic for the film and at no time did I feel threatened — she seemed to enjoy our company.'

The Taylors had a similar experience while filming for *The Island of Dr Moreau*. A tiger shark, held captive in a Pacific atoll lagoon by a net across the entrance, proved to be a gentle creature, easy to work with and co-operative in filming.

'We had to be careful because if we pushed him too hard he stressed out,' Valerie remembers. 'He was a very gentle animal.'

But perhaps the most remarkable story comes from Port Douglas in Queensland where Shane Down has a school of tame tiger sharks in Barrier Reef waters which he feeds by hand from his boat.

The Taylors recently filmed the phenomenon for television. 'He swims in the water with them, totally without fear,' said Valerie.

'He has names for them all. "Sandy" is his particular pet and he can actually wrap his arms around her. The sharks definitely know him, and he seems to be able to do what he likes with them. He calls Sandy "sweetheart".'

This does not mean, of course, that anyone sighting a tiger shark should jump into the water and give it a cuddle.

With confidence and an absence of fear some liberties may be taken, but sharks vary in temperament, even in the same family group. Experienced divers like Valerie Taylor and Shane Down read the sharks' body language and can determine what is safe and what is not. It took Shane Down many hours of patient handfeeding to gain the confidence of his sharks and establish his rapport with them.

And even with divers as experienced as the Taylors, accidents can sometimes happen.

Valerie was attacked in determined fashion by a female whaler at Marion Reef. 'John and I almost cashed in our chips today!' she wrote in her diary. She also received a deep bite on her left leg and calf from a blue shark, a species not normally considered dangerous, while filming off California for the US television show 'Animals, Animals'. The wound was serious enough to mean calling a Coastguard helicopter to take her the 90 kilometres to shore, and she was in hospital for sometime afterwards. Microsurgery was necessary to suture the deep lacerations.

There is also the point that apparent docility of large and dangerous animals — both in the sea and ashore — can be deceptive. One of the problems for African wildlife parks' managements is to convince their tourists that no matter how sleepy, bored or unconcerned the lions look they are still potentially dangerous creatures. When tourist buses or hire cars pull up near a pride of lions the creatures flick their tails, yawn to show lion tonsils in cavernous mouths, and seem utterly uninterested in the visitors' presence.

Every so often a tourist breaks all the rules and goes to pose grinning beside the lions to be photographed or immortalised on home video. Most times they get away with it. But once in a while a lion gets up, stretches languorously and then bites the tourist's head off.

There are similar problems in northeastern US and Canadian national parks with grizzly bears. The grizzlies look like cute teddy bears on a gigantic scale. But if they cuddle a tourist the smile suddenly vanishes. The hug can be for keeps. Bears kill three people a year in North America.

Similarly, there can be two sides to the tiger shark. One of Australia's more notorious attacks took place in Queensland at Kirra Beach, Coolangatta, on 27 October 1937. It was unusual because it was one of the very few on record where more than one shark was involved, and where a rescuer died as well as the original victim.

One of the most inspirational aspects of the records of Australian shark attacks is the fact that in almost all cases there have been people who have gone into the water, regardless of their own risk, to bring the victim ashore. In some cases they have driven off the shark with their bare hands. Generally the rescuers have had charmed lives. Even though a shark has continued to bite and tear at the unfortunate victim it first selected, the rescuer has in most instances remained unscathed.

Coolangatta was an exception. It was late afternoon, a time of day when shark attacks often occur. A group of swimmers were catching waves on a sandbank 200 metres offshore at Kirra Beach. Three of them, Norman Girvan, Jack Brinkley and Gordon 'Don' Doniger, decided to head for shore. Doniger caught a wave which left him with Girvan in a channel halfway to the beach. They were actually joking about sharks when Girvan cried out.

'Quick, Don!' he called. 'A shark's got me!'

Doniger thought he was joking. But when Girvan raised his arm there was blood everywhere.

'It won't let me go!' There was alarm in Girvan's voice now. 'It's got me by the leg!'

Doniger swam across and when he reached Girvan felt him being shaken forcibly. Then Girvan was dragged out of his arms and the shark surfaced, still gripping the unfortunate swimmer.

'It was a big shark,' Doniger later recalled.

'I'm gone! Goodbye!' Girvan cried. The shark dragged him under and neither shark nor victim were seen again.

Jack Brinkley, meanwhile, had been swimming across in response to Doniger's calls. As he started to swim towards Gordon Doniger another shark intercepted Brinkley.

Joseph Doniger, on the beach, had seen the whole tragedy, including the shark that seized Brinkley. Without hesitating, he plunged into the surf and swam towards Brinkley.

'I know there were two sharks,' he said in a statement to police later, 'because the first shark was bigger than the one which attacked Jack Brinkley.'

Joseph Doniger took Brinkley by the shoulders and began the swim back to the beach. The shark attacked again, this time grabbing Brinkley by the left arm below the shoulder. Carried ashore, Brinkley was found to have severe lacerations to his left side and his arm was almost completely severed. In Coolangatta Hospital the arm was amputated and he was given a blood transfusion, but died soon after admission.

Portions of Norman Girvan's body eventually washed ashore. On the day after the attack a large female tiger shark was hooked by fishermen. It was 11 feet 9 inches (3.6 metres) long, 6 feet (1.8 metres) in girth and weighed 850 pounds (386 kilograms). A big mother.

When its stomach was opened parts of Girvan's arms and legs were found. The right hand was identified from an old scar.

The fishermen said that two other sharks were also seen but would not take the baits.

An example of a tiger shark pack attack, with similarities to the *New Venture* tragedy, occurred off Yeppoon on the Queensland coast in November 1988. Though newspapers described the sharks involved as '6 metre bronze whalers' no *Carcharhinidae* has ever reached that size. Whalers do not exceed 3 to 4 metres. It is most likely that the sharks involved were tiger sharks, because of their reported size and grim persistence.

Cedric Coucom, aged 62 years, and his sons James, 33, and Bruce, 17, were at sea on a fishing trip on Sunday 6 November 1988. They ran into bad weather, and by late afternoon were in trouble as their boat *Christie V* began taking in water in giant seas off North Keppel Island.

Cedric Coucom managed to get a Mayday radio call away at 5 p.m., shortly before *Christie V* sank. They donned lifejackets and scrambled into a 4 metre dinghy without food, oars or water. Because the radio call for help had been received and understood they were optimistic about a quick rescue. But the strong winds and rough seas were causing them problems.

'We kept getting swamped and thrown about by the huge seas,' James said.

As the dinghy drifted north they took turns, with one person resting in the waterfilled dinghy, the others holding on to it. At nightfall on the Monday, 24 hours after the sinking, Cedric suddenly cried out: 'Shark! It's got me!'

His sons dragged him into the dinghy but he was shockingly mauled and died within a few seconds. They had no option but to abandon his body to the sharks astern.

The dinghy drifted on into Tuesday, James comforting his brother and telling him not to give up hope. 'The salt water blinded us and we were exhausted by the sun,' he recalled.

Early on Tuesday morning Bruce let go his grasp on the dinghy. As he drifted away the sharks attacked again and though James tried desperately to save him he was too late. 'Tell my family and friends I love them,' were Bruce's last words.

'It was just horrible,' James told reporters later. 'The sharks kept on following the dinghy, nudging it and trying to tip me out. They didn't stop. They just kept on coming and coming.'

When the Mayday call was received on the Sunday, the Coastguard alerted Canberra Air Sea Rescue. But for some reason the aircraft sent out searched the wrong area. A 40 metre ferry was diverted from a voyage to North Keppel Island, but to no avail. Army Iroquois helicopters also failed to find the dinghy in the rough conditions, because it had drifted north of the official search area.

Meanwhile, James drifted on alone in the dinghy without food or water, the craft still battered by the persistent sharks.

At last, at 4.20 p.m. on Tuesday, with less than three hours of daylight remaining, he was sighted by a National Safety Council helicopter. The pilot, Bob Hobson, said: 'Two sharks each twice the size of the dinghy were pounding it and trying to knock James out.

'It's a real miracle that he lived through it.'

James Coucom had drifted 150 kilometres when he was found and winched to safety. His rescuers said he was hallucinating when they found him. Suffering from dehydration, sunburn and exhaustion, he spent several days recovering in Rockhampton Hospital.

A funeral service was held in Yeppoon on 12 November for Cedric and Bruce Coucom. James was able to attend, but newspaper reporters at the service said: 'He looked exhausted, his face badly sunburned, lips blistered.' They also reported that — not surprisingly — he broke down and cried during the service. It was too much to bear.

The body may be resilient and heal quickly. But the mind carries some memories for a lifetime. Wounds of the soul are hard to heal.

Aside from the personal tragedy, the erroneous reporting of the identity of the sharks involved in the *Christie V* drama showed that there were still gaps in our knowledge of sharks in Australian seas.

One man who spent a lifetime trying to correct this situation was Dr Victor Coppleson, an Australian medico who was the father of world scientific research into shark attack. He painstakingly gathered data on shark attacks in Australian waters from the 1920s onwards and published his findings in a book titled *Shark Attack* in 1958. This book, which gained world renown, was subsequently revised by Peter Goadby and reprinted in 1962, 1968, and 1976 under the new title *Killer Sharks*.

Dr Coppleson analysed each shark incident in terms of the time of year, the location and the water temperature, and produced some interesting findings:

> ➤ In Sydney waters, 18 of 19 attacks which he listed for the harbour and inland waters between 1916 and 1965 occurred during just six weeks of the year — between

25 December (Christmas Day) and 7 February. The exception occurred on 8 December.

➤ Ocean attacks also had a timetable, occurring regularly between 7 January and 14 April. But not at other times of the year.

➤ Attacks rarely occurred when the water temperature was less than 70 degrees Fahrenheit (21 degrees Celsius).

➤ The majority of attacks took place over only 48 kilometres of coastline, which included Sydney and Newcastle.

➤ Attacks frequently occurred in cycles, leading Coppleson to believe that a 'rogue' shark might be responsible for a series of attacks.

Dr Coppleson expressed himself as being puzzled by some of the data. Many people swam in Sydney's inland waters in October, November, December, and in April. Thousands thronged the beaches in those months. Why was there only one attack before Christmas Day, against 18 in the next six weeks?

How did water temperature affect sharks? And why was it that 90 per cent of New South Wales shark attacks occurred over only 48 kilometres of coast?

It was true that this area included Sydney and Newcastle, the two major population centres. 'This indicates that shark attacks are directly related to concentrations of population,' wrote Coppleson. 'But though it would seem an obvious rule it is a rule with many exceptions. Here the third great concentration of population is in the Wollongong area south of Sydney. It includes some of the most popular tourist resorts of Australia. Numbers swimming here are as great as at Newcastle, but attacks in this area are almost unknown.'

He pointed out that there was no lack of sharks south of Sydney. It was a favourite area for gamefishermen and there were many records of shark attacks on boats. But not on people.

The other intriguing question was why an area would be free of shark attacks for many years, then suffer a series of attacks in succession. For example, Coogee had never experienced a shark attack until it suffered four in three years between 1922 and 1925. Two were fatal. Nidre Derritt, a 30-year-old woman, had both legs amputated but survived. Jack Dagworthy, aged 16, lost a leg.

At Bondi Beach and nearby Maroubra in 1928–1929 there were three attacks within five weeks and another a short time later. Three attacks were fatal, the fourth victim was seriously injured.

117

Prior to 1934 there had been no attacks north of Sydney heads. But between January 1934 and February 1936 there were five attacks, four of them fatal, between Manly Beach and South Steyne.

A similar pattern was evident in Sydney Harbour and the inland waters. There were three attacks in the Georges River, running into Botany Bay, in 1934.

Coppleson felt, from studying his data, that he was almost able to predict an attack. 'There was some evidence,' he wrote, 'that the attacks were preceded by the appearance of a shark in the area — usually a large one — which heralded its arrival by acting savagely, snapping fish from lines, tearing nets and attacking dogs.

'With these thoughts in mind I read with special interest a report in the *Sydney Morning Herald*, early in January 1940, that dogs were being attacked in Georges River near Botany Bay.

'Because of my convictions I considered writing to the paper a warning that there was a great danger to bathers in the area. However I delayed. At 10.40 a.m. on 23rd January, a 13-year-old boy, Maxwell Farrin, was attacked...'

Farrin suffered terrible injuries and died immediately he was brought ashore. Coppleson then wrote his letter to the newspaper warning that another attack was likely. Eleven days later another swimmer was killed only 400 metres from the spot where Farrin was taken.

Middle Harbour too was to gain a grim reputation, and again many of the attacks came in series. One of the most chilling episodes occurred on 4 January 1942. A motor launch party were picnicking at Egg Rock, near Bantry Bay. It was a particularly hot day. In mid-afternoon Zita Steadman, aged 28, and a companion named Burns went into the water to cool off. They were only a short distance from the beach in waist-deep water. 'Don't go too far out,' Burns warned, 'there are sharks in the harbour.'

Onlookers said that Miss Steadman turned to go closer to shore, then suddenly screamed as a shark surged towards her.

'Burns grabbed an oar from the boat,' Coppleson recorded, 'and began smashing at the shark. It was attacking repeatedly and with such ferocity that it was throwing itself in the air. The flaying oar made not the slightest impression on it. Gradually it drew Zita Steadman into deeper water.

'In desperation Burns leapt into a rowing boat and tried to ram the enraged shark. This failed too, so as he came close he grasped the woman's long black hair as it trailed in the water and freed the body from the shark's grip. The shark was clearly seen. It must have been very large as it had bitten her completely in two.'

In the same area, in the following December, a 15-year-old girl died. There was a gap of 13 years, then another series of attacks, with at least four fatalities between 1955 and actress Marcia Hathaway's tragic death in 1965.

From that time on, until 1996, a period of more than 30 years, there were no further attacks in Sydney Harbour. This was undoubtedly due to a major influence on shark patterns in Sydney waters. The year 1937 saw the introduction of shark net meshing of popular beaches. Meshing not only completely eliminated attacks at the beaches where the nets were set over a longer period; it also saw a dramatic reduction in shark attacks in the general area and in inland waters.

There is an exception to every rule. Though it was not known at the time, *Carcharodon carcharias*, the Great White shark, is warm-blooded and not affected by water temperature like the whalers and tiger sharks. The rapid growth in popularity of SCUBA diving and spearfishing in the years following the publication of Dr Coppleson's book in 1958 saw new attacks in cold water areas, some in cooler months of the year. Great Whites were responsible.

Dr Coppleson received a knighthood for his work on sharks. Sir Victor would no doubt have been interested in the apparent serial nature of Great White attacks on spearfishermen Brian Rodger, Jeff Corner, Rodney Fox and photographer Henri Bource in southern eastern Australia in 1961, 1962, 1963 and 1964. And in the next series of shark deaths, in South Australian waters, with fatalities in 1971, 1974 and 1975, and again in 1985, 1987, 1989 and 1991. Great Whites were believed to have made most of these attacks. Was one shark responsible for more than one human death — following Victor Coppleson's 'rogue' shark theory? Or were there multiple sharks and was the seemingly serial nature of the killings purely coincidental?

Shark experts themselves have long disagreed on whether particular series of shark attacks are the work of one 'rogue' animal, or whether it is just coincidence that patterns of attack often appear to occur in cycles.

The most famous (or infamous) series of attacks recorded occurred in the United States in the summer of 1916. The perpetrator — if indeed it was a single shark — was christened 'The Mad Shark' by New York newspapers.

The key aspect of what is still a puzzling case is that prior to July 1916 there had never been a shark attack recorded in North Eastern America. In fact, in 1891 a New York businessman, Hermann Oelrichs, had offered $500 (a very large sum in those days) for 'proof of an attack by a shark on a living man north of Cape Hatteras'. In 25 years no one had claimed the reward. But that situation was to change dramatically.

The first of the 'Mad Shark' attacks came on 2 July 1916 at the popular resort of Beach Haven, about 100 kilometres south of New York. Charles Vansant, a 24-year-old fine arts graduate from Philadelphia University was swimming close to shore in shoulder-deep water. Taylor Sheridan, who was nearby, heard Vansant suddenly scream and saw him beat wildly at the water with his hands. Then the water around him turned red.

Taylor saw the shark clearly, its fin and back out of the water. He and others formed a human chain and dragged Vansant to shore, the shark still gripping his leg. The shark maintained its grip until they were in 18 inches (45 centimetres) of water, where it finally let go and swirled away. It was described as 'blue grey' in colour and about 10 feet (3 metres) long.

Vansant had suffered massive injuries to his upper left leg. A medical student applied a tourniquet to stop the flow of blood which was staining the beach bright crimson. But Vansant died hours after reaching the hospital.

Four days later, on 6 July, at Spring Lake, a resort 35 miles (56 kilometres) further north there was a second attack. Charles Bruder, a Swiss-born bellboy at a resort hotel, who was swimming a long way from shore raised his arms and called for help.

George White and Chris Anderson, the beach lifeguards, had been watching Bruder and commenting on his distance from shore. At that moment a woman ran up to say that the man in the red canoe was in trouble. The lifesavers launched a boat and rowed to his assistance. As they approached they saw that the 'red canoe' was Bruder's blood in the water.

When they reached him, Bruder cried out that he had been bitten by a shark, then fainted. As they dragged him over the gunwale of the boat the lifeguards felt faint too. The injuries were horrible to see. Bruder's right leg had been bitten off at the calf. His left foot and ankle were missing. The flesh had been stripped away so that the bones protruded two-thirds of the length below each knee. He also had a severe bite out of his abdomen.

Bruder died on the beach before a doctor could reach him. His death caused controversy because many people (especially those with an interest in resort business or property) were reluctant to believe that a shark could be responsible. They suggested that a turtle or 'giant mackerel' might have caused the wounds because of their ragged nature. The wounds were not, they insisted, 'the clean-edged bite of a shark'.

The two attacks caused panic in the resort areas, as much from the dread of loss of earning as fear of further attacks. Fishermen dragged legs of pork and bleeding quarters of lamb as bait to catch the shark. At Spring Lake, the mayor, Oliver H. Brown, instituted a motor boat patrol and had a bathing area enclosed by a shark-proof wire net. Dr A. T. Nichols, shark expert at the American Museum of Natural History, stated that there was 'very little chance of a shark ever attacking anyone'. it was an opinion he would have to revise. The Museum's director, Dr Frederick A. Lucas, added that there was more chance of being struck by lightning than being attacked by a shark. In any case, he added, 'A shark's jaws are not powerful enough to bite through the bone of a human leg'. The evidence, however, was incontrovertible. By 6 July the toll was two attacks and two men dead. Both had been killed in the ocean.

People accustomed to swimming in Matawan Creek some distance to the north saw no reason to be concerned. The town of Matawan and Wychoff dock — an old steamboat wharf — were 11 miles (18 kilometres) upstream from the ocean. No shark had ever been seen there and for generations boys had dived, jumped and splashed naked from the wharf in the old 'swimming hole' tradition.

The summer's day of 12 July was fearfully hot. It was almost tropical; people were sent home from work. A stream of boys headed down to the swimming hole. In the early afternoon, retired sea captain Thomas Cotterell was crossing a bridge over Matawan Creek about half a mile (800 metres) downstream from the swimming hole. To his astonishment he saw a black shape pass under the bridge, moving upstream with the incoming tide. For some moments he stood in disbelief; Matawan Creek had grassy, tree-lined banks and in most parts was barely 10 metres across. What could a shark be doing in the creek?, he asked himself. But he knew a shark when he saw one.

Captain Cotterell ran to the telephone and called the town barber, John Mulsonn, who also happened to be the elected town chief of police. 'Tell them there's a shark in the creek!' he told Mulsonn urgently, 'I saw it myself!'

'Yes, Tom, I'll tell them,' said Mulsonn. Then he hung up the receiver and did precisely nothing. 'A shark in Matawan Creek!… People sure tell a police chief some crazy things!' He shook his head.

But Cotterell himself was so convinced that he continued telling people in the town. Some laughed; others felt sorry for the retired mariner. It was, no doubt, they said, a case of early senility.

At the wharf, a boy named Lester Stilwell who was floating closer to mid-stream than the others, suddenly disappeared below the surface. He reappeared a moment later, screaming, then vanished again with a splash and a swirl. His friends splashed to shore, grabbed their clothes and ran into town shouting that Lester had 'drowned'.

Lester Stilwell was a strong swimmer but he was known to suffer fits. It was taken for granted that this was what had happened. Townsfolk, hearing the news, hurried down to the swimming hole. The crowd included Stilwell's parents and a man named Stanley Fisher. Fisher was 24, a fair-haired, 95 kilogram giant, built like a professional grid-iron footballer. He ran a dry-cleaning business in Matawan and was very popular in the town.

By now many people had heard of Captain's warning. 'A shark?' Fisher said in disbelief. 'I don't care if it is, I'm going after that boy!' He plunged into the creek in his bathing trunks. 'I'll find him!' he said. Others waded in the shallows; men in rowing boats felt with poles for Stilwell's body. There was no visibility in the creek, the mud stirred up by the swimmers cloyed the water.

Fisher made several dives in mid-stream. The watchers lining each bank saw him surface and wave, holding something with the other hand. 'I've got him!' he shouted. Fisher swam towards the bank opposite the wharf, towing the body. He was followed by two men in a motor boat, one of whom was Arthur Van Buskirk. As Fisher reached shallow water and stood up, within reaching distance of the shore, his expression changed. He uttered a sudden cry and threw up his arms.

'The shark! The shark!' people on both banks cried in horror. Fisher fell into a crouch and was dragged backwards below the surface. He surfaced again and swam weakly towards the bank where he dragged himself feebly up the slope and collapsed, lying insensible with shock and pain.

Women screamed, some fainted, and men cried out as they saw that his right leg had been stripped of flesh to the bone from his hip to below the knee. His blood stained the bank while Arthur Van Buskirk made a tourniquet from rope in an effort to stem the bright arterial flow. Dr G. L. Reynolds reached Fisher's side and managed to resuscitate him. Fisher gasped that he had been in less than waist-deep water and had never thought about sharks until the moment he felt his leg seized. Looking down he had clearly seen the shark with his leg in its jaws.

Fisher was carried across the river and rushed by train to a nearby hospital at Long Branch. But he died before he could be placed on the operating table.

Townsfolk ordered a supply of dynamite sticks and gathered together with shotguns, harpoons and a variety of improvised weapons to hunt the shark. As the hunt began, a new motor boat raced up to the steamer wharf with the story of yet another victim.

Twelve-year-old John Dunn had been swimming with his brother William and friends at the New Jersey Clay Brick Co. pier, 800 metres downstream from where Stilwell and Fisher were attacked. People had run to warn swimmers all down the creek. 'There's a shark! Get out of the water!' The boys swam hurriedly to the wharf ladder to scramble out. John Dunn was last to reach the ladder and, as he hauled himself out of the water, left leg trailing, the shark rose up and grabbed his leg. Its jaws closed above and below the knee.

Dunn was taken to a nearby factory where Dr H. J. Cooley of Keyport dressed his wounds. He was then rushed by car to St Peter's Hospital in New Brunswick. There his shockingly injured leg was amputated. But Dunn was fortunate — he was the only one of all the July attack victims to survive.

Lester Stilwell's body was found two days later, by the bank about 100 metres upstream from where the attack took place. He had seven serious wounds: four savage bites to his body, three to his legs. There followed what was perhaps the most extensive shark hunt on record anywhere in the world. Hundreds of hunters took to the creek in boats, dynamiting methodically. They ran wire netting and fishing nets across the creek. The air was filled with the sounds of the detonations of blasting and the reports of shotguns and rifles fired into corners of Matawan Creek where sharks 'might be hiding'. Some sharks *were* caught — surprising in a backwater creek, so far from the seashore. Their presence had never previously been suspected. But when their bellies were ripped open there was no evidence to connect them with the attacks.

The Matawan Creek tragedies and the hunt for the killer were given enormous media attention. During a time of some of the most intense fighting of the First World War, it drove the war from the front pages of New York newspapers. President Woodrow Wilson and his cabinet spent time on top-level discussion about the 'shark menace'.

Meanwhile, coastal resorts were crying out in pain over the damage to the tourist trade. The mayors of ten New Jersey coastal resorts issued a combined press statement protesting about newspaper coverage which had led 'the public to believe the New Jersey seacoast is infested with sharks whereas there are no more than any other summer'. Just more attacks?

The mayors also claimed that their towns had lost more than one million dollars in holiday cancellations, that they had been 'hurt without cause' by the publicity of July 1916. Whatever the pain felt in tourist locations, there was no denying that the attacks had taken place.

America's greatest shark saga finally ended on 14 July 1916 when an 8 foot 6 inch (2.6 metre) Great White shark, weighing 350 pounds (158 kilograms), was caught in Raritan Bay, 6 kilometres northeast of the mouth of Matawan Creek by Michael Schleisser, a Harlem taxidermist, and his friend, John Murphy. Schleisser told how the shark towed his boat backwards in a wild ride until he beat it to death with a broken oar. Inside the shark were 7 kilograms of flesh, including shin and rib-bones, later identified by Dr Frederick A. Lucas, Director of the American Museum of Natural History, as human remains. It is likely that they were those of Charles Bruder, taken at Spring Lake — the location, mode of attack and injuries are all consistent with a *Carcharodon* of the size and weight of the shark caught by Schleisser. A photograph of Schleisser with his shark in *Great White Shark* by Richard Ellis and John McCosker provides the final confirmation — it is without question a young adult specimen of *Carcharodon carcharias*.

The shark was taken to New York and exhibited at the office of *The Home News* newspaper at 125th Street. An article on the following Sunday claimed that 'the yawning jaws and vicious teeth were viewed by at least 30 000 men, women, and children'.

Schleisser's capture ended the series of attacks. The next North Eastern American attack was at Buzzard's Bay, Massachusetts, in 1936. Joseph Troy, aged 16, was savaged on the leg by a Great White. A companion swam him ashore, but he died in New Bedford hospital five hours after the attack. More than 60 years later, there has not been another shark attack in North Eastern America. However, 'The Mad Shark' still swims on, in argument and theory. Controversy remains about whether one shark was responsible for all the attacks or more than one was involved. The principal objection to Schleisser's shark being involved in all the attacks was that Great Whites are an oceanic shark and do not poke their noses into tidal creeks. Not usually, that is. Of course, Matawan Creek is tidal. It was midsummer and extremely hot. Captain Cottrell, who first saw the shark, said that it was moving upstream 'on the incoming tide'. If, for instance, there were an abattoir discharging blood into the creek upstream it is just possible that an oceanic shark — especially a sick or injured shark — might, against all normal probabilities, have been attracted by the scent. It may be significant that the shark did not appear to remain long in the upper reaches. It was already heading on its way back towards the ocean when it attacked the last victim, John Dunn. Or was that perpetrator, against all odds, a different shark?

Evidence from other areas suggests that the Matawan Creek attacks were much more characteristic of *Carcharhinus leucas*, the bull shark. The bull shark is a large and aggressive member of the whaler family, and has been responsible for many human fatalities worldwide. It journeys long distances from the ocean — 3000 kilometres up the Amazon River; 2700 kilometres up the Mississippi — and has killed people in localities as widely spaced as Sydney Harbour in Australia, the surf beaches of Durban in South Africa and

Lake Nicaragua in South America. The Matawan Creek attacks would fit the profile of a bull shark. But in that event it might be expected that, as in other parts of the world, there would have been other attacks in varying severity in the years before and after 1916.

The mystery may never be resolved. In today's world matching of bone samples and the DNA of stomach contents would have been simple and conclusive. In 1916 no such tests were available. Basically there are three possible explanations:

1. Schleisser's shark was 'The Mad Shark' and was responsible for all attacks.

2. Schleisser's shark attacked the two ocean victims. A bull shark went berserk in Matawan Creek.

3. A number of different sharks were involved.

If Schleisser's shark *was* responsible for all the attacks, one reason could be that the shark was ill or injured, causing it to act in an irrational and unusual 'Mad Shark' manner. There is another example on record of irrational behaviour by a sick or injured Great White in the smaller size range.

On 16 February 1966, 13-year-old Raymond Short was part of a holiday crowd enjoying the surf at Coledale Beach, north of Sydney in New South Wales. Members of the Coledale Surf Lifesaving Club noticed patches of sea-weed in the shallow water. Suddenly there was a cry from the surf: 'Help me! Please help!'

Short was only 30 metres from shore. The water around him was tinged with pink, and the 'seaweed' near him now took a new and sinister shape. 'Shark!' cried the lifesaver on tower watch, and the wail of the shark alarm siren sounded. Two Coledale lifesavers ran down the beach and dashed into the surf to help Short who was now screaming in panic.

'It's still got me!' he cried when they reached him. 'Get it off! Get it off!' One of the lifesavers, Raymond Joyce, reached down into the blood-tinged water, clouded with sand from the shore break, and to his astonishment found that he was touching the snout of a shark whose jaws were still gripping Raymond Short's leg.

Other lifesavers arrived; six of them dragged Short and the shark through the shallows and up onto the beach. The shark, a 2.4 metre female Great White weighing about 135 kilograms, refused to let go, even when dragged high and dry. The lifesavers banged surfboards repeatedly on the shark's head, but still it grimly maintained its grip on the boy's leg. Finally the shark

125

succumbed. The jaws were prised open and Short was freed. He was rushed to hospital where he was given massive blood transfusions. His condition remained critical for some days and at one stage it was feared that it would be necessary to amputate his right leg. However, thanks to modern drugs and blood transfusions, he recovered fully, although he carried deep scars on his legs and hands ever after. In 1916, without the benefit of modern treatments, he would almost certainly have been recorded as another fatality.

Some aspects of this case are similar to those of the 1916 attacks. The shark was the same size, species and weight as the one caught by Schleisser. Vansant's killer, too, hung on grimly into shallow water, right to the edge of the beach. But the all-important factor was that the shark that attacked Short had been seriously injured. It had been bitten across the abdomen by another larger Great White. It had numerous partly healed lacerations on its body. 'One wound,' said Dr Coppleson, the medical researcher who personally examined the shark, 'was so severe as to allow the passage of a man's finger straight into the shark's stomach.'

Short's rescuers, Coledale Lifesavers Raymond Robertson, Raymond and Brian Joyce, Clarence Taylor, Warren and Dallas Haberley and Lesley Kennedy, were awarded the Queen's Commendation for Brave Conduct at Government House, Sydney on 18 November 1966. The shark's jaws now hang in the Coledale Lifesaving Club, the characteristic *Carcharodon* teeth reminding us that shark behaviour may not always be what we expect. The question of whether one shark can become a serial killer still remains open for the reader to decide.

THE REAL RISK
OF SHARK ATTACK
chapter eight

WHAT ARE THE ACTUAL CHANCES OF BEING ATTACKED BY A SHARK? That's a question which is asked often enough. People like to know these things. The answer is that records show that, worldwide, there are about 100 shark attacks on humans each year, with fatal results in 20 to 30 per cent of cases.

The United States averages 12 shark attacks annually, with between a quarter and one-third of the victims dying. But the figure varies considerably year by year.

When it is considered that 13 000 people are killed by handguns each year in the United States (1000 of them in New York) and 1000 people die every ten days as a result of motor accidents in Europe, the shark attack figures may seem insignificant. In fact we are told that in the United States the chances of being struck by lightning far outweigh the possibility of shark attack. Between 500 and 600 people there are killed or injured by lightning bolts each year.

Rattlesnakes in Texas and Arizona bite more people than sharks in California and Florida do, and the chances of drowning in the United States are 1000 times greater than suffering a shark attack. And 17 Americans die each year from wasp and bee stings.

Up to February 1996 there were 517 recorded Australian shark attacks, with 185 deaths, since such incidents began to be recorded in 1901. There is an average of one to two attacks a year with 31 fatalities in 30 years recorded on the Australian Shark Attack File kept by the Taronga Zoo in Sydney.

In Australia in the ten years between 1980 and 1990, sharks killed 11 people against 19 killed by lightning, 20 by bee stings, and eight by crocodiles. SCUBA deaths numbered 88, while ordinary drowning accidents claimed 3367 victims. Motor vehicle accidents resulted in 32 772 deaths.

It is common for these kinds of figures to be quoted and compared with the two or three people involved in shark attacks each year. Proof, if you care to believe it, that the danger from sharks is insignificant.

But used in this way the figures can be quite misleading.

In Australia there are some areas and times of year when the shark danger is much greater than average figures indicate. During the green turtle breeding season at the Lacepede Islands in northwestern Australia or at Raine Island on the Great Barrier Reef, each November, the risk of a shark attack on a swimmer can be quite unacceptably high.

This is because tiger sharks circle the islands waiting for sick or injured turtles and hatchlings. They also gulp down baby frigatebirds and gannets who flop pathetically into the water after failing on their first flights. A swimmer splashing on the surface could be a welcome addition to the tiger's opportunistic menu. *Galeocerdo* doesn't mind a pleasant surprise. If swimming in the daytime is dangerous in these areas at those times, then entering the water at night is even more risky. Darkness is the tigers' preferred feeding time.

In cold southern waters there is a different kind of locale and predator but a risk beyond the ordinary, nonetheless, if you were to seek it out.

Carcharodon carcharias, the Great White shark, is most often found near seal or sea lion colonies. Great Whites often shadow pods of migrating whales, to be in hopeful attendance when whales give birth. People diving with sea lions or swimming with whales and calves may unwittingly lift their risk ratio.

The Farralon Islands off San Francisco see a gathering of Great White sharks each autumn with the arrival of semi-mature sea lions and sea elephants. Even in normal months the Farralons are notorious for Great White attacks on divers. When the sea elephants arrive, a surface-swimming diver could be taking a near-suicidal risk.

In contrast, there are many other areas of America and many parts of Australia where there has never been a recorded shark attack in the past 100 years. However, even when no shark has ever been seen in an area, circumstances may change dramatically on a particular day. For example, nothing attracts sharks — Whites, tigers and whalers too — like a dead whale. If a random whale corpse washes ashore even a previously 'safe' spot may carry enhanced risks until the cadaver is consumed, blown up or otherwise disposed of.

Where sharks are concerned, it is unwise to trust some of the more reassuring figures so freely quoted. The location, its proximity to deep water, the seasonal movement of fish or seals, local berleying or baiting by fishermen,

128

the dumping of rubbish or offal — these are the important factors to consider. The past is an indication only, not a sure guide to the present or future.

This is not to disparage figures. Numbers, those ten little symbols so versatile and efficient in general use, are essential tools in the operation of our civilised society.

But within the numerical system there are two kinds of numbers. There are 'true' numbers, like the distance around the earth or the length of a metre, which are scientifically precise and cannot be altered. And there are other numbers which are used as a basis for 'interpretation' — something we love to do since we are a mathematical society. Depending on who is doing the interpreting, there may be different answers from similar sets of figures. They are certainly not precise and may be altered to support a particular need or argument.

Especially beware of the word 'average'. It brings to mind the old joke about the statistician who drowned trying to cross a river which he knew had an average depth of less than 1 metre.

Averaging is a very popular use (or misuse) of numbers. It can produce some curious results.

We hear often enough that the 'average' Australian has particular preferences in relation to beer, sex or politics. But who is this average person? Most of us accept that 'average' means 'most people'.

Wrong! The components of the mythical average person are obtained by taking an extremely small sample of the total population, adding up the multiple statistics (on the basis that they are a typical cross-section) and then making a division. Far from being like most people, the resultant 'average' person as shown on the computer screen may have bits of everyone, but may not actually be identical to any of the individuals originally assessed. He or she may be the rarity, in fact.

To illustrate the point let us assume that the population is roughly divided into people with brown eyes and those who smile at you with blue ones. The computer, which is only as effective as the information fed into its electronic internals, might inform you that the 'average' Australian has one blue eye and one brown eye.

Absurd, of course. But assessing the risk of shark attack by means of the annual average number of such incidents may be just as meaningless. Attacks tend to run in cycles. There may be none for years in a particular area, then several in one summer. Take Florida in the United States for instance. The annual average number of shark attacks for the United States is 12. But in 1995 there were a record 25 attacks in Florida alone, following 22 incidents in 1994.

129

Similarly, we might examine the proposition that in the United States there are 500 'chances' of being struck by lightning as against 12 of being attacked by a shark. '40 to 1, more or less,' a bookmaker would say. 'Place your bets please, gentlemen!'

These odds look good on paper, but in a dispassionate analysis the figures take on a different meaning.

In the United States, thunderstorms, tornadoes and violent electrical disturbances are common inland in the summer months. There are also a lot of people out in the open air — farmers, fruit pickers, field hands, fishermen, golfers, horse riders, trail walkers, mountain climbers, and others too numerous to be mentioned. All of them are potentially vulnerable to lightning strike. The number of people out under the sky, for occupational or recreational purposes, probably runs into millions on any summer weekend. They don't stop what they are doing just because the sky clouds over. Lightning strike, like shark attack, is always unexpected.

On the other hand, the number of people who might encounter the unwelcome attention of sharks is far smaller. Most beachgoers spend far more time on the sand than in the water. The greatest risk of a fatal ocean attack in North American waters is to divers in the Great White shark territory off the California coast. There may be only a few hundred divers who use the areas most vulnerable to attack, such as the Channel Islands and the Farralons. The attack rate in these regions speaks for itself.

If you are a spearfisherman in California, Florida or the Gulf of Mexico you are much more likely to have a shark problem than are snorkellers or SCUBA divers taking pictures in the same areas — because of the obvious danger of attracting and exciting sharks by blood and the vibration of struggling fish. Become a hunter, take the risk of being hunted. Perhaps that's not an unfair equation!

But it isn't practicable to obtain the exact numbers of divers and differentiate their activities and the precise nature of the danger (such as berleying up for sharks with blood and offal) in order to show the particular risk in various categories and localities. Obviously it varies enormously.

However, even taking a widely general view, it is possible that the annual US average of 12 shark attacks, expressed as a percentage of the actual number of people using the ocean, could be higher than the corresponding percentage formed by the 500 unfortunates felled by bolts of lightning. That is, when you take into account the numbers of the much larger land-based group.

Flimsy figures.

There is one certainty, though. That is that the shark attack victims were unlikely to suffer lightning strike. And (you will be one step ahead of me here) those who were lightning victims were certainly in no danger of shark attack.

So how can you rationally compare the two? Who is to say that there really *is* a comparative lightning strike to shark attack risk of 40 to 1? If it makes you feel more comfortable, believe it. But don't try to rationalise it.

Conversely, can it ever be said that a particular beach is 100 per cent safe from shark attack? Or, if there has been one freak circumstance in one year out of many that are incident-free, should you still always be looking over your shoulder?

Take my home beach at Cottesloe as an example. Cottesloe faces the Indian Ocean. It is a pleasant seaside suburb of Perth, capital of the State of Western Australia. The beach is a short walk from the railway line linking Perth and the port of Fremantle, and is one of the most popular bathing beaches in the hot months of the southern hemisphere summer.

In the 1920s it was proportionately even more crowded than today, because it was then the only beach readily reached by public transport. People from inland suburbs would take a sandwich lunch, a towel and the neck-to-knee swimming costume compulsory at the time for 'decency', and would catch the train.

Sunday 22 November 1925 was a day of searing heat. An east wind had been blowing for three days, harsh and hot off the inland deserts. The temperature was well over 100 degrees Fahrenheit (37 degrees Celsius) and Cottesloe beach was packed with 5000 people. The water was typical of summer, emerald in colour, clear and glassy calm, and inviting. It was thronged with bathers cooling off. One of the swimmers was Simeon Ettleson, a 55-year-old red-haired bookmaker's clerk. He was floating on his back, about 30 metres from the shore, dressed in a dark neck-to-knee swimming costume.

Surf club members Reg Bishop, Bert Ireland, Corry Holt and Bill Melrose, were about to go for a row in the club's dinghy, whimsically called the *Diddle-oh*. They were preparing to launch it by the jetty which stretched out from the beach pavilion.

'We were just about to put the dinghy in the water,' Reg Bishop recalled in 1989 in an interview with Gail Williams of the Perth *Sunday Times*, 'when a yell went up and we rowed as fast as we could towards where the sound came from. Then we saw the shark's fin and a swimmer with half his thigh gone.'

The shark, a 4 metre female tiger, had charged between other swimmers to reach Ettleson, tearing most of the flesh from his upper leg. The water around him was red with blood. Four other swimmers were trying to drive the shark away from Ettleson when the boat arrived. Melrose and Holt drove their oars into the water to force the shark away from its victim.

'We managed to get to the man, who was by now floating face down,' Reg Bishop said. 'I still remember the colour of the water. It was red, yellow, and grey with bits of human debris floating.'

As they grasped Ettleson's shoulders to drag him into the boat the shark charged again, taking a huge bite out of the unfortunate man's side so that his organs spilled out into the water.

Then the shark attacked the boat. By now the dinghy had seven people in it, including some swimmers who had climbed in to escape the shark. Despite the extra weight, the force of the charge lifted the bow right out of the water, and left teeth embedded in the timber. In the furore one of the boat's rowlocks was lost overboard, and they had to paddle for shore with one oar and a section of floorboard.

Ettleson was barely alive. 'There was still a slight flicker in his eyes when we got him on board,' Bishop said. 'But he was gone by the time we carried him up the beach in the boat.'

A doctor reached Simeon Ettleson within minutes. But he was only able to confirm what was already only too obvious. That he was dead from shock and loss of blood. Some of the bystanders fainted at the sight.

All the bathers, in the meantime, had fled the water. Many stood at the water's edge, appalled by the tragedy, watching the shark. The tiger continued to swim up and down in an agitated manner in the shallows, lashing the water with its tail.

Constable Dan Hunt and Probationary Constable T. R. Penn brought a .45 Webley revolver and a .44 Winchester rifle from the Claremont Police Station and began firing futilely at the shark. The water deflected the shots.

Fisheries Inspector Brown brought the Fisheries Department launch around by sea and put out set lines with kerosene-tin floats. The shark remained in the area until the following Wednesday, kept there by buckets of blood brought from the Robb's Jetty abattoir. It was finally hooked by a Fremantle fisherman, V. Maiolini, and Constable Hunt, who brought it ashore after a half-hour struggle.

When it was shot at the shark tore the hook and chain out of its mouth, but it was recaptured by Hunt, who jumped into the water and put a rope around its tail. Despite this bravery he was later unable to claim a share of the reward of £200 which had been offered. It was a lot of money in days when many men earned less than £5 a week as a full wage. But it was ruled, in what seems to have been niggardly fashion, that Hunt was 'on duty' at the time, and was therefore ineligible for a share in the reward.

The tiger was exhibited for weeks on coir matting at the surf club. Thousands of people came to see it and it raised £600 for the fledgling WA surf lifesaving movement.

Reg Bishop said he could still smell that shark in the coir matting for years afterwards.

The attack at Cottesloe caused a wave of sharkphobia in Western Australia. Two years earlier a 13-year-old Scotch College schoolboy, Charles Robinson, had been killed in the Swan River while swimming off the school boatshed in Freshwater Bay.

As a result Perth bathers felt endangered in river and sea and the government was deluged by demands for the construction of 'sharkproof' enclosures. A number of 'baths' (pile and picket enclosures with catwalks) were built in the river, and a £3000 shark net system was installed at Cottesloe, scene of the Ettleson tragedy. But the nets filled with weed in heavy weather and did not survive the winter storms. 'The elements beat the nets and blew them away,' Reg Bishop recalled in the Perth *Sunday Times* interview.

As it turned out, the nets were unnecessary. There was never another shark attack at Cottesloe. In the 71 years since Simeon Ettleson took his fatal swim in the heatwave of 1925, hundreds of people have swum there every summer day in perfect safety.

By the 1990s there were few people alive who could remember the 1925 tragedy.

But there was a legacy. Shark tragedies at Cottesloe and elsewhere gave a major impetus to the surf lifesaving movement around Australia. Shark towers were erected at all public beaches, with patrols on summer weekends and holidays. Most Australian beach-goers became familiar with the wail of the siren as the 'shark alarm' sounded... Followed by the headlong rush of people to get out of the water. 'Last one out's a loser!'

The alarms have sounded thousands of times through the years on Perth beaches. But there has been only one other serious attack at a patrolled beach. Ron Sutherland was on leave from the Royal Australian Navy in 1946, and swimming at City Beach only a few metres from the water's edge. There were other swimmers much further out, but a whaler shark passed them all and seized Sutherland's leg, inflicting severe injuries.

Fortunately he was close to shore and was quickly dragged up onto the sand. There were two doctors on the beach who were able to stem the bleeding and save Sutherland's life, though his leg had to be amputated later. After being invalided out of the Navy he later became the chemist at Augusta for many years.

Surf lifesaving patrols, with clubs all around Australia affiliated in a national body, have always been associated with lookout towers and scanning the water for 'man-eaters'. How many lives have actually been saved by pressing the button on the shark alarm is open to question. But volunteer lifesavers provide a unique service in Australia, rescuing people in difficulties in the ocean and treating others for jellyfish stings, sunburn, heart attacks, dehydration, and neck and spinal injuries suffered from recklessly diving into shallow water.

In Western Australia alone, in 1995, 10000 people were helped by Surf Club members and 400 rescued from the surf. Surf Clubs also provided sporting facilities for members of all ages, from juniors to seniors, with competition in surf-belt races and boat, board and ski races. 'Iron man' competitions became a major summer television attraction.

Where do the sharks fit into that picture?

While the shark alarm sticks in the mind of the public, people are individually far more in danger of *drowning*. But, in one of life's ironies, it may be that without the public's perception of the shark 'menace' the volunteer surf lifesaving movement would never have got started. Certainly it would not be the success it is today. Many more people might have drowned at surf beaches through the years. In that sense, sharks may actually have done the Australian beachgoer more good than harm.

At Cottesloe there is the kind of dilemma that often exists about sharks. The beach has seen its one serious shark incident in a century. At the time of writing it had been safe for 71 years. And there was no incident prior to poor Simeon Ettleson's death. The fatal day, 25 November 1925, was one in a hundred years.

Could Cottesloe be accurately described as 'safe' today? Or should we say that there is an 'average' one per cent chance of a shark attack there each year?

The vagaries of shark attack are such that there may be a new tragedy at Cottesloe tomorrow. Or there may not be another in the next hundred years.

The thought does not appear to disturb the people who throng the surf in summer, or the dozens of 12- and 13-year-olds on their boogie-boards bobbing up and down outside the breaker line each day. In fact it is unlikely in 1996 that one person in 1000 swimming there would even have heard of the 1925 tragedy. Time, it is said, heals all wounds.

The concrete pylon that supported one end of the shark net has remained in place at Cottesloe, grey and weatherbeaten. A wave-battered monument to Ettleson.

Another tiger shark in another year, 1994, shattered the theory that working divers using air hoses are not at risk from sharks, with a savage attack at Broome in Western Australia.

Pearl divers encounter sharks on a regular basis. *Pinctada*, the pearl shell, grows in tropical waters in the Indo-Pacific regions. These waters are the particular home of tiger and whaler sharks. While both are dangerous species to humans in some circumstances, pearl divers regarded themselves as safe.

The northwestern Australian coast, from Exmouth Gulf to the Lacepede Islands north of Broome, is famous for the quality of its pearl shell of the genus *Pinctada maxima*, meaning literally 'the biggest'. Pearls cultured in *maxima* oysters are known as 'South Sea' pearls. The largest and most valuable in the world.

The northwest coast carries a particularly heavy population of tiger sharks, too.

Modern pearl divers use 'hookah' apparatus, which superseded helmet suits in the 1970s. Prior to 1994 neither the helmet divers nor those using hookah gear regarded sharks as a problem, though from time to time they saw large tigers.

'They'd come and have a look at us,' said John Monk, a diver in the 1970s. 'But they didn't appear particularly interested. They'd just cruise past and be on their way. But there must have been plenty of them. If you put a line out at night it was snapped up, quickly, and the shark would always be a tiger.'

By 1994, after 20 winter 'seasons' using modern hookah gear, Broome pearl divers had reason to believe that sharks were no threat to them, at least in the divers' professional capacity. It was a perception which changed dramatically in November 1993.

Diver Richard Peter Bisley was 27 years old, and had been working in the pearling industry for four years. He was considered a safe and reasonably experienced diver. On 21 November 1993 he was working on a pearl 'farm' in Roebuck Bay, in 14 metres of water, with another diver, Stefan John Freney-Mills. The farm consisted of rows of captive pearl shell in plastic baskets hanging from wire fences on the seabed. Each shell had had a 'nucleus' inserted carefully in its mantle to induce it to grow a pearl — the standard 'culture' pearling procedure.

135

The diver's job was maintenance: to clean the shell of weed and check that the baskets were placed to take best advantage of the strong tides in the region. Visibility was very poor in Roebuck Bay. But it was a routine job and a task both men were well accustomed to handling.

Air came down to them through twin hoses from a junction connected with a surface compressor. Each had a 'pony' bottle, a small emergency tank which could supply air in the event of a break in the line.

About 3.15 p.m. that afternoon Freney-Mills experienced a sudden drop in pressure in his air supply, sufficient to send him to the surface. He used air from his emergency 20 cubic foot (half a cubic metre) pony bottle in order to ascend to check for the fault.

Bubbles were freely flowing to the surface from the area where Bisley had been working but there was no sign of the diver. When the line was pulled in, Bisley's weight belt was attached, still buckled up, but the hose to the mouthpiece demand valve had been severed, allowing the free flow of air which had forced Freney-Mills to the surface.

It was slack tide, high water. There was no sign of Bisley on the surface and it was evident that he must be in serious trouble without air. Freney-Mills tried to dive again, but was unable to get back to the bottom due to the low pressure in his own supply.

Broome Pearls's operations manager John Kelly, master of the company vessel *Parmelia-K*, was nearby. He was an experienced diver himself and as soon as he was notified he instituted an immediate search of the pearl farm and surrounding area.

Police were contacted and other divers hurried to assist. Three-quarters of an hour after the incident there were nine dinghies with divers and crews searching the pearl farm and the water surrounding it, though they were hampered by the poor underwater visibility of 2.5 metres. By 4.10 p.m. a company Cessna float plane was in the air, with a second aircraft taking off at 5 p.m.

The air and sea search was continued next day, and the signs were ominous. Bisley's mask and demand valve and a bail-out bottle with the shoulder strap severed were found on the bottom by the farm manager Kau Stainton, and he also noticed damage to the fence lines on which the panels of pearl shell were hung. It looked to him as though some large and heavy marine creature had crashed through the panels.

Six days after Bisley's disappearance a tiger shark was hooked on a set line in close proximity to the pearl farm. In its stomach were human remains and clothing, which forensic examination in Perth identified as belonging to Bisley.

While there was some conservationist criticism of the catching of the shark, it was necessary for insurance claims by Bisley's dependents. In the absence of positive proof of death, claims could have been delayed for months or even longer. There was also the relevant matter of diver morale. It was important for men working in the twilight world of shadows with visibility sometimes less than 2 metres to know that the shark responsible was no longer in the area.

Some divers believed that the attack was caused by the shark accidentally bumping into Bisley while chasing fish. Others said that an accidental bump would have frightened the shark as much as the diver. All hoped that the attack was an aberration — an incident unlikely to be repeated.

The capture of that tiger shark resolved the question of Richard Bisley's sad fate. But there are many cases where people have inexplicably disappeared in the ocean. If a body is not recovered, it is usual to assume that the person has drowned or suffered a fatal heart attack. But it is likely that many more people are taken by sharks than are recorded.

The files still remain open on the disappearance of Australian prime minister Harold Holt from Cheviot Beach, Victoria in 1967. A sensation at the time, his death is still perhaps the most famous 'missing body' case on Australian police record, and caused as much public distress within Australia as had the assassination of US President John F. Kennedy in Dallas, Texas, four years earlier.

'How could such a thing happen?' people asked in shock. The basic facts were simple enough: the 59-year-old prime minister had gone for a Sunday morning swim on 17 December 1967 at Cheviot Beach on the Nepean Peninsula flanking Melbourne's Port Phillip Bay. Harold Holt was an experienced skin diver and very familiar with Cheviot Beach. It was his favourite diving spot, where he like to prise abalone from the rocks and spear crayfish (rock lobster). It was his personal delight to barbecue the seafood he caught for his friends at his Portsea beach house.

Holt scorned the idea of having 'minders' or secret service men watching over his security and insisted on living like an ordinary citizen on a weekend away from work. The prime minister said that he felt so refreshed after a weekend at his beach house that the informality was an essential part of the relaxation process.

That fateful Sunday morning he walked with friends to watch lone yachtsman Francis Chichester sail in through Port Phillip Heads. On the way back he suggested a swim and went into the water with Allan Stuart, a young Englishman. He did not have diving equipment that day, but was wearing a bathing costume and sand shoes. He intended only to cool off. Stuart did not feel confident in the water, and soon returned to the beach, but Holt swam out strongly, watched by the others. He appeared to be quite in control in the conditions. But that situation changed dramatically. Newspapers later reported that 'Mr Holt swam out through flat water and disappeared in a sudden boiling of surf which erupted around him while he was swimming strongly'.

There followed the most intensive search in Australian history. Police and army personnel scoured the beaches and headlands for any sign of the missing prime minister. The Navy patrolled at sea. Helicopters flew up and down for more than a week. Navy and SAS divers searched underwater at the spot where he disappeared, and for some distance east and west of it. None of them found so much as a lace from one of Harold Holt's sandshoes.

Wild rumours circulated. Prime Minister Holt had been kidnapped, it was said, by frogmen from a Russian submarine and spirited away. Another version said the submarine was Chinese. There were theories of a secret murder; an assassination like that of Holt's personal friend President Kennedy; an undersea villain lying in wait. All impossible, of course. Holt's fatal decision to swim was a spur-of-the moment matter, and no evil empire could have planned for it.

The usual explanation offered is that Harold Holt drowned. Although he was fit and a strong swimmer, he had no fins that day and there can be strong currents in Cheviot Bay. Nevertheless, there are some puzzling aspects to the case.

A swimmer in difficulties does not disappear immediately. He usually waves his arms and most often calls 'Help!' And if Holt did drown why was no body ever recovered? Bodies usually float, even if they are not washed ashore on the next tide, or are discovered beneath the waves if the deceased were trapped in some rock crevice. It seems extraordinary that such an intense aerial, helicopter and diving search found no trace of the prime minister.

There is one other possibility. Witnesses of Great White attacks have often described the flurry of spray, 'a fountain', thrown up as the shark strikes its victim. Was the 'sudden boiling of surf' described by the Holt witnesses caused by a *Carcharodon*? Was the Prime Minister, in fact, a victim of a Great White shark attack?

Great White sharks do frequent the area. There are large seal and penguin colonies on nearby Phillip Island and in Bass Strait. There have been fatal Great White attacks on humans inside and outside Port Phillip Bay, and in the near vicinity of Cheviot Beach.

At 4.45 p.m. on 14 March 1956, for example, a surf carnival had just ended at nearby Portsea Beach at the entrance to Port Phillip Bay, a short distance from where the prime minister would take his final and fatal swim just over ten years later. A large crowd on the foreshore watched in horror as a huge Great White shark swept between other surfers to seize 26-year-old John Wishart. Wishart had been waiting for a wave to surf ashore and was about 230 metres from the beach with five companions. Wishart was first dragged beneath the surface. Then he reappeared punching desperately at the shark. He was taken below once more and was never seen again.

As in Holt's case, Wishart's body was never recovered. Witnesses confirmed the manner of his death. With Harold Holt we are left to wonder.

Shark behaviour has been a constant puzzle to those people concerned about safety in the water. Scientists have come up with so many conflicting conclusions. Swimmers, surfers, snorkellers, SCUBA divers and others who consider that they may personally be at some risk find it difficult to get consistent advice.

Official organisations have also had their concerns, including the United States Navy. The Navy has craft ranging in size from inflatable dinghies to giant aircraft carriers. It also has a major fleet of aircraft in the US Navy Air Wing, with many units flying from carriers.

Ships may sink in war or peace, aircraft can fall into the sea . . . and men left afloat in lifejackets after such disasters are potential prey for ocean predators.

From this point of view it would seem natural for the US Navy to take a professional interest in sharks. However, the historian of Navy shark research, H. David Baldridge, recalls that such was far from the case in earlier days.

When he began searching through Navy medical files from the Second World War, Baldridge found that there was not even a specific category for shark deaths or injuries. In the best traditions of bureaucracy anywhere, shark attack fell under the heading 'ANIMAL BITE — ANIMAL UNSPECIFIED'.

In 1944 the US Navy put out a training manual, *Shark Sense*. It was aimed at seamen or airmen who might be concerned about finding themselves floating in the sea in a lifejacket. This was a situation which happened often enough in wartime, but since the intention was to keep morale high the manual took a bright and breezy approach.

As an introduction *Shark Sense* stated:

It is evident that the fear of sharks has originated because of wild unfounded tales. The natural conclusion is that the shark offers no unusual hazards to a swimming or drifting man; in fact the chances that a man will be attacked by a shark or barracuda are infinitesimal.

Shark Sense then recommended the kind of action to take in the 'infinitesimal' event that a serviceman should find himself in the water and confronted by a shark.

Man is still the he-coon of all the animals on land or sea… By using his brain he has devised ways to conquer every animal. This does not mean that he can beat every animal at its own game. No man can out-scratch a wild cat, out-wrestle a gorilla, or out-bite a shark.

However, it was suggested that a man could avoid the creature's attack and counter it by some other means of combat in which the animal was less proficient.

What to do with the shark? The man in the water was advised to fire his pistol. The explosion might frighten the shark away. That is, if the wet sidearm was in a firing condition!

The manual continued:

In case of a shark attack and you have no gun: Now this is a pretty desperate counter-measure, but remember that your life insurance company was not happy when you fell into the water. To repeat, in case of a shark attack in the water swim out of his line of charge, grab a pectoral fin and ride with him as long as you can hold your breath.

What then?

If you are fortunate enough to be armed with any kind of knife, and can get to it, cut the shark's belly open. A shark's hide is tough and it will be hard cutting no matter how good your knife is, but the belly is the tenderest part of it. And too, by opening the belly you will let water inside which will kill him almost immediately.

The manual warned that the job was not finished there:

Killing the shark will naturally get blood in the water and probably attract sharks to that spot. Get away from it as quickly as you can!

Where to? And what if you didn't happen to have a knife? The manual was somewhat pessimistic:

Admittedly your chances of whipping an excited shark in the water — unless you are properly armed and trained for just that — may not be 100 per cent.

*But it has been done and your chances of doing it and surviving are greater
than they would be if you did not try it.*

An inescapable conclusion.

The manual went on to suggest a move that the writer may have seen at a
bullfight:

*If you can avoid the shark's mouth by moving a foot [30 centimetres] or so out
of his path it is a miss for the shark and a temporary reprieve for you!*

Olé!

In case the word 'temporary' had something of an ominous ring, the
manual urged the would-be victim to keep trying:

*If you can attach yourself to him by grabbing a fin when he turns for another
attack, you aren't there; you are riding with him, behind his mouth and out of
danger from his teeth. Hold tight and hang on as long as you can without
drowning…*

The manual expressed the hope that:

*After missing his target the shark may lose his viciousness and become his
usual cowardly self again.*

It is reasonable to wonder what the sailors in the water after the mid-
Pacific sinking of the US battleship *Indianopolis* in 1945 thought about the
advice offered in *Shark Sense*. As the manual was on general issue in 1944
some of the men at least must have read it, never guessing that on some dark
future day they would be placed in exactly that predicament.

The *Indianopolis* incident remains one of the more notorious ship-sinking
shark tragedies, and is often bracketed with the 1852 *Birkenhead* and the 1942
Nova Scotia episodes.

The heavy cruiser USS *Indianopolis* was the flagship of the American Fifth
Fleet. She was the vessel that made a top-secret dash to the island of Guam to
deliver the two atomic bombs which would be dropped on Hiroshima and
Nagasaki and which in turn led to a swift ending of the war.

But on her return voyage, hostilities were still very much a reality and by
ill luck she was intercepted by the Japanese submarine *I–58*. It was just after
midnight on 30 July 1945. The cruiser was unescorted and steaming on a
straight course instead of taking the zigzag pattern recommended for
avoiding torpedo fire.

Commander Mochitsura Hasimoto of the *I–58*, peering through his
periscope, could hardly believe his luck. He fired two torpedoes for two

strikes, two flashes of flame and two towering columns of water. A bare 12 minutes later the *Indianopolis*, pride of the Pacific Fifth Fleet, slid below the surface and was on her way to the bottom of the ocean.

She had been carrying a complement of 1196 personnel, and sank so quickly that she took most of her lifeboats and flotation gear with her. About 800 men jumped clear and at daylight were in exactly the situation described in *Shark Sense*: floating in lifejackets with patches of oil and debris and sharks finning all around them.

Naturally the survivors hoped for quick rescue.

But ironically, because of the secrecy of her mission, the *Indianopolis* had been sailing under strict radio silence. The lack of reports and bulletins did not cause official concern at either her point of departure or her destination. The A-Bomb was so secret that hers was to be a voyage no one knew about.

The men floated, huddled together, for one day, then two. After three days they were sure someone must come to find them. But four days after the loss of the ship they were still in their lifejackets in the water. Those who were alive and those who were dead.

Around them swam the sharks. Hundreds of them circling and making passes at the helpless men.

In the *Jaws* film, the sharkfighter Quint, a fictional survivor of the *Indianopolis* disaster, claimed that the sharks killed 600 men. The figure was in fact considerably less, and it may have been that many of those taken were already dead from immersion and exposure. But their horrified shipmates had to watch them torn to pieces, live and dead victims, by the packs of sharks in a blood-reddened sea.

On the fourth day, quite by chance, a reconnaissance aircraft flew overhead, and saw the survivors floating in the sea and the sharks swimming around them. It sent a radio SOS which finally brought help. But aid came too late for the majority of the men of the *Indianopolis*. Only 316 of the original 1196 were saved. They included her captain, who was so tortured by what had occurred that he took his own life in 1977.

The survivors of the *Indianopolis* got together after the war for a reunion every five years. Some of them still had psychological problems, haunted by terrible memories, 50 years later.

After the *Indianopolis* tragedy the Navy took sharks seriously. Ironically, H. David Baldridge himself narrowly missed being a part of the story. 'As a young ensign I came within a whisker of being assigned to that ship for its fateful voyage,' he said. Perhaps the tragedy inspired in him an interest in sharks. In 1976 he wrote an excellent book, titled *Shark Attack*, based on computer studies he had made of Navy and Smithsonian Institute data. Records of attacks around the world.

Baldridge was a member of a Shark Research Panel established in 1958. In that year Dr Sidney Galler of the US Office of Naval Research brought 34 international scientists together in New Orleans to compile information which it was hoped would lead to the development of an effective shark repellent. To know how to repel sharks, the Navy recognised, it had to know more about the creatures. David Baldridge was elected to the panel in 1968 because of work he had done on deterrents with the US Navy and because of his own interest in computer analysis.

The first task was to establish a Shark Attack File — a computer list of every shark attack on record. It involved 348 335 entries describing 1165 cases up to the 1970s. Baldridge's book *Shark Attack* was based on an analysis of the cases, and their circumstances, as seen by a computer. He was at pains to point out that the computer's answers could only be as effective as the information it had received.

The analysis of the data produced some interesting results. For example:

- The records showed 13.5 shark attacks on male humans for every single attack on a female.

- Only about 25 per cent of attacks indicated hunger on the part of the shark. The other attacks may have been territorial or have occurred for some other reason.

- International Orange, the colour most frequently used for lifejackets, may be the most dangerous of all for potential shark attack. Tests showed that it was the colour that most attracted sharks' interest.

- About equal numbers of shark attacks were reported in the two hemispheres of the world, with a slight preponderance (54 per cent) in the southern hemisphere.

- Shark attacks were fatal in only 35 per cent of all recorded incidents.

- Sixty-two per cent of attacks occurred in five feet (1.5 metres) or less of water.

- Sixty-three per cent of attacking sharks were not seen before the victim was struck. But 54 per cent were seen afterwards.

143

➤ Sharks pressed an attack hard only in one case in seven. But in cases where a 'frenzied' shark was involved, the mortality rate climbed to 63 per cent as against 35 per cent for all attacks.

➤ Divers' mortality rate in shark attacks was only 33 per cent of the fatality rate for swimmers, perhaps because they could see the shark and undertake some defence.

➤ But divers formed a high proportion of victims. One diver is on record for every two victims in all other categories. Spearfishing obviously attracts sharks. Divers are in deeper water and often more isolated than swimmers.

➤ In Baldridge's records up to the 1970s no female diver had been attacked below five feet (1.5 metres) of water.

➤ Sixty-five per cent of shark attacks occurred at weekends.

➤ Despite popular belief there appeared to be no preference on the part of sharks for white, black, yellow or brown-skinned persons. But laboratory tests showed that sharks may be attracted by contrasts (e.g. the untanned portion of a suntanned person, or the white palms and soles of a black-skinned person).

➤ Most recorded attacks occurred when the water temperature was over 70 degrees Fahrenheit (21° Celsius).

➤ Most colder water attacks were by *Carcharodon carcharias*, the Great White shark, and the fatality rate was far higher than with lesser species.

➤ The average length of attacking sharks recorded in the Shark Attack File was 2.1 metres (6 feet 10 inches). With some huge sharks of 6 metres or more bumping up the average, more than half the attacking sharks did not exceed 2 metres.

➤ When tests were made with students estimating the length of sharks in tanks, individual estimates varied 19 to 26 per cent in error. Most consistently overestimated the size of the shark.

➤ 94 per cent of attacks on humans are made by single sharks, not pairs or packs. Though it is more common for

144

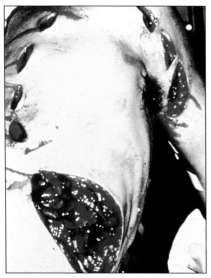
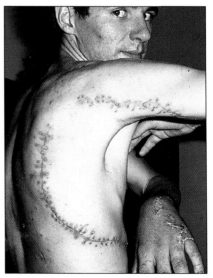

Top: *Lyn Cropp surveys a 5 metre Great White at Albany and wonders what a 6 metre shark, weighing twice as much, would look like.*
Bottom: *Rodney Fox's horrific shark attack wounds; and his scars post-recovery.*
(Photographs: Courtesy Rodney Fox)

These photographs show clearly the differences between the blunt-nosed Tiger shark (**top**) *and the sharper-nosed Great White* (**bottom**). *However the sharks do share one characteristic —* *a liking for human prey. (Photographs: (top) Ritchie Hannstead; (bottom) Peter Newstead)*

Top: *Maurie Glazier (right) and myself. 'Too heavy!' Glazier is telling the photographer who wanted us to lift this Great White's head out of the water. The shark, a female, was almost 6 metres in length and weighed about 2 tonnes. (Photograph: Brian Greenhalgh)*
Bottom: *John Allchin (left) and myself with a Tiger shark at the Monte Bello Islands, the scene of the 1960s British A-bomb tests. (Photograph: Mike Baker)*

147

148

Opposite, top: *Waiting for 'Whitey'. At times the camera gap in the cage seemed uncomfortably large. Great Whites could — and did — get their snouts through the space between the bars. (Photograph: Vic Martin)*

Opposite, bottom: *The author, after a hard day at the office, just off Cheynes Whaling Station in Western Australia. The cold that seeped into our bones and the constant joggling rise and fall of the cage with the swell running inside King Georges Sound quickly depleted our energy, and the taste of whale grease sucked in through our SCUBA mouthpieces induced a feeling of nausea which sometimes lingered long after the dive. (Photograph: Marilyn Edwards)*

Above: *Underwater, in the cage, the sharks seemed even bigger than they really were. Their size took our breath away. (Photograph: Peter Grace)*

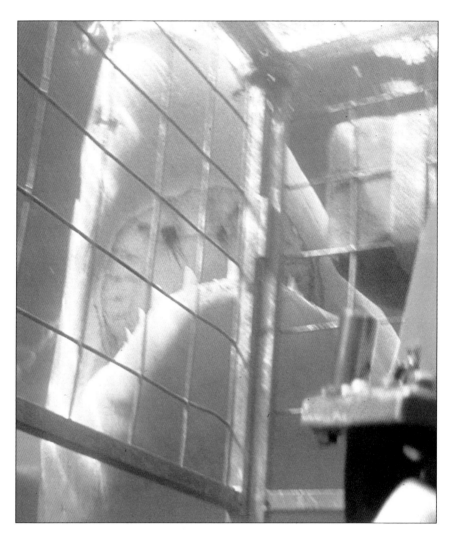

Above: *As the shark's teeth raked the bars of the cage we were able to see clearly the furry parasites clinging to the roof of its mouth, behind those awesome, triangular, serrated fangs. (Photograph: Peter Newstead)* **Opposite, top:** *The Great White is the only shark that will put its head out of the water to look at you in a boat. We called it 'window shopping' or 'counting heads'.* **Opposite, bottom:** *Fearsome jaws show the perfection of Nature's design. It is no surprise that Great Whites have sometimes bitten divers completely in two.*

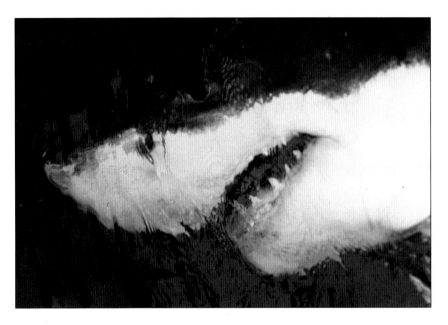

151

Top: *A big Tiger shark comes to take a large fish from the stern platform of Ben Cropp's boat on the Great Barrier Reef.* Bottom: *The shark swallows the bait at a gulp and swirls away while Ben films the action. Later Ben was struck a heavy blow on the head by the tail of another Tiger shark that left him stunned and with a long-term hearing problem.*

sharks to converge in packs on natural food such as a dead whale, or when they are artificially stirred up into a feeding frenzy by 'chum' or berley supplied from a boat.

➤ Victims' bodies are almost always recovered in the event of a fatal attack, with a figure of 96 per cent recovered.

➤ Rescuers are seldom attacked, even though they may be swimming in heavy concentrations of the victim's blood, and even when a victim has been jerked out of the rescuers' grasp by a shark intent on following up its first strike. In 270 cases in the Shark Attack File there were only three fatalities and nine injuries among rescuers.

➤ A study of bathers' activities at beaches showed that, in a typical moment, 46 per cent of the people were facing out to sea, and 19 per cent faced the shore. But an analysis of reported attacks showed that 44 per cent of victims were facing the shore when struck by their shark.

All these findings offer food for thought, and some interesting conclusions may be drawn from such computer analysis of records.

However, Baldridge himself warns that the figures only reflect the information received. We must bear in mind that in the 20 years since he wrote his book there have been changes in human behaviour patterns.

Baldridge reported, for instance, that there were 13.5 attacks on male humans for every single attack on a female. And that no female diver had been attacked at a level deeper than five feet (1.5 metres) of water.

This would seem to indicate that sharks had a strong preference for male human victims, and that female divers were relatively immune. Or, to take it even further, that so long as a woman swam or dived with male companions she could be relatively sure that in the event of an attack the shark would go for one of the men. This claim reminded me of a traditional sea shanty I had heard sung in the Abrolhos Islands off Western Australia:

The Man-Eating Shark

The most chivalrous fish in the ocean
To the ladies forbearing and mild
Though his record be dark
The man-eating shark
Will eat neither woman nor child…

He dines upon seamen and skippers
And tourists his hunger assuage
And a young cabin boy
He'll always enjoy
If he's past the maturity age

A doctor, a lawyer, a preacher
He'll gobble them any fine day
But the ladies, God bless 'em
He'll only address 'em
Politely and go on his way

I can readily cite you an instance
When a lovely young lady from Bream
Who was tender and sweet
And delicious to eat
Fell into the Bay with a scream

She struggled and flounced in the water
And in vain did she cry for her barque
And she'd surely have drowned
If she hadn't been found
By the chivalrous man-eating shark

He bowed in a manner most polished
And soothing her impulses wild
'Don't be frightened,' he said
'I've been properly bred
And will eat neither woman nor child'

He offered his fin and she took it
Such gallantry you couldn't dispute
And the passengers cheered
As the vessel they neared
And a broadside was fired in salute

They soon swam alongside the vessel
And the lifesaving dinghy was lowered

154

With the pick of the crew
And her relatives too
And the mate and the skipper aboard

They hauled her aboard in a jiffy
The shark stood attention meanwhile
Then he turned on his flipper
And ate up the skipper
And went on his way with a smile.

Using Baldridge's figures, a case could indeed be made for the 'Chivalrous Shark'! The vast majority of shark victims *are* male, so the statistics might be taken to indicate a demonstrated preference for men. Or even a forebearing attitude towards women and children, if we chose to mischievously misinterpret the figures.

However, it is an undisputed fact that women and girls, as we have noted, form a smaller proportion of victims. Young children have made the register only in exceptional cases like the Queensland instance where a shark actually snatched a child from its father's arms as he was wading ashore from a boat. But the reasons for this imbalance are, of course, quite unconnected with any imagined chivalrous instincts. The adventurous spirit that leads to a death rate ratio of four young males to one female in motor accidents, sporting accidents, drownings and industrial mishaps is also the key factor underlying the shark attack figures. The majority of women tend to stay close to the beach and keep a close maternal eye on any offspring. In comparison, a greater number of males are more likely to go spearfishing, surfing and SCUBA diving. At the beach, those who swim furthest out, stay longer in the water, take part in horse play or swim off on their own — all behavioural traits proven to attract sharks — are more likely to be male. If more women exhibited these behavioural traits would they be equally likely to attract sharks? The answer is 'Yes'.

In Australia, in the period 1986 to 1996, women figured in some of the most horrific fatal shark attacks.

Peake Bay, north of Port Lincoln (SA), on Sunday 4 March 1985, for example, saw a peaceful scene much like any other summer fine-weather weekend. Some people were sitting on the beach, others were sunbathing, and some walkers paced the tidemark chatting together. Two men and a woman were splashing on the water's edge with children and a dog. Further out, a fisherman in a small dinghy had a line over the side hoping for a bite from a whiting or perhaps a flathead.

Fifty metres from the beach, fins went up in the air as Shirley Anne Durdin, aged 33 years, her husband Barry and another friend snorkelled and dived for scallops. They were on their way back to the beach at the end of their dive to rejoin their friends and their four children, a boy and three girls aged between five and 11 years, who were playing on the sand.

Suddenly there was a shriek. The children and startled onlookers on the beach saw Shirley Durdin struck below the waist by something dark moving at express speed.

Retired fisherman Kevin Wiseman saw the entire attack from a cliff overlooking the bay. 'It was exactly 12.30 p.m.,' he said. 'The first thing I was aware of was a big spray, then a mass of red blood in the water. A chap started yelling: "Help! Help! Help! She's gone!"'

The anguished cry came from Barry Durdin. 'I could see the shark's fin and tail,' Kevin Wiseman said. 'It was a lot longer than Kevin Hirschausen's 4½ metre boat that put out to help.'

Other boats rushed to the scene to find that Mrs Durdin had been bitten in half in the first charge. They found only a headless torso. Even as the boats converged, the shark circled back a second time and made off for deeper water with what remained of Mrs Durdin in its jaws.

The predator was never seen again, though a major effort was made to catch the shark. Port Lincoln fishermen said that a huge Great White had been in the area for a month, attracted by rotten fish and berley which had been thrown into the water at Wiseman's Bay to attract fish for a local fishing competition.

Therese Cartwright first made newspaper headlines two years later, in 1987, when she gave birth to quadruplets. Sarah, Thomas, James and Luke were Tasmania's first quads in six years. In 1994 she had another baby to make a big family.

Despite the time needed to care for five very young children, Therese Cartwright managed to achieve an extraordinary amount. She was completing a Masters course in nursing, had become a keen SCUBA diver, and had developed an interest in Australian fur seals. Once threatened with extinction through depredations by sealers, fur seal numbers have recovered in recent years in Bass Strait.

Therese Cartwright was 34 years old in 1993, and lived with her husband and children in the small town of Exeter near George Town in northeastern Tasmania. On 5 June that year the Cartwrights went to sea in the Australian Maritime College's boat *Reviresco*. Mr Cartwright skippered the boat; Therese and two other divers were to study fur seals at a colony at Tenth Island. All the Cartwright children including the baby went along for the day.

It was a routine which the family had followed often enough before. But this day would be different. The first two divers splashed into the water and dived for the bottom in a trail of bubbles without incident.

But when Therese Cartwright followed and had descended only a metre or so below the surface, she was struck by a 5 metre Great White shark with such force that it sheared a leg from her body in full view of the horrified watchers in the boat. The shark then made off with Mrs Cartwright, heading for deeper water. Her leg was found later, 1.6 kilometres from the scene, but her body was never recovered.

Eleven days before the Cartwright tragedy, John and Deborah Ford were married in St Andrews Church-In-The-Field, in Terrey Hills, Sydney. John was 31 years old, Debbie 29, and they had met at a squash game two years previously. Debbie had a passion for outdoor and water sports.

They decided to spend their honeymoon on the coast north of Sydney. On 9 June 1993, 15 days after their wedding on and four days after the attack on Therese Cartwright they went out for a day's SCUBA diving at Julian Rocks, a popular dive site near Byron Bay. It may have been that the Cartwright tragedy, which had made newspaper headlines, was discussed by divers on the outward trip. Julian Rocks was once well known for pods of mating grey nurse sharks, but there had never been a shark problem in the area.

The dive itself was uneventful. However, at 9.30 a.m., as the divers decompressed 3 metres below the charter boat, John Ford's eyes opened wide in horror at the sight no diver ever wishes to see. A huge Great White shark, mouth open, was charging towards Deborah.

Instinctively, John Ford pushed his wife out of the way and placed himself between her and the shark. As she swam for the surface he took the brunt of the charge. He was dismembered and killed almost instantly. 'He was protecting me. He gave his own life for me,' Deborah Ford said.

Fishermen managed to hook the shark, which was estimated at more than 6 metres, two hours later. During the struggle it towed the boat 6 kilometres out to sea, regurgitated parts of Ford's body, snapped a wire trace and chewed through a net to escape.

'You wouldn't ever see a bigger shark,' said fisherman Ron Boggis. 'In all my life I won't see another bigger one. That thing was as big as a truck!'

Police divers later recovered John Ford's torso from the attack scene, together with his weight belt and fins and a portion of wetsuit. A police helicopter later sighted the shark on the surface south of Point Hastings. 'It looked pretty sick and was rolling around in the water,' a police observer said. But bad weather prevented further searches, with poor visibility and rough seas. By the time it cleared there was no sign of the shark.

These three attacks had a number of factors in common. All were by large Great Whites, and all bore the hallmarks of a typical *Carcharodon* attack. The sharks struck with terrifying suddenness, inflicting horrendous injuries. The victims had no chance to escape or defend themselves.

Each shark had a choice of possible victims. In the case of Shirley Durdin there were a number of other people in the water, and her husband Barry was close by. There were two other divers in the water with Therese Cartwright, and the Fords were also diving in company.

What made the shark select its particular victim? We will obviously never know the answer to that question. But what is certain is that on each of these three chilling occasions the shark made a woman its target. Debbie Ford was saved only because her husband pushed her out of the way at the last moment.

Yet the computer analysis of the Shark Attack File showed 13.5 attacks on males for each attack on a female. Was it a matter, as former US President Richard Nixon once bitterly claimed, that 'There are lies, damned lies, and statistics!!'...?

David Baldridge, compiler of the Shark Attack File said that he and his co-researchers had had difficulty themselves in rationalising their male–female data. The computer showed that 93 per cent of all shark victims were male. This held good regardless of skin colouring. Where white victims were concerned, 93 per cent of 725 cases were male. With black persons 94 per cent of 176 cases were male; and where the victims had yellow or brown skin tones the record showed that 92 per cent of 154 cases were males.

'The first thought was that more men than women are engaged in occupations offering greater opportunity for shark attacks, people such as fishermen, sailors, and so on,' Baldridge said.

So the computer was asked to show instead only the figures on recreational attacks at beaches, where occupations were not a major factor. This time the figure came out at eight attacks on males to one on females. But 8–1 still seemed too high so the scientists, armed with binoculars, set out themselves to find out the reason why.

They discovered that while the numbers of men and women at popular beaches were fairly similar, there were markedly different behaviour patterns. Men swam further out, more often on their own. They indulged in horseplay, kicking and splashing, and they tended to stay much longer in the water.

Attack figures on beaches showed that the lone swimmer, separate from the group, was the most likely victim of an attack. Laboratory tests with splashing rodents showed that sharks would strike at them while ignoring rats which remained still.

In other words it was the more physically energetic and adventurous nature of men which got them into trouble with sharks, rather than any matter of gender. It is a situation which is confirmed in other walks of life. In 1996, research by the Australian Institute of Health and Welfare showed that the death rate from injury of young Australian males was four times higher than the figure for young women. Young men were simply more prone to risk-taking, it was found.

Since the 1970s many more women have taken up diving, surfing, sailboard riding and other adventurous water sports. The tragedies of the Durdins, Cartwrights and Fords indicate all too clearly that there is no such thing as female immunity.

Experience the thrills — take the risk. In similar adventurous situations, it seems, women are as likely to be attacked by sharks as men. Do such attacks, outside the expectations which may arise from interpretation of the figures, mean that the effort of compiling the information for the Shark Attack File has been valueless in terms of predicting shark attack?

Baldridge himself insisted that the key phrase in his research was *assume nothing*, and the two words which were most inappropriate in describing shark behaviour were *always* and *never*.

He also said that one of the weaknesses of the Shark Attack File was the fact that it presented only the human side of a two-sided experience. For true accuracy we should also know the shark's view of the encounter. In this respect we may ultimately have to live with an imperfect picture.

Many experts use the word 'unpredictable' in relation to sharks. Baldridge says that this is incorrect. 'We just don't know enough yet about what makes a shark tick to be able to say what it will do under any given set of circumstances.'

That may amount to the same thing.

There can be no doubting that the information gathered is valuable. Knowledge in any animal study is seldom 100 per cent complete and every experience adds to what we have already recorded. But the current data are still insufficient to enable us to predict what sharks will do. Perhaps we never will entirely succeed in that. However, with each new piece of data, we do obtain a more detailed and fascinating picture.

The certainty is that sharks will continue to surprise us. There is also the probability that, on occasions, the circumstances will be unpleasant.

GREAT WHALES, GIANT SQUID
chapter nine

THE DEAD WHALES FLOATED ABOVE OUR SHARK CAGE, THE SHADOWS OF THEIR huge square heads slack-jawed in death.

Sometimes the teeth caught in the mesh of the cage top and we gently unhooked them. The teeth were smooth and round, 36 of them in the lower jaw set like the tines of a garden rake, fitting into sockets in the upper jaw. They were tusks rather than teeth, each one pure ivory, and some of them were worn and grooved by the years. Looking at them it was not hard to imagine the awesome conflicts between the bulls. The whalers said that they met each other at speed, jaws opened at right angles, with a huge clack-clacking of noise in sperm whale 'talk'.

Great collisions. A battering-ram butting and banging of monstrous heads. The jaws leaving teeth-raking weals on shining skin.

Those teeth would also have known battles with packs of predatory killer whales, and the hunt for squid kilometres below the surface! Deep, deep down in that Abyssalpelagic zone of darkness — the layer of deep ocean that is the home of the giant squid. A nightmare creature we know so little about, lurking there in the awesome gloom.

'Did you meet the Kraken?' I felt like asking the dead whale. 'Did he lash you with hooked tentacles and rapine beak?'

What would we not give to be able to enter the mind of a sperm whale? To be able to travel down with it to the deeps so far beyond our reach…

Sperm whales are the deepest divers. Bulls have been recorded in dives of 2550 metres (8500 feet) below the surface and they are able to stay down almost an hour. 'A minute below for every foot of their length,' said whaler's folklore.

No one knows how big the giant squid may grow. *Architeuthis princeps* is indeed the prince of darkness. Specimens nearly 30 metres (100 feet) in length with the tentacles fully extended have been washed up, and instances of surface encounters with humans have been recorded through the years.

On occasions quite large boats have been attacked by huge squid, which may have mistaken them for whales.

Sperm whales generally seek the smaller squid, which congregate in immense shoals in the ocean's deeper layers. It is supposed by scientists that the whales may stun the squid by the force of their pulsing echo-location signals. But occasional battles have been witnessed between sperms and squid of enormous size. My fishing friends Muriel Thomas and Syd Liddon once saw a big sperm bull wrestling with a huge squid that was wrapped around its head off Shark Bay (WA) in the 1950s. The sight of a lifetime!

At the Albany Whaling Station some of the bulls had big chunks of giant squid tentacles in their stomachs, the evidence of titanic struggles below. In 1978 I myself became the possessor of a squid that would have been about 14 metres complete. The envelope alone was nearly 3 metres long. It took six men to lift it in a tarpaulin. A smaller squid in the same whale's stomach was complete, and was over 8 metres with its tentacles at full stretch.

The curious thing was that the huge squid looked exactly like the squid to be found in a fish shop, but on a much bigger scale. Imagine a man 30 metres high and you'll have an idea of the size comparison.

The big squid had the same familiar physical structure of envelope, golden and black eyes, and two long arms that reach out to grasp the prey. These two predatory tentacles extended two-thirds the length of the body from a cluster of eight shorter primary tentacles.

The suckers on the long arms were circular, each one bigger than a US silver dollar, and they had hooked claws around their rims for more efficient grasp of the prey. Even though my squid was long dead, the suckers still had a residual suction when placed on a bare arm. The feel of the hooks made the hairs prickle on the back of the my neck.

We could only guess at the kind of world where such monsters lived and where the sperm whales made their vertical dives. Do monster squid sometimes triumph over a whale and carry it down to their brothers in the deep?

Viewing the dead whales, we were caught between the hammer of necessity and the anvil of our conscience. We regretted the death of the whales. At the same time the equation was simple. On days when there were no dead whales there were no sharks and we did not shoot a single frame of film.

We needed a daily catch of ten whales or more. When the whalechasers returned at night, invisible in the darkness except for their red and green navigation lights bobbing past Limestone Head, the first four whales they towed in went straight to the slip. They were taken in by the little green tugboat and hauled up by a hissing steam winch by means of a wire rope around their tail. Then positioned on the deck, so that the flensers in their spiked boots could climb the shining flanks at first light. High above the deck and dwarfed by the size of the whale, they swung their hockey-stick flensing knives deep into the blubber. Each slicing blow making a resounding clunk like someone chopping wood.

Additional whales were buoyed out on the pontoon. If there were ten or more then finning sharks and filming divers were able to have their fun in the morning sunshine.

In a sense we were opportunistic 'feeders', like the sharks and birds who were also using the whales further down the food chain. At times there was a bedlam of bird activity around the whales. Huge albatrosses and giant petrels honked at each other, raising their wings in threat and tearing at the carcasses with long hooked beaks. Dark grey skuas, ravens of the sea, shrieked and squabbled over the entrails. Their heads were often bloodied from gobbling like vultures amongst the innards. Silver gulls screeched and fluttered, their snow-white breasts spotted with crimson. On some days the air was heavy with birds flocking about the dead whales, flying, flapping, caw-cawing and landing with heavy splashes.

At the Station we were on the butcher's end of the business. Attendants at the slaughterhouse. The hunt, the pursuit of the quarry, took place far out at sea.

Whaling has been called the greatest of all hunts, and for hundreds of years all the advantages were with the whales. Small-boat whaling with oars and sails and hand-thrown harpoons — 'A dead whale or a stove-in boat!' — required a degree of courage and seamanship we may never see equalled again. Standing by the whales on the flensing deck at Albany, marvelling at their immensity, we wondered how the old-timers could pluck such giants from the sea.

Even in death the sperm whales were majestic. We stood awed beside them. When their dimensions, 15 metres and 50 tonnes of whale, are quoted, they sound impressive enough. But no words can give a real idea of how huge they really were.

Now they were dead. Killed by puny man who would not have a thousandth part of their individual strength but who could call on thousands of horses of mechanical power. Turning it from a hunt to an industrial process. A contest entirely weighted against the whale.

The great change in whaling — the revolution, you might say — came with the invention of the harpoon whaling gun by a Norwegian, Sven Foyn, in 1864.

The harpoon gun was the size of a small howitzer and could be fitted to a steel oceangoing vessel with a range of hundreds of kilometres. The gun was mounted on an elevated bow platform, like the sharp beak of a raptor bird. It could fire a fatal shot at a whale from 100 metres or more instead of the boat's length, which was the maximum distance for 'darting the iron' from a whaleboat.

For all their numbers and years at sea, the Yankee whalers probably took no more than 40 000 sperm whales over the better part of a century. In the period from the end of the 1950s to the end of the 1970s international whalers took 330 000 sperms.

The gun worked so well that over 100 years of use there were few modifications needed. In fact it was too efficient and therein lay the problem. Though it would be wrong to fault the weapon — it was merely the tool and the weakness lay in men's lack of judgement in its use.

Like the chainsaw in the forest, the harpoon gun was too effective, ultimately killing the industry it was designed to serve.

By 1979 the numbers of the world's whales, the mighty blues, the sperms, humpbacks, seis, minkes, finbacks, greys, rights and bowheads, were so diminished that all whaling was banned by most civilised countries of the world.

The slaughter of the whales followed an increasingly familiar pattern. It was similar to the wiping out of the American bison and the near extinction of the fur seal and the sea elephant. The creatures were hunted to a point where there were too few remaining to make it worthwhile. In the case of the dodo, they were slain to the last remaining individual.

A similar pattern continues today, with rampant international overfishing in all the oceans of the world. The stocks of many pelagic species are in peril. What was once the world's most prolific and famous ground, the Grand Banks off Newfoundland, home of Atlantic cod and halibut, closed in 1995 in a desperate last-minute effort to save the fishery from total ruin. Experts were pessimistic about the long-term prognosis.

Overkill is a lesson *Homo sapiens* seemingly never learns.

When I first went out on a whaleship from Albany in 1962 the signs were already there. The humpback herd which made an annual migration up the Western Australian coast had been reduced from somewhere between 12 000 and 17 000 animals in 1949 to 600 survivors.

163

Responsibility for the massacre of the humpbacks did not rest entirely with Australian whalers. Their combined total of kills was tiny compared with the tallies taken by the massive international fleets of British, Norwegian and Russian whalers, working with factory ships down in the Antarctic. That was whaling on a scale never seen before, and it could have only one ending.

When the whales went north in winter there was no respite. Local whalers were waiting for them on the coasts of Australia, South Africa and South America. The *bang!* of harpoon guns was heard wherever whales blew a spout.

When the humpback survivors were belatedly protected in the 1960s the Albany whalers turned to sperm whales, which still swam in numbers in the Southern Ocean.

The great sperm whale, *Physter macrocephalus*, is the world's largest flesh-eater and the biggest of the *Odontoceti*, the toothed whales. Its relations are killer whales or orcas, oceanic pilot whales, dolphins and porpoises.

The sperm whale, the orca and the Great White shark are the apex predators of their individual oceanic food chains.

Others among the 78 whale species are the baleen whales, the family of *Mysticeti*. They include the enormous blue whale, at 30 metres in length and 100 tonnes the world's largest living creature. Blues have hearts the size of a small motor car.

The *Mysticeti* are filter-feeders, straining krill, crustacea and plankton through baleen brushes in their mouths. Among the baleens are humpbacks, right whales, seis, finbacks, the California grey whale and the minke whale. None of them, in the old whaler's estimation, compared with the sperm for strength and spirit. The sperm had a fearsome reputation.

Because sperms sometimes strand and die on beaches they were known to naturalists long before men had the skill to hunt them. Standing beside the dead sperms at Albany makes it easy to understand the almost superstitious awe in which they were once regarded. Sperms were described by nineteenth-century natural history writers as 'fearfully distinguished; from all other species of Leviathan'. They declared that, at the mere sight of a sperm, sharks and fish were 'struck with the most lively terrors...and often in the precipitancy of flight dashed themselves against the rocks'. Others claimed that sperms were 'athirst for human blood'. Which was rubbish, of course. Although sperms swallow quite large squid and sharks, there is no record of an attack on a human being.

The scientific name for the species, *macrocephalus*, meaning 'big head', comes from the huge square head of the sperm whale. The common name,

164

sperm, is associated with the substance called 'spermaceti' in the whale's head. Scientists now believe that it aids the animal in maintaining neutral buoyancy when it sounds to great depths. In earlier centuries the sweet-smelling spermaceti found in the heads of stranded sperm whales was confused by people as having a male sexual function. Hence the name 'sperm' for the species. For whalers it was a source of valuable oil, and oil distilled from the 'case' fetched five times the price of ordinary whale oil.

The character and fighting qualities of sperm whales were a legend among old-time whalemen. Sperm whales have sunk ships.

In 1820 an enraged bull rammed his square head through the timbers of the Yankee whaler *Essex* west of the Galapagos Islands, sinking her in the blue Pacific deeps. Some of the crew sailed their whaleboats to South America, and during 90 days at sea had to resort to cannibalism to survive. They drew lots to see who would be shot and eaten.

Another bull sperm, in 1851, stove in and sank two of the boats of the whaleship *Ann Alexander*. When the captain threw another harpoon, the whale sank the mother ship as well! Her crew were luckier than the men of the *Essex*. They were picked up in the remaining whaleboat by another vessel after only two days adrift.

Closer to home, not far from Albany, a small colonial port on Saturday 4 March 1881, the topsail schooner *Pet*, a 91 tonne vessel sailing with green tuart timber from Bunbury in Western Australia, felt the full wrath of a bull sperm whale.

She was rounding Cape Leeuwin on a fine sunny day, bound for Port Adelaide in South Australia, when the helmsman called, 'Whale on the starboard bow!'

The mate, William Henrietta, ran forwards but had only reached the break of the poop when there was a forceful collision. The ship was shaken and stopped in her course by the impact. Henrietta went below and found 'the whole of the starboard bow stove in'. Water gushed in through the shattered planks of the vessel and she quickly began to list.

The crew barely had time to lower the boats before the *Pet* heeled over and sank. She took with her the captain, Peter Littlejohn, who had been asleep and seemed still drowsy when aroused. He missed getting into one of the boats, despite the shouts of the crew, and drowned.

Herman Melville was the writer who gave sperm whales their place in literature with his epic novel *Moby Dick*. Melville wrote from his own experiences aboard a whaler, and his writing has the breathtaking quality of real-life description. In his book, the whaleship *Pequod* was rammed by Moby

Dick, the great rogue white whale. She sank to share the fate of the *Essex* and the *Ann Alexander,* and Captain Ahab, with his whalebone artificial leg, died lashed to the white whale in a tangle of harpoon lines.

Like many other schoolboys I read *Moby Dick* as a compulsory English text. But unlike some of my classmates (who found it incomprehensible) I relished Melville's descriptions of whaling. Especially the passages dealing with sharks. When I read 'Thousands upon thousands of sharks swarming round the dead Leviathan smackingly feasted on its fatness,' I did not have to close my eyes to see the fins and slapping tails, the vast oil streak on blue tropical waters, the crimson carnage as the sharks gorged on a floating island of whale flesh.

I understood even more about Leviathan when I stood beside sperm whales on the flensing deck at Albany. I had often seen whales before in their own element. But when a whale is seen at sea, only a small portion of the whale's back is visible at the surface as it blows its tell-tale spout. The flensing deck offered an opportunity to stand beside a 15 metre bull and draw in breath at the immensity of the whole creature. It was the only place in Australia, indeed one of very few places in the world, where you could have seen such a sight.

We were able to actually touch the taut, shining flanks and to marvel at the extraordinary evolution of an air-breathing animal which sought its daily food in the permanent darkness kilometres below the surface. We did not enjoy seeing the whales dead. But it did give a better understanding of that mysterious submarine world which was also the home of our sharks.

The colour of the whales' skins was dark blue — almost black — like a Navy submarine. The old bulls, in particular, carried many scars. There were parallel tooth marks from fights or love-play with their own species. There were also sucker marks from squid, including the disc prints of *Architeuthis.* Larger circular scars were a puzzle until I learned later of that impudent rascal, the 'cookie-cutter' shark.

Some of the whales on the slip carried ragged-edged shark bites and we looked at these with narrowed eyes and professional interest. The bigger bites, scalloped out of the whale's outer layer of blubber, and through to the red flesh, measured more than 60 centimetres across. The sharks we had seen were big. But whatever made those bites was a good deal bigger!

They were the personal signature of a *Carcharodon* in the 6 to 7 metre range. The body of such a creature would be as wide as our cage. The distance from the tip of one pectoral side fin to the other, the 'wingspan', would be as great as the length of the larger individuals of most other shark species. The

166

weight would be in tonnes... The bites had been scooped out in the open sea. But what if such a monster were to come grinning in our cage gap?

We tried, without total success, to put that thought aside.

By 1976, as we stood agape beside the whales on the slip at Albany, the groundswell of public opinion was already gathering strength overseas and conservationists of a new breed, for whom the name 'Greens' had just been invented, were calling for an end to whaling. 'Save the Whale' slogans and car stickers were becoming common. The call for an end to commercial whaling came loudest from the United States, once the world's greatest whaling nation.

Albany, of course, was different from any other town in Australia. Whales were the town's bread and butter, and pay packets depended heavily on the industry. Whalers in Albany were still heroes, but there was an air of unease. The newspapers carried stories of moves against whalers elsewhere in the world. People wondered how long it would be before Greenpeace came to Albany. The day would come, perhaps sooner than expected.

Whaling employed the breadwinners of 200 families in Albany. Many others were indirectly dependent on the Whaling Station operations. From the blacksmiths who straightened bent harpoons to the fuel contractors, stock food specialists, electricians, diesel mechanics, truck drivers and the proprietors of the London Hotel where whalers slaked their thirst . . . All had some sort of stake in the whales we had seen on the slip.

There were other problems beside the conservationists.

The whalechasers were old vessels, rusted veterans of whaling operations all over the world, from the Falkland Islands to Antarctica and the coasts of South America. Bought secondhand 'for a song' at the end of their normal working lives, they had been coaxed to sea for years beyond their time.

The whaleships were surveyed each year by Commonwealth inspectors. But the necessary certificates of seaworthiness were being obtained with increasing difficulty. There were stories of holes in rusted upper works being patched with fibreglass and even with cardboard painted over to pass inspection.

Replacements were needed urgently. But to build a new fleet would cost millions of dollars.

Whaleships were specialist vessels. They were high-speed, swift-turning terriers of the sea built for the chase. Their bowels were entirely filled with engines and machinery. They could not be used for cargo or any other kind of fishing or indeed for any other purpose except what they were designed for.

That was killing whales. It was common talk in the town that the company would be crazy to make a major investment in an industry which might be all too shortlived.

And if all that were not enough, there were the Russian and Japanese fleets down 'in the ice', cruising among the Antarctic floes. The reports of the harpoon guns echoing off the bergs, the glittering ice mountains . . .

The International Whaling Commission quota of sperm whales for the Russians in that year of 1976 was 4752 sperms in the northern hemisphere and 3841 south of the equator. For Japanese whales it was 1497 in the north and 301 in the south.

In 1976 the Cheynes Beach Whaling Co. at Albany took 994 sperms. Their quota was reduced in following years to less than 700.

In 1976, also, the word among whalers was that the Russians especially were ignoring all regulations. 'Killing everything with a spout like there was no tomorrow.' Because indeed there would be no tomorrow if world opinion had its way.

The humpbacks and blues had been hunted to near extinction. How much longer could the sperms, the staple fish of the Albany whalers, stand the hunting pressure?

In baseball terms, whaling in Albany was on strike three. The whalers themselves were uneasy about their future. What does a man who has worked half his life in a specialised industry do when his occupation faces extinction? What other careers call for the skills of a whaling master gunner?

When we arrived, the first 'Save the Whale' slogans had been pasted up on Albany billboards. Surreptitiously slapped on in darkness, they were angrily torn down in daylight. But all the indications were there for those who could read them. International film crews like the Cousteaus were preaching the new doctrine of conservation in their television programs. As filmmakers we had been warned to expect some resentment, perhaps even actual hostility.

We were surprised to find that the whalers, both the company and the individuals, could hardly have been more co-operative. Everyone we spoke with was interested in what we were doing. Sharks had been a part of their scene as long as whaleships had been going to sea, and our underwater view was a new perspective. 'What do they look like?' we were asked. 'Aren't you scared?'

No other modern industry, obsessed as everyone is today with the fear of accident and litigation, would have permitted our kind of intrusion into their daily operations.

Cheynes Beach Whaling Co. manager Mick Walters allowed us to moor our boat and shark cage right among the dead whales, where we tried not to hinder the tugboat crew. When a wire broke in the camera a company electrician soldered it. When there was a problem with an outboard motor the engineer took a look. A sudden storm one evening broke the mooring and blew my boat ashore. The tugboat crew roused us at midnight and helped us get it off the lee shore, joking that they supposed we would be 'in the bloody way again' next time there were whales.

Watching the workings of the Station we were aware that the story of our whales and sharks really began far out at sea. Perhaps, to get the whole picture, we should be looking at the apex predators in our food chain. Whalers and sharks, on the continental shelf.

'Sure,' said Mick Walters, when I asked if I could take some surface shots at sea. 'Be at the Town Jetty at 4 a.m.' He grinned and added, 'If you haven't got good sea legs, better take some seasick pills'.

The whalechasers went out long before the rest of the town was out of bed. As they dipped through the darkness of King Georges Sound, the only signs of them were the pinpoints of their red, green and white navigation lights and the deep throb of their engines. As they reached Limestone Head at the entrance to the Sound, the new day's dawn would be breaking, pale pink, over Mt Many Peaks far to the east, and the vessels' bows would begin lifting to the Southern Ocean swell.

One of the visitors on my trip made a sudden dancing, lurching run towards the rail, hand to mouth.

'Poor bastard!' someone said. 'He's got a long day ahead of him!' The whaler's 'day' often ended as late as midnight. For someone already seasick before morning coffee the prospects were unenviable. I averted my eyes, not entirely from politeness. The curse of *mal de mer* can be contagious.

There is no record that seasickness ever killed anyone aboard an Albany whaler. But there have been plenty of people through the years, heaved and tossed, who lost their breakfast and previous night's dinner . . . who may have imagined (by late afternoon) that they were losing something from the previous week. The whaleships had what was sometimes euphemistically called 'a lively action in a sea'.

'Bloody understatement,' said Ches Stubbs, many years a whaling skipper. 'Buggers'll roll in a saucer!'

The ships that had loomed so large beside the wharf as night shadows seemed small indeed in the open sea as they rolled between the swells. *Cheynes II* and *Cheynes III* were 45 metres in length and 437 tonnes. *Cheynes IV* was slightly bigger at 538 tonnes. Occasionally the other boats disappeared from sight in the wave troughs between the shouldering Southern Ocean swells.

The crews came from all nations. In 1976 the three skippers were Axel Christiansen, originally from Norway, Gordon Cruickshank, who spoke with a strong Scottish accent, and Paddy Hart, who had a soft Irish brogue. Kase van der Gaag spent his childhood in Holland and first went to sea in Netherlands merchant ships. The newest of the Cheynes Beach skippers, he held the record of 12 whales caught in one day, and for the biggest sperm caught off the Australian coast. The big bull was 16.7 metres (55 feet).

Why were these vessels, antiques in their trade, but still stout little ships, heading for sea?

In 1976 whaling was still a viable commercial proposition. Whale oil, especially the 'case' sperm whale oil from the spermaceti in the head, had unique properties that could not then be duplicated by any vegetable or mineral oil. It was the 'oiliest' oil, used for purposes as diverse as lubricating the transmissions of nuclear-powered submarines and oiling expensive instruments and wristlet watches. Whale oil was also used in the manufacture of soaps, perfumes, lipsticks and beauty creams. At the Albany Whaling Station the meat and bones were cooked and ground down into stock food and fertiliser. Even the ivory teeth found a market.

In a bizarre touch the flensers, in their spare moments, skinned and dried the bull's penises to windsock size and shape. Some were nearly 3 metres long. They grinned cheekily and sold them to tourists as 'Moby's Dick'.

'The only thing that's not used,' joked Mick Walters, 'is the blow. And we're working on that!'

Even as he spoke in jest, scientists in other parts of the world were nearing the end of their very serious search to find a vegetable oil which would rival the properties of whale oil and be cheaper to produce.

And these whales we were to hunt? What was known about them?

Sperms are not only the most sociable cetaceans, they are also the most numerous of all the larger whales. One reason why they were the last to be hunted. Today there may be more than 1.5 million sperms worldwide.

They live well-organised but curiously segregated lives. Females and calves stay together in family groups of 20 to 30 animals for protection against their only predators, the packs of killer whales. 'When killers threaten the calves,' Ches Stubbs told me, 'the old ladies form a circle with the calves in the centre. They take turns to blow so that one is always watching.'

When male calves reach puberty, at about the age of six years, they leave the family group and form bachelor herds which may have as many as 50 animals.

Sperm bulls do not begin breeding until they are nearly 30 years old. At that time they become solitary swimmers, perhaps because their immense bulk requires too much food to share. Like humans they may live to 70 years or more.

All sperms eat squid, with sharks, large pelagic fish and eels forming an occasional part of their diet. Probably, if sucker scars are any indication, only the old bulls tackle the giant squid. Sperms are found in the Arctic and Antarctic and the tropics in all the great oceans of the world. The cows and calves spent most of their time in tropical waters near the equator. 'On the line' the old whalers called it. The young bulls prefer temperate seas like those of Australia, New Zealand, South Africa and South America. Or the seas off Japan in the Pacific and off the Azores in the Atlantic. The old bulls tend to frequent 'the ice', swimming between the frosted floes and the white crystal palaces of the bergs in the Arctic or Antarctic.

Sperm bulls with Atlantic Greenland harpoons embedded in their hides were sometimes found by old-time whalers in the North Pacific, indicating that they must have found a northwest passage — something which frustrated human explorers for hundreds of years.

Off Albany the whales usually travelled east to west against the set of the current. When the whalechasers reached the continental shelf they altered course and steamed east to meet the whales, with a distance of 8 kilometres between chasers. Above, a spotter aircraft made its own search pattern in an 80 kilometre 'box'.

Aboard the whaler, I was always amazed at how much sea life there was around us. Looking from the shore, the impression might be one of an empty ocean — blue leagues of desert swells reflecting cloud patterns in a sea rolling endlessly beneath the sky. But out on the 'Shelf', with Australia disappearing below the northern horizon, there always seemed to be something to see. There were schools of dolphins, and we passed by spouts of sei whales and minke whales which were not our quarry. Occasionally a pod of killer whales would pass purposefully in the distance, unmistakable with their black and white bodies and knifeblade dorsal fins.

In the 1970s, orcas were seen in the same light as sharks. The whalers had observed them tearing whale calves to bloody rags of flesh.

'Black an' white bastards!' someone muttered on the bridge.

The variety of seabirds was astonishing. Wandering albatrosses, with 2.7 metre wingspans, skimmed the crests of the waves in our wake, gliding effortlessly with scarcely a wingbeat. Flocks of dark shearwaters, or muttonbirds, flitted through the wave troughs, lightly brushing the sea with their wing tips. There were giant black petrels and their relations the speckled

171

cape petrels with thick bodies. Raucous skua gulls, delicate fairy prions and other oceanic birds seldom seen close to land winged around the ship.

Among the smaller birds were the tiny storm petrels, black and white and rather like an oceanic willie wagtail. They were barely as big as a swallow and the sailors called them 'come-to-Jesus birds' from their habit of dabbing at the wavetops with tiny webbed feet. They did indeed look as though they were walking on the water. The storm petrels had a fluttery flight like the wagtail ashore. They looked too frail and delicate to be creatures of the open ocean. It seemed that the first good puff of wind must blow them all away like thistledown. Yet they inhabit the windiest region of the world, the 'Roaring Forties', and are one of the most numerous of all seabirds.

There were spouts of whales ahead. Sperms! The kind of whales our whalers wanted to see. They blew thick bushy spouts, angling to the left at 90 degrees, the 'blow' that characterised sperm whales. We looked expectantly up to the crow's nest at the top of the foremast, that piece of whaling furniture almost unchanged since sailing ship days. But the lookout, showing as a head in a striped woollen beanie, above the top of the barrel, leaned out and made a sideways motion with his hand.

'Cows and calves!' he called down.

The skipper nodded. Cows were not on the list today and no whaler would knowingly take a cow which had a calf. The calves took milk at the breast until they were nearly full grown. Without a mother they would starve and fall victim to the killer whales.

On to the sharks.

But suddenly there was action.

'Blow!' cried the lookout, that age-old call. 'Blo-o-o-w! She blows-oh!'

'Where away?' called the skipper, shading his eyes with a hand as he looked up to the barrel.

'Port, 11 o'clock. About a mile and a half!'

In the far distance a great bushy spout hung on the air. A lone bull sperm. Instantly the atmosphere on the vessel became electric.

'Full ahead!' called the skipper down the voice tube to the engine room. 'Chasing speed!' Bells rang as he pushed the levers on the telegraph to their limit.

'Chasing speed!' replied a muffled echo up the tube from an engineer down in the bowels of the ship.

The engines took on a new throbbing, pulsing beat that shook all the rivets in the ship's tired old hull. But, game as an old racehorse, she increased momentum until she was surging through the waves, cresting through the tops of the swells like an eager steed bounding over fences. Spray threw white either side of the gun platform, and black smoke poured from the ship's funnel. The hunt was on.

The crew moved quietly to their places in readiness. Each man had a job to do.

'Check the gear!' the skipper's voice was quiet but intense.

The harpoon and its equipment had already been carefully examined to ensure that everything, including and especially the gun, was in readiness for firing. But it was checked again. The skipper had binoculars to his eyes, peering into the sun-glitter ahead.

'On screen!' cried the sonar operator in his little cabin on the left of the bridge.

'One mile ahead. Red, slightly on your port bow!' The crackling voice on the radio come from the spotter aircraft. Moments later there was an engine roar and the Cessna did a vertical wing turn above us.

'Keep him in sight!' the skipper muttered.

The throb of the engine was now urgent as a drumbeat, the metal plates vibrating beneath our feet.

'Five hundred yards!' from the crows nest.

'Closing!' from the aircraft radio. 'Ten boat lengths. You'll see him in a minute!'

'Half speed!' the skipper called down the voice tube, and pulled back on the engine telegraph levers. 'Don't run me over the top of the bastard!'

'On screen,' confirmed Sonar.

'You take her!' the skipper called to the first mate, and began running down the catwalk, sliding his hands on the rails either side. As he reached the gun platform a great black back broke the surface ahead of us and I was reminded of the descriptions I had read of sperm whales in *Moby Dick*.

'Close under our lee,' wrote Melville. 'Not 40 fathoms off, a gigantic sperm whale lay rolling in the water like the capsized hull of a frigate, his broad glossy back an Ethiopian hue, glistening in the sun's rays like a mirror!'

Our whale, like Melville's, seemed enormous. Bigger than anything I had imagined. His square head was away from us, pushing up a bow wave like a steamship, and the tail seemed as wide as our vessel. Suddenly the flukes went up in the air, and there was a flurry of spray. The skipper was in the act of unlocking the gun and swinging it to port when the whale dived and disappeared.

He left a huge swirl in the water marking his passage. 'The footprint' the whalers called it.

'God damn!' cursed the skipper making his way back up the catwalk.

'Got him, Sonar?'

'Fifty fathoms going down, 45 degrees red. Angling to port.'

'Keep on track.'

To the engine room: 'Half speed.'

'Half speed it is.'

Now there was a temporary relaxation for us. But not for the bull. He could stay down nearly an hour. But the sonar would follow him all the way, the aircraft would watch for him to reappear. The vessel would be waiting, the harpoon gun loaded and ready.

'Listen to this,' said Sonar. I put the earphones on and heard a sound like castanets, or horses hooves on cobblestones. There was a lot of background noise. Clicks, whistles, squeals. 'The clacks are the bull,' said Sonar. 'Sperm whales talk all the time.'

'And the others?'

'The cows and calves. Maybe some dolphins. If there are pilot whales around they make such a racket we can't even hear the sperms.'

The sound was another new dimension on life deep in the ocean. Did sharks make sounds? Talk to each other? No one could tell me.

Looking around the vessel, I saw the skipper and crew tensed as they waited to renew the hunt and I was conscious that this ship, and the whaling industry itself, were already obsolete. They would all soon be a part of history, disappearing into obscurity like the bull which had just dived before our bows.

'You're lucky to be out on such a beautiful day,' commented the skipper. He added wryly, 'There may not be too many more of 'em!'

These were perhaps the most skilled seamen on the Australian coast. Who else had the task of trying to get chains around the tail of 50 tons of dead whale in the heaving madness of the open sea? The swell rising and falling and threatening to dump the whale on top of the men at the rail. A 35 knot wind screaming around their ears, the sea foaming aboard green around their knees, as they sought to make the whale fast for towing. Repeating the performance, perhaps, until the ship was towing three whales either side. Each one fastened tightly in with chains. That was seamanship.

But what use would these skills be when whaling finished? These Australian whalers, as professionals, were about to become extinct.

Soon enough there would only be memories, and there was a rich store of those...

174

In the two decades of sperm whaling there had been some dramatic events at sea. The time to hear about them, of course, was not the slippery slanting deck of a whalechaser when the crew had a job to do. The 'University of Whaling' was the London Hotel in Albany, where the crew gathered to 'sink a few' after the hard day's work was done. It has been remarked that whaling seemed to generate a thirst in proportion to the size of the quarry.

That was the place to hear how Ches Stubbs lost his foot. Or about the rescue at The Gap...

'There's a guy gone off The Gap.' The message came over radio on the *Cheynes II*, late one afternoon in March 1978. 'Can you help?'

Everyone in the Albany knew about The Gap. It was a death trap for anyone who fell in the water there. No one liked to be involved in a tragedy.

'We'll give it a try,' said skipper Paddy Hart doubtfully. 'We won't reach there until after dark. That doesn't give him much of a show.'

'There's no other vessel in the vicinity,' was the reply. 'You're his only hope.'

It was unusual that *Cheynes II* was heading home early with no whales. A stroke of luck for the man in the water, maybe. But on board the whaler there was a glum silence. The general opinion was that he had no chance. No chance at all. The tourist had fallen off cliffs on one of the most rugged coasts in Australia. The Gap was a spectacular rock formation on the ocean side of the peninsula which protected King George's Sound. Huge Southern Ocean seas smashed continually against sloping granite rocks, throwing spray as high as the cliff tops.

Through the years a number of people had drowned at The Gap, a place notorious for 'king waves' which caught sightseers unaware. Once a person was in the sea at that place with its vertical rocks no one could get to them. Even if they were strong swimmers they were so far from any break in the cliffs where they could get ashore that they almost always drowned. The water was cold and rough, the white foam margin at the cliff edge had little buoyancy for a swimmer.

When *Cheynes II* arrived off the cliffs after dark that day a huge swell was running. They were the conditions in which people fell victim. They were often high up the cliff, believing that they were safe. But they would be swallowed up by a wave which ran up the granite face, caught them in the backwash, and sucked them down to their doom.

Stephen Mathews of Modbury, Adelaide, had been sightseeing at The Gap with a group of friends. He had walked down to take a photograph below a formation called the Natural Bridge when he was swept away.

175

The swell was so high that day that Police Sergeant Terry Goodman, who had established a radio post with lights and a beacon fire on the cliffs, sometimes lost sight of *Cheynes II* as she dropped in the troughs between the waves. It was no place for a vessel to be on a lee shore in the dark. No one knew what the depth of water was on the edge of the cliffs or whether there were lone spires of rock offshore that might rip her bottom out.

But the news from police radio was good. The victim, aged 20, was weak but still afloat. Paddy Hart took *Cheynes II* within 200 metres, as close to the cliffs as he dared.

On the cliffs the police bonfire gave direction. John Bell was flying the whale spotter aircraft backwards and forwards at low level with his landing lights on. Neither the pilot nor the people on the cliff could be of any physical assistance. They could only try to maintain the morale of the swimmer. To tell him to hang on a little longer, that help was on the way.

As they had said, *Cheynes II* was his only hope.

The first problem was how to find the single tiny speck of an exhausted swimmer's head in darkness in that sea. The next difficulty would be getting him aboard a 437 tonne vessel rolling and pitching diabolically as though in protest at her own danger.

The noise of the radio calls, the aircraft roar and the sound of the whalechaser's own engine made it difficult to see or hear. Albany historian Gary Tonkin recalled in 1994, in his article, 'More Stories of the *Cheynes II*: A Dramatic Rescue', that skipper Paddy Hart 'made the brave decision' to cut the engine and order radio silence.

In the quiet that followed a faint cry for help was heard. The lookout aloft in the barrel had a momentary sight of the swimmer's pale face far away in the black water. Without hesitation the vessel's mate, Keith Richardson, stripped and dived over the rail and swam through the blackness in the direction the lookout indicated, towing a lifeline around his waist.

He reached Mathews 70 metres away and tied the line around him. Then willing hands pulled them back to the drifting ship. The engines were fired again while they were still being dragged aboard. It was none too soon. The propeller actually chipped rock as Paddy Hart gave the order 'Full astern!'

'I didn't realise the pressure that was on the guys in the engine room,' Paddy Hart told Gary Tonkin later. 'The engines were shut down and they knew we were in great danger. But they couldn't see what was going on.'

The sonar readout showed a continuous black line, indicating that there had been no depth below the vessel.

Mathews himself, who suffered a broken heel and extensive lacerations, said that when the wave washed him off the cliff he rolled over a shallow bottom for some distance. 'I went over and over in somersaults along the bottom. I didn't even know where the surface was. When I came up I was beyond the breakers. My whole life went before me in those few seconds.'

In later years a plaque to commemorate the act of bravery was placed by The Gap at Natural Bridge. It was hoped that it would also act as a warning to others. But The Gap has continued to claim its victims. Few have been as lucky as Stephen Mathews. There are no whaleships to call on today.

There were other dramatic episodes involving Cheynes Beach Whaling Co. vessels. It was, after all, a hazardous occupation. Whales rammed ships, harpoon lines wound around propellers in lee-shore situations, a spotter aircraft crashed after takeoff, killing the pilot. There were other injuries and accidents, all considered a natural part of one of the ocean's oldest professions.

The day Ches Stubbs lost his left foot brought out the best in the men he sailed with. Especially John Bell, the pilot, who was flying the spotter aircraft that day.

The date was 22 October 1965 and the cause of the accident was simple enough. While chasing a whale, at *Cheynes III's* maximum speed of 14 knots, the vessel dipped her bow in a heavy swell and took a sea-green over the gun platform. It washed several fathoms of fore-runner line across the gundeck. At that moment Ches Stubbs was sighting the gun, with his eyes riveted on a bull sperm whale which was about to surface ahead. As the whale blew its spout he fired, unaware that his leg was now within a bight of the fore-runner. Ches said later that his first impression was of the gun coming back fast towards him. He had heard of guns breaking their mounts, carrying backwards and killing their gunner. He thought this was happening to him.

'Actually I was being dragged into the gun by the fore-runner round my left leg.'

The impact stunned him. When he regained consciousness, he recalled, 'My feet were in the air and when I started thinking clearly again I realised that there was no foot on my left leg'.

Still on his back he asked the seaman above in the crow's nest what had happened.

'You missed the bastard,' the man told him.

'He hadn't realised the reason I was flat on my back. But when I saw the blood spurting out of the bottom of what was left of my leg all the seriousness hit me. What a hell of a way to die! I thought. Bleeding to death out here!'

Despite the pain and shock some of Stubbs' residual humour remained. The crew ran down from the bridge to a gundeck now slippery with the blood spurting from his leg. In their own shock they asked the obvious question: What happened?

'Can't you see? Me fucking foot's gone for cray bait!' shouted Ches from his inverted position. 'Get a tourniquet, quick!'

A little later: 'There was a new shoe on that foot. Better see if you can get it back!'

The situation at that point was actually grim. *Cheynes III* was a full three hours' steaming time from port. If the skipper did not reach a hospital to receive a blood transfusion soon there was a strong probability that he would die from shock and loss of blood.

The company had used various aircraft for spotting. Most were land-based with conventional wheeled undercarriages. By good fortune on that day John Bell, the Albany region's most experienced pilot, was flying a Cessna 303 fitted with floats. Theoretically it was possible to land such an aircraft in the open sea. But only if the weather were very favourable and there was a complete absence of swell. With the high southwest swell running on that October day, landing would be like driving a motor car at 130 kilometres an hour and suddenly encountering a series of house-high humps in the road. Each one immediately behind the other, but presenting different angles.

John Bell was aware of the risk. But he also knew, from the condition of Ches Stubbs as described to him on the ship-to-aircraft radio, that he was the skipper's only chance of survival.

By some sort of miracle he managed to get the Cessna down without flipping it over. There remained the problems of transferring the injured skipper from *Cheynes III* to the aircraft. Most difficult of all would be the takeoff. Trying to get up sufficient speed between and over the bumps of the swells for the aircraft to fly.

It was decided to use the plane's own rubber raft for the transfer. It could only carry two people. Alf Laurence the chief engineer volunteered at once. The other person had to be Ches himself.

There were no paddles and Alf had to use the wooden floorboards. 'We only went around in circles,' Ches said, 'so I started paddling too. But I was pretty weak and it was going to take a long, long time to reach that plane 100 yards [90 metres] away.'

Disregarding the sharks which may have been following the ship in expectation of a kill, Paddy Hart dived overboard and swam the raft to the aircraft.

The two other whalechasers, meanwhile, had been laying oil-streaks to calm the sea. But the first attempt at takeoff was a near disaster. 'We were hitting every wave with a heavy jar,' Ches recalled. 'Then the starboard float dipped into a wave and slewed the plane around, dipping the wing under water. I was in the back seat and water came up green over the window. I swear I was looking down into blue depths. That was how close we were to going over.'

'We'll have to drop you, Alf,' John Bell said. 'She'll never get off the water with this weight.'

'I can't swim a stroke,' said Alf, 'so you'd better get me as close as you can!'

With a couple of kilometres of blue ocean underneath him he launched himself bravely off the float towards the raft, and prayed he wouldn't sink before he reached it.

'Alf took one dive into the water,' Ches said. 'I never saw him come up until he grabbed the raft.'

John Bell, using his radio, had the ships make a wake for him to take some of the peaks out of the swell. Somehow he coaxed the Cessna into the air by running along the crests of the waves. 'It was touch and go,' he said later. 'I wouldn't like to have to do it again.'

Then he had the problem that Ches Stubbs passed out and kept falling unconscious over the controls. Amazingly, the time between Stubbs losing his foot, 65 kilometres from land, and arriving in hospital was only 55 minutes.

'The last thing I remembered,' Ches said later, 'was asking Dr Fitzpatrick for a cigarette and being sick on one of the nursing sisters...'

Fitted with an artificial foot, Ches was stumping the gundeck next season — and for years after that until he retired to carve delicate scrimshaw on whale teeth and to write a vivid book of his recollections, titled *I Remember*. In that time, as master gunner, he took 5000 whales.

He carved me a beautiful tooth with two Great White sharks swimming its ivory surface. While he carved he told me stories about whaling. They included the sad tale of the 'follow fish'.

'When we were whaling humpbacks we mostly found them in pairs,' he said. 'The female was usually bigger, and if she were harpooned the male would not leave her and would be harpooned afterwards. But if the male were harpooned first the female would never stay.'

Whalers always tried to identify the female, and shoot her first. The male, faithful unto death, was called the 'follow fish'.

'It was the opposite with sperms,' said Ches. 'If a cow were shot any bulls in the vicinity would head for the horizon. But the other cows would come

179

to help the wounded one. They would get underneath her and push her to the surface so that she could breath. They had complete disregard for their own danger.'

That was one of the reasons, he said, why whalers hated shooting cows.

Now, out at sea, the big bull was rising and the moment of truth was at hand.

'Coming up,' said Sonar. 'Green. 20 degrees starboard. Angle 45 degrees.'

'Right,' said the skipper down the voice tube. 'Slow ahead!' And the bells rang as he set the engine room telegraph.

'Slow ahead, it is,' came the muffled voice of the engineer back up the tube.

'Half speed ahead!' called the skipper. The radio crackled to life and we heard the spotter plane overhead. 'Four boat lengths ahead! Coming up starboard!'

'Chasing speed!'

The big bull was rising and the skipper aimed to be there to meet him.

Between the chaser, the sonar and the spotter plane, I figured, the whale didn't have much of a chance. That was the way it was intended.

'You take her!' the skipper said to the mate, and ran down the catwalk to the gundeck. There he waved back to the mate.

'Take the way off her!'

All eyes were on the water ahead. In moments the whale would appear. The gun swung from side to side, the harpoon's sinister shape questing like the muzzle of a hound taking a scent.

The harpoon was 6 feet (nearly 2 metres) long and weighed the better part of 90 kilograms. It had four 30 centimetre barbs which opened out like umbrella spokes inside the whale. Screwed on the tip was a long grenade which exploded on a 6 second fuse. Filling the whale's internals with shrapnel.

It took two men to load a harpoon into the barrel of the gun, and in the air it trailed a nylon fore-runner rope with a breaking strain of 8000 kilograms. This was spliced to a thicker rope with 12 700 kilograms breaking strain. In all there was 800 metres of line running through an ingenious system of springs and pulleys to take the shock of 50 tonnes of agonised whale throwing itself about at the other end.

In theory the whale should be killed when the grenade detonated. Dead in a single shot. In practice, more often than not, a second shot with a 'killer' harpoon was required. This was an old harpoon with no barbs, which could be winched back after firing. Its purpose to provide the *coup de grace*.

A good gunner could usually end the stricken whale's flurries with one 'killer' shot. But on a very bad day with a feisty whale, as many as five 'killers' might be required. Skipper and crew cursing alike, because aside from the loss of time — and time was money in whaling as in businesses ashore — no one enjoyed the butchery part of the job.

The whalers respected the whales. They came to know them well in those waters of the Southern Ocean. They watched bulls 'in conference', numbers of males in a circle with their heads in the centre, socialising with each other. They saw the defences against killer whales, cows taking turns to blow with the calves in the centre. Watched cows trying to encourage a wounded member of their pod.

'They be talking to it all the time in their clacking way,' Ches Stubbs said. 'You could hear them on the gundeck.'

'Those were sad incidents,' he went on. 'It made me compare the human race to these harmless mammals. They haven't got that "Up you Jack, I'm alright" system. There is none of the selfishness or jealousy that is so prevalent with human males and females. They look after each other better than we do.'

I thought of what he had told me out on the whalechaser.

But now our bull sperm whale was rising...

'Blow! Blo-o-o-o-w!' from the crow's nest. 'Coming up dead ahead!'

'One boat length!' from the spotter aircraft.

'Coming up now!' called the man in the barrel.

'I see him!' shouted the skipper. 'Take the way off her!'

A huge black back, gnarled and looking like the keel of an upturned vessel, bursts through the water under the bow. Sunlight glinting in a thousand sparkles.

Whoosh!

A thick spout of condensation and water erupts from the nostril on the left side of the whale's head. A hollow roaring sound.

'Now!' says someone on the bridge. 'What the Christ is he waiting for?'

The skipper hesitates, his fingers on a trigger on the long lever behind the gun, squinting down the sights, three seconds' grace in which to check for range, size and sex.

'Bl-o-o-o-ws!' from the crows nest. 'He's up!'

The skipper's lips move silently before the hand squeezes the trigger lever. 'Is he a male, for God's sake? ... How about size? OK... Right then! ... Wait for the roll...'

Bang!

A deafening explosion, fragments of wadding flying through the air, and the harpoon hurtling out with the fore-runner rope snaking behind it. The man still crouching behind the gun.

Whenever I saw that moment it seemed to me to be frozen in time. The deadly shape of the harpoon, on its way. The whale as yet unharmed. Death about to descend from the sky...

A shark attack comes with equal suddenness.

THE SHARK THAT ATTACKED A SUBMARINE

chapter ten

THOUGH ABOUT 100 SHARK ATTACKS ON HUMANS AROUND THE WORLD EACH YEAR are entered in the International Shark Attack File, the number may fall far short of the real figure. This is because no records are kept in certain regions where sharks abound offshore, such as much of Africa, the Arab countries, India, Burma, Indonesia and the Philippines.

Reports are also lacking from Latin areas of the world. Mexico, Chile, Brazil, Argentina, Venezuela, Equador, El Salvador, the Azores and Cape Verde Islands are all places where fishing is an important occupation and where sharks are commonly encountered. Yet there were only 25 reports of shark attacks from these countries on the US Shark Attack File against 1140 from the English-speaking world when Baldridge made his computer analysis in the 1970s.

But even if the true shark attack figure were five or even ten times higher, shark depredations on humans would still pale into insignificance beside the 100 million sharks caught by international fisheries each year. The 1994 haul of sharks was a staggering 3 billion pounds (1.4 billion kilograms) in weight of shark flesh. It was double the 1991 catch. Double trouble for sharks.

While sharks are said to attack humans in a 'cruel' manner, there is nothing pleasant about human methods of catching sharks. Few of us would care to spend our last hours with a steel hook skewered through our jaw, or strangling in the nylon hose of a drift net.

Yet there are worse fates.

Many of the international fishing boats do not have freezer space for shark carcasses. Instead they take the fins for the Asian sharkfin soup market. The fins and tail are sliced off the living shark. The mutilated but still living creature is then slid back writhing into the sea to die a miserable death, while the fins are dried in the rigging.

Humans call sharks 'man-eaters' and regard them as ruthless 'eating-machines'. But we might well ask who is the real predator?

If we were to take a genuinely unprejudiced view, we would have to acknowledge that sharks were here long before us. Shark ancestors were swimming in the oceans before the first insects crawled or flew and before the first living creatures appeared upon the land. They were here before the dinosaurs, and long, long before that Johnny-come-lately, the two-legged upstart *Homo sapiens*. Our own kind, who have so disturbed the world's ecological balance.

Sharks began their evolutionary climb up the ladder of life 370 to 400 million years ago. The dinosaurs had their particular period of terrestrial dominance from 125 million years to 65 million years before the present time.

In contrast, man's ape-like ancestor first stood erect on the plains of Africa no more than 9 million years ago. *Homo sapiens*, the modern human, is a product of only the last 250 000 years. A mere eyeblink in time. Around 3500 years ago our European ancestors were still dressed in skins and blue paint. Hunters of the Bronze Age.

When the word 'shark' is spoken we tend to have a mental image of a creature with a pointed nose, triangular dorsal fin, sharp teeth, and an unnatural appetite for human flesh.

Since the film *Jaws* the popular image has blown up several times in size and increased in nastiness by matching proportion.

But the real facts are that there are more than 360 species of sharks. The smallest is the dwarf shark, *Squaliolus laticaudus*, which matures at 150 mm or 6 inches and could lie in the palm of your hand. Hardly the image of *Jaws*. The largest is the giant whale shark, which may reach 12 metres or 40 feet and many tonnes in weight. Both dwarf and giant are harmless to man.

Indeed, of all the many species, only half a dozen kinds of shark could be described as dangerous to humans, and only three species fit the description of 'man-eater'. The average shark (that word again) is less than 2 metres in length and may eat crabs or sea urchins. Sharks are wonderfully evolved creatures, and may actually have gone further down the evolutionary path than humans in their adaptation to the environment. They are more advanced than the fishes.

Each kind of shark fits a particular niche in the ocean, with a remarkable diversity of shapes and sizes. The Great White, the tiger shark and the whaler family, the three man-eater groups, do fit the popular image in appearance. But there are many others which are radically different.

Take the hammerhead, for instance. Its gargoyle head looks a little similar to the business end of an old-fashioned vacuum cleaner. Head shape apart, the hammerhead's teeth, fins and body are those of a conventional shark. Why the departure from the conventional nose-cone entry?

Your guess is as good as mine. But perhaps the vacuum cleaner shape gives the hammerhead greater sensitivity in scenting and locating prey with its unique sensory apparatus. Watching the hammerhead swim, swinging its peculiar hammer-shaped head from side to side like the sweeping arm of a radar vane, you gain that impression.

The saw shark, on the other hand, has extended its nose as a flattened oarblade which may be a third the length of its body. Studded on each side of this appendage are peg-like teeth. The 'saw' makes a fearsome weapon — no mystery here. The saw-shark swims through a school of small fish swinging and swishing the saw from side to side creating piscatorial mayhem like a crusader wielding a broad sword. Then it sucks up the dead and injured fish in its small mouth, presumably with satisfaction.

There is no relationship between the saw shark and the various species of swordfish except that they all use an extended 'nose' to catch fish. The broadbills, marlin, sailfish and other billfish pursued so eagerly by human anglers are among the world's 20 000 bony fishes. These differ anatomically from sharks in some important aspects.

Bony fishes have swim bladders, their skeletons are composed of calcareous bone, and most have scales. They have one gill slit, where sharks have from five to seven. Sharks have cartilaginous skeletons, which are lighter and more flexible than bone. They have denticles on their skins instead of scales, and they do without the fishes' swim bladder. Some species, like the tiger shark, have large livers which help balance them in the water. Others like the grey nurse may create gas in their stomachs which gives them neutral buoyancy at various depths. White sharks possibly do something similar.

It has often been surmised by experts that sharks cannot rest because of the lack of a swim bladder, and that they must spend their entire lives swimming. Condemned to eternal movement, with no opportunity for repose or reflection, it is no wonder they appear such grim creatures. So it is said.

Personally I am unconvinced.

I have seen schools of grey nurse hovering motionless in reef gutters. No compulsory movement there. At Albany the Great Whites hovered at times, floating like great grey ghosts. Sometimes they sniffed the stern-drive of the boat and the keel from a vertical position, like dogs standing on their hind legs and scenting a bone on a table. They could rise or fall a few centimetres with no apparent fin movement and were obviously able to control their buoyancy at whim.

185

Their interest in the boat was curiosity.

Or were they picking up minute electrical impulses from the equipment on board? They would sometimes 'taste' the boat gently, or mouth the propeller. Their attitude to it showed clearly that they realised that it was an inanimate thing.

Their reaction to us in the cage was quite different.

We were living creatures. The heartbeat and our personal electrical field told the sharks that interesting fact. We were also mammal, and for large Great Whites mammals are preferred prey. Their aggressive movements around the cage carried their own message.

The human preoccupation with danger and therefore with dangerous sharks has meant that we have given a lot of attention to the species with the capacity to kill or injure people and far less study to the many inoffensive species.

The vast majority of sharks are small, though some of the physically less imposing may live a surprisingly long time. The spiny dogfish, *Squalus achanthius*, for instance, which only grows to 1.5 metres, lives more than 30 years, and growth rings in the cartilage of larger sharks show that they may have a similar or even longer life span. Great Whites may live as long as humans.

Sharks' diversity of shapes and sizes, their different colourations and camouflages, depend upon their role in the ocean. They range from the pelagics, ever on the move, to sedentary species like the carpet shark and angel shark. These lie motionless on the bottom, disguised by matching their colouration with the seafloor or reef. There they wait in ambush for their prey to come to them. The tropic nurse shark, *Ginglymostoma cirratum*, sometimes called 'tawny' or 'sleeper' shark, lies asleep in caves all day and wakes to hunt crabs at night.

Where does the name 'shark' come from? That most comprehensive Reader's Digest book *Sharks: Silent Hunters of the Deep* (1986) states: 'Until the mid-Sixteenth Century the word shark in English referred only to human low life.' Or was the name of a piscatorial predator applied to humans in the same sense that a gunman of the old West would insult his enemy by calling him a 'low down coyote'? Who, indeed, likes to be called an 'animal'?

There has been a suggestion that the word was introduced during the time of Queen Elizabeth I by Sir Walter Raleigh, after his voyages to the Caribbean. Or was it a corruption of Aristotle's term 'Selaches' for the sharks and rays?

Shakespeare certainly referred to the 'ravin'd salt-sea shark' in *Macbeth*, as we have already recorded.

Scientific Greeks and Romans, like Pliny the Elder, called them by Aristotle's name of *selachii*, but common folk and fishermen often referred to sharks as 'dogfishes'. The French had a similar name 'chien-de-mer'. French seamen also called Great Whites and whaler sharks 'requins' or 'requiem fish' because of the sharks' interest in corpses thrown overboard from slave ships between Africa and the Americas.

The Spaniards called sharks 'tiburon', the Portuguese 'tubarao', Italians 'squalo', the Hawaiians 'mano'. The Germans call the Great White 'Weisshai', which sounds Japanese. But the Japanese name is 'hohojiozame', the Russian 'seldevaja akula'. And so on…

A shark by any other name?

One of the problems for scientists has been the plethora of 'other names'. There are literally hundreds of them — and frequently a number of names for the same shark in different parts of the world.

Thus the Great White was 'blue pointer' or 'Tommy shark' in South Africa. In Australia it was the 'white shark', 'white pointer', 'white death' or 'Great White'. In Australia the word 'pointer' also referred to the conical snout of the *laminidae*, the mackerel-tailed sharks, and it was the mako which was called 'blue pointer'.

We have seen that scientific checks show that the 'Ganges shark' of India, the 'Zambezi shark' of East Africa, the 'Nicaragua shark' of South America and the 'bull shark' of the Gulf of Mexico and Florida are one and the same creature, *Carcharhinus leucas*.

Similarly the 'grey nurse' of Australian seas is the 'ragged tooth' shark of South Africa and the 'sand-tiger' of the United States. To the scientists it was the same fish whatever the latitude, *Eugomphodus taurus*.

Shark names and identification are often a source of confusion to people who know little about them. From the 1950s to the 1970s there were often glaring errors in reports describing the kind of shark involved in an attack. Different news media would label the same shark a 'bronze whaler', a 'white death' or a 'grey nurse', all on the same day.

Knowledge is more general nowadays, and the grey nurse is no longer wrongfully accused as a 'man-eater'. Authoritative sources like the Australian Shark Attack File kept by John West at Sydney's Taronga Zoo provide accurate information, together with identification on request. But there can still be errors in identification.

A certain means of identifying sharks accurately is, of course, to use scientific terminology. Sharks and their close but flattened relatives, the skates and rays, are collectively known to science as the *Elasmobranchii*. The bony fishes are the *Osteichthyes* — not a word to attempt at dinner with your mouth full, or after a couple of martinis. But because names like *Apristurus*

187

macrorhyncus for the flathead cat shark or *Hypogaleus lyugaeusis* for the blacktip topeshark are themselves such a mouthful, common names no doubt will persist. Most of these have been bestowed by fishermen and they make a colourful collection. The names often tell something of the nature or appearance of the creature described.

For instance, there are the basking shark and the whale shark; the hooked-tooth dogfish; the spiny, whitefin, Portuguese and long nose velvet dogfish. There are lantern sharks, hound sharks, soupfin sharks, bullheads, horned and hooded and guitar sharks, leopard and tiger sharks. There are ribbontail sharks, blackbelly dogfish, birdbeak dogfish, bamboo sharks, bigeye threshers, lantern sharks, goblin sharks — strange creatures these — freckled catsharks, monk sharks, mouse sharks, hardnose and horned sharks. There are carpet sharks, sawtailed catsharks, angel sharks, sleepers, rough skins, pygmy, tail-light and gulper sharks. Even a 'dumb gulper shark'. Perhaps the dumb gulper would prefer its scientific name *Centrophorus larrissoni*, as it is somewhat more dignified.

And there is also little *Isistius brasiliensis*. If you think that its 50 centimetre size makes it insignificant, then think again.

The 'cookie-cutter' shark is perhaps the only selachian known to have made an attack on a US Navy submarine. In fact cookie-cutters damaged no fewer than 30 subs, including a number of nuclear-powered submersibles.

Isistius lives in deep ocean layers in the tropics and swims vertically to the surface at night, rising to make impudent attacks on creatures far larger than itself. Among its victims are whales, dolphins, sharks, even swift-swimming marlin, and broadbill swordfish. The little terrier has a powerful set of jaws. It strikes its victim from below, and bites out a circular section of flesh the size of half a tennis ball. Then, with a flick of its tiny tail, it is gone before retribution can take place from the outraged giant.

We had wondered at the circular scars on the sperm whales on the Albany slip. They were too big for the circular sucker-marks of giant squid which were readily identifiable. But what else could they be?

The US Navy asked the same question.

Their submarines had a listening device which was raised before surfacing to check for approaching vessels. With so many merchant ships at sea today the possibility of collision while surfacing was always a major concern.

The devices were sheathed in rubber. During the late 1970s engineers found that these coatings were being subjected to mysterious semi-circular slashes, about 50 mm in diameter. The engineers scratched their heads but could find no answer. Then the problem was put to a marine biologist.

'*Isistius!*' he said at once. 'The cookie-cutter shark has attacked your submarine!'

The rubber covers were replaced by others made of fibreglass. There was no major damage, except to Navy pride. But if one of the rubber covers had been injured to the extent of flooding, if the listening device had been put out of action and a collision had occurred...then the cookie-cutter would have sunk a Navy submarine.

Sharks are found from the ocean deeps to water so shallow that their bellies scrape the sand, and their dorsal fins are dry. Though we know far more about them than we did 40 or even 20 years ago, we still know more about the surface of the moon than we do about the deeps of the sea. The life of the giant squid, as an example, remains a mystery to us. So does the love life of the Great White shark, though the mating scars on the females give hints of sharp-toothed passion in the depths. No trivial courtship there.

The ocean's average depth is 3730 metres, or 12 230 feet. The safe maximum for SCUBA is between 30 and 60 metres, or 100 and 200 feet, with dives possible to 84 metres (275 feet) exercising extreme care. Rig divers using submersible chambers and breathing air-gas mixtures excluding nitrogen can work in very limited conditions to 1500 feet — nearly 460 metres.

But the Marianas Trench in the northwest Pacific is 11 038 metres or 32 204 feet deep. Far beyond the prying eyes of *Homo sapiens'* present capabilities.

Does anything live down there? One of the deepwater sharks 'Megamouth' is so rare that up to the mid-1990s only nine specimens had been gathered scientifically in the world. One washed ashore on a beach near Busselton, in Western Australia, in 1988 and is now in the Western Australian Museum.

Earlier specimens came from Hawaii, California and Japan, and a later specimen was found in the Atlantic, indicating a wide distribution. But until 1976 (when one accidentally swallowed a US Navy parachute drogue off Hawaii) Megamouth, *Megachasma pelagios*, was completely unknown to science.

Megamouth is a large shark, reaching more than 4 metres, with hundreds of tiny teeth and a huge underslung mouth, as the name indicates. It lives in the midwater zones of the deep ocean and is a filter feeder.

But is it so rare, or is it that we just don't get down deep enough, often enough, to know what's going on?

Are there more unknowns like Megamouth?

The world's largest shark ever known to science was *Carcharodon megladon*. A flesh-eater, it may have been anywhere from 12 to 24 metres (40 to

80 feet) in length. It had serrated teeth shaped like a Great White's, but the fangs were 18 centimetres (7 inches) long instead of 7.5 centimetres. A predator on that kind of scale is difficult to imagine. The mind staggers at the thought of a creature that could probably have swallowed a Volkswagen Beetle or gulped one of today's Great Whites like a salmon.

Megladon lived from 50 million years ago to perhaps 2 million years ago. Recent times, so far as fossils go. It must have been abundant in its day because its teeth are found in fossil beds all around the world. They are also frequently scooped up in scientific trawl nets from the bottom of the ocean.

It is a blessing that *Megladon* is not around today. It would have been an oceanic predator on the scale of the terrible carnivorous land dinosaur *Tyrannosaurus rex*.

Fiction writers have had fun exploring the possibility that some specimens of *Megladon* may still survive in the deepest oceans. Richard Ellis, co-author with John McCosker of the definitive book *Great White Shark* (published by HarperCollins in 1991) speculates that there may be — just may be — the tantalising possibility that some specimens of *Megladon* survived long past their apparent terminal date.

He quotes a report by Australian David G. Stead in 1963 in his book *Sharks and Rays of Australian Seas*. Dr Stead was a scientist and naturalist of world standing and had authority in his field. In 1938 Stead was president of the New South Wales Naturalists' Society. He wrote:

> *In the year 1918 I recorded the sensation that had been caused among the 'outside' (ie deep water) cray fishermen at Port Stephens, when for several days they refused to go to sea to their regular fishing grounds in the vicinity of Broughton Island.*
>
> *The men had been at work on the fishing grounds, which lie in deep water, when an immense shark of almost unbelievable proportions put in an appearance, lifting pot after pot containing many crayfish, and taking as the men said 'pot, lines and all!'*
>
> *These pots, it should be mentioned, were some 3 foot 6 inches [1 metre] in diameter and frequently contained from two to three dozen crayfish, each weighing several pounds. The men were unanimous that this shark was something the like of which they had never dreamed of.*
>
> *In company with the local Fisheries Inspector I questioned many of the men very closely and they all agreed as to the gigantic stature of the beast. But the lengths they gave were, on the whole, absurd. I mention them, however as an indication of the state of mind which this unusual giant had thrown them*

into. And bear in mind that these were men who were used to the sea and all sorts of weather, and all sorts of sharks as well.

One of the crew said the shark was 300 feet [90 metres] long at least. Others said it was as long as the wharf on which we stood — about 115 feet [35 metres]. They affirmed that the water 'boiled' over a large space when the fish swam past. They were all familiar with whales which they had often seen passing at sea, but this was a vast shark. They had seen its terrible head which was 'at least as long as the roof of the wharf shed at Nelsons Bay'.

Impossible of course! But these were prosaic and rather stolid men not given to 'fish stories' nor even to talking about their catches. Furthermore they knew that the person they were talking to (myself) had heard all the fish stories years before! The thing that impressed me was that they all agreed as to the ghostly whitish colour of the vast fish.

What, then, did the fishermen see?

Whale sharks occasionally pass Broughton Island. Ben Cropp photographed a large specimen there in 1965.

But whale sharks reach a maximum size of 12 metres. They do not gobble crayfish pots and their contents. They prefer plankton and despite their bulk have a tiny throat. The fishermen would probably have been familiar with them. Stead himself knew whale sharks, at least in later years, for he wrote a very accurate description of a whale shark sighting off Crocodile Head for *The Australian Naturalist*, which was reprinted in Gilbert Whitely's book on sharks.

Was it all an outrageous invention? Or had the Port Stephens fishermen seen some living ghost from past centuries? A shark so terrible that they lost all sense of size and proportion?

Richard Ellis makes a point. Many, many fossil *Megladon* teeth have been dredged up, he says, and there are numerous impeccable scientific references. 'But not one of these described a tooth as white.' All the teeth recovered to date have been black or brown, indicating fossil origin. On the day a white tooth, indicating freshness, comes up in a trawl we will know that, somewhere out in the wide blue yonder, *Megladon* is still swimming.

I hope I never meet him.

One of the things that *everyone* knows about sharks is that they are excited by blood in the water. Like most shark folklore this may also fall somewhat short of the mark. But it is true that sharks have a phenomenal sense of smell. They have sometimes been called a 'swimming nose' or 'ocean bloodhound'.

In the Lerner Marine Laboratory in the Bahamas, as part of the US Navy's research program, scientists found that lemon sharks were able to detect tuna body juices in a ratio of one part of tuna to 25 million parts of seawater.

Whereas a hound ashore follows a scent in a straight line, sharks swim an S-course up-current. This is because the scent which attracts them is diluted in seawater and spreads wider the further it travels from the source.

It is an experience in itself to see tiger sharks swimming up a bait slick. I have watched them a number of times on Ben Cropp's boat on the Great Barrier Reef and at the Lacepede Islands in Western Australia. The fins come up-current in a series of S-bends until the sharks reach the source and begin their preliminary circling before attacking the target.

Tigers are cautious at first, but once they begin tearing at the carcass of the dead billfish or turtle they are quickly transformed into savagery. Tigers often swim in company, family groups perhaps, and once aroused compete with each other for the quarry. Biting, rolling, threshing, taking flesh and bone in gulps — while smaller fish dash in to scoop up the fragments falling below. Witnessing a tiger shark feeding frenzy sends chills up the spine. Especially if you are a diver.

Hammerheads have a different fluid swimming style as we have just noted, and have the best 'nose' of all. Their peculiarly shaped head allows the maximum passage of water over their olfactory organs as they swing their 'hammer' from side to side.

They can be a pest for gamefishermen trolling for marlin. Game fishing expert Peter Goadby writes in *Sharks: Attacks, Habits, Species*:

A hammerhead will follow a fishing boat for miles… Swimming behind the baits it generally makes a nuisance of itself. Very often the only way to get rid of the hammerhead is by pulling the baits in and running at full speed, circling in all directions to confuse this marine bloodhound. If some spare bait or fish is thrown over whilst circling, the hammerhead might lose interest before it can mutilate the carefully prepared marlin baits. However, sometimes despite all manoeuvres, the hammerhead will show up again behind the baits and grab one.

This also shows the folly of cleaning fish or throwing unused bait into the sea while people are swimming nearby. It also explains — if explanation were needed — why spearfishing attracts sharks.

Humans urinating in the water or even flushing a boat toilet may also possibly attract a shark's keen scent.

But while there is no doubting the questing efficiency of a shark's nasal organs, scent is by no means its only method of locating prey. A shark utilises a number of highly developed senses in its search for food.

Contrary to popular belief, which ascribes poor sight to sharks, most of the larger species also see as well or better than humans in their own environment. It is interesting that while Nature has evolved all kinds of creatures with different sizes, shapes and habits, the basic mechanisms which keep us going seem to be fairly standard.

Each creature, sharks included, has eyes, ears, heart, liver, and lungs or gills for extracting oxygen. The digestive systems of ruminants, the grass-eaters, are somewhat different from those of the carnivores, or meat-eaters. But the principles of the elimination and reproductive systems of the various animals have more similarities than otherwise, whatever the body shape.

Shark's eyes, like our own, have an iris, lens and retina. They can perceive objects in very dim light, obviously, since the major species hunt at night. They have a remarkable mirror-like reflecting layer behind the retina, the *tapetum lucidum*, which amplifies light at night to an extraordinary degree. They can readily distinguish shapes, colours or contrasts in laboratory tests. In fact, corneas from sharks' eyes have been successfully used as transplants for humans.

As mentioned earlier, the colour which has proved to most attract sharks, disconcertingly perhaps, is International Orange. This is the colour most often used for lifejackets, inflatable dinghies and rescue rafts. The high visibility of orange to searching aircraft or helicopters may outweigh the shark-attraction disadvantage by facilitating rescue. But an orange bathing costume or wetsuit may not be the most judicious choice of colour for recreation purposes.

A shark also hears well, sensing sound as vibrations. However, while sight, smell and hearing are undoubtedly important there is another sense, one not shared by humans, which may be most important of all. The visual evidence of the shark's highly developed electrical field sensory equipment lies in the ampullae of Lorenzini.

The ampullae of who…?

Strangely, while the ampullae of Lorenzini are mentioned in every book on sharks, few of the sources mention the origin of the name. Many people, well informed on most physical aspects of sharks, look blank when asked who Lorenzini was. The answer can be found in *Great White Shark* by Richard Ellis and John McCosker.

Stephan Lorenzini was a student who studied under the Danish scientist Neils Stensen. In 1666, while Stensen was physician to the Duke of Tuscany, Ferdinand II, the severed head of a large Great White shark was brought to the Court at Florence, where it no doubt caused a great sensation. Stensen, also known as 'Steno', conducted a thorough scientific examination of the

193

head and gave posterity an accurate description of the teeth, eyes and ears. It was Steno who gave the shark its species name *carcharias*, from the Greek word for 'rough' or 'ragged' teeth.

Lorenzini, his student, was given the task of describing in detail the mucus-filled tubes, or 'ampullae', which appear in most photographs of Great White sharks as small black dots around the nose region. Like a bad case of acne. Since the head was rotten when received and was further decomposing rapidly it may not have seemed the sweetest task of all. But the stink of shark on his fingers would result in immortality for Lorenzini. In fact these ampullae are pores, of a kind — openings in the skin which have been shown to perform an extremely important function for the shark. Lorenzini did such a good job that his name has endured, in shark literature, longer than that of his master.

The ampullae named after Lorenzini, dead now three centuries, are minute canals which respond to electrical impulses. They enable sharks to respond to low frequency sounds and vibrations, such as from a struggling fish, over long distances. These receptive canals, containing minute hairs attached to sensory cells or neuromasts, also extend along the lateral line of the shark's body.

Research over a long period by scientists such as Drs Kalmijn and Dijkgraa of the Netherlands has shown that dogfish sharks can detect weak voltage gradients as low as one hundredth of a microvolt. The tests also show that sharks are more sensitive to electrical fields than any other creature on land or sea.

The importance of this is that all creatures, including humans, have weak electrical fields emanating from their bodies.

The ability to detect the electrical impulses given out by other animals enables sharks and their cousins the rays to find prey such as flounder and crabs even when they are buried and invisible beneath sand. They help the predator sharks, which are also using their keen sense of smell and sharp eyesight, to locate prey at a distance by sensing movement and vibrations.

When we were attracting sharks for filming on the Great Barrier Reef we found, like everyone else in the business, that 'chumming' — chopping up dead fish and making a slick of blood and flesh particles downtide, in the traditional manner — was quite effective. But what really brought sharks more quickly than anything else was for someone to shoot a fish. It was the struggling vibrations of the speared fish, rather than the blood, which brought sharks at the gallop.

From this it may be reasonably surmised that the awkward movements of human swimmers — so lacking in grace compared with fish or sharks —

194

may sometimes be mistaken for a weak or injured sea creature struggling on the surface.

Laboratory tests indicate that while smell and sight are certainly involved in feeding, the electromagnetic senses may play the most important part in the final attack. Especially in dark or turbid water.

Besides attracting sharks, electrical signals can be used for a reverse effect — to send them away. A discovery of great importance, as we shall see in Chapter 15, in the search for a repellent.

The electro-receptor response of sharks to weak magnetic fields suggested to Kalmijn, the scientist, that they may also be sensitive to the earth's magnetic field. This ability may perform the role of an inbuilt compass, enabling the shark to navigate and make seasonal migrations.

Some sharks, including blues and tigers, are great travellers. Sharks can move over great distances for reasons not always clear to us. They may be following school fish, or going to a place where fish school seasonally for spawning. The urge to move on may be a matter of water temperature — too hot or too cold. Or the individual shark may just be a happy wanderer, content to roam.

The major species, Great Whites, tigers, whalers, makos, hammerheads, are found in most of the seas of the world. Great Whites and makos visit the Mediterranean, following schools of pilot whales and tuna or tunny, which in turn follow the sardine runs.

When I was in Sicily in 1958 doing archaeological diving I saw at Martzamemi the traditional tar-painted boats of the fishermen who netted big tuna and sometimes harpooned pilot whales. On their walls were the dried jaws of big mako sharks, and one man showed me with pride the tooth of a Great White, which had been embedded in the bow of his boat.

Shark tagging by institutions such as the US National Marine Fisheries Service laboratories at Narragansett, Rhode Island, has provided invaluable information on Atlantic shark movements.

The Reader's Digest work *Sharks: Silent Hunters of the Deep* reported that up to the time of publication 50 000 sharks had been tagged in a NMFS program that had been running for over 20 years.

One tiger shark tagged in the program swam 2960 kilometres (1850 miles) from New York to Costa Rica. Blue sharks crossed the Atlantic both ways, and moved across the equator from the northern hemisphere to the southern hemisphere. After being tagged in waters off New York State a blue shark swam 5980 kilometres (3740 miles) to Brazil, where it was finally hooked and brought ashore. A tagged mako swam from Virginia in the United States to the West Indies, a distance of 2410 kilometres (1500 miles), at a rate of 28 kilometres a day.

In Australia in 1973 the Fisheries Research Institute in Sydney began a tagging program based on the US model which included marlin, billfish and tuna as well as sharks. The Institute sought the co-operation of professional fishermen and amateur anglers, and in 13 years over 37 000 fish and 3 000 sharks were tagged. The recapture rate with sharks was 2 per cent.

The longest journey recorded was by a mako, which crossed the Tasman Sea to New Zealand, a distance of 2050 kilometres. But more information is expected, especially on the life span of sharks, as years go by and continued tagging produces further results.

In 1990 a school shark originally tagged by CSIRO scientists in 1955 was caught in Bass Strait near Flinders Island. The shark was about 10 years old when first tagged, but it had only grown 17 centimetres since 1955 and was only 195 kilometres from the point of first capture. Obviously a stay-at-home! The 35-year span was believed by Victoria's Marine Science Laboratories to be the world's longest period for a shark between first tagging and recapture.

The Reader's Digest shark book referred to scientific advice that 'some piked dogfish may live as long as 100 years and a similar figure is sometimes suggested for large Great White sharks, *Carcharodon carcharias*'.

The longevity of sharks is of particular concern because population losses cannot be quickly replaced, and sharks are especially vulnerable to overfishing.

Unfortunately, few records are available on the life span or movement of the Great White because, as a solitary deepwater swimmer of great size and speed, it is not easy to tag.

An American scientist, Dr Frank Carey of the US Woods Hole Oceanographic Institute, made the most of a rare opportunity in 1979 when he found a ring of Great Whites feeding off a dead fin whale floating off Montauk. He was able to implant a tiny radio transmitter in one of the Whites while it was distracted by feeding. For three and a half days before it was (presumably) dislodged, the transmitter sent back information to science. Over the period the shark swam at an average of 3.2 kilometres an hour for a distance of 190 kilometres.

At the Albany Whaling Station on the southern WA coast, in October 1967, a Great White shark was hooked on one of the custom shark hooks made by W. Ralph at the Station. The trace broke and the shark swam off. Two weeks later it was caught in a net by Bill McKenzie off Wooded Island near Esperance. Ralph's hook was still in the jaw of the 680 kilogram shark. The distance as the crow flies was about 400 kilometres, indicating an average distance of 29 kilometres a day travelled in an easterly direction. However, if the shark had followed the coast the distance would have been considerably longer.

One of the regrets about the Albany Whaling Station was the fact that the unique opportunity it offered scientists to tag and study Great White sharks in relatively easy circumstances was never utilised. There will never be another chance on the same scale. (Another study which would have been fascinating would have been analysis of the stomach contents of large sperm whale bulls to learn more about *Architeuthis princeps*, the 'Kraken' or giant squid.)

There is a common perception that sharks have a minuscule brain and are among the world's less intelligent creatures. In fact, in laboratory tests sharks have been shown to learn faster than most bony fishes and at a rate comparable with white rats and pigeons. Some sharks, like *carcharias*, have larger brains in proportion to body weight than most fishes, many birds, and some mammals.

In the United States, nurse sharks of the species *Ginglymostoma cirratum* have been trained to come at call, to touch indicated objects, to retrieve a ring thrown into their tank, and to press a target in order to receive food.

In the Harper & Row publication *Great Shark Stories* (1978) shark scientist Eugenie Clark, founder and director of the Cape Haze Marine Laboratory in Florida, tells the tragic story of a lemon shark, *Negaprion brevirostris*, which had been trained to bump a white target at the end of his pool in order to receive a reward of fish. Like many test animals this male shark had become a particular pet, from long familiarity, and was regarded with some affection.

When the target colour was changed to yellow it had unexpected and dramatic results. 'Two feet [60 centimetres] from the target,' Dr Clark wrote:

he suddenly jammed on the brakes by lowering his pectoral fins and did a backflip out of the water, sending spray over Oley, Dr Brown and me. All three sharks in the pen began acting strangely, swimming erratically, fast then slow, bumping into each other as they turned.

The male lemon shark never recovered from this experience. He refused food offered in any way, wouldn't go near even a white target, and died three months later. We felt terrible about his death. For more than a year he had been part of our daily activities… We towed the remains of this once beautiful creature out into the Gulf and watched it sink.

197

Scientists have determined that there are eight orders of shark. These are the saw sharks; carpet sharks; bullhead sharks; ground sharks; dogfish; angel sharks; the frilled or cow sharks; and mackerel sharks.

Curiously, the whaler family and tiger sharks, both dangerous to humans, are classified as 'ground sharks' though they are largely free-swimming pelagics. Great Whites, along with makos, Megamouth and the basking sharks, are all members of the 'mackerel' family, so called from the shape of their tails.

In one of the oddities of Nature some of the harmless sharks, like whale sharks and basking sharks, have very similar body and fin shapes to the man-eaters. Seen from the air, the whale shark, with its square head and brown mottled colouration, looks like a giant tiger shark. In earlier days aerial sightings of 'monster' tigers in tropic waters can be put down to the presence of the plankton-eating whale shark.

Similarly the basking shark, *Cetorhinus maximus*, which may reach 12 metres, nose to tail, looks from a helicopter or light aircraft like the sinister shape of a Great White of enormous size. It has the same mackerel tail, dorsal fin and pectorals and, from above, the head seems to have the conical entry characteristic of *carcharias*.

But *Cetorhinus* is a gentle soul. Like the whale shark it is a filter feeder — despite its great bulk, living on plankton. Don't look for boots, bodies or human skulls inside one of these peaceable monsters.

How, then, do you tell a dangerous shark from one of its harmless cousins? The one sure test is to look at the teeth.

This advice is not intended to outdo some of the wackier suggestions in the US Navy manual *Shark Sense*. It is appreciated that most sharks swim with their mouths closed. If you do get to look at their teeth in the ocean, species identification may not be your most immediate concern.

However, there are often arguments about the identity of a dead shark, and the teeth will give immediate and positive identification. Be careful even at this point and proceed with caution. Sharks can be remarkably tenacious of life. Some apparently moribund sharks have been known to 'come back to life' and snap viciously. People have been seriously injured poking their fingers in the jaws of supposedly dead sharks.

That risk recognised, it is a fact that, while Nature may have given similar shapes to a wide selection of sharks, the teeth of the various species relate specifically to their own role in the ocean. Each shark has teeth adapted to its own particular needs. No two are exactly the same, and most differ quite markedly from each other.

The most spectacular modern shark teeth, naturally, are those of *Carcharodon carcharias*, the Great White shark. In our shark cage by the dead whales at Albany we used to watch with a kind of horrified fascination the teeth occasionally chewed on the bars of our cage. Since they were so spectacular, naturally everyone wanted a Great White tooth. And, as all sharks shed teeth, there was always the chance that one of our cage gnashers would one day send a loose tooth spiralling free as it bit on the bars.

'You'd have to be quick to catch a tooth,' Peter Newstead said. 'Like a slips fieldsman in cricket. But it would be worth a try!'

'You should be filming it,' reproved Vic Martin, wagging a finger.

The incident never happened. But we had long theorised that, with sharks attacking the tough outer skin of the sperm whales tethered to the pontoon on a regular basis, there could be teeth lying on the seabed below.

'The bottom could be littered with them,' suggested Peter hopefully. 'Maybe you could pick them up by the handful.'

It was an interesting thought, with only one problem. The seabed lay only 10 to 12 metres below my boat, an easy dive in ordinary circumstances. But the limiting factor was the presence of *carcharias*, who might make an unwelcome appearance with a mouthful of still operative teeth.

The whaling men had a tradition that after three days without whales the waters around the Station were free of sharks. They used this doubtful statistic to try to cheer divers brought down to do occasional underwater jobs. These divers usually came from Perth. Albany divers were not keen about diving around the Station. They had seen the sharks for themselves.

On one occasion, after several days of rough weather without sharks, the pontoon mooring chains shifted and kinked the heavy flexible oil line connected to the Station.

'Would you mind taking a look?' asked Mick Walters, the operations manager. We could hardly refuse, since we had enjoyed the generous use of his facilities. Anyway, it gave us something to do on a no-film day. And there was the thought of those shark teeth which might be lying about.

The surface crew thought it would be a great idea and put in their individual orders for shark teeth.

I decided that if we ran a rope down through the cage to a heavy weight on the bottom we could pull the cage manually down the line once we overcame the surface buoyancy. The cage could then be tethered to the weight at the bottom, giving us a bolthole to return to in case 'Whitey' appeared with his permanent bottom-jaw grin and unsmiling black eye. We would use our normal cage system of wearing foot-weights without fins, because it would be

199

easier to work on the fuel line. Once that was done we could turn our attention to filling a bag with the shark teeth that might be there if our hunch was correct.

The descent went according to plan. We stepped out of the cage into what was normally *carcharias's* exclusive world, our heads making swivelling motions as we tried to look around 360 degrees all at once. Out in the open we felt naked and definitely nervous. It was a state of mind not noticeably improved by what lay beyond Peter's pointing finger.

All around on the seabed lay great chunks of blubber and bits of whale meat which had been bitten off by the sharks and allowed to sink. The bottom was littered with whale flesh.

It was an unexpected and unwelcome sight.

So much for the three-day theory! The blubber would still be sending out whale slick and scent over many kilometres to attract any sharks that might be around. If one did turn up he (or she) would find us defenceless and unprotected. It was a bit like walking into an 'empty' lion cage at the zoo and hearing a muffled growl behind you.

There was also a complete absence of shark teeth.

If you spend a lot of time in a shark cage with another person you become almost telepathic. In this instance there was no need for the spoken word.

Peter looked at me, and I looked at him.

'Let's get this over with! *Quick!*'

'You bet!'

Shark teeth were forgotten as we moved in slow-motion steps across the bottom, tanks on our backs. We as were as ponderous in our movements as the astronauts on the moon and aware that our return to the cage, even needled by the imperative of an emergency, would be just as slow.

We could see the kink in the oil line and the tangling chain. Fortunately it was a simple matter for us to heave together on the heavy metal links and release the corrugated python of the thigh-thick oil hose.

As we turned back the way we had come, our hearts stood still.

There was no cage!

'What the bloody hell!'

Looking up we could faintly see the reflection of the bars in the murk above our heads. The whale-greasy rope attaching it to the bottom weight had somehow slipped itself and the cage had floated happily back to its normal situation on the surface. Without us.

We had sometimes speculated about whether we could swim with no fins, and with foot-weights around our ankles, in an emergency. Suddenly we found we could, though it was far from easy.

'Where are our shark teeth?' the surface crew asked accusingly when we finally made it to the boat's stern ladder.

Peter said something unprintable.

The *carcharias* teeth we were searching for have been made so famous by *Jaws* that they scarcely need description. Great White teeth from the upper jaw are classic triangles with serrated edges that can shave the hairs off a man's arm. I have won a few beers in pubs proving it.

The bottom teeth, as previously described, are thicker and more rounded. A series of grim spikes that drive in and hold the prey when the shark strikes. As the jaws close with a pressure of some tonnes the shark twists or spins, using its body weight and the cutting action of the upper teeth to tear out a huge chunk of flesh.

Great White upper teeth, the kind people like to wear around their necks on chains, have one flat side — the side which faces to the front when the mouth opens wide — and a slightly rounded rear side. Most people wear them back to front, unaware of the natural situation. Next time you see someone with a white shark tooth, rounded side to the front, you can smile with the benefit of superior knowledge.

The teeth of Great Whites change through a lifetime. Younger *carcharias* live on fish and have slimmer teeth more suitable for catching and disabling small prey. As Great Whites become larger and heavier, past 3 to 4 metres in length, the teeth broaden to become cutting rather than holding devices.

Curiously, the same thing happens with the saltwater crocodile, *Crocodylus porosus*, another man-eater. Young crocodiles eat fish and crustaceans and have more needle-shaped teeth than the adults do. When the crocodile grows to more than 3 metres or so, and loses some of its underwater agility, it turns to surface prey — pigs, cattle, horses and sometimes the occasional unlucky human. The teeth thicken and lengthen to match those of the crocodile's ancestors, the dinosaurs. *Tyrannosaurus* on a lesser scale.

Scientists studying the bones of fossil whales and the ancestors of seals and sea lions have found the marks of shark teeth, including *Carcharodon megladon*, etched into them. They surmise that it was the growth of the large sea mammals which allowed the development of their predator *megladon*.

Megladon is sometimes described as the ancestor of the Great White because of similarities in the tooth structure. But the two may not, in fact, be as closely related as suggested. It is simply a case where the teeth evolved in similar patterns to handle similar prey.

The mako, often a brilliant cobalt blue in colour, may grow to a length of more than 4 metres. It is a deepwater shark, making spectacular leaps as high

201

as 7 metres. It may be the fastest shark of all when hooked on gamefishing tackle and, though it has a similar — though sleeker and smaller — body shape and mackerel tail to the Great White, it has very different teeth. Instead of the familiar serrated triangles the mako has long hooked teeth, like crooked fingers, for immobilising fast-swimming prey like tuna and bonito. The mako strikes the fish ahead of the tail, leaving it helpless in the face of a swirling secondary attack.

Grey nurse, the 'sand tiger' of Florida and the Gulf of Mexico, is a slow-swimming sedentary shark rarely exceeding 3 metres in length, but can also swim surprisingly fast in a short burst of speed over a few metres. It lives on school fish, but feeds on smaller varieties of fish than the mako does. In Australia it follows salmon and herring schools. In consequence its teeth are also hooked and needle-sharp like those of the mako. But they are finer and less robust, given the smaller scale of prey.

Whereas the mako is a bluewater shark and has a vee-shaped mackerel tail for speed, the grey nurse works inshore and has a floppy tail with a long top lobe and scarcely any bottom lobe, so it can swim with its belly scraping the sand in the shallows.

The tiger shark, by contrast, has very distinctive teeth, unlike those of any other kind of shark. They are curved scimitars with pointed tips and a serrated cutting edge on the cusp.

The tiger's favourite prey is turtle and the teeth have evolved to bite and cut through turtle shell. For this reason the tip of the tooth is a strong, sharp spike, and the serrated section of the tooth makes an angled 'tin-opener' cut in the tough turtle carapace once the incision is made.

The whaler family of sharks have 'utility' teeth adaptable to a variety of circumstances. They are spiked and sharp enough to hold prey. But the top row are triangular and able to bite bigger chunks from larger animals if the opportunity does occur.

Hammerhead teeth are curious. The bottom teeth are large, well-developed spikes almost like a Great White's. The top teeth are offset triangles like a whaler's. In the large hammerheads like *Sphyrna mokarran*, the great hammerhead, which may grow to 6 metres, the well-developed teeth give a picture of a predator that should command more respect than we usually accord the species.

The giant whale shark, on the other hand, has thousands of tiny teeth in 300 bands, which give rise to its scientific name *Rhiniodontae typus*, meaning 'file teeth'. The teeth play little part in its ingesting of food. The whale shark is a filter-feeder, straining plankton through its gills.

The nurse shark of the Great Barrier Reef, the Gulf of Mexico and tropical seas, *Ginglymostoma cirratum*, sometimes called the tawny or sleeper shark, has no teeth in the conventional sense. Its bony crushing plates are similar to those of the stingrays. The crushers show that the nurse shark, which also eats crustaceans, probably relies mainly on shellfish for its diet.

The lack of teeth doesn't mean that the nurse shark can't give a decent bite. Because the nurse likes to lie somnolent in caves during the day, some divers have been tempted to pull their tails and inflect other indignities upon them. Presumably this is so that they could boast to their friends, 'I pulled a shark by the tail today'.

Beware the wrath of the meek!

On a number of occasions nurse sharks have decided 'enough is enough' and turned on their tormentors with surprising vigour. The crushing bite can leave nasty bruises and even permanent scars. Sometimes nurse sharks have hung on to their victims — tables turned — with such persistence that their jaws have had to be prised apart.

Don't do it.

In the whole *Elasmobranch* family of sharks and rays, the most curious development is probably the barbed sting of the stingray or stingaree.

This is basically a defensive weapon to protect a creature which lies flat on the seabed like an inverted saucer. The sting, or spike, is close to the base of the tail, and comes erect when the tail curves over the back, in the manner of a scorpion.

The poison, a slime in the barbed grooves of the spike, can be very virulent, causing severe pain and — in the case of humans — hospitalisation. With very big rays, such as the harbour stingray, the sting may be 25 centimetres in length. There have been rare instances of people being killed in Australian waters by accidentally swimming over big stingrays, which have acted defensively. While stingrays are normally not aggressive, it is wise never to swim directly over them. And, of course, avoid treading on rays in shallow water.

Other members of the ray family, such as skates, fiddle sharks and guitar sharks, have no stings or defence mechanisms, and seem to survive quite happily without them. How?

That question remains one of the ocean's many mysteries. But one other member of the ray family has developed an unusual and highly effective defence, as I can personally testify.

The numbfish or electric ray, *Hypnos monopterygium*, a member of the *Torpedinidae*, can put out an electric shock of astonishingly high voltage. The equivalent, it is believed, of at least 200 volts.

Once, when filming on the Great Barrier Reef from Ron Isbel's charter vessel *Sea Hunt*, I was sent down to film the anchor being raised. It was the standard shot most film directors call for on the basis of 'continuity' between sequences. Ron was not entirely happy because *Sea Hunt* was suffering from a bad case of flat batteries. The winch that wound up the heavy anchor chain ran directly off the batteries and made a huge power drain.

'One shot is all you get,' said Ron. I went down the anchor chain in 10 metres of crystal-clear Barrier Reef water and sighted the camera towards the surface. Suddenly I was thrown completely clear of the bottom, performing an impromptu and very undignified somersault.

At the same time I felt a violent electric shock which left me stunned. I was completely bemused because I had never had a similar underwater experience before. It was like putting a wet toe into a 240 volt power socket. Electrifying in every sense.

When I collected my senses my first thought was that the anchor chain must somehow be 'live'. But that was impossible! Then I saw a small, nondescript-looking ray huffily swimming away with an air of injured dignity.

I had evidently landed heavily right on top of *Hypnos*. And paid the price. Naturally I received scant sympathy.

The other divers in the water rolled about laughing so much that they appeared in danger of drowning. The director raged on board about 'unnecessary' delays. But it was Ron Isbel who had the last word.

Told that I had become the victim of an electric ray, he shouted down from the bridge: 'Grab it by the tail, you stupid bastards! And toss it up here. We'll use it to charge the batteries!'

Not me, mate. I was still in a state of shock.

ADVENTURES ON THE SHARK CIRCUIT
chapter eleven

J*AWS*, THE BOOK, WAS JUST OUT WHEN WE MADE OUR FIRST DESCENT IN THE CAGE at Albany. The film was due any day. A tidal wave of promotion surged ahead of both printed pages and screen images. We were warned that the super shark was finning on its way. The world held its breath waiting for what was coming.

When it did arrive *Jaws* was all the shock and horror that the publicity people had promised. Our Albany diving was already planned when I first read my copy of *Jaws*, and naturally a certain amount of reflection followed.

For anyone about to step into a shark cage and face Great Whites, the passage in which Matt Hooper, the scientist, goes down to confront the *Jaws* shark from his own cage is hardly recommended reading.

As our great sharks — the real thing — glided smoothly past our cage at Albany, they turned to look at us with that dark eye which Peter Matthiessen described in *Blue Meridian:* 'Like a black hole in a shroud'. At those times I thought of Peter Benchley's book and wished that I had delayed the reading experience until we'd finished at Albany. Benchley knew his subject. My real-life fisherman friend Sharkey Nelson had many traits in common with the tight-lipped shark hunter, Quint, in *Jaws*. I could also relate to Hooper, the ichthyologist, in his desire to see the great shark underwater.

Once we had been in the cage and had real flesh-and-blood Great White sharks put their heads in through the camera gap and scrape their teeth on the bars, then the fictional account seemed strangely factual.

I could see all too clearly how Hooper could have been hypnotised into his fatal inaction.

When we reached out in real life to try to stroke the grey bodies and white bellies rubbing against the cage, with a sandpaper sound, there was always that momentary crazy impulse to open the cage and swim out with the sharks. It sometimes all seemed rather like a dream.

Hooper's fictional reaction was similar to our own response:

Sharks have everything a scientist dreams of,' he told Ellen Brody. 'They're beautiful — God, how beautiful they are! They're like an impossibly perfect piece of machinery. They're as graceful as any bird. They're as mysterious as any animal on earth. No one knows for sure how long they live or what impulses — except for hunger — they respond to...

'No one knows'... Now, if there was ever anything that could be said about sharks, that was it!

We didn't know ourselves from one day to the next what would happen when we went into our cage. Nor did Hooper in his foray, and, fiction or not, it didn't make good reading in the business we were in.

The first part of his dive was similar to our experience:

Carried by the tide, one of the white squid baits slipped between the bars of the cage and, tethered by twine, fluttered in Hooper's face. He pushed it out of the cage.

He glanced downward, started to look away, then snapped his eyes down again. Rising at him from the darkling blue — slowly and smoothly — was the shark. It rose with no apparent effort, an angel of death gliding towards an appointment foreordained. Hooper wanted to raise his camera but his arm would not obey. In a minute, he said to himself, in a minute.

Hooper stared, enthralled, impelled to flee but unable to move... The fish came closer, silent as a shadow, and Hooper drew back. The head was only a few feet from the cage when the fish turned and began to pass before Hooper's eyes — casually, as if in proud display of its incalculable mass and power.

The snout passed first, then the jaw slack and smiling, armed with row on row of serrate triangles. And then the black fathomless eye, seemingly riveted upon him. The gills rippled — bloodless wounds in the steely skin.

Tentatively Hooper stuck a hand through the bars and touched the flank. It felt cold and hard, not clammy but smooth as vinyl. He let his fingertips caress the flesh — past the pectoral fins, the thick, firm genital claspers — until finally (the fish seemed to have no end) they were slapped away by the sweeping tail.

Our own experience had exactly duplicated Hooper's. His conclusion was what we seriously hoped to avoid.

Hooper raised the camera on the next pass, expecting the shark to turn. Instead, just as ours had, it attacked the cage. Hooper's cage had vertical bars.

The fish rammed through the space between the bars, spreading them further with each thrust of its tail. Hooper, flattened against the back of the cage, saw the mouth reaching, straining, for him. He remembered the powerhead and he tried to lower his right arm and grab it. The fish thrust again, and Hooper saw with the terror of doom that the mouth was going to reach him.

The jaws closed around his torso, he jabbed his fist into the black eye. The fish bit down and the last thing Hooper saw before he died was the eye gazing at him through a cloud of his own blood...

Hmmm. I had built the cage before I read the book. Even then I realised that vertical bars, which could be bent and spread apart by the conical nose and great weight of a large White shark, could be bad news in a confrontation.

Our cage had mesh squares, which a shark (we believed) could not separate. The possibility of a direct attack through the camera gap was the No. 1 problem. As discussed previously, to get the 120 metre or 400 foot load movie camera through, the gap had to be at least 45 centimetres wide. It was a weak point that a determined shark could work on. But there was no option if we wanted film which showed sharks and not just silver cage bars.

Problem No. 2 centred on the tethers from the boat to the cage. Great Whites often throw their tails carelessly around and sometimes get caught in ropes. In South Australia Great Whites had become tangled in cage lines with near-disastrous results for both sharks and occupants.

Our sharks were bigger than the general run of Great Whites at Dangerous Reef. The cage had been lightly built so we could handle it. The downside of this was that the bigger sharks could collapse the cage through threshing and throwing themselves about if they became caught in the cage tethers. Or if they broke the lines they might be off with the cage like a supermarket trolley towed behind a speedboat.

We did not want to be trapped helpless inside the wreckage in either eventuality. There was no perfect answer, but in anticipation of such an emergency I had fitted a quick-release lever (I had read *Jaws* at that point) so that in an instant the bottom of the cage would hinge away like a hangman's drop and allow us to fall through and escape. It would be a desperate measure because we would have no fins and no air. No hope either, if a shark were seriously interested in us in a Hooper situation.

But if the shark were accidentally caught in the tether lines, or was tangled with the cage and panicking, we figured that it would be more interested in escaping from its own predicament than bothering about us. At least for the moment. That should give us time to make the boat.

It was a problematical situation. Until it actually occurred we would not tell whether our emergency plan would work. Or not.

The other countermeasure was to suspend the cage from a high boom, like a gamefishing outrigger going out from the boat. The line to the cage top ran through a stainless steel pulley on the high end of the outrigger, then descended vertically in a straight drop to the cage. This minimised the chance of a randomly flicking mackerel tail fouling slack ropes at low level. There were two other tether lines direct from boat to cage for drawing it in or changing its position. A sharp knife was kept close by so that the ropes could be cut or cast off if things went too badly awry.

'Use your judgement,' I said to whoever was operating the cage lines, usually Maurie Glazier or Peter Grace. 'But for Christ's sake don't cut the lines if it means the shark will take off with us and the cage in tow!'

'Don't worry,' they said. 'We'll look after you.'

Strange, isn't it, how when someone says 'Don't worry' you start to worry?

But we could not have got more competent individuals to care for us. Maurie was a professional fisherman. I had been diving with him for sharks in many locations since the 1950s. Peter was an ocean racing yachtsman familiar with knots and tackle, and knew which line to pull at the right time.

Theirs was an important job. They had to decide when things were becoming simply too dangerous. They had to know when to haul the cage in so that we could bail out through the cage top hatch and on to the boat's duckboard.

At times, getting in and out of the cage, sharks were so close under the duckboard that we could have stepped out and straddled their backs. Like a rodeo rider in a chute dropping onto a Brahmin bull. That would have made an interesting piece of film. Now that our last days in Albany were at hand, Vic was looking for anything which would add to the footage. Anyone crazy enough to try such a rodeo stunt would have been welcome. But there were no volunteers. Getting on the sharks might seem easy enough. But how did you get off, and where?

It highlighted a problem. We had shot an impressive 3000 feet (900 metres) of Great Whites swimming around the cages. But to Vic's critical eye the footage was still on the bland side.

'Drama!' he kept saying. 'We need drama, dammit!'

In some respects we had done too good a job with the cage. It was too safe and worked too well. There had been no blood. Not even a ragged nick or two out of a wetsuit.

208

We began to wonder where we had gone wrong.

'It's a bit ironic,' Peter said, 'when you begin to feel guilty about still being alive.'

We could have faked something, of course. A ploy not entirely unknown in the film industry. Many well-known underwater films have included scenes where a well-proportioned blonde rolled onto her back to show some of her more interesting development, and was (with appropriate shrieks of terror) chased by a plywood fin. There have been a number of instances where the head of a dead shark, with corpse-like grin, reared up out of the water to leer unconvincingly at the camera.

We'd agreed that in our film there should be no chicanery. No buckled cages bent with a kangaroo jack, or 'cry wolf' shouts of 'Help! Help!'

The problem was that as divers we had strong survival instincts which may have run counter to the best interests of the film. The natural inclination was towards a smooth working relationship with our sharks. When surface instructions like 'See if you can't stir the bastards up!' or 'Do *anything* but do *something*!' came down into the cage we could only look at each other and shrug our shoulders.

In the last few days, berleying with whale-meat baits was tried, without any particular success. There was already quite enough dead whale in the water. All that happened was that the baits got in the way of the shots.

Then at last it happened. Two huge female sharks, which we christened Grandma and Dangerous Mabel, turned up and changed our situation from being satisfactorily in control of events to some moments of acute anxiety.

The pair were enormous, each somewhere near the 6 metre mark and maybe 2 tonnes in bulk. They looked mean from the start. When they appeared every other shark vanished with a crack of the tail. That should have told us something.

The cage weighed about 135 kilograms, and if you added the weight of three SCUBA tanks, the fibreglass floats, Peter and myself, there was probably the better part of half a tonne. Yet we had found that the cage was not easy to shift around even when empty!

But when Dangerous Mabel hit the cage on its corner in a moment of pique, it rotated through 360 degrees on the instant. It felt to us as though we'd fallen into a fast-spinning washing machine.

Before we had a chance to pick ourselves up off the cage floor there was another *bang* on the other side of the cage, and Grandma was trying to turn what the surface crew jokingly called our mesh Metal Safety Centre into secondhand scrap.

209

It was impossible to maintain balance. The two sharks appeared to be working in tandem. They tried everything the previous sharks had attempted, including sticking their overblown noses and hideous grins through the camera gap. Then they added some innovations of their own. They shouldered the cage, swatted it with their tails and, in between inflicting physical indignities, peered in inquiringly as though to ask, 'Now, how did you like *that*, dears?'

It looked to us as though they were deliberately trying to make the cage so uncomfortable for us that we'd bail out into open water. Which, of course, would suit them just fine.

If they'd been old ladies ashore they'd have been the kind who did their knitting under the guillotine.

But — as we were constantly reminded — although they were senior females they were still very much sharks.

I remembered Quint's phrase from *Jaws* about the problems of 'dealing with 5000 [2300 kilograms] pounds of pissed-off dinosaur'.

Bang again, so that our back teeth rattled. It was getting beyond a joke. I pointed upwards to Peter. 'Time to go!' He nodded a vigorous affirmative.

As we rose towards the trapdoor in the top of the cage I saw Grandma with her head out of the water in contemplative mode chewing on one of the cage tether ropes.

'She stuck her head right out!' the surface crew told us cheerfully. 'Saw how the cage was attached and went straight to the line and started chomping on it.'

Who said that sharks can't think?

Twice more that day Grandma and Dangerous Mabel gave us a hard time below. Huge old ladies with ragged edges to their fins, pronounced jowls, and great underslung bellies. I was intrigued to note that both carried recent mating scars. Male Great Whites, like many other shark species, nibble the fins and back of their lady loves before and during tender moments.

I couldn't help thinking that they'd be taking a risk with this particular pair of female ogres. If the male's advances were unwelcome the retribution could be awful to contemplate. A blighted romance takes on a different meaning in the shark world.

How do sharks make love? In the case of Great Whites I would imagine that it would be a matter of considerable vigour. The water threshed to foam and bubbles, a pearly cloak to shield the nuptials from prying eyes. No trivial mating there, with animals each over a tonne in weight and sporting the wickedest teeth in the animal world…

Great Whites in fact probably copulate somewhat in the manner of humans. I say 'probably' because no one has ever witnessed such an epic coupling. However, shark mating has been observed in other smaller species.

The male shark is fortunate enough to have two penises, one testis (testicle) to each. The male appendages are bottle-shaped organs called 'claspers', though that is not quite the way they operate. The reproductive organ is inserted singly into the female and the sharks mate body to body, face to face. Do they evidence pleasure? During the process they twine around each other, and it is then that the nibbling takes place. Though done, doubtless, with tender intent, it often leaves distinct lacerations.

Nature has answers for most things. In a number of shark species, including makos and Great Whites, the females have actually grown markedly thicker skin on the backs of their heads and other places susceptible to amorous but damaging male nibbling.

Peter and I, of course, had watched closely for signs of courtship behaviour around the whales, but had to report no luck to Vic.

'They're too interested in the whales,' I said.

Peter nodded. 'Stands to reason,' he agreed. 'Humans don't go to a restaurant to make love. They eat and then go somewhere else.'

Where was 'somewhere else' for the Great White?

Davey Jones's locker perhaps?

Where indeed. I had a feeling that whatever happened, and wherever it happened, it would be a spectacular event.

'Great film,' mourned Vic, with a sideways glance at the cage crew. 'If we could ever get it.' Maternity, the natural end result of shark coupling, like shark sex, wasn't going to be in our film either. For reasons which we were about to learn.

'Did you know,' said John Bass at dinner one night, 'that no pregnant Great White has ever been captured?'

John was a South African shark scientist from Durban who had come to spend a few days with us while on his way to New Zealand.

'We don't even know how many young Whites carry,' he continued. 'Although we do suspect they practise oophagy.'

'*Oophagy*?' queried Vic. 'What's that? It sounds like something disgusting.'

'You're half right,' John Bass smiled. 'At least from the human perspective. Oophagy is infant cannibalism in the womb. Survival of the fittest, you see, at the earliest opportunity of all.'

'You mean' — Vic could hardly believe it — 'that the young sharks actually eat each other in their mother's wombs?'

211

John nodded. 'That's right.'

'No wonder they grow up to be such savage sons of bitches!' Vic shook his head. 'With a start like that! Your first meal is your brother or your sister. And before you've even been born!'

Oophagy, John told us, occurred with the grey nurse, known as the 'ragged tooth shark' in South Africa. The mother conceived a number of foetuses, but usually only two were born. The earlier developers, the stronger ones, ate their weaker brothers and sisters. One shark researcher putting his hand into the womb of a captured grey nurse, to feel if it was pregnant, was actually bitten painfully on the hand by an unborn shark.

The youngest shark 'man-eater' on record.

Nature lays down some hard rules. At Rottnest Island, where my boat is moored in summer and where this book was written, the osprey sea eagles regularly lay three eggs in a nest built like a miniature castle of sticks and sea wrack. Three eaglets are hatched, fierce-beaked and angry-eyed miniatures of their parents. Gradually one emerges as the strongest and the mother concentrates her feeding on it. Finally the strong eaglet, now twice the size of the others, tips his hapless brothers and sisters out of the nest, tumbling them down the sides of the stick-castle to perish below. He or she becomes the sole focus of the parents' attention and goes on to become the hatchling of the year.

With the sheldrakes or mountain ducks that also nest on the island there is a different story to achieve a similar result. The parental home is by freshwater springs near an inland salt lake where brine shrimps proliferate at certain times of year.

Is this where Mrs Mountain Duck lays her eggs? Not on your life. That would be too easy. Instead there is a rigorous test for ducklings before they reach the privileged comfort zone. The eggs are laid in limestone cliffs in remote sea bays facing the winter surf of the Indian Ocean. As many as 13 ducklings may hatch. When she is satisfied that all are out of the egg Mrs Duck marches her brood out of the warmth of the nest. Ignoring their piping protests she makes them jump off a rock into the surf. Then, followed by her little armada of fluffy chicks, peeping away and barely a few days old, she swims off down the rough-water island shore.

At a point closest to the lakes — after an exhausting swim of some kilometres — she comes ashore and marches her brood a similar distance overland. All the way they are harassed by gulls and crows swooping and carrying off weak or exhausted ducklings. A duckling version of Napoleon's retreat from Moscow.

When she reaches the lake, Mother Duck may have as many as six surviving ducklings. Or she may have four, two, one or — sad day — none.

Regardless of how many survive that gruelling first test, only one or two will ever become adults.

Some species seem to breed just to feed other species. At the Murion Islands at Exmouth Gulf I have seen newly hatched baby turtles flippering down the sand to the sea. A running river of tiny black creatures driven by desperate instinct to reach the ocean. Some become confused, go the wrong way and die from exhaustion or lizard predators. Screeching gulls scoop up others at the water's edge, piercing immature shells with strong beaks. In the shallows shark fins cut the surface.

Mother Green Turtle lays 80 to 90 eggs every three or four years. Between monitor lizards, gulls, sharks and fish, only one or two of hundreds of hatchlings in a long lifetime may become adults. Just as well, or the world would be wall-to-wall shellbacks. It is a similar story with crocodiles. Most of the young go to feed some other creature in the food chain.

Nature seems to have laid down a series of queer breeding experiments, contrasting in style. There are those creatures like turtles which have multiple births in the hope that one or two individuals may survive all the dangers and vicissitudes. Other species, including *Homo sapiens* (our own human race), elephants, whales and dolphins, have single births. They care diligently for the offspring through a long period of childhood and adolescence to give it the best chance in life.

But there are contrasts even among similar orders of animals. Among the mammals most of the big creatures have single births. But dogs, cats, rats and pigs all have multiple litters. Lions, tigers and bears have two to four cubs.

Among the sharks are a confusing number of possibilities. The grey nurse, mako and Great White have a small number of progeny and practise oophagy. A tiger shark, on the other hand, a similarly large predator filling the same sort of role in the ocean, may have as many as eighty striped tigelets in a brood and a blue shark 50 or 60 young. Obviously their survival rate is low, otherwise the sea would be filled with the fins of tiger sharks and blues.

'Don't sharks lay eggs?' asked Marilyn, entering the conversation with the dessert. 'We used to find them on the beaches after storms. We called them mermaid's purses.'

John Bass nodded. 'Lots of sharks, particularly the smaller ones, are oviparous and lay eggs. They're not like bird's eggs but square-shaped and flat plastic-looking things. They have tendrils on the corners to catch in seaweed and anchor the egg capsule until it's ready to hatch.'

213

Why had no pregnant white sharks been seen by scientists?

'It is believed that there may be an inhibiting factor,' John explained. 'A hormonal imbalance which extinguishes appetite so that the pregnant female stops feeding. It's Nature's way of making sure she doesn't eat the babies, since sharks normally eat other sharks. And because the females don't feed they tend not to be caught.'

'So they won't be here to eat the whales?' Peter Newstead asked.

'Not if the theory is correct.'

'There goes another shot down the gurgler,' said Vic, looking gloomy again. 'Down the plug hole.' We had been on the lookout for visibly pregnant Great Whites from the cage. Now that avenue, too, was closed. The list of 'non-shots' was lengthening.

It was not until 1985 that scientists did get their hands on a pregnant Great White, and what they found pretty much confirmed the previous theories.

A gravid (pregnant) female, 5.4 metres long, was caught off the Japanese island of Okinawa. A huge creature of *Jaws* dimensions. Another big pregnant female was caught a year later, off the whaling port of Taji in Japan. Both had several near-term embryos about a metre long in their oviducts. There was enough evidence for Japanese scientists to conclude that *carcharias* did indeed practise oophagy, infant cannibalism.

'The ultimate in sibling rivalry,' commented John McCosker in his book *Great White Shark*. 'It would be hard to imagine a more appropriate debut for the fish that will eventually mature into the most feared predator in the ocean.'

Previously some very small Great Whites had been caught in waters near Long Island and New York, indicating that the northeast Atlantic may be a birthing place for some *Carcharodon carcharias*. These little sharks were around the metre to metre-and-a-half mark in length, and were fierce-looking reproductions of their parents in appearance. Deep chested, muscular, and weighing from 9 to 14 kilograms. Ready to take on the world.

Small *carcharias* have been caught in surf beach mesh nets on the Queensland coast. It was long surmised that Moreton Bay, near Brisbane, once a humpback whale birthing area, may have had similar significance for Great Whites. Spencer Gulf in South Australia is another possibility.

No pregnant female or tiny newborn *carcharias* has been recorded from open waters in western or southern Australia. But Shark Bay on the west coast, a place where humpbacks used to congregate with calves, may be a nursery area like Moreton Bay in a similar latitude on the opposite side of the continent.

At Albany, only appetites were on show as Great White sharks savaged the flanks of the dead whales and occasionally evidenced an unsettling interest in us cage dwellers.

Everything comes to an end, sooner or later.

Our last day came and we dropped down into the cage with mixed feelings. It had been a period filled with interest for us. 'A fantastic mix of fear and fascination,' was how I described it to myself in my diary.

Unlike some of the others, Peter and I never underestimated the potential of the great sharks to cause us harm. There were things which could have gone wrong but never did. A good deal of that, we figured, was simply luck, rather than good management.

Later, at the same spot, I would have awesome evidence at first hand of a Great White shark that was savagely out of control. This could have happened at any time during our Albany filming and if it had, someone could have been killed. Yet we had spent more time in cages with Great Whites in a concentrated period than perhaps anyone else up to that time. Due, of course, to the fortunate location.

All that our experience showed was that it could be the first shark, the ninety-ninth or the one-thousandth that caused trouble. Or none of them.

With sharks you never knew.

We had an irrational apprehension that because it was the last day something might go wrong. But instead — such is the way of things — it was an anticlimax.

We had whales, we went down in the cage. Visibility was good, the gear was functioning, our hopes were high.

Not a single shark was seen all day. Emerging at the end of it through the trapdoor in the top of the cage, shivering and blue with cold, I passed up the camera with a full load of film. The trigger pristine and unpressed.

'That's that,' I said. Vic nodded. 'That's that,' he agreed.

I was reminded of shark hunter Quint's remark about sharks in *Jaws*.

'When you want 'em,' he said 'they're never around. It's only when you don't want 'em and don't expect 'em that they show up. Contrary fuckers!'

'Contrary fuckers' indeed.

Well, we had given White sharks our best shot. The film we had in the can was it — for better or worse. Now we were off to the Great Barrier Reef for tigers and whaler sharks and to Moreton Bay for grey nurse lassoing, rodeo fashion.

'Vic Martin's shark circus is on the road again,' I said, wiping my face with a towel.

215

'You'd better believe it,' he grinned. 'Tigers, here we come! Watch out whaler sharks. We'll make you bloody famous!'

We were to have a lot of fun making them famous. From my own point of view it was a relief to no longer be held responsible for the shark action. Vic had made the bookings for the remainder of the shark circuit, and all I had to do from there on was point the camera.

There were also none of the nerve-jangling experiences we had with the Great Whites. We filmed the other species without the protection of cages. Which said a good deal for the respect with which we viewed *carcharias*.

We went to Heron Island off Gladstone, in Queensland, aboard Ron Isbel's charter boat *Sea Hunt*. Heron is one of the loveliest cays of the Barrier Reef, and Ron was one of the best-known charter skippers. He was booked by many of the international film crews and had a laconic sense of humour.

Once he had a French crew aboard. Some fish dripping blood from the duckboard attracted a tiger shark. With a cry of joy the French cameraman grabbed his movie camera and without mask, fins or wetsuit jumped into the water to film the beast.

The tiger shark, attracted by the blood scent and sighting the kicking bare white legs, wheeled and charged. Ron, assessing the situation in an instant, jumped overboard landing hard on top of the tiger and diverting it. His quick thinking saved the Frenchman's life.

Did he receive heartfelt thanks?

A *Bravo, mon ami!* together with a Gallic kiss, perhaps, planted firmly on each cheek?

'No way,' said Ron. 'He was bloody furious! Kept shouting *merde!* Reckoned I'd ruined his shot!'

Both of them had extensive areas of skin scraped raw by contact with the shark. 'That's how close it was,' said Ron.

But the Frenchman never forgave him. Cameramen are a single-minded bunch, whatever language they speak.

We would have been pleased to see tigers almost as close. But despite Ron's best efforts of chumming and berleying in various locations there was not a stripe or a sickle-toothed grin to be seen.

'When you want 'em,' said Ron, paraphrasing Quint, 'the bastards are nowhere to be found. But wait till you're down-current from the boat, with a long weary way to swim, and a bleeding fish on your hands. Then the very last thing you want to see is a bloody shark . . . And that's just when you've got one!'

We did get some good film of hungry whalers dashing in and scooping up fish, sometimes so close that we had to physically push them away. But there

Top: *In 1976 I went out with a whale chaser from the Albany Whaling Station, Western Australia. Here, master gunner Paddy Hart directs the steersman from the gun platform.*
Bottom: *The gun is fired in a detonation of smoke and wadding fragments. The harpoon is in the air with the line snaking behind it. A cruel moment for a sperm whale ahead.*

Top: *The stricken whale stains the blue Southern Ocean crimson with its life blood.*
Bottom: *Whalers watch the last flurry. No one enjoyed the kill. But hunting whales was all the whalers knew.*

Top: *The gaping jaw shows the ivory teeth of a sperm whale bull. Sperms can dive 1800 metres into the midnight world of kraken, the giant squid, and remain submerged an hour below.*
Bottom: *Lynn Cropp with a giant squid taken from the belly of a bull sperm whale. Complete it would have measured 45 feet. Sections of even bigger squid sometimes rolled out on the flensing deck at the whaling station.*

Shooting a scene for the feature film, Orca, with Valerie and Ron Taylor. The shark we caught for this shot was almost 5 metres long and weighed 680 kilograms.
Top: *If Valerie could have given the shark the kiss of life, she would have.*
Right: *Myself with the Orca shark. His bite left permanent scars in the side of my boat. (Photograph: Marilyn Edwards)*
Opposite top: *We used bog mats from my Toyota Landcruiser to form a cradle to lift the shark.*
Opposite bottom: *Valerie Taylor takes stills while Ron Taylor films the shark falling into the water. Ron then reversed the shot to make it look as though Orca was tossing the Great White into the air. (Photograph: Marilyn Edwards)*

221

Remoras seem to hang around with sharks in proportion to size — small shark, small remora; large remora, large shark. So divers are not always pleased to see a big *remora like this one. It usually means a big shark uncomfortably close by.*

Barracuda grow quite large (like this one). They have a protruding lower jaw and teeth like crocodiles. They could do a human a great deal of harm but, in fact, there are no records of fatal attacks.

Top: *A bull shark unexpectedly charges a group of photographers in the Coral Sea during shark feeding, and causes an adrenalin rush. The picture was taken by an American from Florida whose name I have regrettably lost. I hope she sees the picture one day.*
Bottom: *A grey nurse shark, being 'burped' by Bob Webb, before being taken off to Sea World at Surfers Paradise. Burping removed stomach gases caused by the trauma of noose capture.*

was always the feeling that if we got bitten in that situation it would be an accident. The sharks' interest was primarily in the fish.

The important thing in filming whalers while attracting them with fish was to stay together in a group with backs to a coral wall. It was the ascending or descending diver who ran the most risk.

It was surprising how shy the sharks were in general. We had had similar experiences in Western Australia at the Abrolhos Islands and the Dampier Archipelago when we sought out sharks for film and photographs. We could get them to approach the boat on the surface by chumming. But they seemed to shy away as soon as divers were in the water. Curiously tigers, well-equipped and very large sharks, who should (one would think) have nothing to fear, were especially difficult to approach. They kept a cautious distance which frustratingly was usually just outside camera range.

Except when you had no camera and didn't want them.

We learnt how much there was to learn about filming sharks. The most important aspects were season and location. Some places you could never get near sharks. Other spots you had to push them away. But that kind of knowledge only came through experience and many nautical miles, and usually after many mistakes and disappointments. At least we didn't make the ultimate mistake and get eaten.

One of our most interesting experiences on the shark circuit was at Surfers Paradise. We went with Bob Webb and Bill Hookway to film grey nurse sharks.

It was a critical time for the grey nurse.

Divers had discovered that at certain times of year, at a number of locations on the New South Wales and Queensland coast, grey nurse gathered in mating schools. They hung like grey ghosts in reef gullies which might contain as many as 100 sharks. A magnificent sight.

That was soon to change.

The sharks were usually almost motionless in the water, moving their tails slowly to keep them in station against the current. This made them the easiest of targets. Divers using explosive-headed spears killed them by the dozen.

It was like shooting sheep in a pen.

There was no danger to the diver, no challenge. Just that obnoxious human trait, the thrill of the kill. Pleasure in destruction.

So many sharks were killed that the numbers in the gutters dwindled alarmingly. It seemed that the grey nurse, slow breeding like many of the bigger sharks, was in real danger of being wiped out. Legislation was belatedly introduced to protect the species. But the damage had already been done, and we had to travel many sea miles to get even token footage of surviving grey nurse.

The action we particularly wished to film was the live capture of a mature shark — with appropriate government permits. The shark was required for the shark tank at the *Sea World* aquarium at Surfers Paradise.

The capture took place in an unusual way. Bob Webb, sometimes called the 'Underwater Cowboy', had evolved a technique of lassoing big grey nurse in the gutters about 30 metres below the surface, and wrestling them to a standstill.

Bob was a tough customer. In a previous year he and another diver were using SCUBA on Moreton Reef many kilometres from shore. The boat above lost sight of their bubbles. The driver panicked and left the scene, driving back to shore 'to get help'.

When the divers surfaced they found no boat, and a very long way to land. Since they had no other option they began swimming, gradually dropping items of equipment as they went. 'It took me a long time to drop my tank and even longer to discard my weight belt,' Bob recalled. 'Crazy how you hang on to things, worrying about a few dollars, when your life may be at stake.'

Night fell and still they swam. Eventually they lost contact with each other. After 19 hours, totally exhausted, Bob Webb heard surf ahead in the darkness and eventually dragged himself up on a beach on Moreton Island. The other diver was never heard of again.

Why lasso a shark?

In the past, grey nurse caught in nets or brought up on lines usually died in the aquarium. It was found that grey nurse sharks literally had a bellyful of gas when placed under stress. They apparently had the ability to produce gas which acted as a flotation balance like a fish's swim bladder. This was the reason why grey nurse could hover stationary in the breeding gutter in seeming defiance of the scientific belief that such sharks must keep swimming or sink. However, just as a fish's swim bladder can blow up like a balloon and kill it when the fish is hauled up from depths, so a grey nurse's stomach gas can inflate and injure it internally if it is brought to the surface too quickly.

Bob Webb lassoed the shark, slipping a nylon rope noose over its head in an aluminium frame and jerking it tight. This prevented damage to the jaw. Naturally the shark took off in wild panic when it felt the rope, which was attached to the boat above.

When the shark was played to exhaustion Bob was able to approach it down the line and actually take it in his arms.

At that point his task, believe it or not, was to 'burp' the shark to get rid of the gas in its stomach in exactly the same way that a human baby is treated for wind after breast or bottle feeding. As my own daughter Petrana was just a year old, I knew exactly what was required. That delightful, never-to-be-forgotten sound of a baby's wet-lipped b-u-u-r-p! at three o'clock in the morning, which means that everyone can go back to bed!

The sight of Bob Webb with a 2.5 metre, 180 kilogram grey nurse under his arm, gently massaging its belly until the blessed bubbles ballooned from its mouth, was really quite extraordinary. I wouldn't have believed it myself unless I had seen and photographed it. *Eugomphodus taurus* has been relieved of an undeserved reputation as a man-eater. But it still has a big jaw and a mouthful of long and extremely sharp teeth.

Under provocation — and being lassoed definitely fits that description — a stressed grey nurse could do enormous damage to a careless or unlucky human being.

Bob Webb was careful and most proficient in his handling of the sharks. But there was no denying that there was a considerable element of risk.

Once the shark was 'burped' it was raised slowly to the surface, lifted into the boat with a canvas sling, placed in an aerated tank aboard with water pumping through its gills, and rushed to Sea World.

It was found that grey nurse caught in this manner had a much higher survival rate in captivity. Once acclimatised, grey nurse could live many years in an aquarium. They were the ideal aquarium shark. They were big, non-aggressive and with their set of wicked-looking teeth they were everyone's idea of what a shark should look like.

Did we make our sharks — the Great Whites, whalers, non-appearing tigers and the bubble-burping grey nurse — famous?

The film, edited, set to music, with the usual waffling background commentary, did quite well on Australian television. It was shown on the Nine Network, rating a 34, which was pretty good so far as documentary films went at that time. But like so many other Australian documentaries it made no money. In fact Vic said we didn't clear expenses. But the experience, particularly with the Great White sharks, was infinitely rewarding. The kind of memories which last a lifetime.

I was back at Albany again in November 1976, far sooner than I had expected to renew acquaintance with Great Whites.

Ron and Valerie Taylor had been commissioned to shoot the underwater footage for the Dino de Laurentis production *Orca*. The film would star

227

Richard Harris as a grumpy old fisherman and Charlotte Rampling as the beautiful female marine biologist. Bo Derek got eaten in the script. A delicious morsel!

I had worked with Ron on a number of wreck and underwater filming assignments in Western Australia since I met him at the Australian Spearfishing Championship (which he won) in 1962. By the 1970s he and Valerie had established a worldwide reputation as a result of their work in Peter Gimbel's movie *Blue Meridian* and in the live shark filming for *Jaws*.

Ron, who won the World Spearfishing Champion title at Tahiti in 1967, was considered the best underwater cameraman on sharks in the world. Valerie added on-camera glamour and presence and was a skilled still camera photographer. I had written about them in a previous book, *Sharks and Shipwrecks*, published in Australia and the United States in 1975. So, one way and another, we were old friends.

I had returned from eastern Australia, still on something of a high after our own shark adventures, and wondering in odd moments what I was going to do next.

The phone rang and it was Ron.

'We want to film at Albany,' he said, coming straight to the point as he usually did.

He explained about the *Orca* commission. 'We need to catch a White shark,' he said. 'A small one.'

There was a momentary silence. 'I don't think there *are* any small ones,' I said doubtfully. 'Unless you consider a 14 footer [4.3 metre long shark] a small one. We haven't seen anything much further down the size scale than that.'

'Let me explain,' he said. 'In the movie a killer whale — that's the title *Orca* — saves a human from a White shark attack and throws the shark up in the air. That's what we have to film. The shark in the air, and falling back with a splash.'

'Thrown in the air!' My mind boggled. 'You know what these things weigh?'

Ron did, of course. But the vision of trying to propel a tonne of flaccid dead shark through the air, vertically or otherwise, temporarily floored me. I should have known better.

'Easy,' said Ron.

'But how?'

'Lift it up on a mobile crane with a long arm,' he said patiently. 'Let it go and film the fall and the splash. Then for the *up* shot we just reverse the falling part of the film. Easy, like I said.'

Simple. I had a new insight into making motion pictures.

In practice it was not quite so easy as it sounded. With sharks few things are. The sharks have their own priorities.

With Brian Greenhalgh helping we rigged a set-line with hooks and drums, off the Whaling Station, rebaiting every day with huge chunks of whale meat. But the sharks largely ignored the offering. When baits were taken the hooks — the largest available — were straightened with ridiculous ease. It was hard work, everything greasy and reeking of dead sperm from the whale-meat baits. There was a sense of depression because we were not succeeding. And, from the parochial Western Australian aspect, we had been telling Ron and Val for years that our Whites were bigger and badder than those in South Australia. Now I was beginning to feel rather foolish.

At the end of the week bad weather set in, and the whalechasers remained in port. We had the old equation — no whales, no sharks.

'The waiting game,' I said to Ron apologetically. He nodded agreement. 'That's shark filming,' he said. 'A waiting game, if ever there was one.'

He should know. Previously the Taylors had filmed Great Whites in Spencer Gulf in South Australia, with Rodney Fox. Dangerous Reef was the favourite location. Ron was the first person to film Great Whites. His work on *Blue Water — White Death*, and on *Jaws* had been outstanding, establishing his reputation in the international film world. But when Ron filmed live White shark footage for *Jaws* in 1974 in South Australia there were some tense scenes with local abalone divers.

An abalone diver named Terry Manuel had been killed by a Great White at Streaky Bay, only two months before the *Jaws* filming began. Other divers had had serious confrontations with Whites. Among other things, they blamed the berleying by film crews.

'We understand that the sharks can be dangerous at any time,' Neil Williams, one of the pioneers of commercial abalone diving was quoted as saying in the *Port Lincoln Times*. 'We take that risk. But berleying from boats…is educating the sharks to associate divers with food. It markedly increases the threat.'

He had a point, and things were to get worse.

Some film crews, in the human frenzy which followed the release of *Jaws*, actually stuffed wetsuits with horse or seal meat in order to film the human-look-alike dummies being ripped to pieces by the sharks for more dramatic film footage.

That really *was* educating the resident Whites. Sharks have a proven capacity to learn, and the dummying had the potential to teach them that human shapes in wetsuits were easy and satisfactory prey.

229

'It's OK for the filmmakers,' said the abalone divers. 'Those guys are in cages. We're not.' Ordinary swimmers and divers at the nearby beaches of Port Lincoln, and at Aldinga, Port Noalunga and the other beaches on the Adelaide side of the Gulf, were also unprotected.

The abalone divers had their own solution. They said they would catch and kill the 'educated' sharks if filming continued. Meanwhile some of them designed and built their own mobile cages to work abalone. But they regarded the necessity as an imposition.

'I could understand how they felt,' Ron said. 'We work in the water ourselves. The sea is our living too and we'd be angry if it were threatened.'

When the *Orca* commission came up, Albany seemed to offer a solution that would not antagonise anyone.

The Taylors were publicly very much against killing Great Whites. Valerie had been upset that early in 1976 no fewer than 12 *carcharias* had been taken by sports fishermen working out of Port Lincoln in the wake of the *Jaws* publicity.

'It's too many for such a small area,' she said 'The sharks will disappear.'

When *Orca* came up and a shark had to be caught there was some soul searching. I had my own reservations. In previous years I had caught many sharks, including numbers of tigers, whalers and hammerheads, without problems of conscience. They were sharks, weren't they? But now, seeing sharks as a cameraman instead of as a hunter, I had a new understanding of their place in the sea. The Great Whites had awakened an admiration and respect.

In short, where once it would have seemed an exciting challenge to catch a Great White, now there had to be a very good reason.

We agreed that the film justified taking one shark out of the system. In those days they were considered to be plentiful out of Albany. One would surely not be missed. My own personal rule, since becoming a cameraman, was that I would not take a fish except to eat. 'I guess we're eating the shark,' I rationalised. It would be a part of our living, after all.

The assignment was worth a considerable sum of money and most other people in 1976 would have been astonished that we should have given even a second's thought to the propriety of catching a shark. The more so since *Jaws* painted Great Whites as murderous monsters. Nonetheless, it did not sit well with any of us, especially with Valerie Taylor. Once the Australian female spearfishing champion, she had become one of the world's top underwater still photographers. She was now a dedicated conservationist who would not harm a fin or scale of one of her subjects.

Ron was more philosophical. 'It's a pity,' he said. 'But it's the only way to do the shot. Like you said, we're "eating" the shark.'

In a sense, when the time came, the shark made it easier for us. He attacked the boat. It was like a scene from *Jaws*. And like any form of shark attack it was the more startling because it was totally unexpected.

The phone had rung that morning with the news that there were whales. That brightened everyone up. We went through the familiar routine of tying up to the pontoon beside the dead sperm whales. ('Poor things!' said Valerie.)

Aboard my boat *Beachcomber* were Ron and Valerie Taylor and my wife Marilyn. Brian Greenhalgh, our Albany diving friend who had persuaded us to take an interest in Great Whites in the first place, had brought his own boat across from Emu Point with his wife Fran. Because Ron thought he might take some underwater shots if they were available, we had the cage in tow.

We also had on board some large hooks and chunks of whale steak for the set-line.

The sharks were unsatisfactory. We saw some glimpses, flashes of silver in the depths alongside. But there was no active feeding, and while we were still considering what to do the little green tugboat came out, diesel motor pop-popping, and took the last whales off to the slipway ashore.

'That's it, then,' I said in disappointment. 'Goodbye sharks!'

'They don't hang around once the whales have gone?' Ron asked.

'Not in our experience. There's nothing to keep them interested.'

We had been talking with the Greenhalghs aboard while we watched and waited. The discussion, naturally enough in those circumstances, was of sharks and cages and camera techniques. We talked of the dangers of ropes and Ron told us of the shark that got tangled in the cage lines during the *Jaws* filming in South Australia and wrecked the cage.

'Have you thought of filming without the cage?' I asked.

'Often,' he nodded. 'One day we'll do it. It's a matter of the right circumstances. Sometimes it has seemed OK. But there's always that unpredictable factor.'

During the *Jaws* filming Ron had sat on top of a submerged cage with his camera, with his legs inside, ready to drop in. When a White swooped at him he found his SCUBA tank had snagged on the mesh and he was stuck fast — and exposed. He had to fend the shark off with the camera. 'I felt very vulnerable,' he said. 'Nothing happened, fortunately. But it made me think. The Whites were very good at getting out of visibility range and coming from behind you.'

'You needed to have eyes in the back of your head. They seemed to appear where we least expected them,' said Valerie.

231

'I guess you could probably get away with swimming out of the cage,' I suggested. 'So long as you weren't on the surface. I always had a feeling here that the danger was probably in going into the water and getting out.'

It was the old story, we agreed. There might be only one chance in a hundred of something going wrong. But if you did a thing 100 times...

'*Jesus!*' I said, 'look at *that!*'

'That's a bloody big fin!' said Brian Greenhalgh, jumping to his feet.

'Moving fast, too,' said Valerie. 'Quick, where's my camera!'

It was the one time in a hundred.

We had never seen a fin move so fast. It zipped across the water, circled us and then there was a dull watery impact and the cage lifted half out of the water and lay momentarily on its back.

'*Jesus!*' I exclaimed again.

We all knew how heavy and water-resistant the cage was. It must have required an enormous impact to lift it up and lay it over like that. Lucky no one was inside it!

There was a scrunch and the boat moved beneath our feet. The shark had hit the transom. Hard and angry.

'Quick! Let's get a bait over the side,' said Ron. 'This may be our boy!'

A hook and a chunk of whale meat went over with a splash. There were 450 metres of red nylon line coiled in a fishing basket ready for such a moment if the shark should take it.

The shark assaulted the cage once more, and had another biff at the stern of the boat so that everyone cried out together. Then the white float supporting the hook was jerked underwater and the line began to run out at a rapid pace.

'Hook up! There he goes!'

Now pandemonium broke out. We were tied up to the pontoon. Brian Greenhalgh's boat was tied to mine, and the cage hung by yet another line astern. We had to divest ourselves of all this impedimenta as quickly as possible and get the shark out into open water.

If he was able to take a solid jerk on it he could straighten the hook. This meant that if he carried the line around the chains anchoring the pontoon it would probably be the end of the story.

The red line whizzed over the side at astonishing speed.

'Tie a float to the end, quick!'

We had a square red float used for cage baits. There was barely time to get the line through it and tie a bowline knot before it was jerked out of our hands.

The shark was now swimming free. But he was on the end of our line, and the tell-tale float danced crazily across the surface kicking up bright white flashes of spray.

'Cast off!'

Everyone seemed to be yelling at once. Fran Greenhalgh was cast loose in the Greenhalgh boat with instructions to look after the cage. Then we were away with a roar from the Mercury 485 sterndrive.

Dismay!

All morning we had been casting jaundiced eyes on a gamefishing boat anchored nearby, with rods in the holders and baits and lines trailing behind. They were also trying to catch a shark. Our competition, and just when we didn't need it!

Now our red float was heading towards the other boat. We groaned as the line went under her keel. One of their fishermen leaned over and gaffed it up and grabbed our red float gleefully.

'Now it's *our* shark!' he cried, waving the float in triumph, as we ground our teeth. 'It's a free fish and we've got it!'

'No, you bloody well haven't!'

I gunned the boat around the stern of the gamefishermen and Brian scooped up the line on the other side of his hull with a gaff.

'Cut the line!' I shouted, but he had already done it.

'Make fast for'ard. Point me the direction he's taking!'

We left the frustrated gamefishermen with our red float and the memory while the shark headed off into King George's Sound and the deep water.

That was where we wanted him. In that area, free of obstructions, he could swim until he was exhausted and there was no fight left in him.

So we thought.

After an hour he was still swimming strongly and showing no sign of tiring.

'Try bringing him closer to the boat. We may be able to use the shotgun.'

'I'll try,' said Brian, 'but he's still pretty green.'

He assayed a pull on the line which stretched rigid before our bows.

'Hang on!' His voice rose a note. 'He's coming back to us!'

Who was chasing who?

'Keep the line clear. Don't let it tangle in case he runs again.'

Brian was hopping about on the foredeck with coils of line looping and springing around his feet.

'Remember Ches Stubbs!'

Suddenly we saw the fin, much closer than we expected, moving at express speed.

'He's going to ram us! Hold tight!'

There was no doubting the shark's intention. As he reached the boat he maintained his speed and, lifting his head slightly, smashed at full pace into the starboard side. It was just below where I sat at the wheel. He hit with an open mouth full of teeth, and his angry black eyes were looking straight at me.

'Christ Almighty!'

The boat heeled over and moved a metre sideways with the impact. If it had been a bondwood boat we would surely have been sunk. I hoped the fibreglass had held.

'Look under the deck — the starboard bunk — and see if he's holed us!'

Crash! There was another impact at the rear. The shark had just turned my stainless steel diving ladder into a corkscrew.

'The shotgun!'

Brian was down from the foredeck now.

'Ron, you take the line!'

Brian had a 12-gauge shotgun, a .44 magnum, loaded with single-ball buffalo cartridge.

'It should stop him dead.'

My job was with the harpoon. This weapon was exactly like the ones the old whalers had used. It had a heavy wooden handle with a slip head at the end of a spear and with a wire trace attached to a separate rope.

Great White sharks — like most other species — sink to the bottom when dead or mortally wounded. Trying to lift three-quarters of a tonne of shark, if the hook was not secure, we stood a chance of losing him into the depths of King George's Sound. The harpoon was insurance against that happening.

The shark made another attack on the transom.

'Hold him in, Ron!'

'*Now!*'

Bang! The shotgun crashed in my ear and the harpoon thudded home into the gills in the same moment.

'Got him!'

'Like hell we have. Look out! He's running again!'

The shark deluged us with water and plunged below the keel. The line sizzled out through Ron's hands. Fortunately it was wet, and ran slippery and easy without burning.

We now had the shark on two lines. Though he had left deep teeth marks in the boat's fibreglass hull, and there was damage to the diving ladder and chines, we were basically in good shape. It should just be a matter of time...

But it took far longer than anyone expected. The longer it lasted the worse we felt about it.

The shark occasionally turned on his tormentors. But his rushes at the boat became weaker.

Brian kept pumping buffalo shot from the magnum until I thought the shark must sink from the weight of lead. We also had a powerhead on the end of a pole and this too thudded into his battered head.

The shark struggled gamely on. By this time everyone on board felt so sorry for him, so full of admiration for the fight he had made, that if he had been less damaged there might have been a vote to let him go. But at that point it would have been useless. He would just have been fodder for the other sharks.

Finally it was over. Everyone felt badly about the shark. We consoled ourselves with the thought that it was necessary and at least it was done. But that sounded somehow hollow, even to ourselves.

The shark finally lay alongside while we photographed him. He was a male and would measure 15 feet 4 inches (4.7 metres) and weigh somewhere close to 2000 pounds (over 900 kilograms).

Apart from his injuries, he was in perfect condition. Or was he?

'Hey! Look at that!' said Ron.

In a vee-shape across his head was the mark of an enormous bite. Whoever owned the jaws — obviously another Great White — must have been big enough to shake this not inconsiderable shark like a puppy. It was evidently a disciplinary bite. If the perpetrator had wished it could have bitten down hard and taken his head off. Some of the teeth had penetrated in gashes 2 and 3 centimetres deep.

'No wonder he was in such a foul temper!'

This was the one shark in a hundred.

If anyone had been in the water when he first circled the boat at the Whaling Station I am certain they would have been attacked without hesitation. From the fearless and furious way he attacked the cage and the boat I am sure that anyone in the cage would, at the very least, have had a very bad time of it.

It had not been our shark's day. With all sincerity we wished it could have been otherwise.

Brian Greenhalgh looked at the long shape now stilled alongside, at the rows of teeth in the part-open jaw.

'That,' he said, 'must be the ultimate predator.'

'No,' said Valerie beside him. She had tears in her eyes. 'No, not the shark. *We* are the ultimate predators.'

235

It was a moment I remembered more than a year later. The Taylors had returned to Sydney, or were in America or out in the Pacific somewhere. Marilyn and I were in a movie theatre in Perth, Western Australia — the film *Orca* was in town at last. We sat expectantly in our seats. It was a moment we had been eagerly awaiting for months.

The film began. Charlotte Rampling was threatened by a (South Australian) Great White shark. The killer whale surged in to save her. Our shark was flung up in the air and splashed back into the water. It took perhaps less than a second. If we had blinked we would have missed it.

'Is that *all*?' demanded Marilyn incredulously?

'That's all,' I said.

'All that at Albany just for *that*?'

'Just for that. That's show business.' I felt empty saying it.

'I don't believe it!' Her voice trembled with indignation.

There was silence for a while, neither of us really concentrating on the film.

'He deserved better,' I said eventually. And felt a knife-stab of guilt for our one-second shark.

THE GENTLE GIANTS OF NINGALOO

chapter twelve

THE TAIL IN FRONT OF MY MASK, MOVING MAJESTICALLY FROM SIDE TO SIDE, seemed huge as a ship's rudder. I had never seen a caudal fin of that size before, and literally gasped underwater — inhaling a great gulp of air mixed with a certain amount of Indian Ocean through my snorkel.

The towering fin pushed purposefully from one side to the other. A smooth gliding motion, powerful yet unhurried. It traversed an arc of somewhere between 3 and 4 metres as it propelled the vast indistinct mass ahead through the water. A dark bulk which seemed to extend endlessly into the hazy blue beyond.

I tried to think of a word to adequately describe the creature in my mind. Immense, awesome, enormous, incredible... All the extreme adjectives seemed somehow to fall short or sound trite.

'Try *big*!' I told myself. 'And kick a bit bloody harder or you'll be left behind!'

When photographing sharks a station at the tail end is not a bad place to start. Until you're sure that the reception is going to be one of mutual respect.

In this case I knew that the huge creature whose bulk stretched so far ahead of me, like a railway carriage on a misty morning, was officially harmless to humans. Nevertheless, the sheer size of it, glimpsed underwater for the first time as I rolled from the side of the red inflatable, exceeded anything I had ever seen before. This was despite the fact that I'd done my homework and thought I knew what to expect.

I knew, for instance, that whale sharks grew to 12 metres (40 feet) and maybe even more. That they may weigh anything from 1 tonne to 2 tonnes for every metre of their length. That at one time *Rhincondon typus* was considered one of the world's rarest sharks, with only 320 sightings reported to science before 1987.

Figures like these, and seeing someone else's photographs, can tell us a lot about a creature. But nothing compares with seeing the animal alive for yourself. Taking the image, with all its absolute impact, in your own retina. Especially when its belly is comfortably rounder than a Volkswagen and it is the biggest fish in the sea.

Yes, *big*, I decided, was definitely the right word.

Now, reflections aside, the problem was to get from the tail to the head end to look at the rest of the shark. While the movement of that immense vertical tail fin seemed unhurried almost to the point of slow motion, the whale shark was moving through the water at quite a respectable pace.

I could tell from the rapid finbeats of the other divers and the frequent bursts of bubbles from their snorkels that they were having to exert themselves fully just to keep station. Overtaking was obviously going to take a special effort.

Foremost in our pre-dive instructions had been a specific request not to touch the shark. Early divers discovering whale sharks had often grabbed fins and been taken for a tow by the gentle giants. Such extroverted contacts made good stories and even greater photographs. But they were inside the personal space of the shark.

Here, at Ningaloo Reef, where whale sharks gathered after the annual coral spawning late in March each year, it had been found that the huge creatures actually disliked having divers trailing from their appendages. No surprise, really, when you think about it.

Since they are among the planet's most inoffensive animals they didn't bite or threaten. They responded in their own way. They dived.

This meant that the show, for the moment, was at an end. It happened often enough for the message to be received. Divers learnt that, providing they observed certain courtesy rules, whale sharks would let them swim along beside them on the surface like overgrown pilot fish, for long periods. Do it right and everyone got along just fine. If the rules were broken, the sharks simply removed themselves from the scene. It was an effective protest.

The Ningaloo phenomenon — the only place in the world where whale sharks were known to gather in such numbers to a regular timetable — became so important to so many divers that rules had to be established. For the good of both divers and sharks.

Who knows for how many thousands, maybe millions, of years the great assembly of *Rhincondon typus* has been taking place near Ningaloo Reef?

Divers came from all over the world to Ningaloo Reef off North West Cape in Western Australia to see the sharks. No one wanted to see the huge creatures harassed and driven away from their traditional grounds. The Western Australian Government was concerned for the shark from the outset, and had its Department of Conservation and Land Management (CALM) oversee charter boat operations at Ningaloo in the shark season.

Charter boats had to be licensed, their numbers limited, and visiting divers supervised and instructed in the requirements. None of them had to be told that swimming with the whale sharks was a privilege.

The town of Exmouth, on Exmouth Gulf and the base for whale shark operations, is one of Australia's more remote townships. It is 1408 kilometres (880 miles) north of the WA capital, Perth, and 3200 kilometres from Sydney, on the other side of the continent.

American, Japanese, British and European divers have come a very long way by the time they get to Ningaloo Reef. Wherever they start from, anyone going to see whale sharks has spent a good deal of money before they put a fin in the water. No need to ask them whether they care if the whale sharks are driven away. To add force to the message there is a Western Australian Government fine of up to $4000 for riding a whale shark or other form of harassment. But up to the end of 1996 there had been no prosecutions.

'The people who come here come with goodwill towards the sharks,' said Malcolm Toole who operates Exmouth Dive.

'They don't want to be part of sending the sharks away. Once we tell them the reason for the rules, they understand and there are no problems.'

What do the sharks dislike? As observed, they appear to dislike having divers hold on to their fins or tails. They may also have an aversion to SCUBA bubbles, camera flashes and strobe-lights. The high-pitched whirr of a video camera, or perhaps the electrical impulses of its operation, will often result in a dive. Underwater scooters or propulsion vehicles also 'spook' whale sharks. They don't like moving boats to be too close — many of them carry propeller scars.

But they are frequently curious about stationary boats with the engine switched off.

They will sometimes nudge a drifting boat with their noses in inquiring fashion. Or rub against a keel like a cow scratching an itch against a post. You can almost hear them say, 'Ahhh, that's better!'

On that first dive, the benchmark occasion everyone most remembers, my own need was to get from the tail to the head of the particularly large female shark swimming ahead of me. Easier said than done.

I would have to swim in a wide arc, firstly to avoid colliding with the tail and secondly to fin around two other divers ahead of me who had cameras pressed to their masks. Like whale sharks, humans don't like to be bumped unexpectedly in the water (they think of *other* sharks). Nor are they pleased to have their shots blocked by bodies or bubbles of passage between themselves and the subject.

Travelling the length of the shark was a little like gearing up for a sprint in the middle of a mile race. But it was worth the effort. The whale shark was a magnificent sight.

The brown body, with its radiating patterns of silver dollar sized white spots, was a tiger shark shape on an immense scale. Pronounced ridges ran along the sinuously moving body of the shark. The lowest and longest ridge eventually formed part of the caudal ridge in front of the slow-beating tail. Which now, from a perspective alongside the head, seemed a very long way back.

The dorsal fin was huge and sloped back at 45 degrees, again like a tiger's. The pectoral fins were also deep and well pointed. It was easy to see how from an aircraft or even a boat a whale shark could be mistaken for an immense tiger. The stuff of legends. The enormous square head with its metre-wide mouth was a surprise. The mouth was different from that of most of the pelagic sharks, being situated at the very front of the shark instead of being slightly underset. The animal sported a pair of ridiculously small eyes with a pacifically mild expression.

'Are you enjoying your swim?' they seemed to say.

There is always a point with animals, and particularly spectacular creatures like a whale shark, when you would like to be able to talk with them. Impossible, of course, but I believe you can communicate to a degree.

When an angry grey reef shark buzzes you, spiked fins aprickle, the message is clear: *'You're in my space!'*

The feeling with the whale sharks was opposite. One of tranquillity. They seemed content with the morning, and willing to share it with us. Provided we didn't exhibit that painful human aggressive trait and become too pushy.

Humans like to test to boundaries. To find out how far they can go, rather than treating animals with courtesy and respect. It is something of a matter for regret, since it achieves only a negative purpose. Ultimately they reach the point where the creature has had enough and either withdraws or reacts aggressively. Common sense (that rare quality) should tell us that wild animals are nervous about being touched. In the ocean the only physical contacts they are likely to have, other than from their own species and cleaner fish, will be the unwelcome attentions of predators. Similarly, the only creatures which will naturally swim hard at them and prop suddenly in front of their heads will be sharks — rather than tourists with Nikonos underwater cameras.

Whale sharks are not instinctively programmed to welcome such actions.

Imagine a reverse situation where you are enjoying a walk in the park and an unidentified creature of a kind you have never seen before rushes up to you and waves limbs terminating in what appear to be squid tentacles in your face?

What would your reaction be? Ninety-nine per cent of us would run like blazes. The other one per cent might climb a tree. The whale shark dives.

Animals, of course, can become 'tame'. That is to say they become familiar with people and no longer get alarmed. Moray eels and groper can be handfed in a remarkably short time, and then — good intentions established — will put up with all sorts of liberties, including petting and handling by people, in order to get a free meal. Interestingly, it is possible to tame sea creatures far more quickly than animals ashore. Perhaps because they have not had face-to-face experience of humans and because we are not associated *in their minds* with nets or fishing lines.

At the Rowley Shoals, offshore from the pearling port of Broome, I have in a single day tamed big potato cod, 180 kilogram fish, to the point of handfeeding them. By the second day divers were photographed putting their arms around them. Moray eels, despite their fierce appearance, were even more amenable.

Since it is impractical and undesirable to feed a whale shark at Ningaloo and to form that kind of food-based friendship, we have a relationship which is essentially on the shark's terms.

At best they tolerate us. If they don't like what we're doing, or if they're too busy to be bothered with us, they dive. *C'est la vie*, in the world of *Rhincondon typus*.

These thoughts passed through my head as I passed the last of the divers on the whale shark's starboard flank and turned inwards to take my own shot.

As the shark, a mighty behemoth, cruised onwards I stopped swimming to watch the whole amazing length of her pass by. Several bright yellow fish swam out in front of her with a look of serious responsibility, pages heralding the passage of a Very Important Personage.

On her lip a school of very small trevally fluttered their tails, riding on the pressure wave. Some actually swam inside her mouth, and slim black and white remoras slipped in and out of her gills at will. A pair of much larger remoras, *Echeneis naucrates*, were further down her body in a state of agonised indecision. They obviously regarded the divers as predators, and their normal

241

reaction was to duck under to the other side of the shark. To hide behind the great moving body. But because there were divers on both sides they had to keep skittering from one side to the other around her anal fins.

The enormous, spotted, cigar-shaped length of her passed by my mask, and I was able to see that at one time she had been hurt. A crumpled starboard (right-hand) pectoral fin and a deep scar on her abdomen showed that she had been hit by a boat and wounded by the propeller.

The scars were well healed, so the incident must have occurred some years before. How many whale sharks do we accidentally kill?

The tail swept past again and I had to swim backwards to avoid it.

'Magnificent!' I said to myself, marvelling at the spectacle.

There are few animals in the sea so big that you can watch them passing and count the seconds. Whales offer similar size, and some grow considerably bigger. But they are generally far more cautious about divers — and with the human record, who could blame them.

How did this Ningaloo Reef phenomenon begin?

Whale sharks have been around for more than 60 million years. Early contacts with humans may have occurred when *Homo sapiens* first bound logs together and made a raft to cross a strait or gulf, or hollowed out a tree trunk for a canoe to travel a coast.

But early man would not have been a predator.

Rhincondon typus, fully mature, is safe from most things in the sea. The whale shark is simply too big to handle. What protects it from natural enemies also holds good for humans. Some whale sharks have been caught for meat and oil off Indian and Sri Lankan shores. But a *Rhincondon* of any size tended to be too strong. They had an annoying habit of dragging fishing boats under on the end of their harpoon lines. Getting a 10 tonne monster to shore was a performance requiring effort out of the ordinary. Generally speaking there were easier fish to fry.

Scientifically, whale sharks were considered a rare fish, because few specimens had been examined. They were too big for museums. A 10 metre whale shark hardly fits in a glass jar. The combined museums of Europe, in the last century, would not have had enough formalin to preserve an adult specimen.

Though an immature whale shark swam for some years in a Japanese aquarium, there are also obvious difficulties in keeping captive specimens. The amount of specialised food and space required foremost among them. But there is a nice story from the Phoenix group of islands in the Pacific,

242

where the United States Air Force had a tracking station at Canton Island for monitoring space flights.

An 8 metre female whale shark swam into the island's lagoon one day in 1976, and stayed more than a year. The islanders named her 'Mimi' (some versions of the story have her as 'Mini'). Initially she appeared lost in a maze of shallow reefs, and they tried unsuccessfully to lead her out of them. After a time, at her own pace, she found her way into the main lagoon.

Concern was felt that Mimi would not be able to find her proper oceanic food and that she was out of her natural orbit — 'What's a nice girl like you doing in a place like this?' The sympathetic islanders fed her shrimps and small fish. The shark learned to come to a small skiff to be fed, pushing her head up out of the water alongside the skiff, like a dog begging for a bone.

After 14 months, she left the lagoon for the open sea and the normal patterns of whale shark life.

What are those patterns?

The whale shark is something of an oddity. Apart from being the largest cold-blooded fish in the sea, it is a member of the shark order of *Orecto-loboformes*, or carpet sharks. But the whale shark is a roaming pelagic, while it's closer relatives are smaller bottom-dwelling sharks like the Port Jackson, the leopard shark and, more particularly, the wobbegong or carpet shark.

None of us can choose our relatives, of course. But it is curious that these other sharks should lead such different lives. The wobbegong, the whale shark's closest cousin, is a small shark, usually less than 3 metres in length (the size of a large whale shark's tail fin). It spends almost all of its time stationary on the bottom.

The wobbegong's ornate 'carpet' markings camouflage it to blend in with the reef. It is an active carnivore, ambushing smaller prey by pushing off its coiled tail like a spring, with a lightning-quick forward thrust.

The wobbegong has a set of needle-sharp teeth like a grey nurse, and — as some divers have found to their cost — has a decidedly grumpy disposition. While there is no record of a fatal attack by a wobbegong on a human, divers have suffered serious lacerations from wobbegong bites. With some well-placed nips *Orectolabus ornatus* has earned the right to be respected.

It is just as well that wobbegongs do not grow to whale shark size. A 12 metre wobbegong of uncertain temper would not be nice to encounter on a morning swim.

Its larger relative, the whale shark, is fortunately a peaceable soul. The whale shark does have a lot of teeth — 300 bands of them — but they are so small, 2 millimetres, that they present no threat to larger prey. In fact the name *Rhincondon* means 'file-teeth'.

The word 'whale' sometimes puzzles people for the whale shark is no mammal. It is simply big. A 'whale-sized' shark.

The whale shark's diet consists of plankton, shrimp-like crustaceans (krill) and small fish. It is a filter-feeder, swimming with open mouth (an impressive sight) and straining food through its gills. There are two other filter-feeding sharks, neither of them relations.

The basking shark, *Cetorhinus maximus*, grows almost as big as *Rhincondon*, and is sometimes confused with the whale shark in people's minds. It is the second largest shark, growing up to 12 metres. Like the whale shark, the basking shark (so called from its habit of surface swimming) feeds on planktonic crustaceans. Where as the whale shark is a creature of tropical and subtropical seas, the basking shark is found in the colder north and south waters of the Atlantic and Pacific.

We have earlier encountered 'Megamouth', *Megachasma pelagios*, the rare filter-feeder of the deep oceans, which grows to 4.5 metres and consumes crustaceans and deep-layer jellyfish.

There is a great deal that we still have to learn about whale sharks. For many years scientists remained undecided about whether they are *viviparous* (have live young) or *oviparous* (lay eggs). A selachian version of the old conundrum, 'Which came first — the chicken or the egg?'

A whale shark egg 35.5 centimetres ($14^1/_2$ inches) long and the size of a small cushion was dredged up by a trawler in the Gulf of Mexico in 1953. Its skipper, Captain Odell Freeze, felt movement in the large egg case and, opening it with his knife, found a live young whale shark. A surprise for both of them. This might seem to be conclusive proof that whale sharks do indeed lay egg cases, which hatch later on the seabed. But it failed to satisfy the scientists.

'Why have no other whale shark egg cases ever been found?' they wanted to know. 'Maybe that one was an aborted egg capsule — and normally the young hatch inside the mother.'

The jury remained out on the question until 1995, when Dr Eugenie Clark of the United States and Che-Tsung Chen of the National Taiwan Ocean University examined a pregnant 10.5 metre female whale shark.

The shark had been harpooned by fishermen. The *National Geographic* magazine of September 1966 (diplomatically refraining from comment on the desirability or otherwise of harpooning whale sharks) reported that Clark and Che-Tsung found in twin uteruses 'an astonishing 300 embryos from 16 to 20 inches [40 to 50 centimetres] long, proof that whale shark embryos emerge from egg capsules within the body'. The 300 embryos, Dr Clark said, 'far exceeded the largest number reported for any species of shark. Yet this fish was not large as female whale sharks go and probably was young. Larger females likely carry even more offspring'.

The fact that the whale shark is the most prolific of all shark mothers was a surprise in itself for the scientists.

What happens next on the whale shark's long journey through life?

Little whale sharks, recently born and as small as 55 centimetres (21 inches), have been caught in nets off tropical African and Central American coasts. Where the infants go from there is a puzzle. Though there are plenty of records of young immature sharks from three metres upwards in size, there are none of the sightings of *Rhincondon* pups between one and three metres. What is certain is that only a tiny portion of the swarm of 300 infant *Rhincondon* will survive. As with other multiple-birth animals, most will perish or provide food for other creatures in the food chain in Nature's cruel equation for the survival of the fittest.

How long do whale sharks that reach adulthood live?

Dr Geoff Taylor, the primary researcher of whale sharks at Ningaloo, and author of the excellent book *Whale Sharks — Giants of the Ningaloo Reef* (1995), suggests they may live a very long time. 'The whale shark's life pattern is thought to be similar to that of the white-spotted dogfish,' he writes, and he explains further that the dogfish does not reach sexual maturity until 20 years of age and has been known to live past 100 years. 'Preliminary evidence at Ningaloo Reef appears to indicate that the male whale shark does not reach sexual maturity until 30 years of age. If, as with the dogfish, this is less than one-fifth of its life expectancy, then it is not unlikely that the whale shark may be one of the longest living creatures on earth.'

One hundred and fifty years?

It may be that some of the older whale sharks we swam with at Ningaloo were born in a previous century.

Some whale sharks have not reached that kind of milestone due to collisions with shipping. Because of their slow speed and habit of surface swimming, whale sharks are very vulnerable to being run down by ships. Quite a number of collisions were reported early in the 20th century, and one vessel, the *President Wilson*, rammed whale sharks in successive years, 1936 and 1937, in the Red Sea.

Dr Eugene Gudger, Curator of Fishes at the American Museum of Natural History made a lifetime study of whale sharks and published a great deal of what was known about them prior to the Second World War.

In 1941 he wrote a paper titled *The Whale Shark Unafraid* in which he stated: 'Rhincondon fears neither man nor ship!' Perhaps *The Whale Shark Unaware* might have been a more accurate title. Whale sharks in previous millennia had no need to consider men on ships in their evolutionary responses. Many of the whale sharks we saw at Ningaloo were missing portions of fins and tails. Some of this structural damage may have been due to encounters with predatory shark species in early life. But other healed injuries were unquestionably from propellers.

Gudger took measurements from a 9.5 metre (32 foot) whale shark captured off the Florida Keys in 1923. He used them to construct a full-scale model at the American Museum of Natural History. There were displays of smaller specimens at the British Museum and at museums in Paris and Colombo. But generally the world did not know a lot about *Rhincondon typus*. It was a case of 'out of sight, out of mind'.

This is evidenced by the fact that the other American whale shark expert, Dr Fay Wolfson of the Hubbs Marine Institute in San Diego, in 1987 collated all the sightings of *Rhincondon* reported in scientific literature up to that time. The entries numbered only 320. Wolfson's entries may have included sightings by early divers.

Neither Gudger nor Wolfson were ever fortunate enough themselves to see a live whale shark in the wild, though it must have been close to being their dearest wish. A sign of their own times.

Hans Hass, in his book, *We Come from the Sea*, tells of an encounter with a 7.5 metre whale shark in the Red Sea in 1950:

Above the water the mysterious enormous fin was already almost within reach. But still I saw nothing below. Nothing but the empty, blue, bottomless sea. The silver darts of the sun's rays were my only companions...

At last I was able to make out the vague outlines. Then the veil lifted completely. What I saw was so exceptional that I remained hovering in the water motionless. Before me was a shark at least 25 feet [7.6 metres] long. Its entire huge body was covered with hundreds of white spots.

It was hanging in the water almost motionless. Only the large crescent-shaped tail fin was slowly moving to and fro. Near its head the spots were small and numerous, towards the tail they were larger and arranged in rows. Between them ran projecting ridges. The strongest of these terminated in the root of the tail.

The most unusual feature was the creature's mouth. In contrast to all other sharks it was not on the underside, a short distance behind the nose, but right

in front at the foremost point of the head. It was slightly opened and had lips.
In spite of its enormous size the creature looked good tempered and harmless...

Hass recognised the monster as a whale shark and filmed and photographed it in order to share the experience with the world.

The whale shark which approached the Kon Tiki Expedition raft in the mid-Pacific during the great adventure voyage of 1947 received an entirely different description and reception. Thor Heyerdahl, leader of the expedition, recorded the experience in the book, *The Kon Tiki Expedition*:

Knut had been squatting there [by the edge of the raft] washing his pants in a swell, and when he looked up for a moment he was staring straight into the biggest and ugliest face any of us had seen in the whole of our lives. It was the face of a veritable sea monster, so huge and hideous that if the Old Man of the Sea himself had come up he could not have made such an impression on us.

The head was broad and flat like a frog's with two small eyes right at the sides, and a hood-like jaw which was four or five feet [1.2 or 1.5 metres] wide and had long fringes drooping from the corners of the mouth.

Behind the head was an enormous body ending in a long thin tail with a pointed tail fin which stood straight up and showed that this sea monster was not any kind of whale.

The body looked brownish underwater, but both head and body were thickly covered with small white spots... The large round dorsal fin projected clear out of the water and sometimes the tail fin as well. When the creature was in the trough of the swell the water flowed about the broad back as though washing around a submerged reef.

In front of the jaws swam a whole crowd of zebra-striped pilot fish in formation, and large remora fish and other parasites sat firmly attached to the huge body and travelled with it. So that the whole thing looked like a curious zoological collection crowded round something that resembled a floating deepwater reef.

Those aboard the raft saw it as 'incredibly grotesque, inert, and stupid'. Thor Heyerdahl recorded that the men could not help laughing. 'Although we realised that it had strength enough in its tail to smash both balsa logs and ropes to pieces if it attacked us.'

Attacked?

Eric was standing at a corner of the raft with an eight-foot [2.4 metre] hand harpoon. Encouraged by ill-considered shouts he raised the harpoon above his head… He thrust the harpoon with all his giant strength down between his legs and deep into the whale shark's gristly head.

It was a second or two before the giant understood properly what was happening. Then in a flash the placid half-wit transformed into a mountain of steel muscles.

We heard a swishing noise as the harpoon line rushed over the edge of the raft and saw a cascade of water as the giant stood on its head and plunged down into the depths.

The three men who were standing nearest were flung about the place head over heels and two of them were flayed and burned by the line as it rushed through the air. The line, thick enough to hold a boat, was caught on the side of the boat, but snapped like a piece of twine and a few seconds later a broken off harpoon shaft came to the surface 200 yards [180 metres] away.

A shoal of frightened pilot fish shot off through the water in a desperate attempt to keep up with their old Lord and Master… We never saw anything more of the whale shark.

When I first read the story of the Kon Tiki Expedition as a 17-year-old I was completely enthralled. And envious. It was the kind of adventure I dreamt of for myself. When I reached the description of the harpooning of the whale shark I was not offended. It seemed a natural thing to do. If a sea monster surfaced beside your craft in the mid-Pacific, thousands of kilometres from anywhere, some defensive action was surely necessary? It was a case of survival against the sea and the strange and dangerous creatures that inhabited the deeps. Gallant Man against the elements and the beasts. So I thought at the time.

Forty-five years later, after swimming with whale sharks at Ningaloo, I re-read Kon Tiki and squirmed with embarrassment for them.

In 1995, harpooning the whale shark seemed a senseless and stupid act. The poor whale shark's only crime was curiosity. What could have been a delightful mid-ocean interlude became instead an ugly example of humans' thoughtless brutality to an inoffensive creature.

Those 45 years had included a good deal of my own time spent at sea in small boats, occasionally handling very big fish. From that experience I could see the harpooning as having been extremely foolhardy. The line which 'flayed and burned' the men on deck could easily have caught one of them in its coils, dragging him overboard and drowning him. And if the line had not snapped, the whale shark in its struggles to get free, with its immense bulk

248

and strength, could have wrecked the raft, a relatively flimsy affair held together only by cords.

From a seaman's perspective there were surely quite enough natural problems to be encountered on a raft in the middle of the Pacific Ocean, without creating unnecessary additional hazards. In those terms, the word 'half-wit' which Heyerdahl applied to the shark perhaps better described his harpooner.

I was puzzled also by his other descriptions. Thor Heyerdahl, a man I so much admired, described the whale shark as 'the biggest and ugliest face any of us had seen in the whole of our lives'. He added the words 'hideous' and 'grotesque' later in the passage. This did not apply to any of the whale sharks I had seen — creatures of grace and majesty. How could our views be so divergent?

Then the reason dawned on me.

They had, of course, seen the great shark only from the surface, its shape distorted by wavelets and ripples and light refraction. The way we ourselves seem grotesque in a trick showground mirror. The kind of reflection which makes us seem fatter or thinner than we really are.

They were also ignorant about the shark. Little was known about it in 1947, after all, and ignorance breeds fear. Fear tends to incite the 'get them before they get us!' syndrome so familiar in our human dealings with each other.

We knew that the whale sharks would harm no one, and had the incomparable advantage of seeing the sharks in their own element, below the undulating silver skin of the surface. There were no 'trick' images in that underwater world. In the clear blue water of the Leeuwin Current off Ningaloo Reef we saw the smooth lines of the sharks as they truly were.

I'm sure that if the Kon Tiki crew could have seen their shark as we saw ours, as an object of beauty and wonder, then their reactions would have been very different. I felt regret for them at a lost opportunity. They had the chance to observe at length the most seldom seen shark of their day. And they destroyed the moment.

In the 1990s we may wonder what became of that shark. Whether it recovered from its mistreatment to continue swimming the seven seas. Unharmed it might still be swimming today.

It is probably unfair to dwell too deeply on the Kon Tiki incident, which was clearly an accident of misunderstanding. The Kon Tiki crew were men of their time with the common attitudes towards the natural world of their day. A time when the only good shark was one lying dead on a dock.

alf a century on, those attitudes have come around full circle. At Ningaloo Reef we regarded it as a privilege to be able to swim with the whale sharks. In fact I saw myself as doubly fortunate, because it was an opportunity I almost failed to grasp.

Some days may find us in a negative mood. On one such April morning, before the second cup of coffee, the telephone rang and it was my friend Les Valmadre.

'Got you at last!' he cried triumphantly.

Most of the summer I am on my boat at Rottnest Island and only visit the mainland sporadically, so I can be hard to catch.

'What's news?' I asked.

'You have to come to Exmouth Gulf,' he answered. 'The whale sharks are running this month.'

'So…?'

'So my American mate, Doug Seiffert, who runs Tiny Bubbles Expeditions out of Jupiter Beach, Florida, has booked a boat and accommodation at Exmouth. He's had a couple of cancellations. There are two places there if we want them.'

'Hmmm…'

I had a mental vision of black clouds and whitecaps on a wave-spiked sea. April was autumn, a time of unpredictable weather. My boat *Beachcomber III* was still at Rottnest Island and moored in an anchorage open to storms from the northwest danger quarter. If an unexpected cold front pushed up from the Southern Ocean to our latitude of 32 degrees, it could bring gales of 60 knots or more and a giant swell. A recipe for a boat on the rocks. I didn't like to leave her unattended.

'I don't think I can make it.'

'Come on!' said Les. 'The whale sharks are fantastic. This is a great opportunity. You'll kick yourself later if you don't take it.'

'The problem is… '

'I know what the problem is.' Les was becoming impatient. 'You can do it if you want to. Look, think about it overnight and ring me back in the morning.' He hung up before I could reply.

That night I did think about it. Exmouth Gulf, Ningaloo Reef and North West Cape had at one time figured in my life. In 1969 I had taken out a lease on North Muiron Island at the head of the Gulf, with the idea of establishing a fishing camp. The camp was to be an escape from overcivilised life in the city. A parachute out of the rat race. The jump had to wait a little longer. But at Exmouth we had some rare diving and fishing in virgin waters where everything was new and exciting. The sea around the island abounded in fish, sharks, turtles and corals. The Gulf was an old pearling ground. It was a time of high adventure.

'Adventure!' I sat up suddenly in bed. Was my sense of adventure really gone, sunk without a trace? Was the wheelchair just around the corner?

I rang Les in the morning. 'I'll come,' I said.

'I thought you would,' he replied. 'I took the booking.' I could picture him smiling privately under his luxuriant moustache.

When I considered the matter more fully I realised that my appointment with the whale shark was long overdue. My fisherman friend Clem Hill, a man of vast knowledge of the sea, had told me about whale sharks in the 1960s along the back of Dirk Hartog Island. He showed me photographs taken from the deck of the boat he skippered, the *Western Star*, and we speculated then about photographing one underwater.

'They're so quiet,' he insisted. 'You could step off the boat and stand on one'.

In 1965 Ben Cropp, whom I'd known since Mediterranean archaeological days in Sicily in 1958, became the first Australian to film a whale shark. A diving friend, George Meyer, found one off Montague Island on the New South Wales coast on a day of dismal weather. A week later Ben and George, with the odds thousands to one against them, were incredibly fortunate to find the shark again. It became the subject of one of Ben's films, *Whale of a Shark*, and a book of the same title. In the book Ben wrote:

Into my vision swam the most gigantic shark I had ever seen. It was unbelievably large, some 35 feet [10 metres] long. Behind it followed an entourage of circling kingfish, large tuna, and a small whaler shark… George dived and began filming it, sweeping along the full length of the shark and finally grabbing its tail. The shark's reaction was the only unfriendly one it was to make, as it swept George off with one sweep of that gigantic tail. But it was inquisitive and turned back to see what annoying little creature had been hanging on its tail.

It was so uncommon to see a whale shark at that time that the photographs blown up from the 16mm film made newspaper front pages around the world, and appeared in the *National Geographic*.

Ron and Valerie Taylor initially thought that their first whale shark, an enormous specimen which they encountered in the 1970s while returning from an unsuccessful filming trip to Seal Island, must be a Great White.

Then, Valerie recalled, Ron shook his head. 'No Great Whites can be over 30 feet [9 metres],' he said. 'It must be something else.'

Valerie wrote later in *Great Shark Stories*:

Ron cut the motor and we all jumped overboard, abandoning the boat to its own devices. I lay on the surface...eyes straining into the distance.

For a few seconds there was nothing, then, suddenly, like a tanker emerging from a fog, came a head so enormous it hardly seemed real. We hung suspended...as yard after yard of beautiful, spotted, streamlined body flowed past... Ron had dreamed of this moment for years. At last it had arrived, five miles [8 kilometres] out at sea in a howling northerly gale. It could have been a cyclone for all we cared. Here was our shark, bigger and better than our wildest dreams! For the moment fate was our friend.

I saw my own first whale shark in 1977 aboard Ben Cropp's boat *Beva*. Ben was on a voyage filming his series *This Rugged Coast* around Australia and Wally Gibbins and I were doing the diving. We were leaving Norwegian Bay, a deserted whaling station on the Western Australian coast, when just outside the reef passage Ben pulled back hard on the throttles.

'Whale shark!' he cried and pointed. 'Starboard bow!'

The shark was a young one, about 6 metres long, and right on the surface. I could see its white spots and distinctive shape quite clearly as it angled unhurriedly across our bow. It looked just like the one in Clem Hill's photographs.

'Who wants a dive?' asked Ben, and then added, 'You'll have to be quick'.

Beva was a hard-chine Grand Banks cruiser. She had very comfortable accommodation, but with shallow draft and high upperworks she could roll on a wet lawn, as they say. In the rough sea behind the reef she was now tossing about diabolically.

All the gear was packed away below for the long trip to Shark Bay further south. Wally Gibbins and I were fumbling in our diving bags for masks and fins when we heard the throttles open again.

'Too late,' said Ben when we went back on deck. 'Just dived.'

I would have to wait another 17 years for my first underwater sight of *Rhincondon typus*.

Despite the passage of time it was well worth the wait. As Les Valmadre had said, joining Doug Seiffert's Tiny Bubbles Expeditions group was a great experience. The divers were as diverse and interesting a group as you could meet from the United States. The boat, *Nordon II*, was well set up, the crew pleasant and very competent. The weather was perfect and the whale sharks were there in numbers. What more could anyone ask?

In another sense, for me — as for everyone else who was there in the 1990s — it had begun 15 years before at Ningaloo Station at Point Cloates.

In May 1980 the Western Australian Museum was doing a marine archaeological excavation on a recently discovered wreck at the lower end of the Ningaloo Reef. The vessel had been the *Rapid*, an American ship from Boston, wrecked with a cargo of American and Spanish silver dollars in 1811, 18 years before the first European settlement in Western Australia.

The museum excavation, led by Graeme Henderson, included museum staff and divers associated with the museum. Among the volunteers I met Geoff Taylor, a young British medico, and his charming wife Joanna. The Taylors had come to Australia in the 1970s and had become keen divers.

In his book *Whale Sharks — Giants of the Ningaloo Reef*, Geoff recalled that it was a memorable holiday:

> *Living in the station shearing shed and diving and excavating the wreck, strolling along the white coral sand beaches with the surf pounding the reef off-shore and glistening in the tropical sun, we fell in love with this magnificent coast... Joanna and I as relative newcomers to Western Australia and also as novice divers were unaware that in that remote spot there was assembled a 'Who's Who' of Western Australian divers...*
>
> *One afternoon there was great excitement in the camp. A team of divers had been searching for the wreck of a Japanese ship. On their way home they had sighted a whale shark. Museum diver Jeff Kimpton had snorkelled with the shark and then been towed along on its dorsal fin. They returned to camp full of tales of their experience. A whale shark at Ningaloo! I decided then and there that if I got a chance to return to this remote coast I would search out one of these huge yet elusive creatures.*

Two years later Geoff decided to set up a general medical practice in the town of Exmouth, at the northern end of Ningaloo Reef.

For the next 11 years the reef and whale sharks would become a major part of his life. It took almost a year before he realised his dream of swimming with a whale shark. Finally, on 14 March 1982, he and a friend, Peter Moore, dived with three sharks in one day and sighted two more on the surface on the journey home. By the end of the month they had made further sightings and Geoff had shot several minutes of sharks on Super 8 film.

> *Twelve sightings, over a two week period, of one of the rarest creatures in the world — something very special seemed to be happening... There followed a couple of lean years for whale shark sightings. But at Easter 1985 there were*

whale sharks everywhere we looked. On two successive days we dived with ten sharks each day and on the third day, in a one hour sortie along the reef, we encountered another five... It was becoming evident that there was a particular time of year when large numbers of sharks could be found. I had seen whale sharks at other times of the year — July and January — but the biggest numbers were always in the months of March and April.

In the winter of 1985 Geoff answered an advertisement for a medical job in Queensland. He and Joanna decided to accept, to pack up and leave Exmouth. Then the telephone rang. ABC Television in Melbourne had heard that Geoff had been filming whale sharks. Would he be interested in doing some 16mm filming for a television documentary?

'It was the sort of thing I had dreamed of doing. All thoughts of leaving Exmouth rapidly disappeared.' Geoff bought a handwind Bolex 16mm camera and an underwater housing and in April 1986 was finding as many as 15 whale sharks on a single day.

What was the key to their sudden appearance each March and April? Where did the sharks go to during the rest of the year? These were the questions he asked himself.

'It was only at the end of April 1986 that I first learned of the remarkable coral spawning,' Geoff recalled. In fact, the amazing phenomenon of coral spawning had only been discovered on the Great Barrier Reef in the early 1980s.

The spawning, in which all the corals release their eggs on the same night, is tied to the phases of the moon. In Queensland it occurs in late spring, after the October and November full moons. The corals release both semen and eggs which mingle, fertilise and float to the surface forming an oily slick. From this sticky seaborne union is born the coral plankton *planula*, which drifts on the currents for weeks until it finds a suitable place to settle and grow to become new coral.

In March 1984 a Western Australian marine biologist, Chris Simpson, working in the Dampier Archipelago, found that coral spawning also occurs in the west. However, it occurs there in the autumn rather than the spring, after the March and April full moons. As on the east coast, many other creatures besides coral polyps release eggs at the same time. Sea slugs, sea shells and polychaete worms are all included, in a joyous mass release of new life on the reef. The spawning is predictable almost to the hour — seven days after the full moon, one hour after dark.

It is a huge release of protein which begins to drift on the current and attracts other plankton, including the tropical krill, *Pseudeuphausia latifrons,*

254

tiny 10mm shrimp-like creature. In turn, smaller fish come to feed on the krill, and larger fish to feed on the smaller ones. Largest of all, the great whale sharks come to scoop up both the plankton — which is one of their favourite foods — and the small fish that form dense masses known locally as 'bait balls'.

Mackerel, trevally, predatory sharks and even Bryde's whales, along with *Rhincondon typus*, all swim through the bait balls with mouths open, filling their bellies, satiating their hunger, in one enormous feeding orgy.

'It struck me immediately I heard of the coral spawning,' Geoff Taylor recounted 'that it was a natural occurrence of sufficient magnitude to explain the increase in numbers of whale sharks at the particular time.'

The coral spawning did indeed prove to be the key to predicting the arrival of large numbers of whale sharks off Ningaloo Reef in March or April each year.

Geoff found that the number of whale sharks peaked two weeks after the coral spawning. However, a great deal of research and hundreds of hours on the water along the reef and in spotter aircraft were needed before the theory could be established as positive fact.

Geoff own first necessity was to observe a coral spawning for himself:

On March 21st 1987, accompanied by local teacher Les Eadon, I ventured out from the shore at Bundegi Reef at dusk. There is something very lonely about keeping vigil surrounded only by the inky blackness of night, waiting in a tiny inflatable dinghy, floating on the ocean for an event such as coral spawning.

I kept diving down into the darkness to inspect the coral and it looked the same as it always did.

It was 8.25pm and still nothing had happened. I had promised to be home by 9.00pm, but we decided to give it five more minutes. Suddenly I noticed some tiny pink specks floating on the surface which hadn't been there before. Could that be spawn?

Two minutes more and the pink specks were everywhere. We grabbed our SCUBA gear, cameras, and home-made lights, and descended to the coral to watch the mass releasing of eggs and sperm. The sight of all that spawn swirling around the coral heads was like an underwater dance and to see it for the first time was enthralling.

As I attempted to film the spectacle small worms kept crawling in my ear. I made a mental note: 'Wear a hood next year'. When we returned to the surface it was covered in thick slicks of the spawn. The caviar of the reef had a pungent fishy odour and it pervaded everything including our hair.

Plotting the whale sharks' annual program became a major part of the Taylor family's life. Geoff, Joanna and the children, with various diving partners, spent many days on the blue waters outside Ningaloo Reef in a succession of different types of boat. In the end a trimaran sailboat with an elevated viewing position on the mast was found to be the most suitable. The Taylors had some treasured experiences out behind Ningaloo Reef, the spray of the surf constantly rolling on the coral barrier, framing the heights of the Cape Range on the distant land. A highlight was the whale shark feeding frenzy.

Feeding frenzy?

For people accustomed to seeing film and photographs of an animal moving at a giant's staid and measured pace (the stately sounds of a cello dominant in the background music), the notion of 'frenzy' seems contrary to *Rhincondon's* very nature.

Yet such occurrences do take place. Geoff Taylor was both excited and incredulous when Onslow fisherman Andy Young told him of seeing as many as 70 whale sharks milling at dusk 'like excited dogs'. Young had seen it on two occasions, in 1985 and 1988.

Seventy whale sharks in one group! And this a rare animal?

It seemed almost too incredible to be true. But in 1991 Dan Cassidy, fishing from Exmouth and returning along the reef one evening, saw massed whale sharks behaving just as Andy Young had described.

'Would you like to see if they're still there tomorrow?' Cassidy asked Geoff Taylor.

'Would I!'

Geoff and Joanna went out with Cassidy. It was a slim chance that the phenomenon would be repeated but it was worth a try. And so it proved.

The sun was almost touching the horizon when we saw the first animal breaking the surface and then it was gone. Then another appeared, and another, the glow of the setting sun catching their dorsal fins. Soon they were all around us, charging forward, each creating a large bow wave... Tiny creatures leapt out of the water in front of the sharks' giant mouths, endeavouring to escape. In some places the sharks were moving in groups, twisting and turning together, their tails thrashing the water...

A breathtaking sight! Though light conditions were poor in the gathering dusk, the Taylors managed to get some film and photographs.

Next night they went out again. Conditions were identical, but there was not a shark to be seen. That's the way things go with shark behaviour.

To further the research Geoff managed to get a grant from the Australian National Parks and Wildlife Service for aerial surveys, and with assistance from volunteers in Exmouth greatly increased his data on the numbers and movements of whale sharks along Ningaloo Reef.

Any new phenomenon in the underwater world is likely to generate a feeding frenzy among the makers of international documentaries — those elite filmmakers who cater for the television audiences of millions in the United States, Japan and Great Britain. In previous years there had been many successful marine life films, including 'specials' on humpback whales in Hawaii, right whales in Patagonia, killer whales in Canada, Arctic polar bears, and schools of hammerhead sharks in the Sea of Cortez off Mexico — just to name a few of the subjects fixed in the camera viewfinders.

Now the word was out that there was a unique gathering of whale sharks off Ningaloo Reef in remote Western Australia.

The big operators, the *National Geographic*, BBC television, the Japanese NHK company and the American networks, began to respond to signals that something important was going on in Western Australia.

It had been Geoff Taylor's ambition to make his own film, and to this end he had been accumulating footage on Super 8 and later on 16mm film. When films were ultimately made on the whale sharks, Geoff's film was incorporated in seven of the productions, and he appeared on camera, giving expert commentary. But the big corporations had their own teams, a good deal of complex and incredibly expensive gear, and their own way of doing things. The dream of making his own film did not eventuate. 'In retrospect it seems ridiculous in this day and age for a complete amateur to think he could enter the world of professional filmmakers,' he recorded somewhat sadly.

As compensation, the films were shown around the world, and Geoff Taylor deservedly gained credit for his work among the widespread circle of international shark researchers.

It was somewhat ironic that because he had done deals with *National Geographic*, New Zealand television and the Japanese giant, NHK, the film did not appear on Australian television until long after that first release, and then only on daytime television.

However, the international impact was considerable. *National Geographic* followed up the film and used photographs by David Doubliet and text by Dr Eugenie Clark for a major article. Overnight the whale sharks became world famous. By 1993 increasing numbers of international divers were descending on Exmouth for the annual gathering of the sharks. Every year since, groups like our own in 1995, comprising people prominent in the

257

international diving world, have flown into Learmouth, the former military air base south of Exmouth, to see the gentle giants of Ningaloo Reef on the other side of North West Cape.

Les Valmadre and I were the only Australians in our expedition — fortunate last minute inclusions as the result of cancellations. Lucky to be there, as Les remarked, for what proved to be one of our greatest experiences.

The leader of our group was Douglas Seiffert of Tiny Bubbles Expeditions. Doug had recently been diving with sperm whales in the Azores. He had also made previous trips to Australia, to dive with both Great Whites and whale sharks. He was an accomplished photographer who had written articles on sperm whales, manatees and whale sharks for US magazines.

Tom Campbell, a former US Navy 'Seal', was another distinguished photographer whose underwater pictures had appeared on the covers of a number of US magazines. Like Doug, he had been to Australia before. He wrote in the magazine *Discover Diving* about Great Whites: 'One encounter with a predator of this proportion and you quickly realise that you don't own the ocean…'

Charlene Dejori and Cheryl Scorp, from San Antonio, Texas, were the editors of *Ocean Realm*, one of the most successful US dive magazines. Jay Garbose was a Florida lawyer with international diving tastes.

Between them the Americans had an awesome array of underwater cameras, both still and video. They also had a wealth of experience in exotic underwater locations — Truk Lagoon, the Galapagos Islands, South America, the Caribbean, the Red Sea. It seemed that, wherever there was an adventure dive around the world, some or all of them had been there. Now they were at Exmouth.

They were a fair sample of the quality of divers coming halfway around the globe to see the whale sharks off Ningaloo Reef. And next on the boat, after our charter was finished, would be Ron and Valerie Taylor.

The *Nordon II* was a 52 foot (16 metre) charter vessel. John Starling was skipper, Graeme Russell supervised the deck and got people in and out of the water, and Kevin Stone ran the crimson 'mean machine' inflatable. Apart from being good seamen, the crew were all highly qualified divers. They knew what we were after and where we needed help. Ken White from the Department of Fisheries was on the boat for research and was the 'swim-diver' who indicated the direction the shark was taking once the divers were in the water.

By 1995 diving with the whale sharks during their April peak appearance was a highly organised affair. Each day there were as many as a dozen charter boats of various sizes and styles and diver-carrying capacity.

The Department of Conservation and Land Management (CALM) had wisely set a limit of no more than eight divers in the water with each whale shark. But it was found that — for photography — an even smaller number was more satisfactory.

CALM closely supervised operations. But the crews generally were quick to scotch any activity outside the rules. They were also concerned to see that the sharks were not harassed and driven away.

Spotter aircraft circled overhead during peak periods, directing the charter boats to the vicinity of the whale sharks. When our aircraft sighted a shark we scrambled into the bright red inflatable towed behind the mother ship *Nordon II* and sped to the locality. Kevin Stone operated the twin outboard throttles with one hand and a two-way radio with the other. The laconic voice of the pilot came over the airwaves as he stood the Cessna on its wing tip high above our heads.

'Two hundred yards [180 metres] ahead, two o'clock... You read me, Kevin?'

'Roger,' Kevin replies. 'Read you loud and clear.'

'Slow down now. Ten boat lengths on your starboard bow. One o'clock.'

'Affirmative.' Kevin looks over his shoulder. 'You divers ready?'

'Closing,' from the Cessna. 'Two boat lengths dead ahead.'

'I see him.' Kevin cuts the throttles and allows the inflatable to glide. 'Divers, *go!*'

On both sides of the inflatable, fins go up in the air and divers, clutching cameras to their chests, roll backwards into the water. Splash! Splash! Splash! The bubbles dissipate and the huge dark shadow ahead suddenly takes shape in the clear blue water and becomes the world's biggest fish. We pause a moment, awed as always by its monstrous dimensions. Minds numbed for a fraction of a second by the sight. Then — *action*! The shark is receding. Fins kick hard and quick.

The huge mass of the shark, with its silver dollar spots, dwarfs the divers who are making tracks of bubbles with their fins as they now hurry to keep up. Cameras begin clicking as some divers angle down deep on a breath to silhouette the shark against the light. Others fin hard to get ahead for a frontal shot showing the enormous mouth with the little cloud of yellow trevally on the lower lip. The little eye rolling as the shark watches us.

We had good fortune. We saw seven sharks a day, and missed only one day's diving from bad weather, a tropical storm. Yet every swim seemed as much of a thrill as the first.

Each shark was different. By the end of the week we were identifying ones we had seen previously, recognising them by missing portions of fins, by body scars and, in some cases, by distinctive remora (one trailing a length of fishing line).

The sharks always had companions. Sucker fish, small trevally and pilot fish were regulars. Sometimes a shark would be wholly lost in a dense cloud of bait fish clustering around it like a swarm of bees. The shark looking like a moving reef.

At other times larger fish swam with the whale sharks, including spectacular shoals of golden trevally. Ten kilogram fish swimming above the whale shark like a squadron of silver fighter aircraft, while the little fish cowered in the shadow below the shark's large belly.

On one day a whale shark swam right up to the stationary inflatable, nudging it along with its nose. From underwater I saw the yellow arms of Les Valmadre's wetsuit come over the side. I photographed him taking underwater pictures of the whale shark with his immersed Nikonos while he was still in the boat. The shark pushed the inflatable around with its nose, like a water polo player with a ball. Until it got bored and departed with a swish of the tail.

No one used SCUBA. When video was used, by general agreement, the divers videoed towards the end of a swim because the high-pitched sound (or electrical impulses) seemed to often send the sharks into a dive.

By the end of the week's diving no one was ready to go home. The wonder of swimming with the world's biggest sharks still had us in its grip. I wondered why it had taken me so long to catch up with *Rhincondon typus*.

It was only afterwards that I realised how important diving with the whale sharks had been in complementing all those other shark experiences through the years. It was a balance with the other sharks — the whalers, wobbegongs, makos, tiger sharks, grey nurse, hammerheads and, of course, the Great Whites. Putting each one into perspective, in its own place in the sea, somehow put ourselves into a more complete global perspective as well.

Among the celebrities at Exmouth in 1995 was Geoff Taylor himself, his new whale shark book just released. I met him at the boat ramp at Tantabiddi as the small craft ferried international divers out to the charter boats for the day's diving.

'It's a long way from the shearing shed,' he said with a smile, referring to the 1980 *Rapid* wreck excavation where we first met, and which was the experience that began the whale shark saga for him. The expedition members had been accommodated in the Ningaloo sheep station shearing shed.

'What do you think now?' I asked him, as we watched eager divers loading SCUBA tanks and gear into inflatables and aluminium dinghies. The bustle of morning April activity. Getting ready for a whale shark watching day.

'To be honest I don't know,' he said, scratching his head. 'Ask me in ten years' time. We'll have a better idea then, whether having all this attention on the whale sharks has been a good thing.' He paused a moment. 'Or a bad thing.'

It was a beautiful Exmouth morning. The lagoon shining silver in the sunshine. The white feathers of distant surf curling on the reef. The golden beach stretching away to the north. An age-old scene.

What was new at that place was humankind, and what was exceptionally new was the interest in whale sharks. For millions of years they had got on fine without us. For a short time, 1983 to 1993, they had been a focus of attention for one happily obsessed diver. Now they were public property for hundreds of curious people with masks and fins.

All of us would sometimes like to wind the clock back. I sensed that perhaps Geoff might have preferred in his own heart the days of innocence before Ningaloo was 'discovered' by the outside world.

He wrote in his book that his experiences with the whale sharks, especially the glimpses of the rare mass feeding, had for him 'reinforced the fact that we know so very little about the ocean and its inhabitants. As human observers we can only catch glimpses of these creatures of the deep — small pieces in a huge jigsaw puzzle that we cannot hope to complete'.

Nonetheless, at Ningaloo, Geoff Taylor had put some important pieces of that puzzle together. As well as feeling some personal satisfaction in his findings and his contribution to knowledge of these once 'rare' sharks, he also felt a certain responsibility for bringing them to the world's attention. A concern for their future.

He hopes that we, and the rest of the the world, will now watch over the whale sharks well.

HOW SHARKS COMPARE WITH OTHER DANGEROUS CREATURES

chapter thirteen

THE SHARK IS WITHOUT QUESTION AUSTRALIA'S MOST FEARED PREDATOR, HEADING a list of least loved creatures which also includes snakes and crocodiles. Spiders are hardly favourites either.

But the momentary panic at walking into a large and sticky web in the dark may not match the chill of having something large and foreign brush against your leg unexpectedly in the sea. Even if the 'predator' turns out to be seaweed, the heart rate has made a sudden thudding acceleration.

The acute awareness of sharks extends among most ocean-bordering nations. In Australia, the United States, South Africa and New Zealand, the word *shark* induces a predictable reaction. In Hong Kong 'selachiaphobia' could well run as high as anywhere in the world, following a series of deaths from shark attacks at Dragon Boat time in 1994 and 1995. There is a similar nervousness in Japan, Singapore and Hawaii when sharks are in the news.

Curiously, though, in parts of the world where people have the most direct contact with sharks, such as the Pacific islands, New Guinea and the Philippine and Indonesian archipelagoes, attitudes are more relaxed. Or is fatalistic a better word? Whichever you prefer, it is a fact that islanders have learned to live with sharks through thousands of years. They accept them as a part of normal life.

In Australia, where the fear of sharks is integral in the national psyche, there is some foundation for the anxiety. The Australian Shark Attack File, kept at Taronga Zoo, lists 517 attacks and 185 fatalities since such occurrences were first registered. People have been killed often enough by sharks to give reasonable cause for concern.

There may also have been many more attacks than are officially listed. For example, no records were kept in the early days of 'skindiving' in the pearling industry in northwestern Australia and in Queensland.

For nearly 30 years, until the introduction of the helmet diving suit as standard equipment, naked Aborigines dived on the west coast without goggles or fins, bringing up pearl shell on a single breath. Kanakas from New Guinea and the Solomon Islands and Torres Strait Islanders filled a similar role in the Torres Strait and on the Great Barrier Reef. Wherever they were sent below in the tropical waters where pearl shells grow, surface swimmers were very vulnerable to shark attack.

The plunge divers worked 40 or 50 to a vessel. Eight-man teams dived from 16 foot (4.9 metre) dinghies lowered from the mother ship and sculled by a white overseer with an oar at the stern. On a patch of shell the divers perched on the gunwales and customarily entered the water feet first, turning over below the surface to make a vertical dive.

Dives of over seven fathoms (42 feet or 12.6 metres) were not uncommon. Some experienced divers could reach nine and even ten fathoms, without masks or fins. An amazing performance for men without any aids and relying only on a surface breath. In 1872 there were 989 Malay skindivers and 493 Aborigines on 57 vessels licensed out of Cossack on the northwest coast. A substantial number of divers at daily risk from one pearling port alone.

Henry Taunton was on the northwest coast at a time when it was fashionable for young Englishmen of independent means to go adventuring to remote corners of the world for 'colonial experience'. He wrote a book, *Australind*, notable for its descriptions of Australia in the 'Roaring Days'. Taunton spent time with the Cossack pearling fleet.

Roebuck Bay was a bad place for sharks in 1883 and accidents with sharks were painfully numerous in the first season it was worked. There was one patch a little to the northward of Cape Villaret which seemed to be particularly fatal. Here, one calm morning, my dinghy happened to be the last to leave the vessel. The tide was running out strongly and soon drifted us far astern.

Presently all my Malay divers had dropped into the water except an old chap named Ahmun who lingered a few seconds to arrange his chew of betel nut, having done which he also slipped from the gunwale and disappeared.

Few seconds had passed before he returned to the surface, his eye-balls almost starting from their sockets, his features distorted with fear and agony as he called "Oh Tuan! A great shark!" And then he swam frantically towards the dinghy which was distant about ten yards [9 metres].

When he came to the surface I noticed what appeared to my inexperienced eye a peculiar brown halo which surrounded him in the clear green water. But

263

as he began to swim a broad brown trail was left behind him. Then only did I realise that it was the poor fellow's life blood which was discolouring the water.

A few sturdy strokes and he grasped the gunwale of the boat, and his poor head sank down as he repeated in feeble and heart-rending tones "Oh Tuan, in bezar's kali! — Oh Master, a very great shark!"

When we lifted him into the boat a frightful sight met my eye, as fresh in my memory now as I write as if it was only yesterday that I witnessed the tragedy. Half the man's body had been bitten away exposing the pericardium and the heart. In a few moments, with a long-drawn sigh, poor Ahmun passed away...

His blood ran crimson over the pearl shells in the bottom of the boat. The shells that had cost him his life.

Taunton timed his divers and found that they stayed down for an average of 57 seconds a dive. This was remarkable, considering that they made repeated dives over several hours. As might be expected, medically, deaths from drowning after shallow water blackout (due to prolonged breath holding) were not uncommon. But it was the sharks which the divers feared most.

Taunton recorded his personal observation of four attacks with three fatalities in Roebuck Bay in a period of several months. What the total number of deaths was over the 30 year period of skindiving will never be known.

Crocodiles also killed a number of divers in northern Australian waters. King Sound, in northwestern Australia, was especially notorious. John Brockman, an early pearler, described one such attack in his diary. Like Taunton, Brockman had the scull oar in the stern of a dinghy and was waiting for his divers to surface with shells. Suddenly he heard a dreadful scream from beside another dinghy close by. He saw that the white man, Nelson, was attempting to drag aboard a bleeding diver who had been attacked by a crocodile:

The brute had seized the poor fellow by the arm and snapped it off just below the elbow, and Nelson now had him by the other arm and was endeavouring to get him into the boat.

As he was hoisting the unfortunate man on board the wretch came up again and seized the poor fellow by both his legs above the knee, where he held on as quietly as though he had gone to sleep.

Round both dinghies the water was red with blood through which the boys were swimming and climbing into the boats as fast as they could.

The pearlers beat at the crocodile's head with their oars, and jabbed desperately at its eyes. Still the creature held on.

Then, quite suddenly, the crocodile gave his head a turn, taking off both legs just below the hips as if they had been matches, and disappeared with them below the water leaving us with only the dreadfully mangled trunk. Though I have seen death in many forms since then, nothing has ever had such an effect on me as that dreadful scene…

Crocodiles are another predatory creature to have had an effect on the Australian psyche. After a series of horrific attacks in Queensland, the Northern Territory and Western Australia in the 1980s, fear of crocodiles ran second only to the national dread of sharks. Over that ten year period there were eight deaths from crocodile attack, against 11 fatalities caused by sharks in Australia.

Where crocodiles are concerned, the limiting factor — fortunately for the major part of the Australian population — is climate. Crocodiles are reptiles and cold-blooded creatures and they can only breed in the blood-warm waters of northern Australia. Though occasional wanderers came as far south as Port Hedland on the west coast, and Rockhampton in Queensland, saltwater crocodiles are no threat to swimmers further south where most Australians live.

In the North, in 'croc country', people no longer swim in the sea or saltwater areas where there is a crocodile risk.

No longer?

There was a time in the 1960s and 1970s when people were able to swim, almost with impunity, in waters where bathing today would be considered very foolhardy.

This was because crocodiles were hunted for their skins in the years immediately following the Second World War. Hunters shooting at night with spotlights up creeks and rivers took more than 87 000 crocodile skins between 1948 and 1958 in the Northern Territory, when the industry was at its peak. The skins found a ready market in America and Europe for high quality leather shoes, handbags and belts. Hunters shot a further 26 000 Territory crocodiles (according to official records) up to 1971. By that year the animals of the two Australian crocodile species had become so scarce that they appeared threatened with extinction. The government declared each type a protected species.

The hunt had also extended down both the Queensland and Western Australian coasts. By the 1970s there was hardly a crocodile of significant size to be seen. The few survivors were so afraid of men and boats that, for that brief period, it was possible to swim happily in rivers, billabongs and creeks throughout the North.

I remember an occasion north of Broome, in 1974, when I began to cross an estuarine creek which Aborigines had assured me was shallow enough to wade through. Eventually, when I reached neck-deep depth, I finished the crossing by swimming. When I looked at the Admiralty chart that night to see where I'd been I found the scene of my swim listed as *Alligator Creek.*

It was good for a laugh at the time. But I don't think I'd take a similar swim there today.

Under protection the numbers of crocodiles increased much more rapidly than expected. The human population of the North also increased, through expanded pastoral activity, mining and pearling. More crocodiles, more people, more contacts. By the 1980s another major industry, tourism, had become established. As roads were improved and air access became easier thousands of Australians flocked north for winter sun and to see the legendary areas of the Kimberley, the Northern Territory and the Daintree at first hand. They were accustomed to swimming, in the south, anywhere they felt like it. But since 1971 crocodile numbers had expanded each year. And now there was another important factor.

Like the Great White shark, *Crocodylus porosus*, the saltwater crocodile — the 'man-eater' species — eats fish in its early years. But, as *porosus* becomes larger and less agile (at about 3.5 metres), like *Carcharodon* it changes its diet. The Great White begins to prey on seals, dolphins and large mammals — the crocodile ambushes land animals such as dingoes, kangaroos, birds, flying foxes and wild pigs which come to the water's edge.

Crocodylus porosus, found in Australian, Indian, Malaysian, New Guinean, and Solomon Islands waters, is indigenous to a wide Indo-Pacific region. It is not to be confused with the much smaller Johnston, or 'freshwater', crocodile, *Crocodylus johnstoni*. The Johnston seldom grows more than 3.5 metres, has a long slim snout with sharp needle-like teeth, and eats fish, freshwater turtles and crustaceans. Johnstons have often bitten people in self-defence but have never hunted humans as prey. In contrast, the 'saltwater' crocodile is a confirmed mankiller, wherever it is found, once it reaches maturity.

The common name 'saltwater' crocodile is a dangerous misnomer. As an air-breathing animal *porosus* can swim in either salt water or fresh water and is most dangerous in inland freshwater river and billabong systems, because

266

inexperienced people don't expect to find it there. 'Salties' reach a maximum size somewhere between 6 and 9 metres (20 and 30 feet), and may live (without human interference) for 100 years. In their fully mature phase, saltwater crocodiles are huge, heavy and very dangerous animals.

These 'Old Man' crocodiles look like their distant relatives the dinosaurs, with their armour-plated bodies and wickedly exposed teeth. Such outsize specimens are the ones which take prey from river banks. But by the time they are just 5 metres in length they are capable of killing horses, cattle, and young buffalo. Since it is fresh water that bring these animals down to the river to drink, big crocodiles are often found lurking in up-river pools, or where the fresh water meets the salt. These are frequently the kind of idyllic tree-lined lagoons where a tourist has the strongest desire to strip off and swim. 'Fresh water's safe, isn't it?' they ask innocently. Sometimes *porosus* proves them wrong.

By the 1980s, crocodiles born after the introduction of protection in 1971 had grown big enough to be dangerous to large prey.

The difference between the present big crocodiles in Australia and those of previous eras was that the crocodiles of today have grown up with no fear of humans. They have never been hunted, thanks to the protective legislation. Today there is an increasing number of crocodiles of dangerous size and fearless attitude throughout the North. An ironic reversal of the roles of hunter and hunted.

In the early 1980s human awareness of crocodile danger had lagged behind the increase in crocodile numbers and (more importantly) the increase in large crocodiles. This failing was remedied by a series of horrific attacks in the middle of the decade.

In 1974 I was writing the biographies of two prominent Aborigines, Albert Barunga and Joe Nangan. They were men who had grown up in tribal times. As they showed me aspects of their country I did quite a bit of northern creek wading and swimming. They were grand old men and would never have allowed me to unwittingly step into danger. But I noticed that both of them, perhaps from a distant memory, watched me with some unease and preferred to keep their own feet dry.

On a flight up the arrow-straight Prince Regent River, Albert pointed out to me a spectacular waterfall named Kings Cascades. It was an emotional flight. Albert had not been back to his birthplace since his tribe left it in 1943. Tears now ran down his cheeks. 'My poor country!' he said. 'It is all alone now. No more people there.'

The Cascades waterfall ran from a tree-lined billabong high above the river. The water falling in white-lace foaming rapids over a series of terraces, to take a vertical drop to the main stream below. It was breathtakingly beautiful. What a nice place for a swim I thought.

But it was 1987 before I actually went there and had my chance. And in that year all thought of swimming at the Cascades had vanished for ever.

The reason was an American girl named Ginger Fay Meadows, a 24 year old red-headed former model from Charlottesville, Virginia. She had achieved international front-page fame in a way she would hardly have chosen for herself.

In 1987, standing where she had stood only weeks earlier, the Cascades seemed less beautiful to me. There was one patch of shadowed water which looked positively evil. I wondered whether the crocodile that killed Ginger Meadows was still lurking somewhere below the green slime of the surface. To him she had only been prey.

To the rest of the world hers was a story of tragedy which occupied newspaper front pages and television news headlines for several days.

Ginger was desperately unlucky. Although perhaps that could be said of anyone taken by a shark or crocodile anywhere in the world. But few circumstances have been more dramatic or received more international publicity than her untimely death on 29 March 1987 — the day before her 25th birthday.

Ginger had gone to Western Australia for the America's Cup yachting races and had become associated with the US *Eagle* syndicate. The races were sailed off Fremantle and the final was ultimately won in February by Dennis Conner, of the United States, with his strong-wind flier *Stars & Stripes*. When the celebrations and commiserations were over, Ginger was offered a ride around the north of Australia on a luxury motor yacht. The vessel was the *Lady G*, whose next area of operations would be New Guinea waters.

The offer seemed a dream come true. Ginger would be able to see that area of Australia, the wild and untamed North, which had attracted her to the country in the first place.

The *Lady G* had a pleasant trip, calling in at Broome and other places of interest. The Prince Regent River was a legend among travelling yachties, and the skipper Bruce Fitzpatrick had obtained some tourist brochures which showed people swimming at the foot of the Cascades waterfall. 'Don't miss it,' people told him. 'It will be a highlight of your trip. Something you'll always remember.'

On that March morning Bruce Fitzpatrick, Steve Hilton, Madeleine Janes and Jane Burchett, regular members of the crew, and Ginger Meadows, sped up-river in the *Lady G*'s Haines Hunter runabout on the rising tide. They had limited time because they had to be back aboard the *Lady G* before the tide began to fall.

The mood was lighthearted. There were shrieks of laughter when Madeleine Janes slipped and fell into the water getting out of the boat. The girls disembarked on the rock ledge which runs around the foot of the falls, while Bruce Fitzpatrick climbed to the top to take photographs.

There was no sign of any crocodile activity. Though, curiously, a friend working in the New Orleans Beefsteak & Bourbon Bar in Fremantle had warned Ginger before her departure: 'Be careful of crocodiles!' The warning was prompted by television news of a fisherman who had been attacked by a crocodile on the East Alligator River in the Northern Territory. He was decapitated in front of his wife and children.

But the East Alligator River seemed so distant, so remote. The Cascades, with fresh water bubbling down the rocks, were so pleasant and refreshing. No one there gave any thought to predatory crocodiles. It was too nice a morning.

Now the others began to climb the rocks. The terraces were steep and slippery with moss. There was a long vertical reach between terraces. It was hard going even for young people. Jane Burchett had broken her neck in an accident three years before. She was understandably nervous about heights.

'I can't make it,' she said after going a little way. 'You guys go on.'

Jane decided instead to swim around to the left of the falls to see if there was an easier way up. Finding none, she swam back to the boat and met Ginger who was sitting on a rock, enjoying the sunshine. She had also found the climb too steep.

'Take my picture?' asked Ginger. 'The camera's on the seat!' The camera had come to the end of the roll of film. Jane didn't know how to unload the Olympus, so Ginger swam over to the boat to do it herself.

There were now only ten minutes left before the time that Bruce had set for departure because of the tide.

'Shall we see if there's a way up over there?' Ginger asked. She was anxious to see as much as she could of this new country and was now feeling that she'd missed something by not climbing to the top.

'It gets steeper,' said Jane. 'I just swam there that way.' She had a book and was covered with sun cream. She was happy to stay where she was.

'How about that clearing over there?' Ginger persisted. 'We could take our shoes and maybe do some exploring.' Her shoes were runners, white IW Sports.

'OK,' said Jane, always amenable.

But once she began swimming she found that the water felt quite different from her previous swim. She had a strong sense of danger and suddenly became afraid.

'I have to go back,' she said. 'I've lost my nerve!' The water at the foot of the falls now seemed dark and dangerous.

'Come on,' Ginger pleaded. 'We've come this far. Look — I'll go in front!'

Suddenly there was a shout from high above them. Bruce Fitzpatrick at the top of the falls had seen something in the water. He was pointing and shouting at the same time.

'Crocodile! Get out of the water!'

The girls did not register for a moment, looking up with puzzled expressions.

'Crocodile!'

Fitzpatrick yelled so loudly that he almost overbalanced.

Then the girls understood. But they were in a trap. There was no safe place near them that they could reach quickly — the rocks dropped sheer into the water beside them, smooth, green and slippery with no hand or foot holds.

Now everyone was shouting. Bruce began to struggle down the steep slope towards the boat, finding the descent much harder than the climb.

Steve and Madeleine were already halfway down the falls. 'Get the boat!' Bruce shouted to Steve.

Jane Burchett and Ginger Meadows had backed themselves into a shallow ledge and stood trapped in waist-deep water with a rock wall behind them. They could see the crocodile now as it approached between them and the tender. The horned dragon face, the exposed dagger teeth, the blazing yellow eyes looked hideous from where they stood.

Jane screamed loudly out of fright and to try to scare the beast. She took off one of her shoes and threw it. 'I think it hit the crocodile. It stopped and looked disconcerted, as though it had lost its bearings.'

'What shall we do?' asked Ginger, with a note of rising panic in her voice.

Jane was about to say 'Stay here!'. There were still three shoes to throw, and surely Bruce or Steve could not be long with the boat.

But Ginger, on impulse, dived forwards and swam desperately for the nearby mangroves.

Steve Hilton had just reached the boat and saw Ginger begin to swim. She only managed a few strokes in open water before the crocodile was upon her. It seized her in a lightning grab by the upper legs and hips, the jaws extending past her bikini-clad body on either side.

She was dragged under the water. Then the crocodile resurfaced.

270

'She came back clear up to her waist,' Bruce Fitzpatrick said. 'With her hands in the air and a really startled look on her face . . . She was looking right at me, but she didn't say a word.'

'I thought she was reaching out to me for help,' said Jane.

Then Ginger was jerked below the surface once more. It was the last time her friends saw her alive.

Steve took the boat to the spot, revved the engine until the cliffs rang with the sound, but to no avail. 'All I saw was a lot of big bubbles come up.'

Bruce and Steve searched the pool and mangroves in the boat. But although they sighted the crocodile again there was no sign of Ginger. As the tide began to fall they had to abandon the search. To return to the *Lady G*, make an official call to Darwin Radio and give the world the dreadful news. The report that Ginger Meadows was dead. Killed by a crocodile in the Prince Regent River.

Her remains were found by an official search party some days later.

Ginger Meadows's tragedy was similar to most other crocodile and shark attacks. It was so unexpected. So horrifying for the witnesses, so bizarre, that people in the United States and in southern Australia found it difficult to comprehend.

'How *could* something like that happen in 1987?' they demanded. Then, naturally, they looked for someone other than the crocodile to blame. 'Why weren't there warning notices? Why wasn't she told of the danger?'

But the Prince Regent is a remote region; far, far from any human habitation or notices or warnings of any kind. The last people who lived in the area were Albert Barunga's Worrora tribe of Aborigines, and they had been gone from there more than 40 years. They knew about crocodiles, of course. No one needed to tell a Worrora.

But the white people who ventured into the region, like Ginger and the young people from the *Lady G*, were often innocents abroad where dangerous wild life was concerned.

It was true that parties from the great BHP iron ore mine at Kulan Island had sometimes gone to the Cascades by boat. They usually swam in the pool, splashing about after a few beers. 'Downing a few tinnies,' with hilarity and laughter. But because of their noise and numbers they would probably have frightened any crocodile away, unaware themselves that there was a risk.

For people who know, there is often a predictable pattern to crocodilian behaviour. If Ginger Meadows had remained with Jane Burchett the boat would quite likely have reached them both in time. Crocodiles dislike having two targets. They like to be certain before committing to a full attack. Even a shoe thrown in desperation can sometimes buy precious time.

But by swimming in open water Ginger had tragically given the predator its best opportunity, creating the circumstances most favourable for an attack.

'Why, oh why, did she swim?' Jane agonised afterwards. 'If only she'd stayed…'

When I spoke to Jane a year after the event, in doing some research for a book on crocodiles, she said she still asked herself the same question on sleepless nights.

It may remain with her for the rest of her life.

Ginger Meadows's sad fate prompted some people to write to newspapers to protest at the publicity which the tragedy had received.

The search for the body, the arrival of Ginger's estranged husband Duanne to help in the search, the gruesome discovery of the body — all this occupied newspaper space and television time for days. It was, in short, very similar in that respect to the aftermath of a major shark attack.

Those who protested pointed out with logic that people were killed every day in various circumstances. Some of the victims of accidental death, they said, were young women like Ginger Meadows. Like her they might have had a long life ahead, with a family and all the things that make for fulfilment. A happy future — but for some piece of wretched bad luck. Surely the death of anyone, child or adult, cut cruelly short before their time, must be considered a personal tragedy of some dimension?

They were correct in the sense that there can be no comparisons or degrees of importance in personal grief.

If Ginger Meadows had met her sad and premature end in a traffic accident in Fremantle, she would barely have rated a single paragraph in the back pages of the paper. Should a crocodile make such a difference? Was she more important because she suffered a bizarre death? Less significant if it had been a more conventional accident?

The answer, logically, is no. But the fact is that for people with no personal connection with the victim the circumstances do make the difference. At least where 'news' is concerned.

The reason may be that it is not death itself that attracts the general interest. Death, like birth, is everywhere in the world around us. It is the *manner* of dying which engages the attention. Perhaps we all have a subconscious fear of death. The fact that we can have no direct foreknowledge of our own future may create a natural curiosity in the fate of others.

272

Why we should be particularly afraid of a death involving a wild animal, a shark, crocodile or some other beast, does not make logical sense in the modern world. But the fact is that such fear is widespread. It is reflected in the apparently excessive interest shown by newspapers and television in an event such as the tragedy at Kings Cascades. Or when a shark attack takes place.

We are illogically, perhaps, more afraid of some forms of violent death than others. We do fear a shark more than a speeding automobile. Or perhaps, to put it another way, we may be thoroughly cautious where cars are concerned, and sensibly careful to avoid an accident. But we do not experience an actual dread of it happening, or brood about the possibility as we drive along.

On the other side of the coin, we do sometimes think about sharks as we step to the water's edge. Though the danger may be statistically remote, the mere possibility of a shark being around can set the hairs irrationally aprickle on the backs of our necks. Especially if there is cloud or shadow on the water and the other swimmers have gone back to the shore.

When the shark alarm sounds at an Australian surf beach people literally gallop to get out of the water. But the same people will risk life and limb as pedestrians stepping between four lanes of speeding city traffic. They pass nonchalantly between the hurtling metal shapes, though the possibility of death or injury may be more real than the chance of meeting a shark in the sea.

The statisticians, bless them, do their best to give us figures that will allow us to mathematically assess the risk of serious damage from whatever it is that might alarm us. But of course, if the worst does happen (assuming we have some lucid last moments to reflect), it can be absolutely no consolation to know that we are the victim of a rare event or even the exception to a general rule.

The odds of poor Ginger Meadows, for instance, being taken by a crocodile must have been millions to one against. Until she went up the Prince Regent River.

Physical accidents aside, the world is full of creatures that — with a degree of carelessness, provocation or bad luck on our part — could kill us. That is not to say that any of them may or will harm us. It is the possibility which concerns us. Perhaps it all stems from the atavistic memories passed down from our forebears who faced such dangers on a daily basis.

It is intriguing to note that dinosaurs, direct ancestors of crocodiles, passed from the earth 65 million years ago, long before the beginning of the evolution

273

of the human species *Homo sapiens*. But it is a fact that every nation on earth still has its dragon legends. Where do they come from?

Of present animals with a high human-disapproval rating, none has had a blacker name than the wolf — at least in the children's stories and the cautionary tales of many countries. Despite this, researchers can find no instance of a wolf killing any human in modern times.

Things may have been different 600 years ago when wolves were common in Europe. Wolves are natural scavengers and at the time of the Black Death in the 1300s, when survivors fled in panic (spreading the disease) and the dead were left unburied, wolves frequently ate the abandoned bodies of plague victims in isolated villages. Perhaps they also accounted for people who had been left to die and were too weak to defend themselves.

There is no doubt that wolves have the capacity, working as a pack, to kill large prey. They pull down caribou and other large animals in Canada which are faster and heavier than a man. A weak or injured human in the backwoods would theoretically stand little chance against a wolf pack in a disadvantaged situation. But there is no record of its ever happening. Ironically, domestic dogs, bred originally to protect people from wolves, do occasionally kill humans. There are 2 million dog bites recorded annually and 9 to 12 deaths each year in the United States.

Nonetheless, 'Who's Afraid of the Big Bad Wolf?' remains fixed in our folklore, and a long-drawnout wolf howl on a snowbound night in the forest can still make the hair rise on the human head. Even today.

So which are the world's most dangerous animals? How do they rate in comparison to our chosen study, the sharks?

The list contains some surprises. Creatures don't have to be big to be bad for us. Today's greatest killer, by far, is a tiny, fragile winged insect. The bite of the female mosquito, *Anopheles farauti*, kills 2 million people a year through the spread of malaria in Africa and Asia. The disease incapacitates many more, for an estimated 500 million are believed to be infected.

And if we are looking at *really* dangerous creatures the rat flea is up there in the same bracket.

At the time of the Black Death in Europe rat fleas from the black rat, which accompanied the Crusader knights back from the Middle East, killed a third of the population. The plague cut a three year swathe through Europe, the bacillus killing 25 million people.

In Britain and Ireland the effects were particularly devastating. Some experts believe that the death toll there took two-thirds of the islands' population before the plague burnt itself out in 1352. Plague outbreaks

274

returned to trouble Europe on a regular basis until modern times. In London 68 000 died in the 1660s in the 'Great Plague', which ended only when the 'Great Fire of London' consumed the slums.

The plague bacillus still lurks around the world. A sinister presence. But authorities such as the World Health Organisation maintain close checks. The last major outbreak occurred in Manchuria and Siberia in 1920–21, when 70 000 people died.

Australia has had its own mini-epidemics of plague, begun by infected rats coming ashore from ships. In 1909, in Sydney, there were 530 deaths out of 1212 victims. With cleaner living conditions in modern times and reduced numbers of rats (and fleas) we regard plague today as a part of past history. But there is danger in complacency. We enjoy our current plague-free status only through constant vigilance in matters of community health.

Mosquitoes still trouble Australians with outbreaks of dengue fever and Ross River virus — both non-fatal but extremely debilitating diseases.

Few insects cause as violent a psychological reaction as a spider. Particularly if it is large and hairy. Even strong men will flail their arms wildly and shout 'Get it off me!' if a huntsman spider drops from the rafters and lands on their head. Or if they blunder into a large sticky web in the dark.

The world has an incredibly diverse range of spiders, of widely differing shapes and sizes. They undoubtedly do more good than harm and may save many thousands of human lives by keeping down insects which could otherwise cause illness or famine. Only about 20 to 30 spider species are actually dangerous to humans.

Among 2000 or so species, Australia has the equally notorious 'redback' spider, *Latrodectus hasselti*, and funnelweb spider, *Atrax robustus*. Both are capable of delivering a lethal bite. Over the years there were numbers of deaths from these two species until the development of antivenoms. The most recent funnelweb deaths were in 1979 and 1980 — the later case occurring just months before the final development of an antivenom by Dr Struan Sutherland of the Commonwealth Serum Laboratories.

'The redback under the dunny seat' was an institution in the days of old-fashioned 'privies' or pan lavatories. While the site of the bite for people who sat on a toilet was a matter of amusement for others, it was no joke for the recipient, being extremely painful. About 300 people a year in Australia are still treated with antivenom for redback bites, although the outdoor dunny has largely disappeared.

The redback, which likes to live under houses and in dark corners, is closely related to the South African button spider, the New Zealand katipo, and the black widow of the United States. Black widows in the US killed 63 people between 1950 and 1959. Recently redbacks immigrated to Japan in a shipload of timber. There was panic in December 1995 when a series of nests was discovered near Osaka. Despite a huge eradication program, the bad news for the Japanese is that redbacks, once established, are virtually impossible to eliminate.

The large and hairy huntsman spider in Australia has a mild venom and its bite does not pose any sort of a life-threat to people. But it has occasionally wreaked havoc through no fault of its own.

The spider likes the inside of motor cars. In trees it occupies narrow spaces between the bark and the tree. In a vehicle it often decides that the space between the sun visor and the roof-lining is a good place to be. When the vehicle moves, the spider — large enough to span a hand with its hairy legs — commonly abandons its post, descending rapidly on a thread to the nearest low point. Which is often, thanks to standard vehicle geography, the driver's lap.

The descent on the silken thread is often followed by a desperate screech of tyres.

Faced with the spider, people have lost control of vehicles, swerved into oncoming cars on freeways, rolled off embankments, even driven into buildings. Some have jumped out of their cars while they are still moving into lines of other traffic. There have been fatalities from such a comparatively simple cause.

Generally spiders and other creepy-crawlies such as centipedes and scorpions do not cause many deaths. But the fat-tailed scorpion of North Africa has a dark record, with 400 deaths listed in Algeria between 1942 and 1958.

Strangely, the most dangerous of the stinging creatures, whose venom is responsible for most deaths, is one we commonly regard as a benefactor and friend. The honey bee. In North America, Europe and Australia, deaths from bee stings usually involve people who have an allergy. Bees kill five people a year on average in North America and two in Australia. More than sharks. Wild bees in Africa and India are a far more dangerous proposition than domesticated European bees, but records on fatalities are not readily available.

In South America an experiment in interbreeding African bees with European stock went disastrously wrong. The bees were extremely dangerous and aggressive, swarms killing animals and people without provocation. Swarms escaped into the wild and expanded throughout South America and Mexico, moving closer to the United States each year. Their popular name, killer bees, describes their temperament.

In terms of lethal capacity few other creatures can compare with snakes. The World Health Organisation estimates that 30 000 to 40 000 humans die each year from snake bite, most of them in Africa and Asia. The toll in India exceeds 10 000 deaths from snake bite each year. The risk is naturally highest in tropical countries with a low standard of living, where people go barefoot at night without lights. The climate suits snakes, and the humans are generally unprotected and not in easy reach of antivenom.

The poisonous snakes that receive most attention are the spectacular hooded king cobra of India, the black mamba of South Africa, the taipan of Australia, and the rattlesnake of North America. All are large reptiles.

In fact, the small snakes — like the krait, pencil-slim and little more than 30 centimetres or 1 foot in length — may claim more victims. The snake that kills most victims, we are told, is one that many people have never heard of at all. The saw-scaled viper, *Echis carinatus*, whose bite has a delayed rather than an instant effect is a drab creature, thinner than a finger and less than a metre long. Yet it is considered by some to be the world's most dangerous snake.

Another reptile, the African crocodile, *Crocodylus nilecticus*, kills 1000 people a year in Africa. Its slightly larger relation, *Crocodylus porosus*, the 'saltwater' crocodile of India, Burma and Australia, also claims its share of human victims, as we have seen. But for reasons of lesser opportunity it kills a smaller number. Statistically, it finds most of its victims among the primitive tribes living on New Guinea's river systems.

Lions still kill humans in Africa, though because of reduced numbers of lions and reduction of their range, deaths are a fraction of what they were in the 19th century. Curiously the large African herbivores — the elephant, buffalo and hippopotamus — kill more people than the big cats do.

In India, the tiger has always been the supreme predator. In the 1930s tigers may have killed 2000 people a year. One female at Champawat was reputed to have killed 436 human victims. Today the number of tigers has been reduced from an estimated 40 000 in former years to about 4000 individuals. A figure which places *Panthera tigris* on the list of endangered world species.

Nonetheless, the remaining tigers still show why they were once so widely feared. In nature reserve forests at the mangrove-lined mouths of the Ganges and Brahmaputra rivers, tigers still account for unlucky or unwary poachers and beekeepers. They kill around 60 human beings each year.

The leopard is another large cat that may be dangerous to humans. The notorious Indian leopard, the 'Man-eater of Rudyaprayag', killed 125 people in an eight year reign of terror from 1918 to 1926.

But in the 1990s, elephants raiding fields kill more Indians than the carnivores do.

Bears kill three or four people a year in the United States. While the grizzly is rightly feared, the black bear is also a carnivore in its own right, capable of killing large deer. Japan has two black bear-caused fatalities a year and about 20 cases of serious injury.

Domestic animals also figure on the worldwide fatality list. Bulls, cows, horses, pigs, camels, donkeys can all cause fatal accidents when badly handled or encountered in unlucky circumstances.

All the same, with 24 000 gun murders a year in the United States alone, among the most dangerous creatures on earth to *Homo sapiens*, the human race, are members of our own kind.

What happens in the ocean?

There is a similar range of poisonous creatures — and plants — and we should be sensibly aware of them when we enter the realm below the surface. Some of the animals use their venom to hunt. Others use their poison capacity only in defence. Either way we need to treat them with respect.

Sea snakes, like their land cousins, undoubtedly cause many human deaths. They are very similar to land snakes, but have acquired certain modifications for an oceanic life, including a flattened 'paddle' tail and a single extra-large lung. It has been claimed that thousands of fishermen die from sea snake bite each year in Indonesian, Philippine, Malaysian, Burmese and Indian waters. The victims are usually net fishermen working at night, or divers capturing snakes for the skin trade. Exact numbers of deaths are not known because few records are kept in remote areas. There also is a Malay superstition that it is unlucky to talk of a snake bite. It is said to attract the snake spirit, and the next person to be bitten will be the one who has spoken about the snake.

The villain of the piece in the Far East is *Enhydrina schistosa*, the beaked sea snake, which lives mainly on catfish and is common in tropical estuaries and shallows.

Sea snakes have very strong poison, but small teeth. They find it hard to open their mouths wide enough to bite a human. The vulnerable areas, where they can get a grip, are the thin web of skin between the thumb and forefinger, and the side of the foot. Malay people have much smaller hands and feet than Europeans and these are the parts where most Asian net fishermen are bitten. If approached by a sea snake in an aggressive manner, follow the pearl divers' rule. Clench your fists and put them under your armpits.

In Australia, divers and the crews of prawn trawlers encounter sea snakes on a regular basis, but there have been no recorded deaths. Pearl divers and prawn trawler crewmen have been admitted to hospital from time to time with severe symptoms after sea snake bites. But they have recovered after being treated with antivenom.

The most agonising sting in the ocean is said to come from the 13 spikes of the dreaded stonefish, *Synanceia vernucosa*. The stonefish earns its name because its appearance exactly matches a piece of coral rubble or a weed-grown stone. It relies on its disguise and its virulent venom both for protection from predators and to catch its prey.

There is argument about the lethal capacity of a stonefish. Deaths have been reported among Pacific Islanders but no fatalities have yet been recorded in Australian waters. But many people have been stung, and the venom is so painful that sometimes victims become delirious and risk injury by throwing themselves about uncontrollably. Occasionally a secondary injury occurs to the vocal cords from screaming.

The stonefish will not attack a diver or swimmer. The danger is that the fish does not move — the risk lies in treading on it when wading. It is so difficult to see looking through a ruffled surface. The poison is contained in venom sacs surrounding each spike, which is sharp enough to penetrate a sandshoe sole. Anyone wading in coral water should wear thicksoled shoes and watch where they step. Stonefish are a problem for pearl divers picking up shell, because small specimens may shelter undetected in the shadow of a large pearl oyster. They can be a concern for crews of prawn trawlers when they sort their catch because stonefish are sometimes indistinguishable from the weed in the net.

Stonefish have also stung people when washed ashore in storms, or caught in a net. They may appear dead, completely inert and lifeless. But they may revive and can give a sudden vigorous flick which catches people unawares. The results can be very painful if the sharp spines jag on an arm or leg.

The poison dries and crystallises but retains its potency. In Shark Bay, Western Australia, a man was stung when a dried stonefish head, nailed to a wall for ten years as an ornament, fell and accidentally spiked him.

The pain from a stonefish wound may be temporarily relieved by immersion in hot — not scalding — water. But a victim requires hospital treatment for complete recovery.

The stingray is another 'step-on' danger.

Many of the smaller rays like to lie in sun-warmed shallows, disguising themselves by flicking sand over their backs. If a human treads on one unawares, the stingray's natural reaction is to defend itself with the poison-slimed barbed spike in its tail. The sting itself is not fatal (though deaths have occurred due to injury complications), but it can be extremely painful and in some circumstances can cause physical incapacity for weeks. Careless handling of stingrays caught in nets or on lines is another source of injury. Some of the most severe stings come from comparatively small (frying pan-size) rays such as *Urolophus mucosus*, the common small stingray. The venom is contained in mucus which coats the spine.

There are many varieties of batoids or rays, the 'flattened' fish which are close cousins of sharks. They include the stingrays, the mantas which have no sting, and the saw-sharks, guitar fishes, fiddle sharks and skates, which are also stingless.

Rays mainly eat crustaceans, molluscs and sea shells, and are equipped with crushing plates in their mouths rather than cutting teeth like the predatory sharks. The stingray's barbed sting or spike does not play a part in food-gathering, and is purely a defensive weapon.

Some stingrays grow to considerable size. The 'harbour ray' or black stingray *Dasyatis thetidis*, can reach 2 metres across the back and weigh 200 kilograms or more. A ray of this size will have two or even three spines, each as long as a carving knife. The barbs of large rays are so sharp that Aborigines once used clusters of stingray barbs as tips for their fish spears.

Most of the fatalities have occurred from unlucky accidents, through the penetration of the dagger-like barbed spine, rather than the poison. The victims have included swimmers who have inadvertently dived or swum too close to large rays and had their stomach or chest cavity pierced by the barb, which inflicts a similar wound to that of a stiletto dagger.

A recent freak stingray death in Australia occurred at Moresby, near Innisfail in Queensland, in 1988. Twelve-year-old Jeff Zamel was in a dinghy fishing when a large stingray leapt out of the water and landed across his body. The ray lashed out in panic and the barbed spine entered Jeff's chest. He spent two days in hospital and was discharged. But five days later he collapsed and died from cardiac complications.

Like moray eels, mantas and barracuda, stingrays were on the 'black list' of underwater 'enemies' for many years. A good deal of the problem lay in the stingray's appearance. Seen from the surface, a stingray moving along the bottom looks a sinister shape. And apart from the threat of its barbed spine, a dead stingray lying on a jetty looks an ugly creature.

But once divers began meeting stingrays in their own element they found that they were quite different from the popular image. They swam surpris-

280

ingly gracefully. Eagle rays 'wing' their way underwater like a bird in flight. Most rays are attractive creatures in their natural habitat. They are non-aggressive, and easily tamed, and can become very friendly once they become accustomed to divers. No doubt forgiving us our own 'ugly' appearance.

Octopuses, too, had a bad name in days gone by. The French author Victor Hugo was partly to blame. His 1886 novel *Toilers of the Deep* became a bestseller in its time and was widely read in England as well as in France. After being shipwrecked in the Channel Islands, the fictional hero of the book fought a desperate battle for his life with an octopus.

Hugo described the suckers on the octopus's arms:

So many mouths devouring you at the same time… You enter the beast… You become one. The tiger can only devour you; the devil fish inhales you. He draws you to him and bound and helpless you feel yourself emptied into his frightful sac, which is a monster. To be eaten alive is more than terrible, but to be drunk alive is inexpressible.

These lines curled the toes of many readers and became one of the more famous passages in literature. But in fact, far from being predators on *Homo sapiens*, octopuses generally seem shy of humans and are usually comparatively small creatures. Large octopuses certainly exist in Puget Sound on the northwestern corner of the United States, and in the atoll lagoons of the tropical Pacific. But they do not naturally prey on humans or mammals.

Strangely enough the most dangerous octopus to humans is a tiny creature which can sit in your hand. The little blue-ringed octopus, *Hapalochlaena*, carries a deadly venom, tetrodotoxin, similar to the paralysing poison found in some puffer fish. The animal's common name comes from blue pigment cells in the skin which show as iridescent blue rings when the octopus is frightened or excited. The poison is delivered with a bite from the octopus's parrot beak.

Australia has two species of blue-ringed octopus. *Hapalochlaena maculosa* is very common in rock pools of southern coasts and *H. lunulata*, the tropical variety, is found under rocks and stones in the north. Fatalities have been recorded in areas as widely separated as Darwin, Sydney and Port Phillip Bay. They have usually occurred when people played with the animals and placed what they thought was a 'baby' octopus on their hand or arm. In some cases blue-ringeds were slapped on backs in horseplay among people unaware of the little octopuses' lethal capacity.

Nonetheless, considering the number of blue-ringed octopuses that are handled each year, fatal bites are very rare. In that respect it is rather similar

281

to cone shells which also have the capacity to inflect serious injury. But despite careless handling by many shell collectors, cone shell stings are rare and fatalities rarer still.

The giant squid is at the opposite end of the scale to the blue-ringed octopus. *Architeuthis princeps* is one of the world's largest creatures. Some specimens washed ashore have been more than 25 metres in length. *Architeuthis* is formidably armed with hooked suckers on its tentacles and a parrot beak.

It would be extremely dangerous to any humans it encountered. But its hunting grounds are in the abyssal zones of the deep oceans. Though it may rise to the surface at night, sightings are extremely rare. There are recordings of giant squid attacking boats in the North Atlantic, and fishermen from Chile and Peru avoid certain Humboldt Current areas at night because of a fear of large squid.

We know little or nothing of its breeding habits, food sources or length of life. The giant squid remains for us one of the ocean's mysteries.

Smaller squid, harmless to humans, are legion in the ocean and extend worldwide.

A close relative is the cuttlefish, whose white calcarious skeletons wash up by the thousand after winter storms. Unlike squid, which are pelagic and often swim in shoals, cuttlefish are sedentary and live among reefs and rocks. Cuttlefish are intelligent, easily tamed by handfeeding and very curious. They are able to change colours and will sometimes try to mimic the colour of a wetsuit. One was once fascinated by the blonde hair of my diving companion. After several tries it managed to turn its back a very comparable yellow.

A mirror held in front of a cuttlefish — 'Who's a pretty boy, now?' — can bring on a command performance. The cuttlefish primps and preens, changes colours and generally admires itself. One we spent time with at the Abrolhos Islands wanted to keep the mirror. We had to have a tug-of-war, with the cuttlefish turning an angry red — 'I say it's mine, damn you!' — before the tentacles reluctantly let go.

Ordinarily a cuttlefish is no threat to humans, and in friendly circumstances can be a diver's delight. But there was a bizarre cuttlefish-caused death in Western Australia in September 1984.

Diver Albert Jaeger, 26 years old, was found dead on the bottom in 20 metres of water at Rottnest Island. He was last seen alive by companions as he speared a large cuttlefish about 30 centimetres long and then tried to remove it from his handspear. When his body was recovered later his SCUBA tank air supply was exhausted with the reserve lever down. There were bite marks on his ear and round sucker marks on his neck.

Jaeger was physically very fit and an excellent surface swimmer. But he was a very inexperienced SCUBA diver. We can only surmise what happened. It seems likely that when he wrenched the cuttlefish from his handspear the wounded creature wrapped itself around his head and bit him on the ear. And that Jaeger, already almost out of air, panicked and lost his mask and mouthpiece in the struggle. While trying to deal with the cuttlefish — he actually ripped the body from the tentacles — he also lost a fin. From that moment he was doomed. Failing to release his weight belt, and out of air, he had no chance of regaining the surface. So he drowned.

Cone shells, as their name indicates, are vase-shaped and often beautifully marked shellfish. They have developed an extraordinary barbed sting, a miniature harpoon linked to a poison gland which they can dart out in a lightning thrust. Species such as the Geographer cone, *Conus geographus* the textile cone and the tulip cone kill fish. All have the capacity to kill humans and deaths have been recorded throughout the Indo-Pacific region.

Cone shells are valuable to collectors, and commercial gatherers always have an eye out for good quality cones. One cone, *Conus gloriamaris* — Glory of the Seas — is the world's rarest and most valuable shell. A good specimen can fetch thousands of dollars.

Cones are common in Australian tropical and subtropical waters. Many such shells are handled on reefs each year, but to date there has been only one recorded Australian fatality. A 27-year-old man collected a large Geographer cone on a boat trip to Hayman Island in 1934, and was stung on the hand. He died in five hours.

While most people handling shells are aware of the cone's capacity to sting, few realise just how far the tiny harpoon can reach. Many believe that they are safe if they pick a shell up by the base. They think that the sting, which strikes from the front of the shell cannot reach them. But they may be sadly mistaken. Cones can reach surprising distances. The dart can pierce through clothing or gloves.

Tongs are the only safe means of handling cone shells. But after years of reefs being stripped of shells and sealife, there is an increasingly strong perception that live shells should not be handled at all but rather left where they are.

Many of Australia's most important reef locations, including the Great Barrier Reef and the Ningaloo Reef, now enjoy national park status and it is an offence to remove shells or coral. Collecting and souveniring in the past has resulted in sad and empty reefs. The devastated areas warn us that wherever we are, and regardless of whether areas are protected by legislation or not, we need to practise our own individual conservation. 'Collecting' by camera means that the shell or animal remains alive and well. And continues to reproduce in its natural cycle.

The most common stinging creature on the Australian coast, and perhaps the most dangerous, is not a shell or a vertebrate animal but a jellyfish.

Chironex fleckeri, the box jellyfish or 'sea wasp', has killed at least 80 people in Australian waters through the years. That is a figure which puts it in the same league as sharks and crocodiles.

In fact, in the areas where it is most commonly found, from the Kimberley coast around the north of Australia to Cairns, *Chironex* has caused more deaths than shark attacks have. The reported figures may fall short of the actual total because for years the authorities refused to accept the cause of the deaths. *Chironex* was 'the invisible invader' in every sense. It was not identified as a killer until the mid-1950s. Not only was the translucent jellyfish difficult or even impossible to see in the water in most conditions — so far as official Australia was concerned, it did not exist at all.

This was despite consistent recordings of cases which should have shown that a very real danger existed. Studies included in Cleland and Southcott's book *Injuries to Man from Marine Invertebrates in the Australian Region* give details of the case of a 36-year-old man at Proserpine, Queensland, in 1923, who ran from the sea crying out 'I'm stung!' and then collapsed and died. There was a jelly-like substance and deep purple marks on his left arm and ankle.

In another case, at Googarra in 1934, an Italian cane worker aged 28 leapt from the water shouting. He threw himself on the beach and rubbed sand on his legs in agony. Within minutes he had lapsed into unconsciousness and died. He, too, had the whip-like weals around his legs.

A 13-year-old girl at Townsville, in 1941, was swimming with friends near a swimming enclosure when she became suddenly distressed. A man saw translucent tentacles hanging from her chest and shoulders. 'I applied wet sand and after five minutes saw the girl's eyes throw back, and she began to froth at the mouth'. . . Another unexplained fatality.

There were numbers of other cases with similar symptoms and histories of extreme pain and rapid death.

(We now know that neither sand nor any other material should be used to rub the tentacles off the victim's skin, unless the stings have been deactivated with vinegar. Water, methylated spirits, kerosene or alcoholic drinks should not be used instead of vinegar.)

Scientists blamed the common Portuguese man o' war or bluebottle, *Physalia utriculus*, for some of the deaths. But Dr Hugo Flecker, a Cairns medico who had begun compiling Australia's first register of human illnesses and injuries from tropical animals and plants, was not so sure. *Physalia*, with the pretty blue float and long stinging threads, was common all around Australia. Plenty of people got stung south of the Tropic of Capricorn, but none of the southerners died. Was there some other, as yet unknown, factor?

Flecker had been spurred in his search during wartime by an Army doctor named Ronald Southcott. The Army was training commandos and assault groups for the Pacific war north of Cairns in 1943 and 1944. Troops were being stung by mystery sea creatures. Numbers of soldiers were incapacitated and there were some deaths. Southcott, puzzled by the injuries, called on Flecker as a local doctor with experience in the area.

Southcott and Flecker studied and identified some of the details of the problem. But they could not immediately pinpoint the cause. Ten years later it still remained a mystery. Until in 1955 a five-year-old boy at Cardwell died in the tragic circumstances which by then had become all too familiar.

Dr Flecker contacted the Cardwell district inspector of police and requested that the beach be dragged with nets. The local sergeant went out in a boat and recovered several different kinds of jellyfish which were passed on to Flecker for examination.

The Coroner at the inquest into the boy's death refused to believe that a healthy person could be killed by a jellyfish. He brought in a finding of 'death due to allergic shock'. But Flecker found that one of the netted jellyfish had an intensely potent venom. He isolated the poison and found that it rapidly killed laboratory rats and mice.

The creature identified was a translucent *cubomedusa*, or box jellyfish, whose body grew larger than a man's head and trailed 3 metre long tentacles from four points on its abdomen. It was the most advanced of all jellyfish, swimming faster than a man could wade and preying on fish. Tests of the tentacles and their hairlike stinging nematocysts showed that it was also the world's deadliest.

Flecker sent specimens to Dr Southcott, by now a distinguished Adelaide zoologist. Southcott formally identified it as a new genus and named it *Chironex fleckeri* after his old friend and wartime colleague.

Further research showed that there were several different species of dangerous box jellyfish, closely related, in tropical waters. They caused deaths in New Guinea, the Philippine archipelago and elsewhere in the region. Another jellyfish which caused fatalities in the Northern Territory and Queensland was *Chironex quadrigatus*.

There was one other stinger, too, which had a deceptively mild first contact but a strong delayed reaction. People stung felt little pain at first, with a slightly reddened area and some goosebumps. But from 30 minutes to an hour later they collapsed with violent cramps, severe pain and vomiting. Dr Flecker was still working on isolating the culprit when he died in 1957.

Another Cairns doctor, John Barnes, took up the research and in 1961 found that the jellyfish responsible was the 'Irukandji stinger', another *cubomedusa* or box jellyfish. Barnes later found a method of extracting the poison and developing an antivenom for box jellyfish stings. In more recent years important jellyfish research has been carried out by Dr Robert Endean of the University of Queensland.

Today most public beaches in tropical Australia carry signs warning against *Chironex* and the danger of swimming between October and May. Divers and people who do go in the water usually wear lycra 'stinger suits' or other clothing as protection.

The Irukandji stinger, while not fatal, has been a considerable nuisance to pearl divers on the pearling beds of northwestern Australia. Strangely, though it took science half of the 20th century to establish the source of the danger, Aborigines and old local fishermen were always aware of the danger and the types of jellyfish to be avoided.

The list of poisonous creatures goes on. And on. There are fish which are not naturally poisonous in themselves but which carry a residue of ciguatera poison from accumulated weed flagellates in the smaller reef fish they have eaten. Large tropical reef fish, such as barracuda, mackerel, red bass, chinamen and coral trout, may all carry ciguatera at times. It can be confusing because sometimes the fish can be very toxic, while at other times they are free from the poison and people have no ill-effects from eating them. Generally speaking older fish, the large individuals, are the ones to avoid in the tropics because they are more likely to have accumulated the ciguatera toxin.

There have been numerous human fatalities from ciguatera poisoning in the Caribbean, the Pacific and South East Asia, where it is notorious and greatly feared. In Australia there have been only a handful of deaths. But many many people — beginning with explorer James Cook and his crew of HMS *Endeavour* when they sailed the Great Barrier Reef in 1770 — have been made very ill indeed.

Other deaths have occurred from eating genuinely toxic fish such as the Tetratodon family of puffers and blowfish. Many fish, especially lionfish, catfish, gurnards and some roaches, have very poisonous spines. There are stinging nudibranchs and sea anemones that deliver a ferocious boot if roughly handled. And poisonous plants such as 'fire coral' can raise itches and weals.

As a disgruntled companion with a bleeding knuckle once complained to me after a dive, 'Whatever you find in the ocean — if it doesn't sting, it bloody well bites!'.

I'm not sure that he had learnt the lesson, *Look, but don't touch.* An important rule in the ocean, if you wish to keep on enjoying it.

The creatures that can hurt us make up a chronicle of woe. But in fact — with the possible exception of snakes on land — animals do not figure largely in human mortality. On the figures the sea is safer than the land, provided of course that we play by Nature's rules.

In 1996 infectious diseases killed more than 17 million people, according to figures released in May of that year by the World Health Organisation. Tuberculosis made a grim re-emergence, killing 3.1 million more; malaria carried off 2.1 million people; hepatitis B took 1.1 million and measles another million; while whooping cough killed 355 000. Respiratory infections accounted for 4.4 million deaths, and diarrhoeal diseases for 3.1 million. Awesome figures.

The greatest numbers of deaths in the 20th century stem from human conflict. The two world wars in particular. Even in peace we have our problems. Citizen deaths from firearms in the United States in the 20th century will probably exceed 1 million by the year 2000. More than the servicemen killed in the wars. Automobile deaths make another horrendous total.

Is the world, then, such a dangerous place?

You bet it is. It always has been a perilous planet for a weak-bodied creature like *Homo sapiens* — a species whose members like to live together in gregarious swarms conducive to the transmission of infectious diseases. Whose aggressive nature leads to territorial conflicts with neighbours and their own kind in other countries. Whose mechanical inventions include such a high proportion of devices designed to kill — from guns to guided missiles and the A-bomb.

But despite these somewhat cynical observations, the natural world has never been a safer place for humans than it is today. Even the creatures that can hurt us seldom do so. The underwater realm, provided we are careful in the use of our breathing equipment and respect the denizens, is as safe a place as any.

One of the rewards for divers is the opportunity for interaction with creatures once feared as dangerous to humans. For example, in Australia, in the 1970s, we stopped shooting giant groper (fortunately before it was too late) and began handfeeding them instead.

Perhaps the most interesting experience I have had in recent times was at the Caribbean island of Grand Cayman, in August 1995.

All my life I have been aware of stingrays, for the good reasons mentioned earlier. The initial trigger was a newspaper report in Melbourne, in 1945. I was on my way to boarding school at Geelong, and had been swimming in the murky waters of the St Kilda sea baths. Picking up the evening newspaper I found that an Army sergeant had died that day after diving into the baths. He had a stab-like wound in the chest, apparently inflicted by a stingray which had entered the swimming baths through a gap in broken palings in the rundown establishment.

The incident, not unnaturally, made an indelible impression on my 11 year old mind.

Thereafter, though there was no actual phobia, I was always very careful about stingrays. I had seen what they could do. Through the years I read about other fatalities and met numbers of people who had been stung. It was always a painful experience. One friend, Scott Sledge, who worked as an archaeologist with the Western Australian Maritime Museum, trod on a small stingray in a tide pool at the Abrolhos Islands. The spine went right through his Achilles tendon, and the wound was so painful that he had to be airlifted to hospital at Geraldton on the mainland by helicopter.

The problem did not end there. Despite modern drugs the wound became gangrenous and refused to heal. An increasingly large hole appeared in the affected area above his ankle, causing grave medical concern. If the tendon were to be severed by the spread of dying flesh he would be in serious trouble. No one walks without a fully functioning Achilles tendon. After months of intensive (and expensive) medical treatment the problem was overcome and the wound finally healed. But Scott walked with a limp for long after. Today he has the scar and the memory. He too is aware of stingrays.

It was not, of course, the little ray's fault. It simply reacted defensively to what it perceived as an attack by a large and heavy creature. As Scott ruefully conceded, the defence was effective.

I have never been on personal bad terms with stingrays. But I have long been aware that they merit respect. This book, in fact, is largely being written on my boat *Beachcomber III*, in a sheltered bay at Rottnest Island where stingrays frequently patrol below the keel. It is not unlikely that a ray is passing by even as I write this passage. There are two varieties here in Marjorie Bay. A family of blue-spotted eagle rays are often on the search for

One of the magnificent sights of the seven seas. Diver Douglas Seiffert from Florida is dwarfed by one of the bigger whale sharks of Ningaloo Reef.

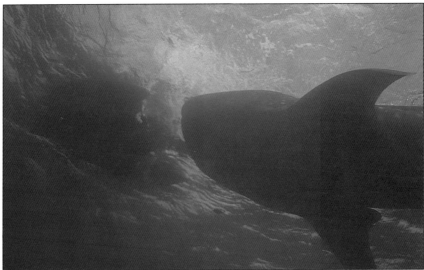

Top and bottom: *Curiosity sometimes brings whale sharks to nudge stationary craft. While Kevin White and diver Les Valmadre watch from above, a whale shark comes up to kiss the stern of the inflatable chase boat. Les's arms can be seen in the underwater picture of the contact.*

290

Top: *Unconcerned, a whale shark tolerates a bubbling buzz of human company.*
Bottom: *Divers watch an uncommon sight — a whale shark filtering plankton behind the Ningaloo Reef.*

291

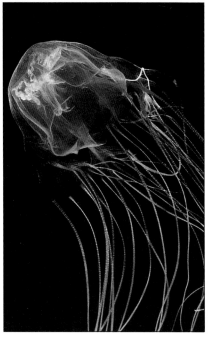

Compared with other dangerous ocean
creatures, the shark blends into the background. However, for the Australian psyche,
the fear of shark attack is still top of the list.
Opposite top: *Sea snakes undoubtedly
cause many human deaths. The victims are
usually net fishermen working at night or
divers capturing the snakes for the skin
trade. (Photograph: Ben Cropp)*
Opposite bottom: *There is argument about
the lethal capacity of the stone fish, but the
poison from the venom sacs around each of its
13 spikes is said to cause agonising pain.*
Top: *The Butterfly fish or Lion fish looks
as delicate and fragile as a bird. But its
appearance belies its venomous spikes, which
give it its other name, the Scorpion fish.*
Bottom: *There are several types of box
jellyfish, all lethal. However, these days
antivenom is available as treatment,
considerably reducing the numbers of
deaths from contact with the tentacles
of this creature.*

Stingrays have a poison spine at the base of their tails for self-protection. Normally humans need to be wary when handling them; there have been a number of accidental fatalities. But at Grand Cayman Island, the rays of the Dasayatis species have become so tame through handfeeding by tourists that they are quite fearless and can be touched and handled without a problem.

Top: *A large female, almost 2 metres across, accepts a piece of local 'ballyhoo' fish from a visiting American diver.*

Opposite, top: *A male stingray charges at the head of a diver: 'Hey, Mister! I'm here too!' The larger females get most of the attention so the smaller males sometimes have to resort to desperate measures or miss out on the handouts.*

Opposite, bottom: *Tiger shark caught in a beach net off a popular swimming beach just north of Newcastle Harbour in 1996. (Photograph: Becca Saunders)*

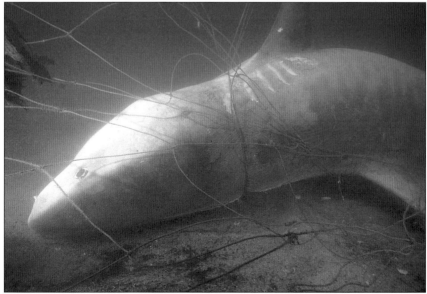

Five seven-gill sharks caught in a net off Merewether Beach, Newcastle, in September 1995. Conservationists are concerned that while beach meshing keeps away dangerous sharks like Tigers and Great Whites, sharks that are not dangerous and other creatures like dolphins, turtles, rays and dugongs also die. (Photograph: Andrew Hodges)

296

lobster shells and 'household' scraps. If herring are caught from the stern then a much larger black ray of the *Dasyatis* genus, almost 2 metres across the back and locally known as the 'Cookie Monster', shows up when the herring are cleaned. Coming up to the duckboard for heads and entrails like a dog begging for biscuits.

The stingrays are all regarded as friends, along with the seabirds, the sea lion, and pods of dolphin which come into the bay to play their own game of 'keep-it-off' with catfish which they throw to each other. A game which the dolphins greatly enjoy, but which is not a lot of fun for the catfish.

But any of my human friends entering the water from the stern of the boat are always warned never to dive or jump in feet first. The water is less than 2 metres deep and, though the risk of startling a patrolling stingray into darting its spine into them is slight, the risk is still there. I still remember reading about the army sergeant at St Kilda 50 years ago.

For all those reasons I was intrigued to find a phenomenon called 'Stingray City' at Grand Cayman island in the Caribbean in 1995. I was diving with Fisheye Dive, an island charter operator. One of their boats took a group of us for a dive on the outer reef which drops away to blue green coral depths. For a second swim, having used our decompression time on the deep dive, we went to a shallow sand area inside the island lagoon of North Sound.

There, at anchor, were at least 20 boats, ranging from dive-boats like our own to large double-decker tourist ferries. There must have been at least 200 spectators and 100 people in the water. The swimmers were surrounded by the moving shapes of stingrays.

The species was *Dasyatis americana*, the 'southern stingray' common in Florida and the Gulf of Mexico. They were large black rays which seemed to me to be identical to the *Dasyatis thetidis* I had left behind at home. They were big rays. Some were almost 2 metres across, though sizes of a metre or so were more common, with others of around 50 centimetres swimming among them.

I had seen concentrations of rays before but never concentrations of rays and people. Certainly I had never seen swimmers scooping up large rays and lifting them above the surface to have their photographs taken with them. An armful of live and co-operative stingrays is not a common sight elsewhere in the world.

At first I was appalled, knowing the capacity of such rays to deal a serious or even lethal wound if startled or mishandled.

'Doesn't anyone ever get stung?' I asked our dive guide.

'It has happened,' Jim conceded. 'But very rarely. The rays are very good at putting up with people.'

We watched others, waist-deep, lifting rays out of the water the way children pick up cats, with a two-armed, chest-high heave. But with never a sign of concern or bad temper on the part of the rays.

'Both the rays and the people are totally confident with each other,' Jim explained. 'The rays seem to actually enjoy being cuddled.'

There was a reason, of course. The rays were fed by the tourists, and anyone with a plastic bag of a local Grand Cayman fish called ballyhoo, or (better still) fresh squid, was guaranteed an attentive troupe of instant stingray friends. The rays were quite fearless in their quest for food and had modified their natural behaviour remarkably at Stingray City. Normally stingrays are night-feeders and prefer to remain flat on the bottom. This is so that, if they are threatened by their enemies the shark or (in cooler waters) the sea lion, they can clamp to the bottom and curl their tail and spines up in defence.

At Stingray City the rays often 'fly high' just below the surface. They literally swarm over a diver until his food is exhausted. At the same time they allow themselves to be touched, stroked and handled with total confidence.

Being lifted out of the water is the supreme test for any sea creature. The first time in the thin, unsupportive atmosphere of air, with all the unfamiliar sounds of people's voices and boat engines, must have the potential to be traumatic. But the rays seemed to accept the lifting and handling in relaxed fashion. It concerned me until I became used to it, because lifting a ray chest-high out of the water means that the regions likely to be pierced by the spine in the event of a ray suddenly panicking would be chest, neck or face. Or an eye.

'I must confess it makes me nervous,' I said to Jim.

'You'll get used to it,' he said with a grin. 'Here, take this and see for yourself,' and he handed me a bag of ballyhoo.

The rays were marvellous. I was not unused to feeding large tame sea animals from our own days of handling groper and potato cod and moray eels on the west coast of Australia and on the Great Barrier Reef.

But feeding stingrays on the sea floor was a new departure.

As with all sea creatures some caution was necessary. A moray eel has teeth like a wolf, a groper has hundreds of tiny teeth in a jaw that could take in your head let alone your hand. Food needs to be proffered in a way that precludes the animal including your fingers in the mouthful.

Unfortunately, on the Barrier Reef some people have teased the animals by offering food and jerking it away again to prolong the contact or to get a better photograph. This may mean that, next time, the animal will naturally snatch, and someone else may be badly bitten. Food should be offered so that the creature can approach calmly of its own accord, confident that no trickery is involved. Just like offering titbits to your dog.

The stingrays are different, in that their eyes are on top of their disc-like body and their mouth underneath. This means that when your hand and the piece of fish or squid drops below their nose it disappears from view. The stingray has no teeth but does have crushing plates which can give loose fingers a painful pinch. When offering food the hand should be held perfectly flat with the fish balanced on the palm, so that the ray can scoop it up easily. It is exactly the same as giving a horse an apple or carrot using your a flat palm.

It was extraordinary kneeling on the bottom and watching the rays nuzzling the divers and moving over them like underwater vacuum cleaners. Naturally I looked to see what the tails were doing, and I saw some curled in the strike position. But the spines never seemed to be extended.

Many of the tourist divers were inexperienced and clumsy in their movements and unintentionally rough in the way they handled the creatures. But the stingrays always seemed to remain calm and confident.

The largest ones were females. The males were quite tiny and sometimes comic in their attempts to get attention. The big females were easily identified and had names like Darth Vader, Big Mamma, Stubby, and Ray Jay. Naturally, divers sought them out first for photographs. The little rays tended to be ignored as insignificant, or worse, trampled under flippers.

It was amusing to watch them desperately trying tricks to attract divers, finally flying into diver's masks. 'Hey! I'm here too!'

It is believed that rays move in family groups. Two or three large females are leaders, accompanied by some small males and others of various sizes and generations in between. They may live at least 40 years.

In the week when I dived, there were sometimes more than 100 people in the water, matched by what appeared to be at least an equal number of stingrays. A phenomenon in every sense.

It began in a small way years ago when island fishermen came into North Sound to clean their catch of fish. Three rays regularly came to eat the leftovers and began to associate the boats with food. In the 1980s, as described in a booklet *Swim with the Rays* by South African Mike Nelson, divers became interested in the rays and began handfeeding them. Their numbers increased until today Stingray City is a major tourist attraction. The rays (and the people) have since appeared in the Cousteau television series and in the *National Geographic*.

299

Stingrays anywhere can be handfed and can quickly become tame if food is available on a regular basis. But it could take years before they are confident enough to be handled like the rays of Stingray City. And it could be quite dangerous to be overfamiliar with stingrays in other locations.

Some scientists grumble about Stingray City as 'modifying natural behaviour' and making the animals 'too dependent' on human beings. This is a charge levelled wherever fish or dolphins or other wild animals are fed for the benefit of human enjoyment. I think it is a specious objection.

Species that will accept handfeeding from humans include giant groper, potato cod, Maori wrasse (Napoleon fish), snapper, morays, stingrays, dolphins and even sharks. There are well-known shark-feeding stations in the Maldive Islands in the Indian Ocean, on the Great Barrier Reef and in the Bahamas.

Sure, for a tiny fraction of the particular species it is 'unnatural' behaviour. Better than shooting them with a speargun, of course. But from the frowns of disapproval and pursed lips of the purists you might get the impression that it is a fate worse than death.

Baloney.

The obvious advantage to the creatures is an immediate free lunch. A temporary stomach-filling satisfaction. But there is a long-term benefit which may be far more significant. Humans, it is acknowledged, have had a devastating effect on wildlife on land, as evidenced by the tragic list of extinct and endangered species and ravaged forests and habitat.

We have the capacity to inflict similar damage in the sea. There is widespread evidence that the deterioration has already begun. The two human factors essentially involved are greed and ignorance. To protect the other living creatures on our vulnerable planet we need to change the way that people and governments think.

If people everywhere can be brought to see the animals as living, interesting creatures, and to view coral reefs as worth preserving, then there is some hope for the future.

Human interaction with sea creatures, such as occurs at Stingray City, is important as a public relations exercise. For thousands of visitors to Grand Cayman it engenders genuine goodwill towards the animals. The films and magazine articles increase people's awareness of life under the surface, and its importance to us all. They remind us that a planet without animals would be a dull and tragic desert. Inspire us, perhaps, to ensure that such a global disaster never occurs.

We should remember that before the advent of oceanariums dolphins were 'porpoises' and were shot or harpooned, without restriction, for bait or in order to remove competition for net fishermen. Orcas were 'killer whales' and murderous beasts. The great whales were being hunted remorselessly to extinction in all the seven seas by the fleets of as many nations. The oceanariums with their dolphin shows and television programs like *Flipper* brought marine mammals to our attention and changed the whole viewpoint of the English-speaking world. They led to the 'Save The Whale' campaigns of the 1970s and 1980s. The ultimate result was the cessation of international whaling and the near deification of the dolphin. The oceanariums are criticised today by the Green movement as 'unnatural'. But without their important and timely educational role our thinking might be no further advanced than it was in the 1950s.

For these same reasons Stingray City has its own important role in matching humans up with animals and finding that we can be friends after all.

We may even think more kindly of the shark.

THE GLOBAL SCENE: SHARK ATTACKS AROUND THE WORLD
chapter fourteen

THE SURF WAS RUNNING HIGH AND HOLLOW AT NAHOON REEF, NEAR EAST London on South Africa's southeast coast in the winter of 1994.

The morning of 4 July broke as a fine sunny day with little wind. The glassy swell rolling in with huge peaking crests from the Indian Ocean made conditions perfect. Some of South Africa's best surfriders had taken their big-wave boards to Nahoon that Saturday.

André Carter, 31 years old, was a professional surfer who had represented South Africa as a Springbok. He was lying on his board 200 metres offshore, paddling back after catching a wave, when he felt a jolting impact which shoved him and his board violently sideways through the water.

'It was the most powerful force I have ever felt in my life,' he said later. 'I felt myself pushed then pinned. Nailed to the board by a crushing weight and compression.'

He twisted his head to look over his left shoulder and was greeted by a sight which horrified him. 'I saw a big black shiny head. A huge shark with its teeth embedded in my thigh and the board. I was gripped between the board and the shark's mouth. The filling in a huge sandwich.'

The shark may have been surprised by the rigidity of the fibreglass board. It released its grip. As it turned and surged back for another bite Carter rolled off the board, and the shark bit out an enormous crescent-shaped chunk of foam and fibreglass. As it spat the second mouthful Carter grabbed his damaged board. Though he was bleeding badly from multiple gashes, he managed to catch a wave which peaked at the critical moment. He surfed it right in to the beach, leaving a trail of blood behind him.

His two companions, John Borne and Bruce Corby, were nearby when Carter was first struck. When Borne saw Carter gripped by the 4 metre shark he paddled towards him through the blood-reddened sea.

By good fortune he caught the same providentially breaking wave that saved Carter. But Bruce Corby, 22 years-old, was unluckily left behind.

Borne shouted 'Shark! Shark attack!' as he approached the beach to alert the people on the shore that André Carter had been hit and was badly hurt.

Bruce Corby came in shortly afterwards. 'I asked him if he had seen what happened,' Borne recalled. 'Did you see that, Bruce?'

'John, I've just lost my leg!' Corby gasped.

It was only when Borne saw the blood behind Corby, crimson in the white foam, that he realised how seriously he was injured.

Corby's right leg had been completely severed by the shark, bitten through at the knee joint.

Fellow surfers tied a tourniquet on Corby's leg in an endeavour to stem the bleeding. But he had already lost a critical amount of blood. Not long after being carried ashore he lost consciousness and stopped breathing. Attempts to revive him were unsuccessful and he was pronounced dead soon after his arrival at hospital.

Carter was also severely injured, with massive lacerations to his buttocks and thigh which required more than 400 stitches.

The incident was the first shark attack in East London since a 14-year-old boy died in 1960. It was one of the few cases on record where a Great White had attacked multiple victims.

It was also the first major test for South African legislation passed three years previously to protect the Great White shark. The new law had penalties of up to $20000 or six months imprisonment for any individual killing a Great White in South African waters.

In past years major efforts had been made to catch 'killer sharks' involved in fatal attacks. In 1994 revenge killings by communities were a thing of the past, though there was still a good deal of ill-feeling in the immediate East London area.

Dr Leonard Campagno was a shark researcher and marine biologist who had played a major part in having Great Whites protected in South Africa. Now he appealed to the public not to make the incident the subject of a vendetta against sharks. 'Trying to foster a human mentality of seeking revenge on animals is not the answer,' he told news reporters. 'Sharks have rights too. It's their world as well as ours. The revenge attitude goes back to the bad old days when the only good shark was a dead one.'

Campagno, the senior research scientist at the J. L. B. Smith Institute of Ichthyology at the South African Museum in Cape Town, was adamant that hunting and fishing for Great White sharks in previous years had reduced the adult breeding population to the point where they should be listed as an endangered species. He believed that there were only about 1200 specimens of *Carcharodon carcharias* left around South Africa's 3000 kilometre coastline. 'As slow breeders,' he said, 'it could take years of protection to restore the original numbers.'

From his hospital bed, victim André Carter agreed, with reservations, that nothing would be achieved by hunting the shark. 'It would be senseless to go on a hunting spree for that shark, as many East London people want to do,' he said. 'But obviously I feel hostile and angry towards that particular shark. It killed my friend.'

The Great White also received support from what would once have been an unlikely source.

Theo Ferreira was at one time one of the more prominent anglers and hunters of Great White sharks in South Africa.

'Then one day,' he recalled, 'I hooked a 15-footer [4.6 metre shark]. I towed it into harbour and pumped five bullets into it and stabbed it six times through the gill plates.

'That shark just refused to die. After mutilating it until the sea turned red with blood, I realised for the first time that we were dealing with a magnificent creature with a mighty will to live. I felt embarrassment and remorse, and I haven't hunted the Great White since.'

Not only did he put his rods, reels and flying gaffs aside; Ferreira vowed that he would make up for some of the damage he had done. He formed an organisation called the Cape Town White Shark Research Project to study Great Whites and assist in the preservation of the species. An important goal was educating people about the big sharks.

He and his son Craig still hunt Great Whites today. They attract them to their boat as they did in their gamefishing days with slicks of pilchard and fish oil and animal baits to bring the sharks alongside. But instead of hooking them and fighting them to the death with game tackle, they now use a handspear to place identity tags in the hard muscle area at the base of the sharks' dorsal fins. Then they watch them go on their way with a smile. The tags will help in tracing sharks' seasonal movements and providing information about their habits.

'Two White sharks are never alike in their behaviour,' he told newspaper reporters. 'We know them by sight and get quite attached to individual creatures. We can actually pat some on the head like dogs. But we're very careful. We know we're dealing with a predator who is the "King of the Heap".'

The Ferreiras have made the transition from foes to friendship. Will tourists one day feed Great Whites by hand the way visiting divers feed potato cod on the Great Barrier Reef? Perhaps they'd need to count their fingers (even arms) afterwards.

But, to be serious, handfeeding of Great Whites has already been done.

Carcharodon cacharias is probably the most intelligent species of shark. Most sharks, in fact, are capable of learnt behaviour. In the United States shark researchers such as Dr Eugenie Clark have successfully taught lemon and nurse sharks to nose targets and ring bells to receive food.

In South Australia Valerie Taylor handfed a Great White at water level from the stern platform of the charter boat *Trade Wind*, during a shark-filming expedition with her husband Ron Taylor.

'First we threw out pieces of fish tied to a line,' Valerie recalled.

'As the shark reached for the fish we would pull the line away, drawing it closer to the boat.

'Soon the shark, realising he would only receive a reward by coming close, started popping up next to the stern duckboard, like a dog begging for a biscuit.

'The White has one characteristic not found in other sharks. He will lift his head above the surface to get a better view of what is happening. This can be rather disconcerting, until you get used to it.

'This shark was lifting his head out of the water and looking right at us. Ron suggested I try handfeeding him.

'Since White sharks can rise above the surface to a bait or to take a seal lying on the water's edge, the idea was not without some risk. But we both thought it was worth trying.

'The shark watched me climb down.

'My weight caused the platform to sink a little. I offered a fish by waving it about underneath the surface.

'Whitey glided over, raising his head out of the water next to the fish rather than under it.

'I had to actually put the fish in his mouth. He took it in one big splashy bite. Then he took another five fish, one after the other. I gave him a pat on the head with each one.'

In a short time the shark learnt not only to take a fish from Valerie's hand — he also learnt to come from a particular angle to the sun to avoid the shadow of the boat and so suit Ron Taylor's camera angle.

In Cape Town, in 1996, Theo and Craig Ferreira hoped to attract visitors from diving clubs in Britain and Europe to see their Great Whites. They also planned to establish a sponsorship scheme from business corporations and enthusiasts to 'adopt' individual Great Whites at $2000 a time, to provide funds for the White Shark Research Project.

The concept offers some interesting thoughts. Corporate sponsors usually require some return for their dollars. Are there commercial possibilities with Great Whites? Could it mean that we may live to see a Great White with a Coca-Cola logo on its tail? Or will some future assailant in a fatal attack carry the Nike sports emblem and the famous slogan '*Just do it!*' on its dorsal fin?

There are no smiles, of course, in a real-life fatal attack.

One of the more unusual and sadder stories from South Africa concerns a young skindiver named Gerjo van Niekerk. He was attacked by a Great White on 17 September 1989 while diving in Smitswinkel Bay, and was lucky enough to escape with lacerations across his torso.

In a newspaper interview after the attack he said that he was determined to continue diving because he loved the sport. Attacks on divers are also rare enough that he might reasonably have thought that the odds with a Great White would be millions to one against another serious encounter. Lightning never strikes the same spot twice, we are told. Surely that should also apply with sharks?

Alas, no. Always beware of statistics. Don't bet your life on theoretical odds. You could be a million-to-one-chance loser.

Only two months later van Niekerk was attacked again, this time fatally. He died on 26 November 1989, torn to pieces, while diving for abalone. A human leg was washed ashore on Melkbosselstrand beach and identified by his parents. A pitiable portion of him left to tell a tragic tale.

The only other person known to have experienced two Great White shark attacks was a Californian, Rodney Orr. He was attacked off the north coast of San Francisco in 1961 and survived with a severe fright and minor injuries. Twenty-nine years later, in 1990, another Great White gripped his head in its jaws. Miraculously he escaped again, more fortunate the second time around than Gerjo van Niekerk.

The Californian coast has had more White shark attacks reported — 50 up to 1991 — than any similar shoreline in the world. One tragic story concerned two kayakers in 1989. The shark in question may have initially erred in its identification of the surface shapes. But the end result spelt disaster for the paddlers.

John McCosker described the incident in *Great White Shark*. On 26 January, 1989 Tamara McCallister and her friend Roy Jeffery Stoddard, both 24 years old, left Malibu Beach in California in sea kayaks. They intended to make a short trip to a point a mile and a half (2.4 kilometres) north of their starting point. The journey should have taken less than an hour in unsinkable craft which were entirely suitable for the sea conditions. There was no initial concern when the two were delayed some hours in their arrival. But when the pair were still missing 24 hours later an extensive search was begun. It was successful, in that the kayaks were located. But the news was not good.

The kayaks had been lashed together and drifting 80 kilometres up the coast, towards Point Conception. One of the craft had major gouges and three large holes in its underside. Indications of a Great White shark attack from below, with the kind of damage characteristic of previous attacks on surfboards.

On the third day, Tamara McCallister's shark-torn body was found floating 70 kilometres northwest of Malibu, and about 8 kilometres offshore from Ventura. John McCosker reported:

She bore the unmistakable wounds of a massive White shark bite, including a 13-inch [33 centimetre] gouge from her left thigh. Warren Lovell, the County Coroner, concluded that she had sustained other bites and had bruises on her hands, but no water in her lungs. That last condition suggests that she had not drowned before she was bitten and the damage to her hands would indicate that she had fought with her attacker. Tamara McCallister is therefore listed as the 50th verified White shark victim in California, and her companion, whose body was never found, was presumably the 51st.

What could have happened?

Lashing kayaks together for stability at rest is common practice among ocean paddlers. Sometimes they pause to eat. They may wish to get out of their craft for a swim. Or they may just be pausing to relax on a beautiful morning.

Since it was winter and the water was cool, a swim was probably not the reason. Tamara's body was clothed when recovered. The two paddlers had probably just paused to enjoy the day. Until their peace was shattered, and their interlude turned into a nightmare.

The shark obviously attacked from below, in the usual fashion, and in the surprise may have tipped one or both of the paddlers into the water. It seems most likely that Tamara was attacked first and tried to defend herself. Roy Stoddard may have heroically tried to protect her. Like John Ford with his new wife at Byron Bay, in Australia, devoured before her horrified eyes in 1993, Stoddard may have been killed and eaten by the shark.

The Great White has a demonstrated intelligence. Its poise and confidence in the water have already been remarked on. But sometimes the smartest of sharks does some apparently silly things. White sharks occasionally attack very strange surface objects.

In the days when most boats were made of wood I once saw a 50 foot (15 metre) ketch with a Great White tooth embedded in the stempost at the bow. The tooth and other scars were revealed when the craft was hauled up on the slip after striking an 'unidentified object' out at sea. Obviously the object was a Great White and the shark at that point probably had a sore mouth.

The shipwrights told me that it was not an isolated instance. Shark teeth were occasionally found in wooden keels and rudders. Especially in the timber undersides of fishing boats, which tended to attract sharks with blood and offal when processing their catch at sea. What the shark hoped to achieve if it did subdue a 50 foot vessel is an open question. Presumably it mistook the craft for a whale. Even so, a whale of that size would be beyond the ordinary lethal capacity of even a very large *Carcharodon*.

With today's craft most often constructed of fibreglass, aluminium or steel, teeth are no longer found embedded in hulls. But presumably an errant shark still occasionally hurls itself at the overhead shape from far below to have its teeth scrape jarringly on metal.

Fortunately for the shark it still has a few thousand spare teeth to work through its system. Where a human biting hard by accident on a foreign object would have an expensive trip to the dentist, and might never achieve quite the same smile again, the shark has no such problem. A new tooth moves forwards to take the place of gapped or damaged fangs. Convenient.

At the Farralon Islands, 42 kilometres west of San Francisco, shark researchers in the sea elephant season have sometimes attracted this kind of Great White attack by towing a surfboard with a mounted video camera. The sharks attacked the towed target with vigour, showing that even though the surfboard had little resemblance to a sea lion — no fins, for a start — they were attracted by the surface movement like a fish to an artificial lure.

Study of individual sharks at the Farralons showed that the Great Whites averaged one sea elephant kill each over about three months. One huge female named 'Stumpy' (because of a missing section of tail fin) was the most successful. She killed three elephant seals in a season. It was surmised that she may have been pregnant and required the extra protein.

The camera pictures that the scientists obtained, showing White sharks hurtling up from below to make a strike on the target board, may have made disturbing viewing for surfboard riders. In fact, many more surfers are bumped than are actually harmed. In Australia, while admittedly there have been a number of surfer deaths, so many boardriders have been bumped through the years — with quite a number having their boards actually bitten — that such incidents are no longer recorded as 'attacks'.

Sharks off the northwestern American coast have even bitten at floating pine logs out at sea, which look even less like a sea elephant. The characteristic triangular *Carcharodon* teeth have been found embedded deep in the bark as evidence of yet another identification error.

Could there be such a creature as a shortsighted shark?

It does seem likely that many attacks on humans are a case of mistaken identity — one reason, perhaps, why so many divers survive a strike from a creature with such awesome lethal potential as the Great White shark.

In *Great White Shark* Richard Ellis and John McCosker list 11 *Carcharodon* attacks in Californian waters in the 1960s, and 33 in the 1970s and 1980s. There were to be more, including some fatal confrontations, in the 1990s.

The concentration of Californian attacks seemed to occur in an area between Monterey Bay and Tomales Point — a 190 kilometre stretch of water centring on San Francisco and the Farralon Islands. McCosker reported that this section of coast had become known as the 'Red Triangle' or 'White Shark Attack Capital of the World'.

For some reason there were few attacks south of Point Conception — though the unfortunate kayakers were a sadly spectacular exception to that general rule.

The Farralons, where Whites lie in wait for young elephant seals and sea lions, have rightly been regarded as the most dangerous area of all.

Al Giddings, now a world-renowned underwater photographer, gave McCosker a graphic account of a *Carcharodon* attack on a diving friend at the Farralons in November 1962. McCosker records in his book that he returned to the site with Giddings years later. Giddings recalled for him 'the moment forever embedded in his memory'.

At the time there was a comfortable theory that SCUBA divers were safe from sharks. Al Giddings and Leroy French were partners in the Bamboo Reef Diving School which taught SCUBA diving and arranged boat trips to adventure locations such as the Farralons.

At the end of the day's diving Giddings was checking that everyone was back aboard before raising the anchor. Realising that his partner had not returned, he looked out behind the boat and saw with a shock that Leroy French was thrashing on the surface, his arm gripped in the jaws of a Great White shark. Giddings courageously leapt into the water and swam to aid French. The diver was wearing a black wetsuit with yellow SCUBA tanks. He had just surfaced after a dive to 130 feet (40 metres) and had moved his mask to his forehead and taken out his mouthpiece. It was at that point that the shark first grabbed him by the arm.

Swimming towards him, Giddings saw a daunting sight. He told John McCosker:

I saw a great tail come up over Leroy's head behind him. He couldn't see it [the shark] but he could see reflected in my eyes the terror and total amazement and could hear the rush of water behind him. And, of course, he had been hit once, so he knew it was coming again.

Before my unbelieving eyes the tail went up, then went down alongside him. Leroy disappeared and was gone. I continued to the spot where he had disappeared, and as I was looking around frantically he popped up next to me, clawing, spitting, and screaming, in a way I would not have thought humanly possible.

Somehow I swam behind him, grabbed the union of his tanks and took off with him. We got him to the boat and he was lifted out of the water, blood all over him, blood all over me too, still in the water. We got him on deck and applied a tourniquet.

The drama was watched, wide-eyed, by the other divers and pupils of the Bamboo Reef Diving School. Their reactions were what we can imagine... Enthusiasm for diving diminishing by the second to a rapid round zero. As John McCosker commented, 'It was not good for business'.

French was airlifted to hospital by Coastguard helicopter. He had serious wounds to his left arm, buttocks and legs. It may be that his tanks saved his life, preventing the shark from grabbing him with the species' preferred grasp across the abdomen. A grip which fatally immobilises natural prey such as sea lions and elephant seals, and which all too often kills humans. The shark apparently bit most other exposed portions of French's body.

'Two years and 450 stitches later,' Giddings recalled, 'he was walking again.'

In December 1994 a Great White killed a 42-year-old commercial sea urchin diver at San Miguel Island, now Santa Barbara. The diver was severely mauled on the leg. Crew members saw the shark, which was positively identified as a Great White. They were administering cardiac resuscitation to the unconscious man when the Coastguard helicopter arrived. But he was dead 45 minutes after reaching hospital in Santa Barbara.

A diver seized by his air tank at Point Lobos on the central California coast, in July 1995 was more fortunate. 'He was at 40 feet [12 metres], and had a lucky escape because the shark, apparently, chomped on his air tank and released him,' ranger Chuck Bancroft told Reuters News Service. The shark was a Great White between 12 and 14 feet (3.7 and 4.3 metres) in length. The diver escaped with puncture wounds to the shoulder and thigh.

In an analysis of Great White attacks, McCosker marvelled at the low fatality rate of humans. Of 116 worldwide *Carcharodon* attacks recorded in his book only 14 were fatal. The proportion of Californian fatalities was even less. Six out of a total of 50 attacks.

From this he developed his 'Bite and Spit' theory. McCosker suggests that the shark's technique is to hit prey, such as an immature elephant seal, so hard with a massive first strike that the unfortunate animal is immobilised. Then the shark backs off and waits while the prey weakens through shock and loss of blood until it is helpless to defend itself. This is practical in a survival sense because a sea lion (for instance) has jaws like a land lion and is capable of inflicting considerable damage even in a dying condition. 'One hit before I go!'

The sharks are particularly vulnerable around the eye and gill area, and caution, in the unforgiving world of Nature, is common sense.

However, there may be another aspect. Crocodiles, another attacking creature, may give us a clue.

I once spent some time with a crocodile victim, Val Plumwood, while researching a book, *Crocodile Attack in Australia* (1988). She had been canoeing on the East Alligator River in the Northern Territory at the start of the wet season, November 1985. A crocodile attacked her canoe and, when she paddled to the bank and climbed up into the branches of a tree to escape its unwelcome attentions, the crocodile leapt up vertically, seizing her by the lower limbs and torso and dragging her down into the water.

It was a terrifying experience. 'Once it got hold of me I had no chance at all. I couldn't believe the strength — the sheer power was enormous,' she told me.

The crocodile took her in a series of 'death rolls', the normal technique to disorient and eventually drown prey. In the dark water Val Plumwood managed to grab some mangrove roots and, though seriously injured, tensed herself enough to tear free from the wicked jaws.

She dragged herself back into the tree and — horror of horrors! — the crocodile leapt and caught her again. 'This time I felt pure despair!'

Once more the violent threshing and death rolls. 'I really hoped it would finish me quickly. I thought I'd rather go through anything than one more of those rolls!'

Then her waving arms touched the tree again and she found a handhold. This time when she broke free she went for the steep bank, clawing her fingers into the mud. Twice — a living nightmare — she slithered back and expected the crocodile to grab her again. On the third try, miraculously, she clawed herself over the crest of the bank.

'I reached the top in utter amazement, because I never expected to get away, and I stood up and set off on a sort of hysterical flopping half-crawl half-run, trying to put distance between me and the river…'

She was seriously injured with badly bleeding teeth wounds 5 centimetres deep, and stranded in a remote part of northern Australia with rain and darkness falling. But, through courage and keeping her head, she escaped the crocodile and survived the ordeal in the bush, making it to hospital where she successfully fought a near-death infection.

In so many ways it was similar to shark attacks, where divers survive despite terrible injuries. Though many, like Val Plumwood, have the legacy of a lifelong trauma.

Why? How is it possible that they escape from such an efficient predator?

In the case of the crocodile, a cold-blooded reptile, scientists suggest that it was likely that the reptile had used up its immediately available energy. Crocodiles often exhaust themselves in fighting with other crocodiles or in subduing large prey — one reason why they often store the body of a victim for some time until they recover well enough to eat it.

Large crocodiles who are trapped and struggle too hard to get free, frequently die from sheer energy loss.

There may be some similarities here with a Great White shark. Particularly with very large specimens of *Carcharodon* who have to move 1 or 2 tonnes of body mass through the water fast in order to make a strike. The charge takes place at express speed. For a big shark it probably demands a huge output of energy. The initial impact, the threshing and thrashing movements involved in throwing the victim about, consume even more strength.

When the Great White shark — which is only slightly warm-blooded — backs off, it may be as much out of the need to take a break as a calculated hunting technique.

In that moment of grace the prey has a chance to escape. In Nature the attack is successfully completed more often than not. Though some sea lions and sea elephants do get away. They can be seen in the rookeries ashore with fearful healed scars they will carry for the remainder of their lives.

Some of the escapees struggle ashore only to die of their wounds. When we were diving on the 1629 *Batavia* wreck at the Abrolhos Islands off Western Australia in 1972, a stricken sea lion came ashore and lay by our tent for a week. It had a fearful shark wound in its side. There was nothing we could do, except sorrow for it. On the eighth day it died.

The reason for the high human rate of survival is the fact that most divers and surfers are in company. There is often a nearby boat with radio to summon medical aid and transport to hospital. Humans are usually rescued by their friends during the lull in the 'Bite and Spit' procedure. Rescuers, such as Giddings, often ignore the risk to themselves, swimming to rescue friends and sometimes strangers through blood-reddened waters. Courage and the instinct to save an endangered fellow are among the most admirable traits of *Homo sapiens*. In this way human victims are usually quickly removed from the water. Then, thanks often to the rapid transportation to hospital afforded by helicopters, blood transfusions, surgery and modern drugs save lives that would otherwise be lost.

The shark goes disappointed and without its dinner.

Is caution the keynote in 'Bite and Spit'? Or could the need to pump more oxygen over the gills also be a factor? Only the sharks can tell us.

While California, with its high population of marine mammals — sea elephants, sea lions and sea otters — has lived with the notoriety of its Great White shark incidents, Florida on the opposite side of the United States has had its own share of shark attacks.

Florida normally averages 12 to 14 attacks a year. But in 1994 there were 22 attacks, and in 1995 a record 25 attacks were registered with the International Shark Attack File at Gainesville.

They included the case of the student marine biologist, William Covert, mentioned in Chapter 1. Covert, 25, was from Michigan and a graduate of Michigan State University. He was working at a holiday diving job, catching tropical fish in order to pay his way through further studies. Late in September 1995 he failed to return from a dive at Islamaralda, on the Florida Keys. Shark-torn fragments of his sweatshirt, tracksuit pants and SCUBA gear were recovered from 10 metres of water. His weight belt had been bitten through.

'Jagged and punctured pieces of his T-shirt, sweat pants and SCUBA gear were recovered,' Miami police reported.

'We think he was attacked and eaten by a 10 or 12 foot [3 or 3.7 metre] bull shark, based on two experts who examined the clothing,' Sheriff's spokeswoman Becky Herrin told Reuters News Service. 'The shark apparently ripped off Covert's arms as the diver tried to wriggle free,' she continued.

Shark attacks in Mexican and South American waters are not as well documented as similar incidents in Australia, the United States and South Africa. This is not due to any lack of sharks or victims. On the contrary the waters of Mexico, both on the Pacific side and on the east coast in the Gulf of

Mexico, abound in sharks. Nor is it because the sharks are better behaved than their relatives in the waters of English-speaking countries.

It is simply that the recording systems are less efficient. With so many people involved in coastal fishing it may be, as in some Asian countries, that a shark attack is not considered an especially remarkable event.

In San Salvador, there were two attacks in one day in 1993. An 18-year-old surfer was killed by an unidentified shark at La Libertad Beach, 29 kilometres from the capital, in September 1993, according to Reuters News Service. Another bather was badly injured at nearby La Paz beach on the same day. An oysterman was killed a month previously when a shark attacked fishermen at La Union, 175 kilometres east of San Salvador. Naval authorities said that they believed the same shark was responsible for all the attacks. But no information was available to back up the theory.

In tropical waters it is largely the tiger shark, *Galeocerdo cuvieri*, and the bull shark, *Carcharhinus leucas*, that cause problems with human swimmers and divers. Further south, in colder Chilean waters where seals and sea lions gather, our old acquaintance *Carcharodon* is again found in numbers. Chilean divers, particularly commercial divers working on 'hookah' apparatus (like Australian abalone divers) for shellfish, are very vulnerable to Great White attacks. There have been a number of recorded fatalities among commercial divers and spearfishermen in Chile.

But what is perhaps the greatest loss of human life to sharks — certainly in American waters — since the Second World War has gone unrecorded for lack of evidence.

The opportunity for the sharks occurred during the periodic waves of illegal emigration from Cuba known to the US press as the 'Cuban rafters'. Cuban refugees from the Castro regime took to the water by the thousands during the 1980s and early 1990s. In trying to reach Florida they posed a major problem for US and Cuban coastguard authorities.

The strait between Cuba and the Florida Keys appears temptingly narrow. In May 1997 Australian distance swimmer Susie Maroney made the crossing, covering 180 kilometres in 24 hours. Hers was the first success in more than 50 attempts by other swimmers over the years.

The difference between Susie Maroney and the refugees was her shark cage and support vessels. The refugees, most of whom had no knowledge of the sea, often set off on makeshift rafts or sometimes even the inner tubes of tyres. When the fastenings of these crazy improvised craft broke or came untied from the violent movement of the waves in the open sea, many people perished miserably.

In 1980 some 125000 Cubans left on craft of all kinds. There was a regular trickle of illegal emigrants in succeeding years. More than 4000 crossed in 1993 and a major exodus occurred in August 1994, when 30000 Cubans attempted to reach Florida during an amnesty lifting restrictions on emigration. In this period the Cuban Coastguard rescued 3398 who were in trouble even before they left Cuban waters. The US Coastguard picked up thousands more drifting helplessly in the approaches to Florida. Thousands of others died through the years from drowning, dehydration or shark attack, when their flimsy craft disintegrated and immersed them in the waters of the Gulf Stream.

Though the distance from Cuba to Florida is comparatively short for a well-found vessel, the stretch of water is subject to fickle weather changes and to strong winds. The ever-flowing current of the Gulf Stream may carry unlucky rafters far out into the Atlantic Ocean, well away from land.

US experts estimated that from 50 to 60 per cent of randomly departing rafters may have perished at sea. The sharks undoubtedly took their share.

In 1993, while 3778 people reached the Florida coast, 725 others were notified as missing. There were hundreds of other unknowns who failed to complete unrecorded voyages. For them it was a fatal drift.

The Gulf Stream has a heavy population of sharks, including tiger sharks, blues and the dangerous oceanic whalers, which have been responsible for many deaths in recorded ship disasters.

The Cuban Government clamped down on illegal departures in September 1994. But it was difficult to prevent refugees surreptitiously sneaking away at night on their crazy craft, hoping to reach the land at the end of the rainbow. Convinced they would find their pot of gold in the United States.

Sometimes the sharks of the Gulf Stream found them instead.

Half a world away, on the other side of the Pacific Ocean, the islands of New Zealand are natural territory for sharks of many species. New Zealand waters are rich in fish, dolphins, whales, seals and sea lions. There is a great diversity of habitat from the warmer North Island to the Norwegian-like fiords of the South Island.

New Zealand whalers, working out from the Bay of Islands, the Tory Channel and other locations, often had Great Whites attracted to dead whales, especially in the sperm whale fishery.

Zane Grey made New Zealand famous as a gamefishing location in the 1920s and 1930s. He fished there for mako, thresher sharks, tiger sharks, marlin and the Great White, and declared New Zealand waters 'unsurpassed' for the variety and quality of the gamefish.

Encounters between sharks and divers were inevitable once New Zealanders took up spearfishing and SCUBA diving. There have been 65 attacks and 13 fatalities since 1936 in New Zealand waters. In a series of fatal attacks near Dunedin, in colder South Island waters, in 1964, 1967 and 1968, *Carcharodon carcharias* was the culprit.

In fact up to 1987, Dunedin, the southernmost major city of New Zealand, below 40 degrees latitude, had more attacks — four fatal, four non-fatal — than any other region of the North and South Islands. Because of the colder water *Carcharodon* was responsible for most if not all of the attacks.

A fortunate survivor of a New Zealand Great White attack was Kina Scollay. In November 1995 Scollay was diving in the Chaltham Islands from the fishing boat *Harvest*. He was 22 years old and an accomplished diver. He accepted a dare to free-dive to the bottom below the boat — in 18 metres, or 60 feet, of water.

To prove he had reached the bottom he picked up a rock. As he was ascending, rock in hand, he was seized around the waist by a huge Great White.

'I got no warning that the shark was around,' he said later in hospital, in a newspaper interview.

'He took me in his jaws in one hit.

'I remember everything about the attack. In fact every time I shut my eyes I see that shark coming at me. I can't help thinking how lucky I was.'

The shark first grabbed Scollay around the waist, but was foiled by his lead belt. Then it seized his leg. Scollay beat at the shark's head with the rock as he was dragged along under water, striking at its eyes until it let go.

'I must be the luckiest man alive,' he said. 'I was saved by my weight belt and that stone in my hand.' He was flown to Christchurch from the Chatham Islands and underwent emergency surgery for severe wounds to his leg and gashes to his abdomen.

'There was a lot of pain on the flight to hospital,' he said. 'But I'll go diving again.'

In the warmer waters of Hawaii, problems for surfers and swimmers were more often caused by tiger and whaler sharks. But in the case of William Goins, swimming near Haleiwa, Oahu, on 18 May 1926, there was no doubt about the identity of the attacker. Goins gave a sudden shriek and disappeared. Two days later a 3.5 metre Great White was hooked and Goins's remains were found in its stomach.

More than 60 shark attacks were recorded in Hawaiian waters between 1886 and 1993, with about 12 fatalities. In 1992 there was a spate of attacks, including two fatalities. In 1993 three surfers were bitten and one surfer was knocked off his board. They all survived. Two people were bitten in Hawaii in 1994.

However, shark researchers such as Kim Holland, an associate of the Hawaii Institute of Marine Biology, believe that the risks of shark attack in the islands are not high.

'When you think how many people are in the water every day, 365 days a year,' he told Reuters News Service, 'the total number of attacks is incredibly low. These animals aren't just biting anything that is the right size in the water. If they were we'd have dozens of attacks a week.'

Holland and his research team believe that there are more tiger sharks than previously thought. His research group has been catching tiger sharks and fitting them with sonic transmitters. The sharks are then followed by surface craft tracking their movements through the transmitters' signals. These tiger sharks have been mature animals of about 3 to 4 metres in size. They travelled considerable distances, and were found to move between the surface and depths down to 300 metres on reef slopes.

One of their favourite foods appeared to be stingrays. The researchers often found that the tiger sharks they caught had stingray barbs embedded in their faces. A study of sharks' highly developed immune system, Holland said, might one day hold the key to fighting human diseases such as cancer and AIDS.

Sharks saving lives, perhaps?

In Hong Kong, each year, June is the time of the Dragon Boat Festival, or *Tuen ng* — a major Chinese celebration dating back to the 4th century BC. Legend has it that the origin of *Tuen ng* occurred when a poet named Qu Yuan lost favour with the Emperor and decided to drown himself. He threw himself in the river and fishermen launched their boats and raced to save him. Sadly they were too late. But he has lived on in the Dragon Boat races tradition.

Today, the Dragon Boat races each June are a major Hong Kong event and in 1995, 40 crews from other countries, including Australia and New Zealand, and 129 Chinese boats took part.

But by the 1990s June had also become known in Hong Kong as the time of shark attack. After a ten year period free from shark incidents there had come a horrific series of attacks which induced an atmosphere of near hysteria among some residents of the famous former British colony.

A woman was the first victim, killed off Sai Kung in 1991. In 1992 there were two victims. An elderly man was taken by a shark at Silverstrand. Ten days earlier a woman had been killed at nearby Sheung Sz Wan beach. There were more deaths in 1993 and 1994.

317

Then three people were killed in the Dragon Boat month of 1995.

Schoolteacher Tso Kam Sun, 44 years old, was the first victim. He was a former champion swimmer who had represented Hong Kong in the Commonwealth Games. His body was found at Silverstrand on Thursday 1 June. He was still in his diving wetsuit, and his right leg had been cleanly severed at the hip.

On the following day, Friday 2 June, Herman Lo Cheuk-yuet, 29, was attacked by a shark at Sheung Sz Wan. He also lost his right leg.

The two attacks proved disastrous for local business. At Repulse Bay, Hong Kong's best known beach, holiday crowds dropped from the 100 000 watching the Dragon Boat races on the Friday to 10 000 on the following day. People stayed away from the beaches despite the glorious sunshine. And despite the fact that normal summer Saturday crowds at Repulse Bay numbered 20 000 to 30 000 people. The attacks produced a response from beachside business people similar to those in the town of 'Amity' in *Jaws* fiction.

In an attempt to play down publicity which was adversely affecting the tourist trade, official sources introduced a curious form of 'doublespeak' in which the word 'shark' was never mentioned. Reuters News Service, repeating an official police statement, said: 'Herman Lo Cheuk-yuet was attacked by a giant fish about 6 or 7 feet [1.8 or 2.1 metres] long. The right leg was eaten by the fish. The left was wounded.'

Tso Kam Sun's death was reported in other news sources as being from 'a possible shark attack', though the cause of death was obvious.

Journalists at the *South China Morning Post* reported that in Lo's case the Police Public Relations Bureau 'refused to say that it was a shark attack, but admitted that a "fish" could have been responsible'.

'What sort of fish?' asked a reporter.

'It was a shark-like fish,' said the police spokesperson.

Eleven days later, on 14 June, came a third, particularly savage, attack. At the exclusive Clearwater beach Wong Kwai-yung, 45 years old, became the next victim.

Ms Wong had been swimming with a group of friends only 15 metres from the shore, in water described as 'chest-deep'. As she cried for help the attacking shark struck with terrific force, severing her left leg at the hip and taking off her left forearm. When she was dragged from the water she was dead from shock and loss of blood. Her body was terribly mutilated. There were no less than seven other bites on her abdomen and two on her right thigh. The injuries raised the question of whether more than one shark was involved in the attack. No one was able to identify the shark or sharks responsible.

The spate of shark attacks in successive years, and the three fatalities in June 1995, naturally sparked a good deal of controversy in Hong Kong. There were some who defended the sharks.

A correspondent of the *South China Morning Post*, Ms Sive Bresnihan wrote: 'Respect and acceptance should be shown to our Sai Kung shark. I believe it should be left alone as its victims died through the predator's natural instincts. If we, the people of Hong Kong, kill that shark, we will be no better than the beast itself.'

That was all very well, grumbled newspaper columnist Tim Hamlett in reply: 'Sharks have two thirds of the world to swim about in; the average Hong Kong resident does not even have room for a horizontal bath. Our need is greater than theirs.'

In Australia, there was a tart comment from the *Sydney Morning Herald*: 'The outpourings from Hong Kong shark lovers look a little strange in a territory which consumes more shark-fin soup per capita than anywhere else in the world.'

In previous years people with reputations as 'shark experts' had been brought to Hong Kong to advise the authorities or to attempt to get rid of the sharks. With mixed results.

Australian Vic Hislop, with a 'Down Under' reputation as a shark killer, was brought to the colony in 1993 to rid local waters of the menacing sharks. The sharks eluded Hislop's hooks and chains, prompting a response from Hong Kong's own marine experts. Professor Brian Morton, of the University of Hong Kong's Swire Marine Laboratory, said: 'Supposing this guy [Hislop] gets one shark, supposing he gets two, do we know he's got the right shark? Do we know how many more there are?' He suggested that the killing of one shark might give swimmers a false sense of security, 'prompting them to return to the water before it is safe to do so'. Professor Morton speculated that the shark or sharks involved might be the species *Galeocerdo cuvieri*, the tiger shark, which was found in Hong Kong waters.

Following the first two attacks in 1995, Ocean Park Aquarium curator Michael Stewart was quoted by the *South China Morning Post*, on 3 June, as saying: 'You're more likely to be killed by a bus or breathing the air than you are by a shark'.

Small consolation for Wong Kwai-yung who lost a leg and an arm to the shark at Clearwater ten days later.

The Hong Kong authorities reacted by erecting warning signs and temporarily closing several beaches. In 1995 the annual Sai Kung Dragon Boat race course was protected by 2 kilometres of commercial fishing nets. The competitors were forbidden to celebrate a win by throwing themselves in the water in accordance with tradition. However, the authorities couldn't prevent several of the crews being swamped during the race.

Fortunately the sharks stayed away.

In 1996 Hong Kong brought in a real shark expert, Dr George Burgess, from the Florida Museum of Natural History. As the keeper of the International Shark File at Gainesville he was familiar with the details of attacks around the world.

Possible attractions for sharks, such as fish farms which were adjacent to attack sites at the Clearwater Bay beaches, were identified. Dr Burgess advised that rising sea temperatures and the inshore movements of ocean currents were keys in shark attacks. Most of the Hong Kong attacks had occurred in June when sea temperatures reached 25 or 26 degrees Celsius.

In June 1995, in view of the success of anti-shark nets at beaches in Australia and South Africa, contracts were let for installing shark nets at 22 Hong Kong beaches, for a total cost of 80 million dollars.

'The total force a shark would have to exert to break through the net would be 10 tonnes,' said Harold Kram, managing director of Maritime Mechanics, contracted to install 50 per cent of the nets. He said that after South Africa installed nets in 1960 there had not been a single fatal accident at a netted beach.

However, there was one unexpected downside to the nets. They trapped floating rubbish to a disconcerting degree. Three nets alone off the New Territories beaches caught 42 tonnes of refuse in 1994.

The Hong Kong shark attacks had an interesting and sinister aspect. Unlike other areas of the world where there is about a 60 per cent survival rate in shark attack situations, Hong Kong victims invariably died. What kind of shark was responsible? The injuries were usually massive. All three victims in 1995 suffered the loss of a leg at the hip. We are already familiar with the shark that makes that kind of fearsome first strike. *Carcharodon carcharias* is found in Hong Kong waters.

The Great White is also found off Japan, and in recent years Japan has shared Hong Kong's shark attack woes. However, most of the victims were divers and fishermen rather than recreational swimmers.

Shellfish diver Kazuta Harada was gathering abalone in the Inland Sea, off the island of Gyogo, in October 1992. He was working below a fishing boat, wearing an old-fashioned copper helmet diving rig which was fitted with surface communication. On a routine dive the crew were startled to hear him cry, 'Shark! Pull me up! Pull me up!' But by the time they hauled in his lifeline and the heavy rubber air-hose Harada was gone, torn from his suit. Only the helmet and the shredded canvas corslet remained. Later they learned that the shark had earlier attacked another diver who escaped by 'playing dead'. It was identified as a Great White from a surface photograph of its dorsal fin.

The incidents killed the annual summer tourist trade at Gyogo. Normally the island played host to thousands of visitors. But because of the shark incidents tourist traffic dwindled to a mere trickle.

Other shark deaths in Japanese waters included a net fisherman, an angler and a female abalone diver. There were also attacks on fishing boats. Fishermen appeared on television showing huge *Carcharodon* teeth which had been embedded in their hulls.

Back in Africa, while the Great White was blamed for many of the fatal onslaughts of the 1990s, it is more likely that the bull shark, *Carcharhinus leucas*, sometimes called the Zambezi shark in Africa, was responsible for the attacks on members of the United Nations peacekeeping forces in Somalia.

At Mogadishu, capital of the wartorn nation, the surf rolls in from the Indian Ocean. Arroyo Beach at Mogadishu was named by US Marines after a comrade killed in a firefight with Somali gunmen in the emergency of 1992. When they arrived, the United Nations peacekeepers had been delighted to find the beach and its azure blue water. They saw it as some compensation for the arid inland of Somalia and the problems of peacekeeping among hostile factions in a violent war zone. But in May 1993 a French diplomat's secretary was fatally mauled by a shark. In October a Russian helicopter crewman was killed. An American soldier and several Somali children were also attacked, in one of the highest shark attack rates in the world. Indeed, between 1978 and 1985, according to Reuters News Service, 30 people were estimated to have been killed off Mogadishu, a single point in the lengthy east African shoreline of Somalia.

The United Nations provided a temporary solution to its problem by installing a $60 000 shark net at Arroyo Beach. When the UN forces thankfully departed at the end of one round of hostilities they left the net and the memories. How long the net remained in place without UN maintenance, and subject to depredation from local fishermen filching materials from it, is open to question.

The net had been part of an interesting interaction between sharks and humans, those newcomers to the ocean. When the peacekeepers departed the sharks continued to swim the blue waters off Arroyo Beach and Mogadishu. As they always had.

THE SEARCH FOR A SHARK REPELLENT
chapter fifteen

THE SEARCH FOR A SUCCESSFUL SHARK REPELLENT PROBABLY BEGAN WITH OUR ancestors in prehistoric times. A jab with a sharpened stake or perhaps a coral rock desperately flung to keep the finned adversary at a safe distance. Basic techniques of this kind presumably enjoyed a degree of success. Along with the occasional regrettable failure. But the primitive means may have been just as effective as some of the more sophisticated 20th century attempts at keeping sharks at bay. The search for a repellent has had a history of frustration and failed attempts.

Modern methods of shark control include chemicals and dyes released in the water, poison syringes, carbon dioxide darts, explosive-headed spears, sonic waves and electric shocks. Even distillates of the body fluids of a small Red Sea fish called the Moses sole.

And, of course, there have been the enclosures — nets, iron bars, wooden palisades — used to fence off areas of water to keep sharks safely on the outside of the barrier and the bathers safe inside. A derivative of these orthodox enclosures, in more recent times, is the mobile shark cage (i.e. people cage) like the one whose bars became so familiar to us at Albany. Its purpose was to provide safety in filming or photographing large and dangerous sharks such as the Great White.

Active shark devices have ranged from the simple to the complex. Jacques Cousteau and his divers in their early encounters with Red Sea and Indian Ocean whaler sharks — working from the research vessel *Calypso* in the 1960s and 1970s — used the 'shark billy'. This was a short broomstick, or similar piece of wood, with three or more nails in one end and a loop of cord at the other. It was only one step advanced from the sharpened stake. But it was simple, very inexpensive, and a lot better than nothing at all.

Divers swam with the cord looped over one arm, without undue inconvenience. If sharks came too close they could be fended off with a strong thrust of the 'shark billy'. The nails would not injure the shark. But they prevented the wood slipping on the shark's skin, and were just sharp enough to carry a defensive warning. It was basic. But it was preferable to trying to fend off sharks with the bare hands like a rugby player warding off a tackle with a stiff arm.

The essential difference being, of course, that a rugby player has yet to have his arm bitten off.

Hans Hass, as we have seen, simply shouted at his sharks.

In their turn Ron and Valerie Taylor developed a chainmail steel suit resistant to shark bites, and US researcher Walter Stark and New Zealand diver Wade Doak placed their faith in a wetsuit banded in sea snake patterns, which they called a 'Zebra suit'.

Visual deterrents have worked with other predators in other situations. Indian villagers in tiger country have painted eyes on the backs of their shirts. Tigers — like most man-eating sharks — prefer to attack from behind, and were disconcerted by the painted eyes. The simple stratagem reduced tiger attacks by more than 50 per cent. There is no record of anyone yet painting eyes on their SCUBA tanks or fins, but someone is bound to try it sometime.

Since we live in a scientific age it has been assumed that science would solve the problem in a sophisticated way. It took a surprisingly long time. There were many shark repellent theories and devices through the years which showed some promise. But none were 100 per cent effective. Some of the greatest disappointments were with systems which apparently worked in laboratories and captive situations but did not stand up to tests with sharks engaged in a feeding frenzy in the open sea.

For example, shark fishermen who catch sharks for a living in Australia, Africa or Mexico will tell you that sharks, like crows, seemed disturbed by corpses of their own kind. They may be initially attracted by dead or dying sharks, mainly cannibalising on the livers. But sharks will avoid an area once dead sharks are lying decomposing on the bottom. This is one reason why professional fishermen never clean their catch on the fishing grounds, and why they continually move the position of their nets or long-lines.

US Navy scientists searching for a repellent during the Second World War took this practical experience as a logical starting point. In laboratory analysis they found that the repelling elements in rotting shark flesh were acetic acid and the rank odour of ammonia. They also examined the ink ejected by squid and octopuses when threatened by predators, and combined these elements into a nigrosine dye called 'Shark Chaser'. Throughout the war Navy lifejackets carried a 127 gram packet of Shark Chaser which could be expelled into the water in a dark cloud when the wearer pulled a release tab.

The dye packets were probably beneficial in giving peace of mind to individuals left floating in the sea after ship sinkings or aircrew baleouts. But a major limitation was the fact that the dye dispersed rapidly. Even if effective it would not give lasting protection to a person who might be in the water many hours. In the case of the US cruiser *Indianapolis*, survivors had to float for four days before rescue.

In examining the limitations, Dr Victor Coppleson, in *Shark Attack*, cited the case of two US airmen. Their reconnaissance aircraft ditched in the ocean east of Wallis Island in the mid-1940s.

The pilot, Lieutenant A. G. Reading, was knocked unconscious by the impact of the aircraft hitting the waves. His radio man, E. H. Almond, pulled him out of the cockpit before the plane sank and inflated his lifejacket, thus saving Reading's life at some risk to his own. But Almond's trousers were ripped off in the desperate struggle to get free of the cockpit. A significant factor.

Reading soon regained consciousness, and the two men calmly prepared their emergency drill. They tied themselves together with cords, and pulled their dye-marker tabs. But they were disconcerted to find that they soon drifted away from the dye stain.

'Reading was fully clothed,' Coppleson reports, 'but Almond was wearing only briefs with his legs bare.'

> *After about half an hour sharks appeared. Soon afterwards Almond said something had struck his right foot. His foot was bleeding and he tried to hold it out of the water. Then the sharks struck again and both men were dragged under for a moment. The water around them was now stained red with blood. There were five sharks altogether. Not only did Almond's right leg have numerous wounds but his left thigh was also badly lacerated. He felt no great pain, he said [to Reading], though the sharks continued to strike at him.*
>
> *Reading hit at the passing sharks with his binoculars, but almost immediately they again struck at Almond. Both men went under together and when they surfaced Reading found himself separated from Almond. Reading received a sharp whack on his cheekbone from the tail of one of the sharks. This shark continued to attack Almond, who was now under water.*
>
> *The sharks kept circling and every now and then Reading would feel one with his foot. He was rescued at midnight after 16 hours in the water.*

Miraculously Reading was still unscathed. But there can be no doubt that the loss of his trousers cost Almond his life. The whiteness of his exposed limbs, possibly scratched in the exit from the cockpit, attracted the sharks. And the dye repellent proved tragically ineffective.

There were many other harrowing stories of men and sharks in the Second World War.

The British had their own equivalent of the sinking of the *Indianapolis* when the Royal Navy Cruisers *Dorsetshire* and *Cornwall* were sunk by Japanese torpedo bombers in the Indian Ocean. Coppleson records the response.

Captain A. W. Shelton Agar VC of the Dorsetshire *realised that greater danger to the hundreds of men in the water came from sharks rather than from dive-bombers.*

Captain Agar and those still alive decided that the only way to keep the sharks off was to bring all the dead bodies floating in lifejackets into the centre and make a circle of live men around them. They remained in this way in the water for 36 hours, fighting off sharks with 60 corpses in their midst.

If ever men had need of an effective shark repellent…

Shark Chaser was the result of hurried wartime experiments. When peacetime allowed more testing it was found that the dye was ineffective when sharks were aroused in a feeding frenzy. At Shark Bay, in Western Australia, sharks actually ate the packets of dye and chemicals.

With Shark Chaser discredited, the US Navy took a different line of research. A device called Shark Screen, invented by Dr C. Scott Johnson, was developed for sailors and airmen who might find themselves immersed in the ocean in an emergency.

Shark Screen was one of the more promising inventions, and in my opinion still has a good deal of merit. It was like a large black garbage bag with an inflatable collar. When a man climbed inside the bag he became a dark and shapeless mass unlikely to attract sharks. The plastic wall cut off such odours as those of blood or urine. The collar, coloured orange or yellow, acted as support when inflated and could be readily seen from the air. It was perhaps the most effective of the inventions of its time.

After the conclusion of the Vietnam War the US Navy abandoned its shark research programs on the basis that no US service man or woman had suffered an on-duty shark attack since the Second World War. The very provision of deterrents such as Shark Chaser, it was suggested, might rather have had the negative effect of heightening anxiety about the risk of shark attacks when statistics showed that the actual danger was negligible.

Peacetime operations, of course, are quite different from those during a war. When ships are sunk suddenly by torpedoes or long-range missiles far from land, hundreds of men may be thrown together into shark-infested water. That was the unenviable situation of the crew of the *Indianapolis* in 1945. To suggest that there is no risk in such cases may be as inappropriate as overstating the danger of shark attack. The risk of sharks, high or low or non-existent, will always depend upon time and tide and place. And the particular circumstances.

Some of the repellent devices introduced through the years were quite effective in killing sharks — if that was all that was required. The human race has ever been ingenious in inventing tools of slaughter. Though (digressing for a moment) it is a strange thing that men who hunt for a living have always tended to be conservative, resisting 'newfangled' things. Through the centuries they have tended to change time-honoured methods with reluctance.

Rapid advancements in weaponry have usually occurred during wars. When hostilities ceased (or subsided for the moment) the technological advances filtered through for civilian uses.

As an example, the .303 cartridge was designed for lethal use in the Lee Enfield rifle against Great Britain's enemies. The rifle was the standard weapon used by soldiers of the United Kingdom and British Commonwealth forces in the First and Second World Wars. However, about the time when the .303 rifle was retired by the Australian Army the cartridge took on a new and unexpected role against sharks, along with other forms of ammunition.

The new hybrid underwater weapon was the 'powerhead' or 'bangstick'.

It was invented by an American named, aptly, Scott G. Slaughter. In an issue of the *Saturday Evening Post* in 1956 he described his shark-killing exploits in the Gulf of Mexico, armed with his particularly potent device.

Like many effective inventions its principle was quite simple. It consisted of a sliding chamber on the end of a spear or pole, with a fixed firing pin. The chamber contained a shotgun shell or rifle cartridge. When the chamber hit the shark it was forced backwards and struck the firing pin. *Bang!* The cartridge fired and the lead shot or slug entered the shark's body. But the really lethal effect was caused by the expansion of the gases that followed the projectile and ripped the unfortunate creature apart internally.

Scott Slaughter failed one day to return from a bluewater rendezvous with his sharks in the Gulf. Perhaps they had the last laugh. At any rate he passed into history — but his invention was adopted by divers in many countries. In Australia it was called a 'smokie', from the smoke and bubbles released on impact. It could be used with a very short handspear or even contained in a leg-sheath, like a knife, for defensive purposes.

But most divers used the powerhead as an offensive weapon. It was adapted to several forms of ammunition. Shotgun shells were popular, but it was the .303 cartridge that was best suited for firing from a speargun. The projectile had a slim shape for travelling through the water. The propulsion charge, designed as a mankiller, packed a fearful punch. War surplus supplies of the ammunition in the 1960s and 1970s were still easily available and inexpensive. And all that the bullets needed for waterproofing was a dash of women's nail varnish to prevent water entering the centrefire section.

A somewhat similar device was the Shark Dart. This was a chamber containing a soda siphon carbon dioxide cartridge leading to a hollow spiked nozzle. When the dart struck a shark the CO_2 gas was fired into its internals through the nozzle. The charge blew the shark up like a football bladder. It was effective, but it was a very cruel death for the shark. Similarly, a strychnine-filled hypodermic needle carried on the end of a spear also killed sharks. But in an agonising and inhuman way.

Of the three methods only the powerhead killed instantly and was perhaps the 'kindest' form of offensive weaponry. If that word is appropriate.

All the systems had their drawbacks.

The most immediate downside of the powerhead was that divers for a time went crazy, killing sharks in their hundreds. Most of the victims were harmless species like wobbegongs and grey nurse. Few really large sharks were killed, though Wally Gibbons, one of the best spearfishermen Australia has produced, shot a 360 kilogram tiger at Heron Island. As recorded elsewhere, the grey nurse population on the east coast of Australia was decimated and reduced to a dangerously low level. The overkill eventually resulted in *Eugomphodus taurus* being declared a protected species.

The defensive use of weapons is another matter. For example, take the Great White. Like the crocodile, it is an ambush animal. It begins its charge from behind and below, out of the quarry's line of vision. Divers who become victims seldom see the shark before they are hit. In such circumstances defensive handheld weapons are not a great deal of use.

There is also the point that powerheads, shark darts and the like require some skill and practice in their use. In the 1960s and 1970s, when most divers were spearfishermen — predators themselves — the proficiency was there. Today, when cameras make most of the shots, powerheads carried for defence

327

can be as dangerous, in agitated and unskilled hands, to the user or to other divers as they are to potential marauders.

Surfers, who figure prominently as shark victims, are also likely to have little advance warning of a shark attack. And there is no place on the board or about their person where they could safely carry a powerhead.

Finally, law enforcement agencies in many areas have frowned on the use of powerheads and shark darts. They see them as easily concealed weapons which could be used on land by criminals. Police in Western Australia placed a ban on powerheads from the outset.

As diving is generally regarded as a modern sport, we tend to see the question of dealing with sharks as a modern problem. Sport diving is certainly an innovation which has achieved its major impact with the wide use of SCUBA since the Second World War. There is a natural tendency among modern divers to think that real diving only began in the postwar years. This is something of a misconception.

Divers have been going down under water for thousands of years in various capacities. Long before there were written records, early hunters sought fish and shellfish. Others dived for salvage of lost objects. In the wars between the Greek City states and the Persian Empire, 400 years before Christ, divers were used to cut the anchor cables of enemy ships, to open boom gates and remove obstructions — even to sink unsuspecting enemy vessels anchored at night, by boring holes in their hulls with augers.

The Egyptian queen Cleopatra, on the royal barge in 78 BC, had a diver go down to put a salted herring on the fishing line of the Roman general Mark Anthony, as a joke.

By the 17th century divers were attempting major salvage, breathing air trapped in heavy bells. Using this primitive but quite effective method, divers raised nearly half the cannon from the wreck of the warship *Vasa*, which sank in Stockholm Harbour in 1628. The guns each weighed between 775 kilograms and 3 tonnes, and the ship lay in 30 metres of icy water, with low visibility. In those circumstances the salvage was a very considerable achievement.

In 1629, divers raised eight chests of treasure (out of a recorded ten) from the submerged wreck of the Dutch East India Company vessel, *Batavia*, lost on a coral reef of the Abrolhos Islands off the Western Australian coast. Her shattered hull lay in a depth of 3 to 7 metres, which was comparatively shallow. But a huge surf rolls regularly over the wrecksite from the Indian Ocean. The divers had only oar-powered ship's boats for surface support and were free-diving, holding their breath. The chests of silver each weighed 360 kilograms.

When we began excavating the *Batavia* wreck in 1963 (see my book, *Islands of Angry Ghosts*) we had to cope with the same turbulent conditions and, even with all the advantages of modern equipment, it was far from easy. We wondered how those divers of a previous century had managed. And wished, of course, that they had been less efficient.

When the Spanish Plate Fleet of 11 galleons was wrecked off the Florida coast in 1715, Spaniards based in Cuba mounted a major salvage expedition. Indian divers recovered a huge amount of treasure. But a third of the divers died during the operations, driven unmercifully hard by their Spanish masters.

Pearl divers fished the waters of the Red Sea and Persian Gulf and the coasts of Sri Lanka long before Rome became a civilisation. The banks of pearl shell became exhausted from overfishing in the 16th and 17th centuries. The Australian pearling industry began in Torres Strait and northwestern Australia in the 1860s, using hundreds of Aboriginal and imported skindivers, and has continued with helmet divers — with a break during the Second World War — until the present time.

Jacques Cousteau and Hans Hass are generally given credit as the fathers of modern diving. But the frogmen of the Second World War (irrespective of which side they were on) have yet to receive in full the acclaim they undoubtedly deserve. Using dangerous oxygen equipment (designed for lack of surface bubbles) these men risked their lives on a regular basis. They usually dived at night in unfamiliar waters, handling high explosives. In the case of Allied frogmen, both the Germans and Japanese regarded such operators behind their lines as spies, and if they were captured they faced the probability of being shot or beheaded. Many of them died violently on what we would regard today as suicidally dangerous missions. They knew the risks and they accepted them in a tradition of courage that has seldom been equalled.

In today's diving the first objective is to stay alive. But we should salute those early divers. In my own case they were an inspiration in the immediate postwar period — in the years before the world heard of Hass and Cousteau.

Many divers, from the pearl seekers of Cleopatra's day to the commando frogmen of the Second World War, listed sharks among their potential dangers.

The Roman historian, Pliny the Elder, has already been quoted in his account, in 77 AD, of Arabian pearl divers' experiences: 'The one safety lies in going for them and taking the offensive, for a dogfish [shark] is as much afraid of a man as a man is of it.'

The Sri Lankan divers, in contrast, relied on magic spells. The great Venetian traveller Marco Polo visited their pearling grounds in 1299. He wrote:

There are in the Gulf of Mannar a multitude of great fishes [sharks] which would kill the pearl fishers going down to the sea. But provision against that danger is made by the pearl merchants in this way. The merchants take certain magicians called Brahmans who with their enchantment and diabolical acts control these fishes so they can hurt no one.

The Brahmans, he said, lifted their spells at night so that thieves diving at night would not be protected.

We may smile patronisingly today at these supposed superstitions. But the spells may have been more effective than we imagine. As Pliny observed, boldness can be an effective technique with sharks. The divers, believing that no harm could come to them, may have displayed a confidence that stood them in good stead.

Both wild and domestic animals are quick to sense fear. We do not have to look far to find a first-rate example of animal reactions in our own street. Any postie who has delivered mail on foot or from a bicycle has first-hand experience of the psychology of *Canis familiaris,* Fido, the domestic dog. Most dogs are territorial and will challenge a stranger on their own territory. Run from a growling dog on his own patch and the certainty is that the hound will run after you. Perhaps taking a piece out of your trousers in the process. But hold your ground, look the dog in the eye and talk to it, and you may get a wag of the tail. At worst, most dogs will back off with a subdued growl which says, 'I'm only doing my job'.

There are similarities in behaviour between dogs and some species of shark. This applies particularly with the *Carcharhinidae* or whaler sharks, the species most likely to be encountered by pearl divers in tropical waters and which were called 'dog-fish' by the Romans.

What did wartime frogmen do about sharks?

With the dangers of depth charges, hand grenades lobbed in the water beside them, submarine nets in the dark and machine guns strafing the surface — plus the ever present risk of being poisoned by their own oxygen equipment if they drifted below 10 metres in the darkness — sharks were well down their list of perils.

Nonetheless, sharks were considered when frogmen began operating in tropical waters during the latter stages of the war. In a fine book, *The Frogmen* by James Gleeson and T. J. Waldron, published in 1950, Captain Dennis

Lilleyman, a British commander of X-craft submersibles, is quoted as requesting advice on how to deal with sharks during a raid. Lilleyman commented: 'The advice I got from the authorities was as follows: *Before the operation drop some dead horses into the area and the sharks will be fully occupied with those.*'

The question of where he would find a convenient source of dead horses, and who would drop them into the area of attack, was not addressed.

With further experience, he formed his own entirely sensible conclusions:

A shark underwater is an exhilarating sight. It has a beauty of movement and its perfectly streamlined body powered by rippling muscles makes it capable of amazing speeds… If a swimmer dressed in a frogman suit and oxygen set swims directly underwater towards a shark the chances are that the shark will be surprised at the appearance of this unusual underwater creature and will be nervous if the direct approach is made towards him, and in consequence will turn away and 'beat it'… If, on the other hand, the swimmer turns away from the shark or makes for the surface the shark may then have a go at him. The initial movement of a swimmer on a direct encounter is therefore of great importance.

Some creatures in Nature, though appearing both appetising and defenceless (a bad combination for survival), nonetheless appear immune from shark attack.

In the 1970s US researcher Dr Eugenie Clark found a small flat fish in the Red Sea called *Pardarchirus marmoratus*, otherwise known as the Moses sole. When it was placed in an aquarium tank all the other animals died. Sharks that tried to eat it turned away violently as they opened their mouths. It was found that the sole secreted a milky fluid which was poisonous and unpalatable and which effectively protected it from predators.

The discovery was hailed as a breakthrough in the search for a shark repellent. But the difficulty was that a swimmer needed to be able to disperse a kilogram of the material per hour for it to be effective. This fact killed the possibility of using the chemical as a practical repellent. The Moses sole released a small concentrated burst in moments of danger directly into the predator's mouth. A swimmer or diver would have to carry a possibly heavy and bulky container of chemical against the chance of a shark confrontation, and would have to be aware of the shark in advance — often an impossibility, as we've noted.

The chainmail suit developed by Ron and Valerie Taylor was an innovative approach to self-protection against sharks.

Ron got the idea from a steel-mesh glove used by abattoir workers to prevent their razor-sharp knife slipping and cutting the hand they used to steady the lamb or beef they were boning. He took the idea to an American, Jeremiah Sullivan, and they developed a suit made up of 400 000 stainless steel rings.

The suit, as demonstrated on television by Valerie Taylor — with blue sharks chewing on her chainmail-clad arms — was certainly effective against smaller sharks. But, while shark teeth would not penetrate the steel links, a human could perhaps be crushed or suffer broken limbs or internal injuries in a Great White attack. Also, the suits were expensive, costing more than $5000, and they were a considerable weight in the water. Most ordinary divers did not see them as a practical option.

The US Navy conducted tests of suits made with Kevlar, a lightweight plastic material used in the manufacture of bulletproof vests, sailboards, yachts and sports car bodies. But the suits were too stiff. Worse than that: while the suits could stop a revolver bullet, shark teeth still got through them.

A less expensive product was the 'banded' wetsuit which, to be made in its simplest form, only required a can of paint. It was developed in the 1970s by American marine biologist Walter Starck. He was also the inventor of the 'Electrolung', an invention ahead of its time, which utilised mixtures of gases and allowed divers to swim at far greater depths than they could with SCUBA, without risk of the 'bends'. It was claimed that divers could use it as deep as 300 metres (1000 feet).

Starck had observed that Pacific banded sea snakes swam among sharks with apparent immunity. Striped pilot fish swimming at the shark's nose also appeared to enjoy privileged status. Were the bands and stripes a 'Keep Off' sign recognised by predators?

Starck decided to find out and tried a wetsuit painted with white stripes. He was delighted with the results. Wade Doak, a New Zealander, joined Starck on his radically different dive-boat, El Torito, in the South Pacific and in 1975 wrote the interesting and informative book Sharks and Other Ancestors on their marine study adventures.

They called the striped wetsuit the 'Zebra suit', and for them it seemed to work. But when it was tested by the US Navy and by Valerie Taylor the results were less impressive. In fact, in an experiment made by the Taylors at 'The Horn', a notorious shark spot at Osprey Reef in the Coral Sea, Valerie Taylor was bumped and jostled by out of control grey reef sharks. 'In 30 years of diving I have never had to push grey reef sharks away before,' she said. Valerie believed that by breaking her silhouette the stripes had made her invisible 'It was almost as if the sharks could not see me.' She also said, 'I was sceptical from the first...'

It may have been that Starck and Doak's confidence in the suit made it work for them, as the Brahmans' shark spells had given confidence to the Sri Lankan divers. In contrast, Valerie's negative attitude may have produced an opposite result. Or were there just different reactions from different sharks in different places?

Whatever the reason, the striped suit went the way of the other experiments. Each one stuck with the same label: 'It seemed a good idea at the time.'

Even enclosures, which should surely have been 100 per cent effective, had their problems. Many 'sharkproof' zones in rivers, estuaries and oceans were created early in the 20th century when swimming first became a fashionable relaxation. Constructed with netting, bars or wooden piles and palisades, they worked well in calm conditions when the materials were new. But fierce ocean storms and surf smashed sea baths and drowned nets under tonnes of seaweed. Rust rapidly rotted out wire mesh and steel bars. Teredo worms ate palisades and weakened wooden structures.

Enclosures died a natural death in most places with the advent of large public swimming pools.

In Australia, with a spate of shark attacks in the Sydney region in the 1920s and early 1930s, there was so much public concern that in 1934 the New South Wales Government set up a Shark Menace Advisory Committee, with Sir Adrian Curlewis, a famous figure in the Surf Lifesaving Association, as chairman. The Committee's recommendation — controversial at the time — was that the NSW Government should subsidise a program of systematic meshing to control sharks off Sydney beaches.

The dramatic success of the beach meshing silenced critics and delighted those who had voted in favour of the program.

In *Shark Attack*, Victor Coppleson put the results in perspective with past years: 'Without meshing — assuming the previous rate of attacks on the Sydney beaches had been maintained — there would have been about 14 attacks on these beaches between 1937 and 1956. Actually there were none.'

Since the introduction of meshing, over a period of 60 years there has not been a single fatality at any of the meshed beaches. There were only eight incidents in Sydney Harbour.

Catch figures showed a huge reduction in the numbers of potentially dangerous sharks caught as the years progressed.

In 1940–41 nets caught 751 sharks in one summer and 1500 were taken between Palm Beach and Cronulla in 17 months. More than half, 900 in all, were large Great Whites, tiger sharks and whalers — 'potential man-eaters', the newspapers claimed. By the summer of 1980–81 the catch was down to 163 sharks per season. The individuals were smaller and there was a marked reduction in the dangerous species. In the 1990s, despite increased numbers of meshed beaches and a more efficient operation, the catch remains at between 120 and 180 sharks per year.

The meshing program was eventually extended to beaches north of Sydney and to Newcastle. In Queensland, where attacks had brought bad publicity, a system of long-lines was tried as an experiment. This was abandoned when a young surfer tangled in a line and drowned. The NSW system of meshing was introduced and still operates on the Gold Coast.

What is shark meshing? Contrary to widespread belief, the shark nets do not enclose a beach or form a protective barrier. The nets are set parallel to the beach, in panels of netting with a 30 cm mesh, hanging 6 metres deep below the surface. Each panel is about 150 metres in length and is supported by floats at regular intervals, with conspicuous buoys at either end.

Sharks could, of course, circumvent the nets and reach the beach. But they seldom appear to do so. Is the long-term success of the program due to a decline in stocks through 'catching out' the potential maneaters? Or have the sharks become 'educated' and learnt to avoid the nets and the beaches where they are set?

There are still many unanswered questions, partly because Australian authorities have not used the meshing program fully for research. Though the contractors are required to note the species and numbers caught, the shark carcasses from the nets are simply dumped at sea 6 kilometres offshore without further study. The concern has only been with the effectiveness of the program. Though most beachgoers (and beach businesses) in Sydney and on the Queensland Gold Coast have been happy enough with that aspect, it seems a shame that the opportunity for scientific study of sharks and their behaviour has not been utilised.

In contrast, shark meshing has never found favour in the United States, though Florida has sometimes had 20 or more shark attacks in a summer.

But when South Africa had its own shark attack crisis in the 1950s, and the Natal coast was declared the 'Shark Attack Capital of the World', the Australian system was adopted. Today the Natal Sharks Board has the largest and most sophisticated shark-meshing organisation in the world. And the success rate in reducing South African attacks has been similar to the Australian experience.

South Africa, in the 1950s, had the world's highest incidence of recorded shark attacks, with as many as six attacks a year off Natal beaches.

The summer holidays of 1957 — including the month which quickly became known as 'Black December' — saw seven attacks with five fatalities in as many months. The summer came to a bloody climax with two fatalities at Easter time in 1958.

The attacks received a lot of publicity, mainly via radio news broadcasts, and mass hysteria ensued. Thousands of people fled the beaches and the holiday resorts.

The panic reached its peak in April 1958 when two attacks at Uvongo prompted people to cut short their Easter break.

The mass evacuation of thousands of cars from the coast caused a huge traffic jam on the roads heading inland.

The attacks were an economic catastrophe for the hotels and resorts along the coast that were dependant on the holiday trade. It is estimated that the loss of income cost the equivalent of $200 million in today's money.

Shark fever in South Africa reached a peak when the government sent a naval frigate to drop depth charges off Margate and Uvongo.

Police were sent to sea in small boats, armed with hand grenades to drop on any sharks that might be sighted! Futile gestures, of course, since explosions actually attract sharks to feed on dead and dying fish. But they indicate the strength of anti-shark fear at the time.

The City of Durban had already quietly begun shark meshing in 1952, the techniques modelled on those developed in Australia.

The Natal Sharks Board was established in 1964 and began a meshing program at all Natal beaches. It was immediately effective.

Between 1978 and 1984 the nets caught 8333 sharks. Ten per cent were potentially dangerous Great Whites, tigers and bull sharks — known in South Africa as Zambezi sharks.

In line with the Australian experience, human fatalities ceased at meshed beaches.

The Natal Sharks Board extended its operations to other beaches outside Natal, and by the 1990s it had become a major organisation with modern headquarters at Umhlanga Rocks.

Unlike Australian netting operators, the Natal Sharks Board — which was meshing 46 beaches in 1987 — tagged and released sharks still alive in the nets and brought the dead sharks ashore for scientific research.

Whereas in Australia the meshing was contracted out by government and local authorities to private operators, the Natal Sharks Board had its own fleet of small boats and carried out the entire operation itself. The headquarters at Umhlanga Rocks was equipped with research and conference facilities. Visitors were able to see films and hear lectures on sharks. They could watch them being dissected and see the whole scientific process.

At first glance the beach meshing programs in South Africa and Australia, which were extended in 1996 to Hong Kong, might appear to be the logical answer to shark attack. There is no denying the effectiveness of meshing. But meshing programs do not come cheaply. Though the dollar expenditure might be considered to be balanced by income from tourism, the costs limited the operation to centres of population. People swimming at unprotected beaches elsewhere, including surfers and divers, still took their chances.

Environmentalists have had strong concerns about mesh netting. The major proportion of sharks caught in the nets are harmless to humans. The nets also catch and kill dolphins, turtles, rays and (in Queensland) dugongs. Sometimes they entangle the humpback whales travelling the coast on their annual migrations.

The question the conservationists ask is whether this wastage of innocent marine life is fair exchange for human bathers feeling safe at the beaches.

They take the argument a stage further by stating that even so-called 'man-eaters' have their own right to life. Their concern is that the population of some kinds of sharks — and in particular the Great White — appears to be seriously declining. That we may be close to a point where *Carcharodon carcharias* could become an endangered species.

This is not a universally accepted view. In any age there are dissidents, and this is particularly so where emotional subjects like the relationships between sharks and humans are concerned.

One such dissident is shark hunter, Vic Hislop of Hervey Bay, Queensland. Born outside of his time, Hislop would have been considered a hero in the 1950s and '60s, 'ridding the seas of a menace' to quote the popular newspaper phrase. In the 1990s he ran a permanent exhibition at Hervey Bay, centred around a giant *Carcharodon* and entitled the *Great White Death Shark Show*. At a time when the conservation moves to protect sharks were gaining ascendancy, Hislop and his vehemently opposing views led him into the centre of controversy. Hislop was quoted in the Brisbane *Courier-Mail*, 28 November 1987, as saying, 'If sharks had legs they'd be running around chewing up people, spewing 'em out just to chew up more — plus all the things they just maim and shake and leave to die.'

Does Hislop still hold such extreme views? I asked him that question in 1997. 'Look, I'm a conservationist,' he responded with an injured tone. 'I'm more of a conservationist than the greenies because I'm out on the water every day and I see what really goes on.

'I'm on the side of the gentle creatures, the whales, dolphins, dugong and turtles. If sharks breed up because they're protected and other fish — just as wonderful in evolutionary terms — are being thinned out be overfishing, what do you think is going to happen? I'll tell you. The innocent creatures will feel it hardest because they'll become the shark's main food instead of fish. You can also bet that there'll be a lot more attacks on human beings.

'Sharks scarce? Don't you believe it! There are more sharks out there than anyone ever thought of. No one ever sees a tiger in Moreton Bay but if I put a set-line out I'll catch two or three any night. Some of them will be very big, very dangerous sharks.

'What will become scarce if government and other idiots take protection too far, is the gentle creatures. In ten years time let's see how many dugong there are, eh? And I don't want to hear any nonsense about disease, pollution or boat propellers. They'll be inside the guts of tiger sharks.'

Hislop, who suffered some bad press in newspapers and a blistering interview from Channel Nine's Terry Willesee on *A Current Affair* for his capture of a 2.5 tonne, 7 metre Great White in Victorian waters in 1987, denies he is anti-shark.

'Most species of shark are harmless,' he said. 'It's only the Great Whites and tigers that are dangerous. I don't hate them either. they're my living. But you have to understand what they are. They're pristine killers, creatures from the Ice Age. They eat their own young. They'll eat anything. they'll eat you too if they get a chance. They're indiscriminate hunters and if they breed up we'll have a huge problem.

'Anyway, who catches the most sharks? The Queensland government have caught 49 Great Whites in the beach nets since 1992. I've only caught five Whites and they've been used commercially in my exhibition. to educate the public. The Shark Show employs five people and gives them a living. In that regard I'm just like any other fisherman catching something out of the sea to feed his family. But I'm supposed to be the bad guy...'

He shakes his head. 'How do you make any sense of that?'

Regardless of the controversy about protecting sharks, there are still those with an open mind where shark repellants are concerned. There is a need for an invention that would protect people and ward off sharks without killing the creatures needlessly, and that would spare the innocent by-catch of dolphins and turtles. There is also a requirement for a method that could be effective for individual divers, surfers and swimmers, regardless of where they swim.

Most of the obvious (and not so obvious) possibilities have already been rejected as failing to give 100 per cent cover. Bubble curtains, underwater shouting, bangsticks, shark darts, chemicals, sonic waves, striped or steel-mesh wetsuits, the Moses sole, even the Brahmans' spells and Japanese ricepaper charms of history, have not provided a satisfactory answer to a worldwide problem.

But there was one field left which had not been fully explored.

In February 1996 the Natal Sharks Board announced that it had found an answer based on an electrical field which forms an elliptical zone of safety around a diver or swimmer.

In that month they launched an interesting-looking black and yellow device which came in two sections. It was called the POD, the initials standing for Protective Oceanic Device. Scientists of the board had been looking at the idea, on and off, for about 20 years. One of the thoughts behind the invention first occurred to a Natal Sharks Board researcher in the 1970s when he was using an electronic probe to 'age' the carcasses of sharks brought in from the nets. (Dialetic properties of raw fish muscle and skin change as freshness is lost.) If the shark responded with muscle movement to the electric current it meant that it was a 'fresh' corpse and could be used for animal or human consumption.

The researcher noted that the eyes and jaws areas were particularly susceptible to the current. Presumably this would cause discomfort to a live shark, leading to the idea that an electric field targeting these areas might prove an effective shark repellant.

It was well known from the past experiments of scientists that sharks were very much more susceptible to electric current than humans were. Researchers such as Dr Dijkgraaf and Dr Kalmijn in the Netherlands in the 1930s had found that sharks could detect voltage gradients as low as 0.01 microvolts per centimetre. In fact, sharks were found to have the most acute sensitivity to electric current of any ocean or land animal. Their 'ampullae of Lorenzini', the pits or pores in the pointed snouts, enabled them to detect electrical signals so weak that they would not register with a human being.

Graeme Charter of the Natal Sharks Board formed the theory that humans might be able to comfortably surround themselves with an electrical field which would not affect them but would be intolerable to a shark. He spoke about his thoughts on the matter. But for some years the development of a repellent was not considered a practical option for the Natal Sharks Board, mainly because the batteries and other components available at that time were too heavy. However, in 1992, with the development of nickel cadmium batteries to an advanced level, it was decided to examine the possibilities of a device utilising an electric field.

Graeme Charter and electronics expert Norman Starkey were given the task of turning theory into practice.

Using copper loops as probes set some metres apart in a large tank, they found that by passing a low voltage battery current between them they were able to create an electronic field which deflected cruising sharks in the tank from their chosen course. Further tests showed that they could also turn them away from baits while feeding. Bull sharks that had been gulping fresh fish down hungrily lost all interest when the current was switched on, and departed with a flick of their tails.

The next step was to test the device with a diver in the ocean.

In the 1990s Ron and Valerie Taylor were probably the world's best known shark-filming couple. Their films had been popular in South Africa where interest in sharks naturally ran high. With the Taylors' vast experience and their acclaimed photographic skills they seemed the logical people to undertake the tests with wild sharks in an open ocean.

At first the Taylors were sceptical.

'Here we go again!' laughed Valerie. 'We've had the bubble barrier, the striped suit, queer noises, Navy dye packets, the Moses sole — you name it. We've seen them all.'

They were also aware that other electronic devices, some tested by the US Navy, others actually patented, had also been unsuccessful. 'But imagine if it *did* work,' said Ron, looking further ahead. 'If the principle is right it could do away with nets and beach meshing!'

The Taylors had been among the foremost opponents of beach meshing. They had spent time rescuing turtles and harmless animals caught in the deadly nylon. They also saw the dead ones, pathetic corpses tangled in the nets. They understood the difficulty in trying to change entrenched public opinion. To get rid of the nets it would be necessary to come up with some acceptable alternative.

They decided to test the South African device.

On arrival they were shown demonstrations of the electrical field which provided impressive results with large bull sharks in a tank. The Taylors saw enough to convince them that the next step was worthwhile. Diving with the sharks.

'They really didn't want us to go into the tank at first,' Valerie remembers with a smile. 'They thought we were crazy.'

The bull sharks they were about to join were certainly a dangerous species of shark. The largest of the whaler family, the *Carcharhinidae*, they had earned a grim reputation on the Natal coast. The sharks in the tank were big, mature animals, capable of aggressive behaviour.

'I suppose if you were the owner of the tank,' Valerie recalled, 'you'd have to be concerned. It would have been a terrible thing for them if a couple of well-known divers jumped into their tank and got chewed up . . . They'd seen their sharks tear a giant groper to pieces. They thought the sharks might do the same to us.'

But if the device wouldn't work in the tank it would be small value in the open sea. There was only one way to find out. Splash! Splash! In went the Taylors while the watchers held their breaths.

There was nervous tension as the pair set their tanks back against the wall and crouched waiting for the bull sharks to react. At first the sharks swam boldly up to them. But as the fizz of bubbles around the metal loops showed that the electric current was flowing, the sharks turned sharply away, their eyes flickering and jaws working, as had been noted in the early experiments.

'It worked perfectly, every time,' said Ron. 'But I had a feeling that the limits of the tank made the charge more concentrated. I couldn't help wondering whether it would work as well in the open sea.'

'What about with Whites?' asked Valerie.

Everyone thought hard at that point. Great White sharks had by far the largest body mass of any of the dangerous shark species. *Carcharodon* would obviously require a burst of more powerful electric current. Would they need a charge that would be too uncomfortable for humans? What if the whalers were somehow more susceptible, and big sharks like Great Whites and tigers were less affected? Or if, as Ron had suggested, the device only worked well within the confines of a tank?

Once again, there was only one way to find out. Ron and Valerie Taylor and a team from the Natal Sharks Board, headed by Graeme Charter, travelled to Cape Town at the southern tip of the African continent.

There the currents from the Atlantic and Indian oceans converged. The fish-rich waters sustained a huge population of seals, penguins and cormorants. Great White sharks, their predators, swam with them in greater numbers than perhaps anywhere else in the world.

The site chosen for the experiment was Gansbaai, near Dyers Island. It was a place where a deep channel runs between rockbound islands and where the seals and penguins haul ashore to breed. The sharks patrol the channels. 'The water was stiff with Great Whites,' Valerie said. 'As soon as we started berleying there were fins and tails breaking the surface. We may have had ten Whites around the boat at one time.'

Initially the divers worked with a cage. But the metal bars seemed to confuse the electrical field. Voltage had been raised from 12 volts for Zambezi (or bull) sharks to 48 volts for Great Whites, and Valerie kept receiving shocks in the cage. The results were inconclusive.

Next day a fierce storm swept through.

When it was over they were dismayed to find that the cage had broken free and washed away. The divers had the option of packing up and going home, or going into the water with the Great Whites without cage protection.

It would be the supreme test of the POD. But the device had successfully turned sharks away from baits around the boat. Even when sharks were actually chewing on meat from culled seals they spat the baits out and turned tail the moment the current was switched on.

Ron Taylor suggested that four divers should enter the water. 'We could watch each other's backs and even if the POD didn't work the numbers should deter the sharks and give us a fair chance of survival,' he said.

Most divers would want more than 'a fair chance' of surviving. However, Valerie was confident.

'We had never knowingly swum with Great Whites without a cage before. But I always believed that if you stood your ground with a shark — any shark — you gained his respect. He's used to prey that try to flee from him. Sharks don't expect you to stare them in the eye. It's outside their experience. They may circle you, and look at you. But generally speaking you're pretty safe.'

She added, 'It's the shark you don't see that gets you.'

There were some high pulse rates as they entered the water. But they were relieved to find that the POD proved as effective as it had in the early tests.

The Whites made passes at them, employing the surprise techniques they used in attacks on seals.

'They'd whoosh past and disappear into the murk,' said Ron. 'When they returned you could never tell which direction they'd be coming from.'

'Very sneaky,' said Valerie. 'They were very sneaky sharks. One got to within five feet [1.5 metres] behind me before I realised he was there.'

Nonetheless, the electrical field turned the sharks away every time, and after a period of exposure they seemed reluctant to come close.

The test crew were jubilant. *Carcharodon* was the ultimate shark. It was a major breakthrough, offering all kinds of promise for the future. Further tests only enhanced the POD's reputation. Graeme Charter and Norm Starkey took it to Australia to test it with the Taylors on sharks on the Great Barrier Reef, in the Coral Sea, and off New Guinea. The sharks found there were different varieties from those on the Natal coast. The Natal Sharks Board wanted to be absolutely certain that its device worked on all the dangerous species.

It worked so well, in fact, that when it was demonstrated in 1994 at Milne Bay in New Guinea, at Bob Halstead's tourist shark-feeding operation, the biggest sharks left the area at speed, and two years later had still not returned.

Why had the Natal Sharks Board succeeded where others failed?

The South African Council for Scientific and Industrial Research had tried unsuccessfully for 34 years to design an electric cable system to replace shark nets. A good deal of work had been done with electronics in the United States to the point where actual patents had been taken out. But no device had been produced previously that was practical in the field.

Though the principle of the POD was simple enough, the electrical field, the voltage and the pulse rate were variables, and it was important to get the right combinations. The Natal Sharks Board had better facilities for research and live-testing than most of its rivals, and sometimes in science there is a certain amount of luck in the circumstances that lead to success.

Is the device always 100 per cent successful?

'Used correctly it has never failed us,' said Valerie Taylor. 'But we had one bad scare filming with Great Whites at Neptune Island in South Australia in March 1996, which showed us how divers might get caught out.

'We were filming our own documentary, with divers in a cage and sharks all around. I had the POD and Ron was filming without protection. I thought I had him covered with the electric field. But he got around to the opposite side of the cage and the metal bars interrupted the current flow. Immediately a huge White made a lunge at him.

'I saw Ron swimming, literally, for his life, trying to get back to my side of the cage. I sped over the top, zapped everyone in the cage with the current, and drove the shark off. But it was a very near thing. It was perhaps the closest call in all our years of shark filming. That shark was so quick! It just showed how careful and alert you always have to be when you're dealing with big predators. The POD does work and works, well. But you need to be vitally aware of every situation.'

Like most effective inventions the POD is basically a simple device. But it needs to have the right combination of factors. Graeme Charter, now director of the Natal Sharks Board, explained its function in the literature that accompanied the official release in February 1996:

> The shark POD (Protective Oceanic Device) consists of three components linked by electrical cables.
>
> The main body of the diver unit, containing the battery, is strapped to the SCUBA tank. The foot probe is attached to one of the diver's fins. Separated by at least 1.5 metres the two sections create an elliptical electrical field around the diver when the current is switched on.
>
> Sharks are most sensitive to electrical fields. Pores (ampullae of Lorenzini) in the shark's snout enable it to detect electrical signals of an extremely low voltage. For example, if a field could be generated by an ordinary torch battery with electrodes 1600 kilometres apart the shark would be able to detect it.
>
> The field being detected is measured at 100 millionth of a volt per centimetre. The design of the shark POD is such that the electrical field it produces will repel sharks coming from any direction.
>
> Correctly used, the electrical field is not strong enough to cause any discomfort to humans. However, the field is far greater than the tolerance of sharks. In field trials the sharks were repelled from 4 to 7 metres away.

The commercial POD has a rechargeable battery with 75 minutes running time, is shock resistant and is submergible to 50 metres.

The Natal Sharks Board, in 1997, was working on future applications which included the possibility of barrier protection for beaches. If they succeed in producing a successful system there need be no more sharks drowned in beach meshing nets. No more dolphins, dugongs, turtles or other harmless creatures sacrificed for our personal safety. In short, a better deal for humans and marine mammals, all round. This would surely make the POD one of the more significant marine inventions of modern times.

SHARING THE PLANET
chapter sixteen

I N THE YEAR 2001, AS WE LOOK BACK AT RECENT HISTORY, WE WILL BE REMINDED that in the past hundred years alone humans have caused vast damage to the earth in forest clearing, land degradation, air and water pollution and the killing off of animal species. We will see that repairs are mandatory. We will also be reminded that in the past 80 years the world's population has quadrupled to 5.8 billion people. If such increases go unchecked a figure of 10 billion is possible by the end of the 21st century. That will *really* test the resources of the planet.

The end of a century is traditionally a time for reassessment. A time for reflection on the way we were and the way we are.

Newspapers are the mirror of their times. There is a treasure store of random information in most dailies between the front page and the sports columns. And we can source extra information, including warning signals, by linking apparently unconnected stories to establish a pattern. Indicators of the directions in which we are moving.

The brightest news in 1996 was undoubtedly the successful launch of *Mars Surveyor*. The American space agency satellite set off in November on the first leg of a circuitous 700 million kilometre journey to the Red Planet. When it reaches Mars's orbit, after 10 months, the satellite is primed to send back information on climate, atmosphere and landscape. Later a tiny six wheeled vehicle will touch down on the surface to send back pictures of the terrain.

The Mars project was sparked by analysis of meteors which suggested that life may have once existed on Mars. May indeed still exist. And if there are living organisms on Mars, why not intelligent life elsewhere in space?

It is possible that the voyage of *Mars Surveyor* may one day be set alongside the great voyages of history such as Colombus's departure for the

New World in 1492. Or Magellan's circumnavigation of 1518. For those addicted to the long-running television odessey *Star Trek* it might mean that today's space fiction is translated into fact far sooner than they'd imagined.

'We're looking for Spock out there,' said a NASA spokesman at the launch of *Mars Surveyor,* speaking of the alien hero of *Star Trek.* Where once that might have been taken for humour, in 1996 it was an entirely serious, if metaphorical, statement.

Although we have become accustomed to scientific marvels, the skill level in such projects is still breathtaking. What is even more of a wonder is the fact that we have come so far along the road of scientific inventiveness in so short a time. And the pace is accelerating!

The *Mars Surveyor* launch was the best of the good news I found in my morning paper. There was less cause for euphoria in another story I noted the day before. It was headed 'FROG LIMB ALERT'.

> *Minnesota, USA: Bruce Nelson was catching frogs for catfish bait last year when he realised something was horribly wrong – some of the frogs had stumps for legs, others had as many as four tangled hind legs.*
>
> *'You see deformed things all the time in Nature, but nothing like this,' he said.*
>
> *Across the midwestern state of Minnesota, into neighbouring Wisconsin, South Dakota, and even as far away as Quebec and Vermont, scientists are seeing the same kind of misshapen limbs, along with frogs with tails, missing or shrunken eyes, and smaller sex organs.*
>
> *Scientists have had a hard time finding wetlands in Minnesota with no deformed frogs.*
>
> *'It scares me,' said Judy Helgen, a scientist with the Minnesota Pollution Control Agency.*
>
> *Scientists are not sure what is causing the deformities. Theories run from pesticides to parasites to radiation from ozone depletion — or a combination of factors.*
>
> *'There's a reasonable assumption that if there's an external substance influencing amphibian development it could also influence human development,' said David Hoppe, who is on a State-financed team of scientists researching the problem.*

Another article in the same issue of my local paper carried news of an alarming decline in human and animal male sperm counts. A US researcher had startled a congressional meeting in 1994 by stating: 'Each man in this room is half the man his grandfather was!' That was one way of putting it — it certainly made the point.

The decline in male testosterone potency is thought to extend to all members of the animal kingdom. While no falling graph has been cited for shark would-be fathers, that may only be due to lack of research on them. If so many other species are being downgraded in the potency of their testes, then it is a reasonable assumption that sharks may be sharing a similar low.

The cause of falling testosterone levels, and many other linked health problems, is a combination of pollutants from plastics, DDT, defoliants and other chemicals which disrupt hormonal balance by mimicking the female hormone, oestrogen. The chemicals, called POPs (for persistent organic polluters), do not readily dissolve. They are carried by air and water and accumulate in our fatty tissues.

They are part of the worldwide story of pollution. We are familiar with the scientific alarm over the depletion of the ozone layer in the earth's atmosphere. It is well recorded that the accumulation of CFCs, or chlorofluorocarbons, has caused recurring holes in the ozone layer above the Antarctic. The situation became serious enough for 86 countries to sign an agreement at Helsinki in 1989 to scale down all CFC production. A deadline of the year 2000 was set for elimination of all CFCs.

Another November 1996 article concerned President Bill Clinton, who made his own impassioned plea for the environment on a visit to Australia. Speaking at Port Douglas in northern Queensland, President Clinton voiced his concern at global warming: 'We must work to reduce harmful greenhouse gas emissions. Those gases released by cars and power plants and burning forests, affect our health and our climate. If they continue unabated, the consequences will be nothing short of devastating for the children I see here and their children...'

The side-effects of these trends already touch every living creature on land and in the sea. Sharks among them.

It is a fact that seals and sharks and other creatures in the food chain — even in the remotest areas, including places which never see a human — have traces of DDT in their fatty tissues and mercury in their livers. Pollution has spread from the tropics to the poles.

Like many forms of animal life, and despite the fact that they live in the deep sea and are seemingly well out of the mainstream of human movements, sharks have already suffered a good deal from overfishing and from pollutants.

Numbers of the Great White shark, in fact, appeared to drop so alarmingly between the 1970s and the 1990s, that serious fears were expressed that

346

Carcharodon carcharias might follow *Megladon* into extinction if the population losses were not checked.

As we've noted, in 1991 South Africa became the first country in the world to legislate to protect the Great White. Penalties for killing a *Carcharodon* in the waters of the Republic were severe, with fines of up to $20 000 or six months imprisonment. During the 1990s Great Whites were also protected in California and Florida, off the coast of Namibia, in southwest Africa, and in the Canary Islands and the Maldives.

In Australia, in 1996 Tasmania was the only State that had full protection legislation for *Carcharodon*, though South Australia had banned commercial fishermen from trading in jaws and teeth since 1994.

The New South Wales Department of Fisheries held a meeting in September 1996 to discuss the desirability of full national protection for the Great White. The meeting was attended by scientists, conservationists and representatives of the various State governments. It came about as the result of pressure by a number of organisations, scientists, and other people, including Ron and Valerie Taylor, Rodney Fox and Ian Gordon.

At the meeting the scientific and conservation representatives supported the case for national protection. Government fisheries representatives from the various States were asked to vote on the issue. New South Wales, South Australia, Tasmania and the Northern Territory were in favour of protection. Western Australia, Queensland and Victoria had reservations. As a result of the meeting New South Wales, in January 1997, banned fishing for the Great White, and Queensland (despite the September vote) followed suit in February and May 1997.

Announcing the decision, NSW Minister for Fisheries Bob Martin said: 'Years of irrational hatred and indiscriminate hunting have taken their toll. It's time to stop demonising the species and to start recognising it as a fine example of top-of-the-chain evolution.'

The ban was instituted under existing legislation, the *NSW Fisheries Management Act 1994*. It became an offence to take a Great White or for a person to have a Great White in their possession. The maximum penalty was a $20 000 fine or six months in prison.

However, despite the fact that a small percentage of the annual beach-nets catch were Great Whites, Martin said, there would be no downgrading of the beach meshing program. 'We faced this dilemma when we protected the grey nurse. As magnificent as these shark species are, I'm afraid we have a higher duty to protect the beachgoing public of New South Wales. Nothing will be done that would prejudice their safety.'

For the sharks it was perhaps a case of 'win some, lose some'. But conservationists saw the protection for *Carcharodon* as a triumph. While the ban in Queensland came as something of a pleasant surprise for protectionists, it was regarded as important because it indicated that, with New South Wales, Tasmania and Queensland offering full protection, it would be only a matter of time before the remaining States accepted the principle.

The Queensland penalty of $75 000 for catching a Great White, announced by Queensland Primary Industries Minister Trevor Perret on 1 February 1997, and applying to the grey nurse as well, showed that his government was serious in its intentions. 'Scientific evidence shows that action must be taken to prevent any further decline in these species,' Perret told reporters at a press meeting at Sea World on Queensland's Gold Coast. 'Shark numbers are declining because of low birthrates and overfishing.' He condemned in particular the 'shocking practice of live-finning for the Asian seafood trade'.

As in New South Wales, Perret said, the Queensland beach meshing program would remain in place — at least until some other equally effective means of protection was established.

While most people approved of the ban — a complete public turnaround from 20 years before — there were, as expected, some who could not agree that 'man-eaters' deserved protection. One predictable opponent of the bans was the outspoken Hervey Bay shark hunter, Vic Hislop. He described the New South Wales Government ban on taking Great White sharks as irresponsible.

Hislop was reported in the *West Australian* newspaper as saying: 'For a government to protect something that can tear your children apart in seconds is brainless. I hope that the next time a person is taken by a Great White shark in NSW someone is held responsible for [having protected] these creatures.'

The Queensland ban, which more directly affected his activities, brought an even stronger response. 'Criminal!' he told news reporters, and was quoted as adding: 'People with vested interests lied to the government to force the decision.'

He went on: 'Of about 350 species of sharks there are about 340 which deserve to be protected. These include the grey nurse. But the Great White is a killer. As fish stocks around the world are more and more depleted and sharks have less and less food to choose from, they will increasingly attack people.'

While the ban on catching *Carcharodon* in Australia pleased the conservationists — but not Vic Hislop — the world situation on shark fishing is less satisfactory. As indeed it is with all forms of fishing — from the plundering of the great shoals of oceanic tuna, with attendant destruction of dolphins, the mass depletion of cold water orange rougheys, to an ominous resumption of pirate whaling. The world picture shows grim portents for the future.

It is significant that two of the world's most influential and widely read magazines, *Time* and *National Geographic*, each with a different readership and agenda, have chosen to address the problem with unusually lengthy articles.

The *Geographic* was first out, in November 1995. The lead article for that issue was titled 'DIMINISHING RETURNS — EXPLOITING THE OCEAN'S BOUNTY'. The article began with the significant words: 'The unthinkable has come to pass: the wealth of the oceans, once deemed inexhaustible, has proven finite.'

There followed over 36 illustrated pages — a series of detailed examinations of fisheries around the world. From the devastated Grand Banks of Newfoundland to Morocco, Senegal, the North Pacific salmon fishery, the Philippines and the oceanic tuna industry, the articles dealt with fish ranging from tiny anchovies to giant sharks. The *Geographic* reporters came to some glum conclusions.

They found that fishermen everywhere said the same thing, in different languages: 'Too many fishermen; not enough fish.'

The classic disaster was off Newfoundland, Canada. Catches on the Grand Banks, once the Atlantic's most bountiful fishery for cod and halibut, dropped so low that the Canadian Government closed the fishery in the desperate hope that it might one day recover. The move put 40 000 Newfoundlanders out of work.

Despite this, Spanish and Portuguese vessels continued to fish the grounds just outside Canada's 200 mile (320 kilometre) limit, some illegally using fine-meshed nets to take undersized fish.

Like Newfoundland, each area has its own problems. But one universal cause for concern is the supertrawlers whose enormous nets can engulf 60 metric tonnes of fish in a single haul. Other negatives are the mist-fine drift nets, 30 kilometres long, which kill all kinds of sea creatures beyond the intended quarry, and the tuna purse seines with their unacceptable dolphin kills. With modern satellite navigation systems, global positioning is able to put a vessel within metres of any known reef or rock, or fish spawning ground.

But, by and large, it's not the equipment that is the problem. It's the way it is used — the ocean equivalent of the bulldozer and chainsaw in the rainforest. The enormous technical improvements of the past 20 years have created fishing fleets so efficient that they may, in the end, make themselves obsolete, through lack of enough fish to sustain the economic effort of catching them.

In the process small village fishermen from Africa to Mexico are being squeezed out of existence in the 1990s by the big internationals. The traditional fishing grounds are being ruined by overexploitation. For poor people who need fish to feed their families, as well as to earn a living, actual survival may be threatened.

In addition to taking too many fish, trawlers often damage the seabed, dragging chains and otter boards which destroy fragile ecosystems and spawning grounds. In these terms, today's catch may mean that there is literally no tomorrow. Environmentalists call the big trawlers 'strip miners of the sea' because of the damage they leave in their wake.

There is also the major problem of the 'by-catch'. This comprises fish, squid, shellfish and other sea creatures that are not the intended target of the fishermen but are taken by the trawl nets which, of course, cannot discriminate between creatures. The by-catch species are innocent bystanders caught in the crossfire.

In the Gulf of Mexico a Texas prawn trawler may take a dozen pounds (5.4 kilograms) of other sea life for every pound (450 grams) of marketable shrimps, or prawns. The average by-catch ratio for shrimp boats overall is four to one. A good deal of the by-catch consists of juvenile fish which, when shovelled back into the sea from the sorting tables, are dead. The figures quoted apply to shrimp or prawn fishing boats around the world.

The *Time* magazine article of 28 October 1996 had a similar theme to that of the *Geographic*. 'GLOBAL AGENDA: TREASURES OF THE SEAS' it was headed, with the subtitle 'We've plundered the ocean's gifts — can we now protect them?' *Time's* reporters not unexpectedly saw essentially the same problems that concerned the *Geographic's* writers.

They reported that the world fish catch in 1950 was about 20 million tons (18 million tonnes) a year. By 1989 the figure had hit 86 million tons (78 million tonnes). Significantly, and despite bigger and more technically efficient fishing vessels being launched in the past ten years, the overall figure has dropped since and is declining. More effort, more expense, for less fish.

'Thanks mainly to the trawlers and their high-tech gear, 70 per cent of the world's fish stocks are being strained up to and beyond their ability to sustain commercial quantities of fish,' *Time* reported.

The overfishing includes sharks, which are our particular concern, and perhaps this is the most wasteful fishery of all. For many of the sharks are simply stripped of their fins, and their wasted carcasses are thrown back into the ocean. The fins, hung in the rigging to dry, go to Asian markets for sharkfin soup. A questionable luxury, rather than an actual necessity in anyone's diet.

Many of today's shark fisheries are in subsistence-economy areas. In parts of South East Asia, east and west Africa, Mexico and South America, catch records are poor or non-existent. This makes it difficult to get an accurate figure of the annual world shark catch. But scientists estimate that 100 million sharks are caught internationally each year.

The *recorded* 1994 catch was 1.4 billion kilograms of shark. It was double the 1991 catch. How long can shark populations sustain such pressure?

As we have already noted, sharks are slow breeders. When populations are significantly reduced it may take another century for them to recover. The most threatened species may face extinction. Yet sharks and other fish are a major source of protein for many nations of the world — especially countries like China and Japan. The world will always be hungry for fish and fish products. What, then, is the answer?

Conservationists' hopes were initially raised by the prospects of fish farming. After all, they pointed out, land-sourced foods are produced by farming. We grow fruit, grain, chickens, sheep and cattle in a controlled way for human consumption. If we had to go out and kill a wild creature or pick a berry to eat, in the old hunter-gatherer tradition, civilised life as we know it would be impossible. Yet fishing still involves hunting wild stocks, at risk of wind and weather, often 'by guess or by God'.

'This is crazy!' conservationists say. 'It makes no sense.'

Fish farming has had its successes. The Chinese have been practising aquaculture for centuries, growing fish and prawns in their irrigation systems as a natural by-product of rice farming. In 1992 fish farming — including crustaceans — was a $25 billion industry worldwide. Twenty-five per cent of all salmon are now raised artificially. There are 50 countries breeding shrimps or prawns. Some 200 species of fish, crabs, shrimps and shellfish are grown around the world for human consumption.

But nothing is easy. Or so it seems. In the salmon industry it takes 3 kilograms of fishmeal to produce 1 kilogram of salmon. The fish are clustered so thickly in some floating pens in bays that their excreta fouls the bottom below, creating 'dead zones' for other life and breeding grounds for disease. Farms may 'kill' one area and have to be moved to the next. The shrimp farmers in Thailand and Vietnam clear extensive mangrove swamps and other important fish breeding areas. With over-intensive stocking, sometimes 500 000 animals to the hectare, the areas become contaminated. The shrimp farmers move on, to clear new areas, seeking clean ground and leaving devastation behind them.

Most people who spend time in or on the ocean have seen environmental situations which have caused them concern. I saw a turtle farm on the British

Grand Cayman island in 1995. There, part-grown turtles were packed so tightly in their tanks that there seemed to be more turtle than water. They writhed and struggled up through the bodies of other turtles just to come to the surface to breath. Turtles are tough, and so they lived. But what kind of a life was it for creatures that are normally free-ranging swimmers in the open ocean? It was like putting ten humans in a small car and having them live, eat and perform all their natural functions in that confined space. Cruel! We need to display humanity in our dealings with animals along with our economic pragmatism.

The other problem facing fish and shark populations in the modern world is the pollution or destruction of natural habitats. *Time* magazine examined coral ecosystems: 'Already some experts estimate ten percent of the earth's reefs have been mortally wounded. Thirty percent are in critical shape and may die within the next 10 to 20 years. And an additional 30 percent are coming under such sustained attack that they may perish by 2050.'

'I used to be reluctant to say the sky was falling in,' said palaeobiologist Jeremy Jackson of the Smithsonian Tropical Research Institute in Panama. 'I'm not any more. Today, when I go for a swim on a reef in Panama I cry.'

Significantly, 1997 is the International Year of the Reef.

Off Western Australia, in areas as remote from the mainstream of civilisation as the Abrolhos Islands and the Ningaloo barrier reef, I saw not long ago hectares of dead coral where 30 years before there were brilliant coral gardens.

What is killing the coral?

No one seems to know. Some blame an influx of a marine snail named *Dropella*, which has recently multiplied in huge numbers. But is this increase because of overfishing of the bald-chin groper and the spangled emperor fish? These species previously ate the snails and their eggs and kept the shellfish numbers down. Because the fish are easily caught and good to eat, they have been heavily overfished for years — with amateur fishermen on holiday the worst offenders.

Interference with natural populations on a massive scale can bring all kinds of unexpected and often unwelcome results.

Knowledge is all-important in the sea, as on the land. Ashore, necessity has turned our farmers into practical scientists. The good farmer knows when to leave a field fallow, when to add trace elements. When to sow, when to reap. He or she knows how much stock the property will carry. Abuse of the land will leave it exhausted and unable to grow a crop. Too many animals cause overcrowding, disease and soil erosion. Farmers practise husbandry learned over many centuries, caring for their fields and their animals because that is their own key to survival.

We need to practise similar husbandry in the sea. Fish farms will work when the problems are erased. The coral reefs may still be saved, at least in many parts of the world, if — a big if — we learn how to protect the environment.

There will be a sustainable yield for fishermen among free-swimming ocean fish and sharks if sensible quotas are observed and the resources are not irresponsibly raped until the industry is ruined.

To take one example: lobster fisheries, worldwide, are among the most vulnerable fisheries because demand always exceeds the supply of the delicious flesh, and they are readily fished out if greed overcomes commonsense. But in Western Australia, mercifully distant from intense international competition, careful management of the commercial rock lobster industry has been fostered through the restriction of boat licences and lobster pot numbers, together with the use of closed seasons. As a result, the industry is in better shape in the 1990s than it was in the 1960s. There has been similar success with abalone fishing and culture pearling.

The sea's resources *can* be managed.

Perhaps we should say they *must* be managed, if there is to be a future of quality for humankind as well as for fishes.

And sharks . . .

Meanwhile, it may be time again for me to dust off the shark cage down in the back garden. The project? This time we hope to film tiger sharks off the Muiron islands at the North West Cape. *Galeocerdo cuvieri* — Sharkey Nelson's 'mean striped bastards' — can grow to 5 or 6 metres. Huge and powerful animals at that size, they have teeth that can crunch through a full-grown turtle's shell like a biscuit.

How will they react to the shark cage? How will we react to them?

It will be interesting finding out.

REFERENCES

Baldridge, H. David 1976, *Shark Attack*, Everest Books, United Kingdom.

Benchley, Peter 1974, *Jaws*, Doubleday, New York.

Brockman, John, personal diary, Battye Library, Perth.

Brown, Theo, W. 1973, *Sharks: The Search for a Repellent*, Angus & Robertson, Sydney.

Bruce, Barry 1995, 'The Protection of the White Shark', *Southern Fisheries*, South Australian Primary Industries Department, Vol. 3, No. 2, Winter 1995.

Caldwell, Norman 1936, *Fangs of the Sea*, Angus & Robertson, Sydney.

Coppleson, Victor 1958, *Shark Attack*, Angus & Robertson, Sydney.

Couch, Jonathon 1867, *A History of the Fishes of the British Isles*, Groombridge, London.

Cropp, Ben 1964 *The Shark Hunters*, Rigby, Adelaide.

Cropp, Ben 1969, *Whale of a Shark*, Rigby, Adelaide.

Cousteau, Jacques-Yves & Cousteau, Philippe 1970, *The Shark: Splendid Savage of the Sea*, Doubleday, New York.

Doak, Wade 1975, *Sharks and Other Ancestors*, Hodder & Stoughton, Auckland and Sydney.

Edwards, Hugh 1975, *Sharks and Shipwrecks*, Lansdowne Press, Melbourne; Quadrangle, New York.

Edwards, Hugh 1976, *Tiger Shark*, Angus & Robertson, Sydney.

Edwards, Hugh 1988, *Crocodile Attack in Australia*, Swan Publishing, Perth.

Edwards, Hugh 1996, *Islands of Angry Ghosts*, Angus & Robertson, Sydney.

Ellis, Richard 1975, *The Book of Sharks*, Grossert and Dunlap, New York.

Ellis, Richard & McCosker, John 1991, *Great White Shark*, Harper Collins Publishers, New York.

Gilbert, Perry 1963, *Sharks and Survival*, D. C. Heath, Boston DC.

Gleeson, James & Waldron, T. J. 1950, *The Frogmen*, Morrison & Gibbs, London.

Goadby, Peter 1975, *Sharks: Attacks, Habits, Species*, Ure Smith, Sydney.

Goadby, Peter 1976, *Killer Sharks*, Angus & Robertson, Sydney.

Goadby, Peter; Taylor, Ron & Taylor, Valerie 1978, *Great Shark Stories*, Harper & Row, New York.

Greenberg, Jerry & Greenberg, Michael 1981, *Sharks and Other Dangerous Sea Creatures*, Seahawk Press, Florida.

Grey, Loren (ed.) 1974, *Shark, The Killer of the Deep: Zane Grey*, Belmont Tower Books, New York.

Hass, Hans 1952, *Men and Sharks*, Jarrolds, London.

Hass, Hans 1952, *Under the Red Sea*, Jarrolds, London.

Hass, Hans 1972, *To Unplumbed Depths*, Harrap, London.

Hemingway, Ernest 1967, *The Old Man and the Sea*, Jonathon Cape, London.

Heyerdahl, Thor 1951, *The Kon Tiki Expedition*, George Allen & Unwin, London.

Hugo, Victor n.d., *Toilers of the Sea*, The Readers Library Publishing Co., London.

Matthiessen, Peter 1971, *Blue Meridian: The Search for the Great White Shark*, Random House, New York.

Mead, Tom 1961, *Killers of Eden*, Angus & Robertson, Sydney.

Melville, Herman 1951, *Moby Dick*, Everyman's Library, J. M. Dent & Sons, London.

Nelson, Mike 1988, *Swim with the Rays*, Blueline Press, Colorado.

Pennant, T. 1812, *British Zoology*, Vol. IV, Wilkie & Robinson, London.

Pepperell, Julian; West, John & Woon, Peter (eds.) 1992, *Shark Conservation*, proceedings of international workshop held at Taronga Park Zoo, Sydney, 24 February 1991, published by Zoological Parks Board of New South Wales.

Reader's Digest Services 1986, *Sharks: Silent Hunters of the Deep*, Reader's Digest, Sydney.

Stead, D. G. 1963, *Sharks and Rays of Australian Seas*, Angus & Robertson, Sydney.

Stubbs, Ches 1985, *I Remember*, self published, Albany.

Taylor, Geoff 1995, *Whale Sharks: Giants of the Ningaloo Reef*, Harper Collins Publishers, Sydney.

Tonkin, Gary 1994, 'More Stories of the *Cheynes II*: A Dramatic Rescue', *Maritime Heritage Association Journal*, Vol. 5, No. 4, December 1994.

Weldon, Kevin (and contributors) 1987, *Sharks*, Golden Press, Sydney.

Whitely, Gilbert Percy 1940, *The Sharks, Rays, Devil-Fish, and Other Primitive Fishes of Australia and New Zealand*, Royal Zoological Society of New South Wales, n.p.

INDEX

Abrolhos Islands, W.A. 50, 105, 110, 225, 282, 328–9, 352
Adams, Darren 3–4, 8, 12
Albany, W.A. 44, 167, 175, 228–36
Albany Whaling Station *see* Cheynes Beach Whaling Station
Aldinga Beach, S.A. 60
Almond, E.H. 324
Amazon shark 30 *see also* Whaler sharks
ampullae of Lorenzini 193–5, 338–43
Aristotle, descriptions of sharks 84–6, 89
Australian Shark Attack File 187, 262

baiting and sharks 191–2, 229–30
Baldridge, H. David 139, 142–4, 155, 158–9
Baleen whales 164
Bantry Bay, NSW 118
Barnes, John 286
Bartle, Robert 35–42, 72, 99–100, 104
Barunga, Albert 267, 271
Basking sharks 188, 198, 244
Bass, John 212, 213
Batavia (shipwreck) 50, 110–11, 328–9
Bay of Islands, N.Z. 315
Beach Haven, N.J. 120
behaviour
   sea creatures and human contact 297–301
   sharks 94, 139, 330
   see also Great White sharks
   Tiger sharks
Bell, John 177–9
Bishop, Reg 131, 133
Bisley, Peter 135–7
Blacktip topeshark 188
Blue sharks 31, 113, 195
Blue whales 164
Blue-ringed octopus 281–2

Bluebottles 284–5
Bondi Beach, NSW 9–10, 117
Botany Bay, NSW 118
Boundy, Ray 103–4, 105
Bource, Henri 34, 65, 67–72
Bowring, Pat 9–12
Box jellyfish 284–286
Bronze Whaler shark 37, 115
   see also Whaler sharks
Broome, W.A. 241
Broughton Island, NSW 190, 191
Brown, Theo 100–2, 109
Bruder, Charles 120, 124
Bull sharks 13, 30, 104, 107–8, 120–4, 187, 321, 339–40 *see also* Whaler sharks
Buzzard Bay, MA 124
Byron Bay, NSW 11, 157

Campagno, Dr Leonard 303, 335
cannibalism, infant 214
Cape Leeuwin, W.A. 3, 165
Cape Naturaliste, W.A. 3
Caracalinga Head, S.A. 63–4
Carchardon megladon 189–90, 201
Carcharodon carcharias see Great White Sharks
Caernarvon, W.A. 29
Carter, Andre 302–4
Cartwright, Therese 11, 104, 156–7
Cayman Islands 288, 297–300
chain mail suit 323, 332
Charter, Graeme 339–43
Chatham Islands, N.Z. 316
Che-Tsung Chen 244–5
Cheviot Beach, Vic 137–8
Cheynes Beach Whaling Station 17, 43–4, 161–2, 168, 196
   filming 44–59, 87–8, 93–8, 207–10, 215, 228–36
   whaling trip 169–82
Cheynes II (whaling ship) 29, 169–82

City Beach, W.A. 133
Clark, Dr Eugenie 197, 244–5, 257, 305, 331
Clarke, Norman 21–2
Cleaner fish 90
Clearwater Beach, H.K. 318
Cobia kingfish 90–2
Coledale Beach, NSW 125–6
colour, and shark attraction 193
Coogee, NSW 117
'Cookie cutter' sharks 188–9
Coolangatta, Qld 113–14
Coppleson, Dr Victor 23, 116–19, 126, 324–5, 333
coral collecting 283–4
coral death 352
coral spawning 254–5
Corby, Bruce 302–3
Corner, Jeff 63–4
Coronation Beach, W.A. 14
Cossack, W.A. 263
Cottesloe, W. A. 109, 131, 133–4
Coucom, Cedric, James and Bruce 115–16
Cousteau, Jacques 168, 299, 322, 329
Covert, William 13, 313
crocodiles
   African 277
   freshwater 266
   saltwater 201, 264–73, 311
Cropp, Ben 105, 191, 192, 251, 252
Cuba 314–15

Dampier Archipelago, W.A. 92, 225
Dangerous Reef, S.A. 229
Dijkgraa, Dr 194, 338
Dirk Hartog Island 251
Doak, Wade 323, 332–3
Dogfish sharks 194
Dragon Boat Festival, Hong Kong 317–21
Dunedin, N.Z. 316
Dunn, John 122–3, 124

Dunsborough, W.A. 37
Durban, South Africa 82–6, 335
Durdin, Shirley 104, 156, 158
Dwarf sharks 184
Dyers Island, South Africa 340

Eagle rays 288, 297
East Alligator River, N.T. 311
Edmunds, Damon 8–9
Edwards, Marilyn 96–8, 213, 231, 236
Egg Rock, NSW 118
electric field shark repellent 338–43
Electric ray 203–4
electrical field sensors, of sharks 193–5, 338–43
Ellis, Richard 124, 190, 191, 193–4, 309
environment
  degradation 345–7
  fish stock depletion and 349–53
  shark protection and 336–7, 347–9
  whaling bans and 163, 168
Esperance, W.A. 196
Ettleson, Simeon 109, 131–2
Exmouth Gulf, W.A. 135, 213, 239, 250
  see also Ningaloo Reef
eyesight and sense of smell, of sharks 192–3

Farralon Islands, CA 11, 12, 128, 130, 308–9
Ferreira, Theo and Craig 304–6
filming
  at Cheynes Beach 44–59, 87–8, 93–8, 207–10, 215
  at Ningaloo Reef 253–7
  Blue Water, White Death 33, 228, 229
  for Orca 227–36
  Heron Island 216, 225
  problems 50–1
  Surfers Paradise 225–7
fish farming 351–3
fish stock depletion 163, 347–53
Fitzpatrick, Bruce 268–70
Flathead cat shark 188
Flinders Island, Bass Strait 196

Florida Keys 246, 313–15
Ford, John and Deborah 11, 104, 157
Fox, Rodney 34, 72, 229, 347

game fishing 20
Ganges shark 30–1, 108, 187
  see also Whaler sharks
Gansbaai, South Africa 340
Gap, The, Albany 175
Georges River, NSW 118
Georgetown, Tas. 156–7
Geraldton, W.A. 14
Gibbons, Wally 252, 327
Giddings, Al 309–10, 313
Gimbel, Peter 33, 228
Girvan, Norman 114–15
Glazier, Maurie 92, 95, 105, 208
Goadby, Peter 27–8, 116, 192
Good, Darren 31–2
Googarra, Qld 284
Grace, Peter 95, 208
Grand Banks, Newfoundland 163, 349
Great White Shark
  attacks by 5–8, 21–2, 34, 38–41, 120–5, 137–9, 155–8, 302–21
  behaviour 94, 139
  electric deterrent 340–3
  electrical sensors 193–4
  eyes 205–7
  feeding 305
  filming at whaling station 44–59, 87–8, 93–8, 207–10
  first filming of 33
  historic descriptions of 22–3
  lifespan and movement, recording of 196–7
  Jaws 33–4, 89, 205–7, 228
  method of attack 8–12, 71, 99–100, 104–5, 311–13
  Mexico and Central America 313–15
  New Zealand 315–16
  North East America 120–4
  protection of 347–9
  size of 28–9
  South Africa 302–4
  South East Australia 60–72
  teeth 199–201
Greenhalgh, Brian 50, 95, 229, 231, 235
Greenhalgh, Fran 231, 233

Grey Nurse sharks 21, 94, 185–6, 187, 202, 212, 225–7
Grey reef sharks 31, 107, 109
Grey, Zane 20, 315
Gudger, Dr Eugene 245–6
Gyogo, Japan 320–1

Haleiwa, Oahu 316
Hammerhead sharks 184–5, 192, 202
Hapalochaena 281–2
Harada, Kazuta 320–1
harpooning 162–3, 177–82
Hart, Paddy 170, 175–6
Hass, Hans 85, 246, 323, 329
Hathaway, Marcia 102–3, 108, 119
Hawaii 316–17
Hayman Island, Qld 283
Heron Island, Qld 216
Heyerdahl, Thor 24, 247–9
Hill, Clem 29, 251, 252
Hilton, Steve 268, 270
Hislop, Vic 319, 336, 348
Holt, Corry 131–2
Holt, Harold 137–9
Honeymoon Island, W.A. 1–8
Hong Kong 317–21
Hooghly River, India 31
Hopetoun, W.A. 1, 4, 8
Hopkins, Gary 100–2
Humpback whales 163–4, 214

Ingleman-Sundeberg, Catherina 96–8
International Whaling Commission 168
International Orange, shark attractant 193
Isbel, Ron 94, 204, 216

Janes, Madeleine 268–9
Japan 320–1
Jaws (book and film, Benchley) 33–4, 89, 205–7, 228
Julian Rocks, NSW 11, 157
Jurien Bay, W.A. 35–42, 100

Kalmijn, Dr 194, 338
Kelly, Walter 67–70
kevlar suits 332
Killer whales 164, 171
King Georges Sound, W.A. 17, 43, 175
Kings Cascades, W.A. 267–73

Kirra Beach, Qld 113–14
Kon Tiki expedition 23–4, 247–9
Koputai (paddle steamer wreck) 9–11, 13
Krill 254–5
Kruppa, Dietmar 68–9
Kulan Island, W.A. 271

La Libertad Beach, San Salvador 314
La Paz Beach, San Salvador 314
Lacepede Islands, W.A. 128, 135, 192
Lady Julia Percy Island 67–8
Lashman, David 1–8
Lemon sharks 31, 107, 192, 197, 305
Lighthouse, Reef, W.A. 14
Lilleyman, Captain Dennis 330–1
Lodestone Reef, Qld 103
longevity, of sharks 196
Lorenzini, Stephan 193–4
Lucas, Dr Frederick A. 121, 124

McCallister, Tamara 306–7
McCosker, John 124, 190, 193–4, 214, 309–11
Mako sharks 32, 195–6, 201–2
Malibu Beach, CA 307
Manly, NSW 118
Marion Reef, Qld 112–3
Marjorie Bay, W.A. 288
Maroubra, NSW 117
Martin, Vic 49–52, 86, 94, 208–9, 211–12, 214, 215
Martzamemi, Sicily 195
Matawan Creek, N.J. 121–3
Mathews, Stephen 175–7
Meadows, Ginger Fay 268–73
Megamouth 189, 244
Melkbosselstrand, South Africa 306
Melrose, Bill 131–2
Mexico 313–14
Middle Harbour 100–1, 102, 118
Milne Bay, PNG 342
Minke whales 171
Mogadishu, Somalia 321
Montague Island, NSW 251
Monte Circeo, Italy 34

Monterey Bay, CA 309
Moresby, Qld 280
Moreton Bay, Qld 94, 214
Moses sole 322, 331
Munglinup Beach, W.A. 7–8
Murion Islands, W.A. 213, 250, 353
Murphy, Dennis 103–4, 105
Murray, Ken 100–2, 108

Nahoon Reef, S.A. 302
Narragansett, Rhode Island 195
Natal Sharks Board 335–6, 338–43
Natal, South Africa 30, 82–6, 334–6
Natural Bridge, Albany 175–7
Nelson, Mike 299
Nelson, Ted 'Sharkey' 26, 107, 110, 205
New Zealand 315–16
New Zealand katipo 275
Newcastle, NSW 30
Newstead, Peter 44–59, 95–7, 199, 208, 214
Nicaraguan shark 30, 108, 187 *see also* Whaler sharks
Ningaloo Reef, W.A. 237–42, 245, 253–61, 352
Norton, Linda 103–4
Norwegian Bay, W.A. 252
Numbfish 203–4
Nurse sharks 197, 203, 305

Oceanic whitetip 31, 107
Octopuses 281–2
oophagy 211–12
Orcas *see* Killer whales
orders, of sharks 198
overfishing 163, 347–53

Parramatta, NSW 31–2
Peake Bay, S.A. 155–7
pearl shell diving 72 85, 135, 262–5, 329
Phillips, Allen 63–4
Piked Dogfish sharks 196
Pilot fish 90–2
Pinctada *see* pearl shell diving
Plumwood, Val 310–12
Point Cloates, W.A. 253
Point Conception, CA 307
Point Moore, W.A. 14
Port Fairy, Vic 67–8, 70

Port Lincoln, S.A. 5, 155–7
Port Philip Bay, Vic 22, 137
Port Stephens, NSW 190
Portugeuse man o' war 284–5
powerhead 326–7
Prince Regent River, W.A. 267–73
Protective Oceanic Device (POD) 338–43

Ragged tooth sharks *see* Grey Nurse sharks
Rainbow Coast, W.A. 3
Raine Island, Qld 128
Rangiora Atoll 102
Raritan Bay, N.J. 123
Ratcliffe, Jill 68, 70
Rays 21, 187, 203–4, 279–81
Reading, Lieutenant A. G. 324–5
Remoras 90–2
Repulse Bay, HK 318
Rodger, Brian 34, 61–3, 65, 72
Roebuck Bay, W.A. 135, 263–4
Rottnest Island, W.A. 18, 110, 212, 288
Rowley Shoals, W.A. 241

Sai Kung, H.K. 317
San Miguel Island, CA 310
San Salvador, shark attacks 314
Sand Tiger sharks *see* Grey Nurse sharks
Santa Barbara Island, CA 310
Sarra, Maurizzio 34
Saw sharks 185
Schleisser, Michael 123, 124
Schonhofer, Werner 14–15
School sharks 196
SCUBA diving
  development of 18–20
  shark attack risk 130, 328–31
Sea snakes 278–9, 332
Sea wasp 284–6
Sei whales 171
Seiffert, Doug 250, 252, 258
Shark Attack File 143, 158–9, 313
  Australian 187, 262
shark attacks 183
  chances of Ch.8
  first recordings of 24
  statistical analysis of 143–55, 158–9

see also under Great White
Shark
Shark Bay, W.A. 161, 214
shark behaviour 94, 139
  see also under Great White
  sharks
  Tiger sharks
shark cages 5, 205–7, 333
  filming from 17–18, 44–59,
  87–8, 93–8, 207–10, 215
'Shark Chaser' dye 324–5
Shark Dart 327–8
shark eggs 213–14, 244
shark killers 20, 326–8
shark mating and breeding
  210–14
Shark Menace Advisory
  Committee (NSW) 333
shark net meshing 119, 133,
  319–20, 333–6
shark protection 336–7
shark repellent 102, 195,
  Ch. 15
Shark Screen 325
shark tagging 195–7
Sheung Sz Wan Beach, H.K.
  317
Short, Raymond 125–6
Silverstrand, H.K. 317
Silvertip 31, 107
Slaughter, Scott G. 326–7
Sleeper sharks 203
Smitswinkel Bay, South Africa
  306
South Steyne, NSW 118
spearfishing competitions 36,
  61–7
Sperm whales 160–2, 164–7,
  169–82
Spring Lake, N.J. 120, 124
Squid, Giant 160–1, 197, 282
Starck, Walter 332–3
Stead, David G. 190–1
Steadman, Zita 108, 118
Stensen, Neils 193–4
Stilwell, Lester 121–3
Stingray City 297–300

Stingrays 203, 279–81, 288,
  297–300
Stoddard, Roy Jeffery 306–7
Stone, Kevin 258–9
Stonefish 279
Stuart, Allan 137–8
Stubbs, Ches 29, 169, 175,
  177–9, 181
Sugarloaf Bay, NSW 102
surf lifesaving movement
  133–4
Surfers Paradise, Qld 225–7
Swan River, W.A. 30, 108, 133
Sydney Harbour, NSW 100,
  118, 333
Sydney Heads, NSW 20

Tantabiddi, W.A. 260
Tawny sharks 203
Taylor, Dr Geoff 245, 253–7,
  260
Taylor, Joanna 253–6
Taylor, Ron 33, 51, 227–36,
  323, 332
  shark conservation 347
  testing electric deterrent
  339–43
  whale sharks 251–2
Taylor, Valerie 33, 51, 112–13,
  227–36, 323, 332–3
  feeding great whites 305
  shark conservation 347
  testing electric deterrent
  339–43
  whale sharks 251–2
Thevenard Island, W.A. 92,
  107
Tiger sharks 15, 23, 192, 353
  attacks by 128, 131–2, 136
  behaviour and method of
  attack 105–7, 109–10
  size of 27, 28, 30
  tagging 195–6
  teeth 202
  Valerie Taylor and 112–13
  Zane Grey and 20
Tigers 277

Tiny Bubbles Expeditions 250,
  252, 258
Tomales Point, CA 309
Tonkin, Gary 176
Toothed whales 164
training
  of sharks 197, 305
  of stingrays 298–300
Turtles 106–7, 128, 213
Tyrrenian Sea 34

US National Marine Fisheries
  Service 195

Valmadre, Les 250, 258
Vasa (shipwreck) 328

Walters, Mick 169, 170, 199
Warner, Lee 35–42, 72, 99–100
Watson's Bay, NSW 20
Webb, Bob 225–7
Weir, David 1–8, 12, 16
West, John 187
Whale sharks 188, 191, 202,
  248–54
  Ningaloo Reef 237–42, 245,
  253–61
Whaler sharks 21, 28, 30, 31–2,
  85, 107–8, 187, 202
  filming 216, 225
whaling 17–18, 25–6, 29,
  162–3, 167–9
  banning 163, 168
  on *Cheyne II* 169–82
White-striped shark-sucker 91
Whitely, Gilbert Percy 20–2,
  191
Wiseman's Bay, S.A. 156
Wobbegong 243
Wong Kwai-yung 318, 319
Wooded Island, W.A. 196–7

Yeppoon, Qld 115

Zambezi shark 30, 187, 321 *see
  also* Whaler sharks
zebra suit 323, 332–3

OTHER BOOKS
BY HUGH EDWARDS

God and Little Fishes
Islands of Angry Ghosts
Wreck on the Half Moon Reef
Pearl Divers of Australia
William Bligh
Skindiving
Sharks and Shipwrecks
Joe Nangan's Dreaming
Tiger Shark
Sea Lion Island
The Pearl Pirates
The Crocodile God
Australian and New Zealand Shipwrecks and Sea Tragedies
Sim the Sea Lion
Port of Pearls
Salute to Western Australia
Crocodile Attack in Australia
The Remarkable Dolphins of Monkey Mia
Kimberley — Dreaming to Diamonds
Gold Dust and Iron Mountains
Pearls of Broome and Northern Australia
Meekatharra — The Gold Beyond the Rivers

Hugh Edwards has also received the following awards:

Sir Thomas White Memorial Prize for the best book published by an Australian in 1966 for *Islands of Angry Ghosts*

Western Australia Week Non-fiction Award 1984 (shared) for *Port of Pearls*

Best Australian Television Documentary 1980 for *Wreck at Madman's Corner* (underwater camera work)